GENERATIONS OF SETTLERS

Dellplain Latin American Studies

No. 8* *Studies in Spanish American Population History*, edited by David J. Robinson

No. 9* *The People of the Colca Valley: A Population Study*, Noble David Cook

No.10* *Tierra Adentro: Settlement and Society in Colonial Durango*, Michael M. Swann

No. 11* *Andean Reflections: Letters from Carl O. Sauer While on a South American Trip Under a Grant from the Rockefeller Foundation, 1942*, Edited by Robert C. West

No.12* *Credit and Socioeconomic Change in Colonial Mexico: Loans and Mortgages in Guadalajara, 1720 - 1820*, Linda Greenow

No.13* *Once Beneath the Forest: Prehistoric Terracing in the Río Bec Region of the Maya Lowlands*, B. L. Turner, II

No.14* *Marriage and Fertility in Chile: Demographic Turning Points in the Petorca Valley, 1840 - 1976*, Robert McCaa

No. 15* *The Spatial Organization of New Land Settlement in Latin America*, Jacob O. Maos

No.16* *The Anglo-Argentine Connection, 1900 - 1939*, Roger Gravil

No. 17 *Costa Rica: A Geographical Interpretation in Historical Perspective*, Carolyn Hall

No. 18 *Household Economy and Urban Development: São Paulo, 1765 - 1836*, Elizabeth Anne Kuznesof

No. 19 *Irrigation in the Bajío Region of Colonial Mexico*, Michael E. Murphy

No. 20 *The Cost of Conquest: Indian Decline in Honduras Under Spanish Rule*, Linda Newson

No. 21 *Petty Capitalism in Spanish America: The Pulperos of Puebla, Mexico City, Caracas, and Buenos Aires*, Jay Kinsbruner

No. 22 *British Merchants and Chilean Development, 1851- 1886*, John Mayo

No. 23 *Hispanic Lands and Peoples: Selected Writings of James J. Parsons*, edited by William M. Denevan

No. 24 *Migrants in the Mexican North: Mobility, Economy, and Society in a Colonial World*, Michael M. Swann

No. 25 *Puebla de los Angeles, Industry and Society in a Mexican City, 1700-1850*, Guy P. C. Thomson

* indicates a book in the series that is now out of print

Dellplain Latin American Studies

PUBLISHED IN COOPERATION WITH
THE DEPARTMENT OF GEOGRAPHY
SYRACUSE UNIVERSITY

GENERATIONS OF SETTLERS

Rural Households and Markets on the Costa Rican Frontier, 1850–1935

Mario Samper

Dellplain Latin American Studies, No. 26

LONDON AND NEW YORK

First published 1990 by Westview Press, Inc.

Published 2018 by Routledge
52 Vanderbilt Avenue, New York, NY 10017
2 Park Square, Milton Park, Abingdon, Oxon OX14 4RN

Routledge is an imprint of the Taylor & Francis Group, an informa business

Library of Congress Cataloging-in-Publication Data
Samper, Mario.
Generations of settlers : rural households and markets on the Costa Rican frontier, 1850–1935/Mario Samper.
p. cm.—(Dellplain Latin American Studies ; no. 26)
Includes bibliographical references and index.
ISBN 0-8133-8021-9
1. Agriculture—Economic aspects—Costa Rica—Central Valley—History. 2. Land use, Rural—Costa Rica—Central Valley—History. 3. Land tenure—Costa Rica—Central Valley—History. 4. Rural families—Costa Rica—Central Valley—Economic conditions. 5. Peasantry—Costa Rica—Central Valley—History. I. Title. II. Series.
HD1805.C46S26 1990
338.1'097286'5—dc20 90-45671
CIP

ISBN 13: 978-0-367-01569-5 (hbk)
ISBN 13: 978-0-367-16556-7 (pbk)

To my family, in Costa Rica and Colombia.

To the elderly people from whom I learned so much about history and life.

Contents

List of Tables

List of Figures

Acknowledgments

In the course of several years mainly devoted to the preparation of this study, I acquired numerous intellectual and personal debts. The attempt to record each one has made me acutely aware of the fact that this is in many ways a collective effort, although I am, of course, solely responsible for the content and whatever shortcomings or misinterpretations there may be.

I should first thank professors Tulio Halperín, James Parsons and Richard Herr for their generous support. I must also express my deep gratitude to several Costa Rican and foreign colleagues whose stimulating criticism was invaluable, or who provided indispensable data and counsel: Víctor Hugo Acuña, Guillermo Carvajal, José Antonio Fernández, Elizabeth Fonseca, Edwin González, Lowell Gudmundson, Elizabeth Kuznesof, Héctor Pérez, Arodys Robles, William Roseberry and Rosalba Salas, among others.

My wife Cecilia Villarreal spent long hours helping me enter data into the computer and allowing me to draft the manuscript, while pursuing her own professional career. Our children -Alexandra, Jimena and Daniel- made it sometimes difficult and always worthwhile.

Brunilda Hilje, Alba Camacho, Rosalba Salas and Mario Sáenz helped follow the paths of settlers through the national archives and the real estate registry. Anabelle Fonseca worked long days with me tracking down and interviewing their descendants, and María Isabel Padilla transcribed the often almost unintelligible tapes we had recorded. Damaris Gamboa and Giselle Cordero also cooperated in secretarial tasks. Gerardo Mora also worked late helping me process data from probate inventories. In the archives of the Ospina family, in Colombia, Constanza Toro completed the data collection which I began on one of my trips.

The History Department of the Universidad Nacional provided constant support for my research activities during these years, and a framework for discussion of preliminary results. The Centro de Investigaciones Históricas at Universidad de Costa Rica, and especially my colleagues in the quantitative history program, also contributed significantly. The staff of the Archivo Nacional, Registro de la Propiedad, Registro Civil and local parishes was extremely helpful. Those in charge of the historical archives in Medellín, the Fundación Antioqueña de Estudios Sociales, and the public notaries and parish offices in southwestern Antioquia allowed me to obtain valuable information. I received an Inter-American Foundation research fellowship for part of my fieldwork in Costa Rica and Colombia, as well as a Fulbright scholarship for graduate studies at the University of California. None of these institutions is responsible for the content of this book.

The people who shared their personal knowledge of history with me through interviews were essential to this research project, and I sincerely hope they find their lives reflected here, to a certain extent, and in the appropriate manner.

Mario Samper

Chapter 1

INTRODUCTION

This is a study on peasant-farmers, neither fully traditional and subsistence-oriented, nor totally mercantile in their productive activities, their values, and their social relations. The following analysis focuses on a specific region of Costa Rica: the northwestern section of the Central Valley. There, as in several other regions of Latin America and the Caribbean which hardly conform to generalizations based on areas where vast haciendas and their conflictive interactions with Indian communities have been historically predominant, effective land settlement was, to a large extent, carried out by a geographically mobile and personally free population, most or all of which came from areas settled during colonial times.

This process, together with an active interest by merchants and certain public policies which favored access to land, however inegalitarian, cleared the ground for an export-oriented rural economy in which household production of commodities such as coffee played a fundamental role. Credit, processing and trade networks linked local producers, often relying primarily on family labor, to the world market. In the process, increasingly specialized peasant-farmers obtained tangible benefits while they also entered into a situation from which they found it difficult to disentangle themselves as it became less favorable over time.

In the nineteenth and twentieth centuries, rural households in this region and elsewhere in Costa Rica interacted in various seemingly contradictory ways with other productive units and social forces. Such relations involved both economic antagonism and complementarity, as well as the combination of sociopolitical alliances and confrontations among the same collective actors. The underlying social dynamics are, no doubt, relevant to an understanding of the current dilemmas of this rural society, and of the manner in which the descendants of settlers have sought to deal with them.

This is also a story of individual men, women and children who need not be anonymous, except insofar as required by respect for the privacy of their relatives regarding certain situations in the past. In the course of their lives, members of settler families were actively involved in multiple exchanges between rural households and their markets or, more generally, their changing societal environment: as commodity producers who also grew or made much of what they required; as consumers of foodcrops and manufactured products, some of which tended to displace local agricultural production or craftsmanship; as part-time or full-time wage earners, whether on other peasant farms or on haciendas; as participants in labor exchanges among domestic, household-based units, and sometimes as small-scale contractors of seasonal or permanent workers; as sharecroppers, tenant farmers or persons who bought and sold land; as lenders and as borrowers, often simultaneously; as individuals with various complementary or contradictory socioeconomic and sociopolitical insertions in an agrarian society which underwent deep transformations in the course of a few decades.

Individual members of rural households were also involved in complex, often conflictive interrelations within the co-resident family unit: working together on the household plot under kinship relations which were far from egalitarian, with a division of labor by sex and age which also represented a distribution of power; struggling together for subsistence or prosperity of the household, and also competing among each other for immediate benefits and for inheritance rights; and contributing with their work to the viability of the domestic unit, then leaving it out of a shared necessity to recreate peasant farming on the more distant frontiers.

At a more general level of analysis, the generations of settlers studied here were collective participants in the development, in Costa Rica, of a set of social relations which can be discussed with reference to an historically specific concept of agrarian capitalism. In relation to the rural society upon which we will focus, peasant-farmer households controlled much of the land and of commodity production, including export crops. Yet in the final analysis, the local owners of wealth, accrued from various economic activities of the colonial period and enhanced by direct access to British trade and credit after independence from Spain, organized and controlled the production of agricultural commodities for the local and European markets, in the way they found best suited to their interests, given local conditions regarding land, labor, and other factors. By combining direct and indirect control of agroexport production, they minimized risk and concentrated their investments in the most profitable activities and areas. In so doing, given the initial abundance of land relative to population, they allowed for a parallel, complementary rather than mutually exclusive expansion of market-oriented agriculture on variously-sized productive units, both in previously- and in newly-settled regions.

Public policies, which were clearly designed by the local elite after Independence, played a major role with respect to the social heterogeneity of commodity production. Instead of restricting access to the land and forcefully recruiting laborers to work on haciendas, nineteenth-century governments actively promoted land claims, large or small, as well as settlement on the frontier and coffee cultivation on all types of holdings. Far from opposing such policies, merchants -and later processing firms- advanced credit to rural households for them to invest in coffee production, and owners of large tracts of land in certain areas sold parts of it to reap a handsome short-term profit and attract settlers to the region.

Peasant-farmer settlement on or near the initially large land claims not only made the remaining estate land more valuable, it also created a potential source of labor for the estate itself, at least on a seasonal basis. Domestic units also supplied agricultural products and livestock for local consumption. This, together with imports from other regions or countries as transportation networks improved, made it possible for the estates to slowly shift away from food-crops and cattle, so as to concentrate on one or several specifically commercial agricultural products. As rural households themselves shifted into agro-export cultivation, primarily of coffee, they supplemented estate production and permitted economies of scale in processing, transportation, and marketing by the merchant-planter elite.

Although it had significant colonial antecedentes (for example in livestock raising, sugarcane and tobacco cultivation) household-based commodity production in Costa Rica's Central Valley, and especially its major export component was, to a large extent, created by the very expansion of agrarian capitalism in Costa Rica. Widespread peasant commodity production in this country is something more than the survival of a precapitalist past in a mercantile environment; it is a result of the historically specific way in which capital accumulation took place in this rural society at the time. To be sure, peasant-farmer access to the land and successful involvement in commercial agriculture was one of the factors which made wage labor continue to be a scarce commodity through the early stages of agro-export growth, and thus restricted the establishment of very large coffee plantations during that period in Costa Rica. Yet market-oriented production based on household labor, and especially coffee production by domestic units, was not only a goal for peasant-farmers themselves, but also fostered actively by the ruling elite of merchant-planters, in the context of a generalization of mercantile relations in the countryside. By facilitating access to the land and providing credit, while establishing a monopoly over processing and the export-import business, owners of capital contributed to the rise of a strong sector of commercial peasant farming while pursuing their own economic objectives. In so doing, they indirectly expanded their control over production in a highly profitable manner, yet they also strengthened a domestic production sector which would continue to be a major component of rural society, despite subsequent changes in the original conditions.

It is in light of these historical processes that we seek to understand the interlinkages between rural households and their markets, as well as the concrete social meanings of the various ways in which members of these households participated in complex, seemingly ambivalent networks of social relations. A comprehension of the early establishment of such interactions will be our starting point for an historical analysis of how they were redefined during later stages, as the initial setting was fundamentally altered in the specific region and in Costa Rican society as a whole. Land/labor ratios declined rapidly during the latter part of the nineteenth century and in the early decades of the twentieth; by the turn of the century there was not much unclaimed agricultural land within the Central Valley, and the settlement frontier had moved on to peripheral areas of the country. Even though major sectors of the rural population had attained material benefits from agro-export growth, social distance had also increased. Accumulation of capital was accompanied by a growing importance of rural wage labor, though not by a widespread proletarianization of peasant-farmer households, whose members devised alternative strategies for survival.

As land gradually became scarce in former frontier regions, by the combined effect of settlement itself, demographic growth and landholding concentration, rural households perforce were placed in situations which, despite individual variations and greater or lesser opportunities for success, imposed certain options on their members. The outcome of the domestic units' decisions or actions with respect to such options, not necessarily of their own choice, affected not only their short-term conditions but also their long-term viability. Components of household strategies in face of trends and fluctuations which threatened the sustained reproduction of domestic units included, among others:

- agricultural intensification and specialization in land use patterns, with increasingly higher labor inputs per area and certain inherent risks, i.e. greater vulnerability;
- non-agricultural activities and forms of employment of household members in a gamut from artisanal production, processing of agricultural products and transportation, to professional training, e. g. in education;
- part-time, seasonal, or permanent wage labor on other productive units within or without the region;
- selective migration of growing numbers of children and grandchildren of former settlers.

Quite often, rural households followed several of these paths simultaneously or shifted from one emphasis to another in response to changing internal and external conditions. As a result of such partly imposed and partly chosen options, the landholding foundations of domestic production in this region eroded in the course of several decades, with varying impacts on specific rural households. Subdivision of holdings through sale and inheritance was a generalized process with different meanings for various types of productive units. Pressures in this direction differed over time, in response to the relative availability of material resources, factor intensities, social differentiation within the region and inheritance systems which slowly adapted to societal changes. The general direction of this adaptation was from absolute partibility toward a system of preferential inheritance, partly based on legal modifications but especially on the need to counteract extreme fragmentation of holdings, so as to maintain viable, even if very small, economic units.

In any case, these options, dilemmas and strategies of rural households require an historical explanation with reference not only to the specific regional case, but also to Costa Rican society and to a broader comparative context which, to be meaningful, must also refer to certain relevant conceptual issues. The Costa Rican case exemplifies one of the several different ways in which rural societies have become increasingly mercantile without necessarily following the classical path of "prior" or "primitive" accumulation, i.e. expropriation of the landholding peasantry as a prerequisite for agrarian capitalism. Quite the contrary, peasant-farmer access to the land and household agro-export production essentially resulted from the very process by which agrarian capitalism reorganized the Costa Rican landscape, the technical organization of production, societal and domestic relations, socio-political interactions and value systems. It also shows how rural commodity production, and more specifically mercantile relations between direct producers and owners of capital, can develop over a relatively long period under forms of land tenure and social interaction which have little to do with abstract, classical definitions of "agrarian capitalism" or "capitalistic relations".

In Costa Rica, as in several other Latin American cases which will be discussed comparatively in the final chapter, peasant farming is still of great significance in the export sector of the economy, a century and a half after production based on family labor became a fundamental component of production for the world market. The question, clearly, is not whether peasant commodity production will someday disappear, but why and how it came to be so important in the course of that very same process of capital accumulation which otherwise might have hindered or destroyed it. And the question is relevant to understand the role that peasant-farmer households are playing today in these societies, both as economic units and as collective actors on the socio-political arena.

This book will first present certain conceptual issues regarding household commodity production and agrarian capitalism, and it will also refer to specific issues in Costa Rican historiography. It will then focus on the regional case-study, addressing the following aspects and questions through empirical analysis:

1. A characterization of land use and other economic activities, at a regional level and per types of productive units, at three points in time representing early settlement, an intermediate situation, and systematic out-migration. Questions addressed in this connection included:

- What were the main changes in the composition of rural households' movable and immovable possessions during the period?
- How did that composition reflect greater or lesser market orientation and/or need to work for wages or hire laborers?
- How does the composition of movable and immovable possessions of domestic units compare to that of larger and smaller units?

- Were there significant subregional variations in the composition of household possessions, and how can they be explained?

2. An analysis of variations in the way productive factors were combined in selected cases over several generations, from initial settlement to outmigration.
   - At what rate, and to what extent, was land use intensified in terms of product per area and the various inputs at a regional, subregional and productive-unit level?
   - How did the allocation of factors of production to agriculture, crafts, processing and transportation vary over time?
   - In what ways did transformations in rural production and market involvement affect the distribution of productive tasks and labor requirements over the year in the various types of units?

3. A discussion of the strategies used by domestic units in response to new possibilities and dilemmas raised by their active insertion into product, land, labor and credit markets in the region, as it was transformed from a settlement frontier to an area of out-migration.
   - To what extent did the characteristics, motivations and socioeconomic prospects of settlers change during the period under analysis, and for what reasons?
   - How did domestic units react to changes in their social environment, e.g. early opportunities for accumulation and, later on, the increasingly limited options available to them?

The specific questions regarding the regional case study will then be set in a broader comparative and conceptual framework, to address issues such as the role of peasant farming in the development of agro-export production; the reasons for substantial variations in the relative importance of various types of productive units in given regions, over time; and the contradictory nature of social relations when independent peasant farmers are a major part of the rural population but their societal context is in many ways akin to agrarian capitalism.

Primary sources of information on the Costa Rican case include a series of population and production censuses, parish records, probate inventories, real estate registry, oral history, and others. Systematic population counts were available for 1843-44, 1864, 1883, 1892, 1927 and 1950 with the original household-level information in 1843-44 and 1927. These were used for follow-up on individual cases, while all five provided general data on demographic trends and occupational characteristics.

Coffee production censuses were taken regionally in 1878 and nationwide in 1935, the latter providing information on crop mixes and other productive characteristics of coffee farms at a cantón level. Regarding other products, there is some statistical information, of doubtful precision, for 1884, 1888, 1892, and 1905, which was used to obtain an overall picture of changes in land use. The first modern agricultural censuses were taken in 1950 and 1955.

There are well-kept parish records throughout the Central Valley covering much of the period under analysis, and aggregate statistics have been derived from them in several studies. These were used to supplement census information and outline demographic changes, but information from the original records also helped the tracing of individual cases and certain specific research questions.

Probate inventories, wills and other inheritance-related legal documents were of primary importance in characterizing the various types of production units. They provided a relatively precise view of land tenure, land use and movables per household, as well as inheritance practices and personal information, which served to present three chronological cross-sections at critical points in time: 1850-1859, 1895-1904, and 1926-1935. They also were the basis for identification of specific cases which were followed throughout the period, through these and other sources. Information from the real estate registry, available for most of the period, complemented that from the probate inventories. It was used to validate data on land tenure, use and disposition, as well as to study changes through time of individual properties. While a complete study of notarized purchases would have gone beyond the scope of this study, landholding transactions were followed-up retrospectively and prospectively for case studies of selected units of production, identified through probate proceedings.

Oral history was another, extremely valuable source for information unavailable from written sources. Elderly descendants of the deceased in 1926-1935 were sought out in towns and remote areas, and more than fifty were interviewed. Their testimony was of great qualitative importance to understand key aspects of rural households toward the end of our period, and certain projections beyond.

From these sources, as well as from the bibliography, an overall view was obtained of agrarian changes from initial settlement to large-scale out-migration, especially with reference to population and production. It was also possible to characterize specific types of productive units, and study variations in their internal organization, reproductive strategies and external linkages. Certain technical and social aspects of production and exchange could not be covered appropriately, for lack of sources. Many other topics were dealt with only tangentially, especially political and cultural aspects which are undoubtedly important. Nevertheless, the socioeconomic groundwork presented here should stimulate further research on the Costa Rican case, as well as a cross-regional and cross-national comparative discussion.

Chapter Two outlines the main issues to be discussed, while dismissing others which have no sound historical basis in the Costa Rican case. It also outlines a conceptual framework, specifically refered to domestic units and their economic interaction, concluding with a preliminary typology. Chapter Three provides the essential background on early settlement up to the mid-nineteenth century. Chapter Four presents the agrarian situation, especially that of rural households, in the 1850's. The fifth chapter discusses the relevant transformations during the latter part of the nineteenth century, ending with an analysis of productive units at the turn of the century. Chapter Six continues into the 1930's and beyond, with an emphasis on the increasingly acute dilemmas faced by peasant households toward the end of the period, and how they sought to solve them. The final chapter situates the Costa Rican case within a wider comparative context, especially with respect to Colombia, where the author has done primary-source research on a comparable region. Other, relevant Latin American cases are discussed upon the basis of existing secondary sources. Questions addressed comparatively are also related to the relevant historiographical and conceptual issues raised in earlier chapters.

Chapter 2

DOMESTIC UNITS AND SOCIAL ENVIRONMENT

Three initial topics will be dealt with in this chapter, providing a basis for a contextualized presentation of the specific case study in following chapters. First, the indispensable historical background is briefly summarized for those unfamiliar with Costa Rican history. Second, a discussion is undertaken of the major historiographical issues which are relevant to our regional case, and those which are not. Third, a conceptual framework for the historical analysis of domestic units and their interactions among each other, with different types of economic units, and with societal processes is presented.

An Historical Context

From late colonial times well into the twentieth century, land settlement and peasant farming have been outstanding features of Costa Rican rural history. The territory of this country is relatively small, just over fifty-one thousand square kilometers, if we include the Partido de Nicoya, annexed in 1824, shortly after Independence from Spain. Even so, population at the end of the colonial period was concentrated in a few small regions covering less than five percent of the territory: mainly in the Meseta Central, where more than four fifths of the population lived at the time, and in certain sparsely settled peripheral areas (Figure 2.1).

The Meseta is an area some 40 km. long and 20 km. wide, set within the tectonic depression known as the Central Valley, which is four or five times larger. It is flanked by mountains to the north and south. Soils here are mostly of volcanic and sedimentary origin, and quite fertile. This *graben* is well-watered, with numerous rivers and creeks running down from the slopes of the volcanoes and other mountains. The climate is temperate, and most agricultural lands in the Central Valley are at altitudes between 800 and 1600 meters. Most inhabitants of this region were either of Spanish descent or "*mestizos*", although several small Indian towns remained within the Meseta Central under Spanish colonial rule.

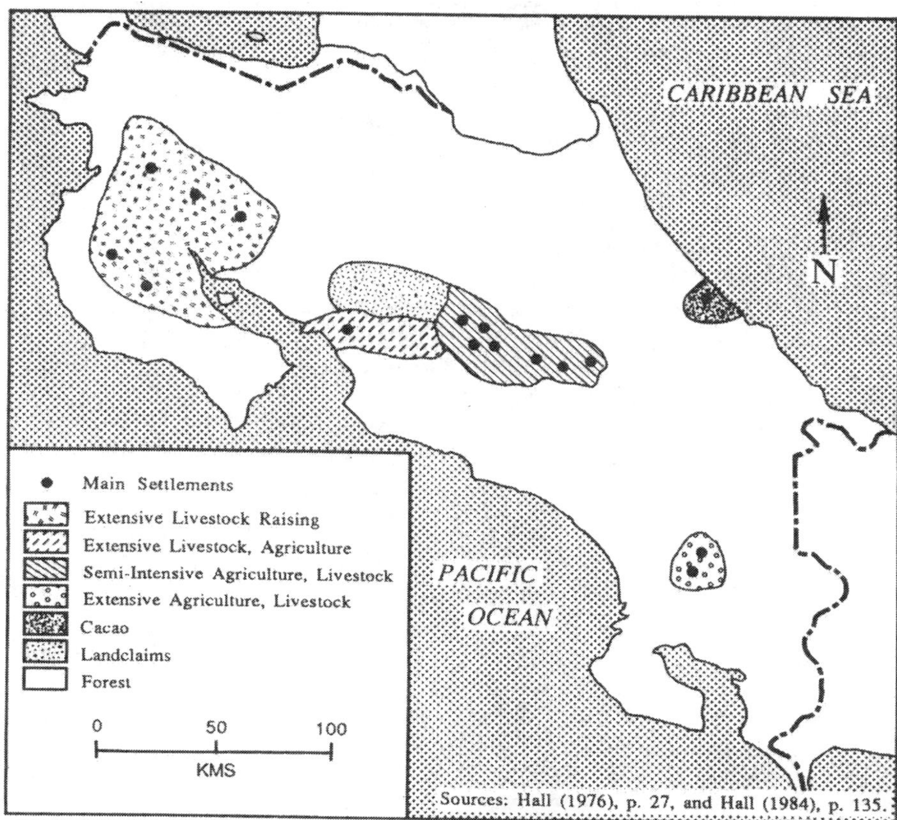

Figure 2.1 Late-colonial settlement and land use in Costa Rica

Other inhabited regions of the country, toward the early nineteenth century, were the Pacific settlements of Liberia, Esparza and Nicoya, where about nine percent of the population lived. This part of the country is dryer, and the climate quite warm. Soils are often less fertile than in the Central Valley, except for the sedimentary ones near certain rivers. The other two, very minor areas of colonial settlement were: Matina, on the Atlantic coast, where there had been some cacao cultivation; and the Indian settlements of Térraba and Boruca, in the southern part of the country.

Elsewhere, save for a thinly spread out indigenous population not subject to colonial rule, especially in the Talamanca area, the remaining territory was almost uninhabited and was covered by forests. Population densities in Costa Rica were, therefore, quite low throughout the colonial period, just over one person per square kilometer at the time of Independence from Spain.

In the following century, despite fluctuations, the country's population grew from roughly 65,000 to almost half a million inhabitants.[1] During this same period, extensive land settlement spread throughout the Central Valley and then into the peripheral territories. In the century after Independence, occupation of new lands in Costa Rica was mainly carried out by the local population, except in two specific regions: the Atlantic coast, where Jamaicans came as hired laborers to work on the banana plantations after construction of the railroad in the 1870's, and the northern plains, where Nicaraguan immigrants had settled before many Costa Ricans arrived from the central highlands.

In most cases, the centrifugal movement from the coffee-producing regions, which gradually expanded within the Central Valley, sought to reproduce a market-oriented type of rural production. Locally-produced consumption goods were necessary in the early years on the frontier, when communications were very poor. But livestock raising, maize production, sugarcane and coffee, especially, were economic activities with which the settlers hoped to and often did reenter the market as commodity producers. The goal of settlement was, quite clearly, other than mere subsistence.

This movement of population, and the associated changes in landscape, land tenure and land use patterns, followed several routes within and beyond the Central Valley. However, during the nineteenth century it was especially important in the region on which this case study will focus, the Northwest. First, in the middle decades of the century, this was the main area of peasant-farmer settlement, a process which fundamentally altered landholding and land use in the course of a few decades. Then, toward the latter part of the century, it became one of the major regional sources of out-migration toward various other parts of the country. Let us briefly introduce these generations of settlers, before discussing certain specific issues of interpretation to which we will return in the following chapters.

---

1 Hall (1984), p. 143.

From the early through mid-nineteenth century, people from the main area of Colonial settlement in Costa Rica's Meseta Central (Figure 2.2) moved westward, beyond the city of Alajuela, to a previously unsettled region in the northwestern part of the tectonic depression known generally as the Central Valley, even though it actually includes a number of smaller valleys. Population grew rapidly in the areas of settlement, as immigrants continued to arrive, and large families were the rule. Towns were founded, mule tracks emerged and cartroads were constructed, and the landscape fundamentally altered by the efforts of settlers who, in doing so, redeveloped social ties in a new, challenging environment.

During the latter part of that century, forests were transformed into pastures, maize fields, sugarcane and coffee plantations. Initially-large land claims were partly broken up, and while some estates employed wage laborers, family-based domestic units played a very significant role in commercial agriculture. The ever more numerous peasant farms became smaller, especially due to partible inheritance practices, but agricultural intensification and a gradual specialization in coffee compensated for diminished areas from one generation to the next. It was not until the turn of the century that serious limitations to the independent establishment of new rural households within the region became apparent, though out-migration had already begun.

Between the late-nineteenth century and the 1930s, children and grandchildren of those who had settled the northwestern area joined the growing number of Costa Ricans who opened up new agricultural frontiers beyond the Central Valley. The abundant and virgin soil which received their forefathers had been made productive, but also scarce. Not only had the landscape changed, but also the apparent egalitarianism of early settlement had given way to increasingly conflictive social relations, despite a persistent element of complementarity.

Increasingly difficult access to land within the northwestern area and technological limitations -not to be overcome until the middle of the twentieth century- restricted the local options available to the descendants of the original settlers. Given the existence of agricultural frontiers beyond the Central Valley, emigration by members of domestic units was an alternative, once again, for members of households seeking to avoid excessive fragmentation of their lands.

Out-migration and market-oriented specialization were but two components of complex strategies devised by rural households, first to take advantage of opportunities and then to face increasingly adverse conditions. They involved constant adjustments of labor capacity and material resources, technical and social organization of production, household consumption and reinvestment, even personal relations, values and expectations. Their outcome was of major consequence in terms of the overall reproduction of domestic units, both within the Central Valley and in the areas of settlement opened up as of the late nineteenth century. There is a need to understand the conditions under which these processes took place, the underlying social changes, and their implications for future generations.

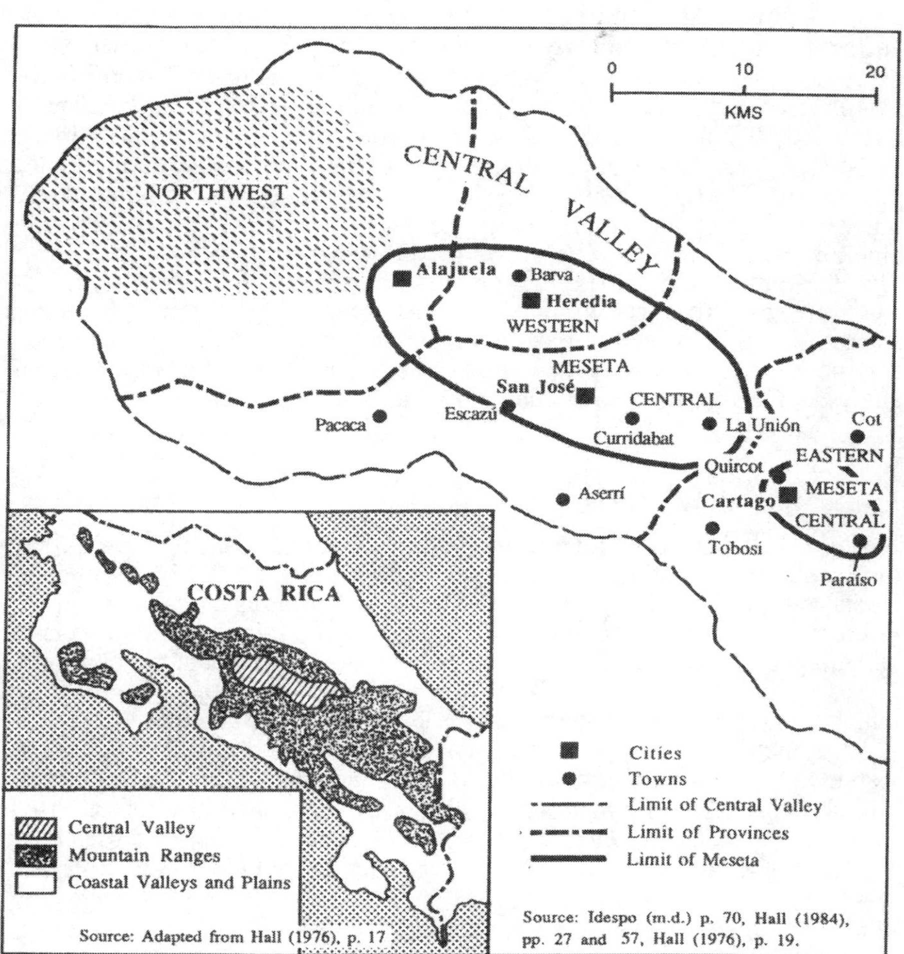

Figure 2.2 Regions of Costa Rica around 1848

The fundamental processes and the dilemmas faced by peasant-farmers during colonization and agro-export development were not unique to Costa Rica. Elsewhere in Latin America and the Caribbean, as in various other previously unsettled parts of the world, successive generations of settlers effected similar agrarian transformations -with certain critical differences- during the nineteenth and early twentieth centuries. This study presents and discusses a specific case of agro-export development with significant smallholder participation, in a context of geographical expansion through land settlement as well as major societal transformations, especially those associated with the generalization of mercantile relations and commodity production. The questions raised should be relevant to many other cases, but especially to an understanding of "atypical" processes of agrarian change and the role of peasant commodity production in agro-export growth. Matters of historical interpretation regarding the Costa Rican case-study are, therefore, set within the context of conceptual issues from the start, and will be placed in a comparative perspective in the Epilogue. At this point, it is necessary to identify the major points for an historical analysis of the regional case-study in Costa Rica.

Issues and Non-issues

From the mid-nineteenth century, as a consequence of processes outlined in the previous section, several generations of rural households in Costa Rica's Central Valley faced a series of progressively more acute dilemmas, regarding which they devised various strategies either to take advantage of perceived opportunities or to ensure economic survival despite increasingly limited options. The context for such decisions was a rapidly changing agrarian environment, where extensive land settlement led to the development of many new productive units, large and small, in the framework of a booming agricultural export economy. A relatively poor, though inegalitarian colonial society was being transformed by coffee-based outward growth and by the expansion of domestic markets for other agricultural products, as well as for labor, land, and credit. Social relations were deeply affected, with members of rural households becoming more and more involved in these markets, often simultaneously, as independent commodity producers, as wage-workers and/or contractors of labor, and as participants in various land-tenure or credit transactions.

The changing socioeconomic and sociopolitical conditions under which these multiple market insertions took place were, of course, a given fact for individual households, but the aggregate result of economic decisions by numerous domestic units decisively influenced the overall process. An explanation of the specific (but not necessarily unique) characteristics of agrarian capitalism in Costa Rica requires an analysis of the complex interactions between peasant households and their social environment.

In the period and area on which this regional case-study focuses, there was a parallel and intertwined development of domestic or household production units and of larger economic units based primarily on wage labor. The various linkages among them were partly complementary, insofar as entrepreneurial and petty commodity producers shared certain common interests, despite their antagonisms. At first, a relatively open agricultural frontier provided real opportunities not only for landgrabbers but also for middling peasant settlers, many of whom succeeded in an increasingly commodified rural economy. Thereafter, conditions evolved less favorably for mercantile peasant-farmers than for the larger estate-owners, as local access to land became difficult for a rapidly growing population and as formerly scarce labor became more and more abundant.

Peasant-farmers, whether in previously-occupied or in newly-settled regions, tended to specialize rapidly and extensively in market-oriented production, with its inherent risks and potential benefits. Consumption needs were satisfied only partly by diversified subsistence production. Specialization in and within agriculture was the dominant trend on peasant farms, even though export-oriented agriculture had begun on the larger estates. Intensive commodity production was, in fact, one of the means by which domestic units first consolidated their hold on the land, and then sought to counteract its more limited availability in later stages. Given the legal and social norm of partible inheritance, land subdivision was closely associated with agricultural intensification and specialization. On the other hand, a gradually receding settlement frontier -within and beyond the Central Valley- offered an outlet for certain members of domestic units, and also diminished or delayed the pressures for fragmentation, but could not counteract the latter process completely. Part-time wage labor and non-agricultural activities were an occupational alternative for some household members, not only due to the reduced size of holdings, but also because specialization in coffee (the main export commodity) led to strong seasonal fluctuations in family labor-time requirements on domestic production units. In the long run, the very existence of such domestic, household-based units was threatened by severely restricted options, and decisions tended to be more costly for them in many ways. However, peasant farmers neither disappeared nor reverted to subsistence-oriented or consumption-oriented agriculture. Persistent smallholder commodity production, seasonal wage-labor, continued out-migration and the presence of a growing landless population in the region attest to the complexity of individual and collective peasant strategies for economic survival from the mid-nineteenth century into the 1930s, and are still characteristic of the area.

The active and multi-level participation of numerous domestic agricultural production units in commodity, land, labor and credit transactions throughout the period was a feature of agrarian capitalism in Costa Rica. However, peasant-farming was not equally prevalent in the various regions or subregions, as will be seen in the following chapters. Domestic units, further discussed in the next section, did in fact control a major part of the land and of commercial agricultural production in the specific region studied here, the northwestern section of the Central Valley. This is also true of several other areas of Costa Rica and, for that matter, of

Latin America. Their successful commodity specialization was, nevertheless, far from autonomous. Rather, it resulted from a conflictive interaction between peasant-farmers and merchants, moneylenders, owners of processing mills and of estates. These relationships involved both association and confrontation, mutual benefit and direct or indirect exploitation, in ways which varied from case to case and over time.

The social reality to which we refer would hardly be in accordance with an idyllic version of a homogeneous rural society of equally-poor subsistence farmers, nor would it fit into an explanatory model based primarily on primitive accumulation or expropriation of the peasantry as a prerequisite for capital formation, and wage labor as the predominant social relation. The conceptual issues underlying alternative characterizations are undoubtedly relevant to an understanding of the specific nature of agrarian capitalism and agro-export development in Costa Rica. They will here be addressed through an empirical case-study and some comparative analysis, rather than abstract discussion of a theoretical nature, once certain basic concepts have been set forth. But first let us state, in summary fashion, how these issues relate to prevalent conceptions regarding the history of agrarian change in Costa Rica and Latin America.

The alleged uniqueness of Costa Rican rural history, an idea tied to that of a presumably more egalitarian land-tenure situation, vis-à-vis certain other Central or Latin American societies, merits a closer look in light of several "atypical" agrarian changes in various regions of the continent. There is a need to discuss possible explanations of the rather obvious discrepancy between cases where a landed peasantry played a significant role in agro-export development, on the one hand, and often-used typologies based on the "latifundia-minifundia" dyad or on a view of peasants as traditional, subsistence-oriented producers, on the other. Among such cases, one might mention certain coffee-growing areas in Colombia, Venezuela or the West Indies where peasant production was especially important.[2] Even in countries where very large estates undoubtedly predominated in coffee production, such as El Salvador, Guatemala or Brazil, peasant households played a role both as providers of labor and as commodity producers, whether within or without the export

---

2 Specific historical and bibliographic references to these and other cases will be made later. At this point, suffice it to state that there is a vast literature on Colombia, which will be our primary comparative counterpart. Many studies of specific aspects or areas were published between James Parsons' 1948 doctoral dissertation, *Antioqueño Colonization in Western Colombia* (1949), and Marco Palacios' revised edition of *El café en Colombia, 1850-1970* (1983), while studies on the subject continue to appear. Other areas where peasants played a major role in coffee production have not been studied in such detail nor by so many researchers, but at least the following should be mentioned: William Roseberry, *Coffee and capitalism in the Venezuelan Andes* (1983); Gisela Eisner, *Jamaica 1830-1930* (1961); Douglas Hall, *Free Jamaica, 1838-1865* (1981); Fernando Picó, *Amargo café* (1981); and Laird W. Bergad, *Coffee and the Growth of Agrarian Capitalism in Nineteenth-Century Puerto Rico* (1983).

sector.[3] Domestic units were also significant in other areas of market-oriented agriculture throughout Latin America, despite the existence of vast estates and of very inegalitarian rural societies, from Mexico to Argentina.[4] But with few exceptions, their historical significance has been systematically minimized, both in the various national historiographies and in many comprehensive studies. As Lowell Gudmundson has stated:

> For nineteenth-century Latin America, even such penetrating analyses as those of Stanley and Barbara Stein and Bradford Burns fail to allow any room for smallholder agriculture in their transitionary typologies.[5]

In the case of Costa Rica, where the economic significance of domestic rural commodity production is undeniable, it has frequently been typified as an either "backward" or "precapitalist" remnant of something akin to a "golden age",[6] gradually disappearing as capitalist relations expand and mature. The major importance of market-oriented peasant farming has also been considered an exceptional or anomalous trait, rather than a basic feature of the way agrarian capitalism developed, historically, not only in this but in other comparable cases. Costa Rican history generally, and that of mercantile household production in its rural areas, has usually been

---

3 The role of market-oriented peasant farming within economies where large estates clearly predominated has not been dealt with systematically, but several local studies have pointed out its importance in specific regions despite landholding concentration: For El Salvador, one might mention Ernesto Richter's "Proceso de acumulación y dominación en la formación socio-política salvadoreña" (1976), which documents peasant coffee production, or David Browning's *El Salvador, Landscape and Society* (1971). For Guatemala, where Indian-peasant communities and vast estates were clearly differentiated in terms of their main productive activities, but linked by coercive labor recruitment, one can mention, among various others, J. C. Cambranes, *Coffee and Peasants in Guatemala* (1985) and Humberto Flores, *Proletarización del campesino de Guatemala* (1977). For Brazil, there are many studies of the *colonato* system of foreign immigrants on *fazenda* lands, among the earlier of which are E. Viotti da Costa, *Da senzala à colonia* (1966), and Thomas H. Holloway, *Migration and Mobility: Immigrants as Laborers and Land-owners in the Coffee Zone of São Paulo, Brazil, 1886-1934* (1974).

4 In the case of Mexico, formerly an archetype of nearly absolute *hacienda* domination, various studies of *rancheros* derived from David Brading's *Haciendas and Ranchos in the Mexican Bajío* (1978). For Argentina, another stereotypical case of vast estates in control of the land and of exports, see Eduardo Archetti and Kristi-Anne Stölen, *Explotación familiar y acumulación de capital en el campo argentino* (1975).

5 Gudmundson, Lowell, *Costa Rica Before Coffee* (1986a), p. 158.

6 Regarding Costa Rica, traditional historiography and some more recent studies abound in this type of characterization, e. g. Carlos Monge Alfaro, *Historia de Costa Rica* (1974) and Mitchell Allan Seligson, *El campesino y el capitalismo agrario de Costa Rica* (1980). For a solid critique of such positions, see L. Gudmundson (1986a), pp. 1-24.

viewed in isolation, or contrasted with an oversimplified idea of how agricultural production is organized elsewhere in Latin America.

There have, nevertheless, been some recent, stimulating efforts to situate Costa Rican social, economic and political history in a comparative framework. Ciro Cardoso and Héctor Pérez have focused primarily on divergences vis-à-vis other Central and Latin American processes in which agrarian change followed very different socioeconomic and sociopolitical paths, although at the same time they have indicated certain similarities with other formerly peripheral areas of Spanish America.[7] Lowell Gudmundson, and his commentators in a 1986 symposium on coffee in Costa Rica,[8] have suggested various avenues for comparative analysis in the context of Latin American transformations with much more affinity among them, as well as common discrepancies with the hacienda, latifundia and plantation models. And a comparative research program on Central American rural history is now underway at the Universidad Nacional in Costa Rica, gradually involving other specialists in the field.

Among the various historical cases of major agricultural regions which do not fit into the formerly accepted stereotype of rural Latin America, there are equally important similarities and differences, which only a joint effort based on comparable case-studies can fully describe or discuss. A few such elements will be brought up, toward the end of this book, primarily as regards the Costa Rican and Colombian cases, but also with respect to other regions of Latin America and the Caribbean. It is hoped that this will contribute to the development of a broader framework for systematic comparison, in terms of the various combinations of diverse and interrelated productive units; of consumption and market-oriented agriculture; of family and wage-labor; and other components of interaction between domestic units and their markets. It may also elucidate relations between direct producers and capital, or between peasant-farmers and a merchant-planter elite.

The alleged singularity of the Costa Rican case involves both a mythical element and one which is based on distinct historical processes. On the one hand, certain specific features tend to be exaggerated, and characteristics in common with other rural areas of Latin America are left

---

7 In *Centroamérica y la economía occidental* (1977), Ciro Cardoso and Héctor Pérez systematically compared the economic history of Costa Rica to that of the other Central American countries, stressing differential factors, while in the second volume of *Historia económica de América Latina* (1981) they emphasized similarities with settlement of "empty areas" elsewhere in Latin America. Héctor Pérez (1977, 1986) has also written comparative essays on export agriculture in Costa Rica and Argentina, and on the sociopolitical history of Central America.

8 Lowell Gudmundson has followed up on the comparative references in his doctoral dissertation both in "Rancheros and revisionism" (n.d.) and "La Costa Rica cafetalera en contexto comparado" (1986b), published together with comments by Catherine LeGrand, Elizabeth Kuznesof and William Roseberry, in *Revista de Historia* 14 (1986), pp. 31-39.

aside or unemphasized, so as to stress differences rather than affinities. This leads to idealized versions of Costa Rican rural history, which in turn substantiate the collective illusion that "Costa Rica is different" in Central or Latin America. Implicitly, there is the hope that these partly-true, partly-imaginary differences will suffice to cast away the contemporary demons which lurk in a turbulent geopolitical milieu.

On the other hand, certain undeniable specificities should forewarn us about merely substituting one ideological construct with another, or renouncing both complexity and diversity so as to enunciate an all-encompassing but simplistic formulation. Our research questions will be set within a basic conceptual framework, but answers need be sought in detailed study of concrete historical processes, then subject to comparative analysis, before any empirically-based generalizations can be attempted.

The fabricated issue of an absolute specificity or "uniqueness" of the manner in which agrarian capitalism developed in Costa Rica tends to disappear once we set aside frequent stereotypes on Latin American rural society, past and present. Dicotomies which forcefully insert historical peasantries into isolated compartments hinder, more than they help, by oversimplifying analyses of mutually-exclusive categories: traditional peasant versus modern farmer; culturally conservative or innovative mentality; subsistence producer versus entrepreneurial type; proletarianized peasant laborer as opposed to rural petty bourgeisie. Regarding these and other preconceived polarities, more often than not we find a combination of features of one and the other "ideal type", rather than a clear-cut differentiation in totally distinct segments of the rural population. The same is true for economic units which combine seemingly contradictory elements in their multi-level interactions, and even for specific individuals who participate in various kinds of mercantile relations. However, this does not preclude the theoretical and practical usefulness of inquiring why one or another feature tends to prevail under certain historical circumstances, or why such features tend to associate in certain ways.

To explain successful market-oriented specialization by peasant-farmers in nineteenth- and twentieth-century Costa Rica, in contrast to certain other areas of Latin America, factors such as the following have been stressed in the literature: [9]

- lack of a numerically important indigenous (or other) servile population;
- low demographic density throughout the colonial period;
- weak foreign immigration during the nineteenth and early twentieth century;

---

[9] The summary outline below is based on a large body of literature on the economic and social history of Costa Rica, specific references to which will be made in following chapters. However, Héctor Pérez clearly defined the major features on which there seems to be a consensus, in proposing his own model of agroexport development in Costa Rica: "Economía política del café en Costa Rica, 1850-1950" (1981).

- restricted concentration of agricultural land already under production;
- limited scope of agricultural exports prior to Independence; and
- relative importance of domestic-type holdings in the Costa Rican countryside, specifically in the Central Valley, before and during agro-export expansion.

The abovementioned factors, and additional ones which might be added to the list, are linked to three relevant characteristics of early nineteenth-century rural society in Costa Rica:

- A weakly developed local structure of production, especially as regards the international market (before coffee), despite the fact that there were local market exchanges as well as longer-distance trade.
- A scarcity of labor, due to the abovementioned demographic factors and the non-existence of forced labor recruitment on any significant scale at the time.
- A limited economic impact of expropriations of mainmort possessions during the late Colonial period and shortly after Independence, even though there was early liberal legislation to that effect.

Thus, all references in the literature on Costa Rica emphasize the lack of certain premises for the type of transition to agrarian capitalism which was linked to the expropriation of indigenous communities and/or forced labor recruitment elsewhere in Latin America. Nevertheless, an explanation based primarily on the absence of a given set of factors entails a degree of circularity: the absence of one or two factors, e.g. of a strong demographic pressure or of rapid concentration of productive land, is assigned a causal relationship with other factors, such as the scarcity of potential wage labor or the quantitative predominance of economic units employing household labor. To a certain extent that may be true, but actually the latter factors also influenced the former ones, inasmuch as productive landholding concentration (as opposed to formal ownership of large, unproductive tracts of land) was seriously hindered by difficulty in obtaining labor. And population growth would have led to greater pressures -and made more labor available- if independent household economic units had not been so numerous. Furthermore, all these interrelated factors can only be understood as components of a specific historical situation, determined by a complex set of positive socioeconomic, sociopolitical and cultural conditions, not just the absence of processes found elsewhere. For example, an explanation of the process of land settlement after 1830, in which many Costa Rican peasants were able to consolidate their situation via rapid market-specialization, requires consideration of several other variables, including:

- the specific manner in which expulsion from the previously-settled Meseta Central was combined with attraction to the northwestern section of the Central Valley, a variable combination involving quite a variety of economic and cultural components;

- government policies in favor of claims on public lands, which allowed for the formation of large landholdings but also permitted many peasants to acquire land;
- subdivision of some of the largest land claims, whether to obtain a profit or attract settlers, with the end result that more medium and small farms were established;
- an active role of merchant capital in promoting peasant farmer specialization in products for the local or international markets; or
- the prior productive experience of the settlers, the economic means available to each family, the material support provided by parents to their sons and daughters when they moved out to the frontier, and their expectations as migrants.

Another risk of explanations based primarily on the absence of certain conditions is the fact that a secondary role is almost inevitably assigned to the initiative or creative actions of concrete men and women, who individually and collectively transformed their own and others' social environment. Certainly there is a need, at some point, for categorization, factor-identification, and indication of trends, so as to transcend a historical narrative based on isolated events and outstanding individual protagonists. However, the frontier was not settled by abstract entities or forces, but by many very real, if often anonymous people sharing values, motivations, experiences, limitations, and hopes. It was they who opened up the forest, planted maize and raised cattle, sold sugarcane or coffee, formed new households and succeeded or failed in attaining their vision of a better life. It was also concrete people who claimed vast portions of public lands, inaccessible until the first mule-trails or cartroads; who often sold land to the first settlers at a profit, and other times sought to obtain still more land by whatever means and methods. Men and women of flesh and blood were involved in the various marketing and financial networks, in agricultural work or in processing of agricultural products, whether in dominant or subordinate positions. Relationships among them were multiple, variegated and in many ways contradictory. If merchants and estate-owners exploited those whose labor created wealth, and did so by various means, they also found that there were certain clearly-defined limits to such exploitation, due to objective conditions and subjective factors. We can analyze their interaction in terms of class relations involving both alliances and antagonisms, but we must also seek to understand how such social interrelations were created, over time, by historical individuals and groupings of individuals.

Though a systematic treatment of large numbers of cases requires quantitative analysis, the history we are reconstructing need not be one of anonymous actors. Insofar as possible, reference will be made to the active roles of those who perhaps unknowingly tilled the fruitful soils of an agrarian society undergoing deep changes. Appropriate categories will be used as analytical tools, but hopefully not as substitutes for historical knowledge, e.g. regarding relations between direct producers and owners of capital, regarding mercantile production on domestic units and multiple economic insertions in the context of a transitional process, and the specific characteristics of agrarian capitalism in the Costa Rican or other cases. On the other hand, it is not simply a matter of exemplifying, but rather of attempting to reconstruct, whenever possible, the direct involvement of men, women and children in the shaping of their own individual, family, communal and class history.

This study does not intend to judge the aims and motivations of the various historical actors, but rather to understand the process by which, given certain limits and potentialities, these persons, families, groups of relatives and neighbors, or strangers brought together by necessity and joint venture, settled new lands and built roads, towns, small or large enterprises, communal ties, affinities and differentiations. In doing so, they shaped a series of socioeconomic and sociopolitical relations among themselves, between peasants and merchants, between day-laborers and estate-owners, or within rural communities and households. The complexity and apparent ambigüity of such relations, involving both alliances and conflicts, cooperation and exploitation, are a challenge to the historian, but attempting to understand them should also bring us closer to the contraditory reality of our own society today.

The primary research focused on the process by which a major part of the peasantry shifted from the mixed livestock/agricultural production of early stages of settlement which, contrary to prior assumptions, seems not to have been primarily for self-consumption, to relatively specialized forms of commodity production, specifically for export. In a parallel or, rather, imbricated manner, wage labor developed in the recently settled areas, in response to needs both of the larger estates and of domestic units themselves. For many such households, market integration of their members as commodity producers or through wage labor were not mutually exclusive but rather complementary options. The dynamic interaction between one and the other process is the intermediate perspective adopted here regarding the productive and reproductive strategies of domestic units in the area and period.

In discussing such issues, the question arises as to the seemingly contradictory requirements of domestic, household-based units of production and consumption within mercantile economies, which have been observed in various other cases. (But not wherever we find peasantries, since the peasant-farmers to which we refer participate in an economic environment in which not only products, but also land and labor tend to become commodities, and are therefore not a universal, timeless category of agricultural producers relying on household labor.) On the one hand, there is a need to ensure not only personal and family subsistence, a heavy requirement in itself, but also cross-generational survival of the domestic production/consumption units themselves. This sets a limit to risk-taking by the household members, and both self-consumption and diversified productive activities act as insurance against natural or market-induced calamities, as well as other unforeseeable circumstances. On the other hand, commodity specialization can offer lucrative opportunities which peasant-farmers are very much aware of and willing to take, when the expected gains seem to compensate the risks or when they are forced to for other reasons, such as the diminishing size of holdings from one generation to the next.

Peasant-farmers' responses to this dilemma have varied historically, and have been influenced by specific factors, an understanding of which will shed light on linkages between the strategies of domestic units and social, economic, political and cultural processes which affect their internal decision-making and resource allocation. In turn, peasant households collectively are a basic component of that very same social environment which each domestic unit seemingly confronts as an isolated entity. In other words, the productive and reproductive options of domestic units reflect both their internal composition and the macro-context of which they themselves, together, are a major component. There is little use, then, for either "externalist" or "internalist" perspectives. In the former, domestic units are passive recipients or victims of their "circumstances", the "laws of market exchange" or "capitalism", depending on the viewpoint adopted. In the latter, the internal dynamics of a "smallholder", "peasant" or "petty commodity" mode of production becomes the motive force of its own history.

Even though peasant farming was the initial focus of the research reported here, an isolated analysis of "typical" domestic units would clearly have been insufficient. A model of interactions among various economic units and an appropriate typology—both of which are outlined in the following section—became necessary to take into account specific characteristics of this rural society, such as multiple economic insertions of members of peasant-farmer households, and as a tool to study a far more complex social reality. Furthermore, various types of productive units had to be considered, so as to discuss their interactions and the impact of overall changes on a specific grouping. As a matter of fact, in empirical analysis it would probably have been extremely difficult to even identify more than a few exceptional domestic units relying exclusively on family-labor, given the intricate interweaving of peasant commodity production and wage labor, and these would hardly be representative of a significant part of the rural population. Therefore, a more realistic approach required taking into account all household-based economic units, and comparing them with other types of productive units, with respect to specific variables and research questions.

The growth of peasant-farmer commodity production in nineteenth- and early-twentieth-century Costa Rica was impressive, but it was not self-generated in isolation from other social forces which played a major role in shaping rural society. Certain segments of the Costa Rican peasantry were relatively successful first in acquiring land, and later in ensuring reproduction of rural domestic units by means of a strategy based primarily on agricultural intensification and market-oriented specialization. This certainly defined important characteristics of the way in which members of rural households participated in their markets. On the other hand, this process was actively fostered by merchant capital, initially acting on its own and then as an extension of agroindustrial and financial capital during the coffee boom. Inherent shortcomings and contradictions of this partly complementary interaction would only become acute or apparent once socioeconomic conditions were substantially altered in later stages of settlement. The above raises two types of questions:

First, which were the objective and subjective factors which made such a strategy feasible and effective, in contrast to adverse spiritual and material conditions for peasant market specialization, and how did such factors come about, combine, and change over time? In various regions and periods we find situations in which such a process was clearly successful, and others in which it was not. The question is not, therefore, a merely academic one, but rather one directly related to social aspects of economic development in rural areas. Once again, Costa Rica is not as exceptional in this regard as we are sometimes led to believe, and comparison with other regions at least within Latin America should provide a better understanding both of the specific case and of broader processes. Of course, a systematic comparative analysis of such factors in multiple cases is beyond the scope of this work, but it is hoped that their historical discussion for Costa Rica and an outline of elements for comparison may contribute to a joint effort along these lines.

Second, why did the seemingly successful strategy of Costa Rican peasant-farmers not allow them to escape the dilemmas asociated with their growing involvement in a market economy which they themselves helped to develop? Once they were fully market-oriented and tended to specialize in a specific export commodity, they were more prone than ever to suffering the consequences of changing conditions in their economic, social and political environment, and they faced the need to defend their own interests under increasingly difficult circumstances. If toward the middle of the nineteenth century there was an accesible agricultural frontier, with real opportunities to acquire land in the northwestern section of the Central Valley, by the turn of the century that situation had changed radically in the region, and half a century later the main areas of settlement beyond the Central Valley were also disappearing. If during the latter half of the nineteenth century price trends for coffee were favorable to producers, despite short-term fluctuations, the opposite was true after the turn-of-the-century economic crisis, in real values vis-à-vis industrial goods and other imported items. In the early twentieth century, instability on the international market affected the income of highly specialized producers more and more violently. Furthermore, while the extremely high death rate of 1856-57 in Costa Rica had been, in the final analysis, a boon for the surviving peasantry, the reduction of mortality after the late nineteenth century, together with restricted access to land, led to growing social-demographic pressures in the region, while less outlets were available for "surplus" population. And even though liberal legislation made possible peasant access to the land (while at the same time allowing vast claims and even greater de facto acquisitions), by the turn of the century it had become an obsolete legal framework. Relations between peasant-farmers and the merchant-planter elite became increasingly conflictive. While there were still conciliatory mechanisms and elements of association between direct producers and those controlling economic and political power, their relations were redefined in terms of less compatible objectives. Basic structural contradictions became more apparent toward the end of the period, and also skewed the social effects of short-term economic fluctuations. New solidarities arose not only among wage-workers, but also among small-scale commodity producers in the region. These, in turn, led to a reformulation of their interactions with the socioeconomic and sociopolitical elites.

Costa Rican society today, like other historically similar societies, continues to undergo a process of social polarization and faces once again, by a combination of structural and conjunctural crises, the societal dilemmas raised by an inadequacy of productive, social, and political patterns. Any solution or outcome will necessarily involve a significant agrarian component, and current rural issues derive from historical transformations and continuities such as those mentioned above. The social actors today are not the same as in the past, and the specific issues at stake are also quite different, so that historical experiences cannot be directly applied to the solution of contemporary problems. But perhaps an understanding of comparable bygone situations can help to raise relevant questions about the present and inquire into the future implications of certain options, even though today's answers will surely differ from yesterday's.

A Conceptual Framework

This section will present certain intermediate-level tools for an analysis of increasingly mercantile production/consumption units, in areas where peasant farmers were actively involved in three interrelated processes of agrarian change:

- At a regional scale, a variable combination of attraction and expulsion factors led first to migration from previously settled areas to an agricultural frontier, with permanent settlement there, and later to out-migration of offspring. Unclaimed land, initially abundant, became scarce due not only to local demographic growth, but also to socioeconomic pressures. Emigration was one of the options open to descendants of former immigrants.
- At the level of productive units, land use patterns became more intensive, primarily in terms of labor inputs and resulting yields per area. This higher intensity was closely associated with market-oriented specialization, both in and within agriculture. Productive activities on such units were correspondingly reorganized, technically and socially. This was reflected in resource allocation, members' involvement in economic decision-making, and surplus disposition.

- Where micro and macro-social processes intersect, economic interaction was based upon a differentiation involving both complementarity and inequality, reciprocity and exploitation, in a movement from emphasis on the former to the latter. The conditions under which the members of productive units participated in production and exchange varied, as certain products and then labor were transformed into commodities. The social meaning of transactions in land and credit also changed fundamentally over time. Opportunities for accumulation, which had been open to many, tended to become a privilege of the few.

The basic concepts which will be discussed below focus on the characteristics and implications of the complex socioeconomic interaction (which is also a sociopolitical one) among direct producers, as well as between them and owners of capital. The analytical model, categories, and typology presented here are relevant both to the internal organization of productive units, especially domestic ones, and to the multiple, changing ways in which they -and their members individually- are or were involved in multi-level social relations. There is a need, especially, for a framework allowing us to perceive as clearly as possible the dynamic linkages among numerous variables such as population, access to the land and to other resources, technology for production, processing or transportation, and the ties -whether of association or conflict- among houshold members, between peasants and merchants, or between day-laborers and estate-owners.

A conceptual characterization that stresses agrarian capitalism or a transition toward fully commodified social relations is probably valid at a very general level, but it is insufficient to comprehend the specific historical process discussed here. Rather than entering into abstract theoretical issues, some very basic analytical tools should help us, then, build upward from the study of specific economic units, through their various exchanges and interactions, to the broader agrarian changes in which they or their members were active participants.

The concept of a rural domestic unit where production and consumption are organized around the household (hereafter "domestic unit"), is of primary importance: it will be the starting point for an inquiry into the multiple and changing ways in which members of rural households were involved in the product, labor, land and credit markets which developed over time in a previously unsettled region, rapidly involved in commercial agriculture. The main characteristics of such domestic units, as can be derived from numerous case-studies and an equally prolific theoretical literature, but especially from empirically-based models of rural households' economic organization may be outlined.[10]

---

10 Among such models, de Vries' (1978) "specialization" versus "peasant" model was especially useful, together with Hymer and Resnick's (1969) discussion of rural households' options between production of agricultural commodities, non-agricultural activities, and consumption of manufactured goods. Deere and de Janvry

The main type of production and consumption units which will be studied here is an agrarian economic unit based primarily on labor of household members, both for agriculture proper and for crafts or other activities. This is not to say that domestic units are necessarily self-sufficient in terms of labor or production; instead, they often participate quite actively in various exchanges. Therefore, rather than existing as isolated, self-enclosed entities, they are closely linked to other economic and social forces, relating to them in ways which constantly redefine the options available to individual domestic units.

In contrast to a frequent assumption of the anthropological and economic literature on peasantries, whether in the marxist or chayanovian tradition,[11] the domestic units with which this study deals are historically specific elements of a mercantile agrarian economy, rather than the basis for a universal or ahistorical "peasant economy" or "simple commodity mode of production". Far from being mere remnants of a precapitalist past, such domestic units result from and participate in the development of product, credit, land and labor markets. They are so enmeshed in the fabric of societal interrelations that their internal dynamics are unintelligible without

---

(1979) also provide a well-structured diagramatic interpretation of the multiple interactions between domestic units and their markets. Leaving aside the vast theoretical literature on the economics of peasant production, two basic reference models are of course those set forth by A.V. Chayanov (1966) and W. Kula (1976), with an ongoing and seemingly unending discussion of the chayanovian versus marxist perspectives, as in Lehman (1986). Broad overviews of the factors of agrarian change include Slicher van Bath (1963) and Boserup (1965 and 1981). The contributions by the abovementioned authors, as well as certain exceptions to their models, are discussed in Samper (1983), pp. 3-19. Despite innumerable case studies, the recent literature on Latin American peasantries includes few comprehensive works, with solid theoretical and empirical foundations, such as Goodman and Redclift (1982), de Janvry (1981), or Piñeiro and Llovet (1986).

11 The idea of a "peasant" culture and worldview, existing in very diverse historical periods and societies, underlies much of the anthropological contribution, from Kroeber to Wolf and more recently, e.g. Foster, "What is a Peasant", in Potter (1967), p. 46, Georgescu-Roegen and Thorner, in Wharton (1970), p. 61-99, and Dalton (1972), p. 385-6. The concept of a specifically peasant rationality, set forth by Chayanov's Organization and Production School in the early 20th century, has been applied in a modified form by marxian and non-marxian researchers to the analysis of a wide range of societies; e.g. Bartra (1974), Kula (1976), Archetti and Stölen (1975), and Hunt (1979). Chayanovian approaches have been criticized by Vilar in Anes (1978), by Harrison (1975, 1977) and by many other marxists, especially in the *Journal of Peasant Studies*. At the same time, the concept of a simple commodity mode of production, whether formally "subsumed" or structurally "articulated" to other modes, ultimately refers to a peasant economic system which, though subordinate, would be found in feudal, capitalist and other types of societies. In partial contrast to the simple commodity mode of production, a long-enduring "domestic mode of production" has been conceptualized, initially based on a strongly communal "self-sustaining economy", and finally ruptured by commodification of products and especially of labor, as in Meillassoux (1983).

reference to their multiple interactions. Their history cannot be explained merely through reference to a hypothetical "peasant rationality", nor did rural societies with major peasant-farmer components simply "drift" toward agrarian capitalism. The logic of household production was distinct from that of capital accumulation, but they were neither mutually exclusive nor completely independent from each other.

The various productive uses of household labor are the outcome of an intertwining of factors which are both internal and external to each domestic unit. It may be useful to discuss the ways in which components of domestic units are combined, in response to their specific requirements, as well as to historical conditions affecting them. To do this, there is a need for categories which allow us to insert microanalysis in a broader perspective, but without resorting to an explanation of individual units exclusively in terms of macrosocial variables. The following paragraphs outline the internal dynamics of domestic units as they interact with their social environment.

Conceptually, for purposes of clarity, a domestic unit will first be discussed as if it were an abstract economic entity, with a certain number and type of members (P), as well as a certain quantity and quality of material resources (R). With the technical means and labor force at its disposal, whether belonging to the household or not, the domestic unit produces an output (Q), which to a greater or lesser extent fulfills its requirements for direct or indirect consumption and productive use or reinvestment (Figure 2.3).

At this level, variations in the weight of each component lead to significant changes in the internal dynamics of each domestic unit and in its external interrelations. For example, with fixed resources and a growing number of members, a domestic unit which previously had "surplus" material resources vis-à-vis family labor capacity (and therefore had to obtain additional labor or find other uses for part of its resources) would move into a situation of equilibrium, and end up having a deficit of material resources. This last situation could also lead to output being less than that required for simple reproduction of the domestic unit, or -from another viewpoint- to an inability to fully occupy household labor given the material resources at its disposal. Deficits might also result from the specific conditions under which domestic units participate in the various markets, e.g. for products, material resources or labor (Figure 2.4).

Let us refer, first of all, to the members of domestic units, or more specifically to the composition and organization of such rural households. In the type of agrarian societies where domestic units are actively involved in market relations, they are often based on nuclear families, rather than on very extended, multi-generational households.[12] Sons and daughters who

---

12 Laslett, Medick (1976) and Levine (1977), among others, have shown that to be the case in many areas of preindustrial and protoindustrial Europe, where transition to capitalism cannot be equated with household nuclearization. Recent research on

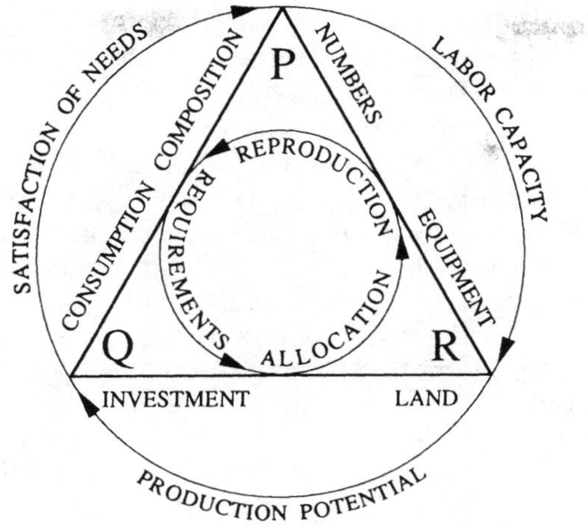

Figure 2.3 Basic components of domestic units

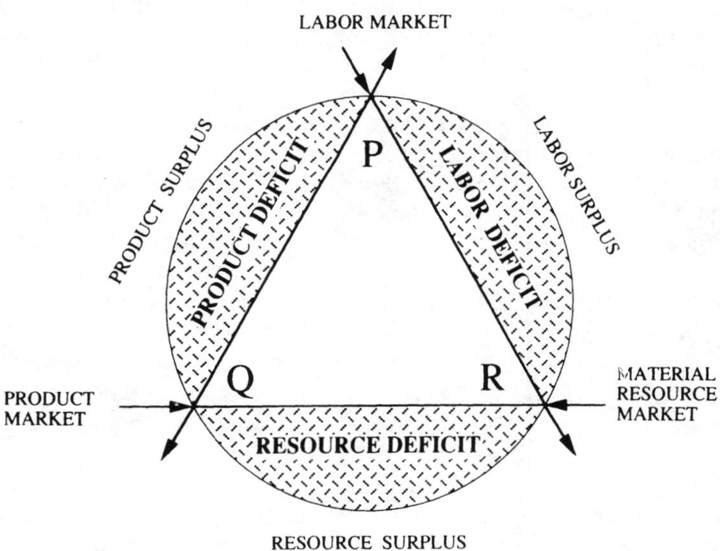

Figure 2.4 Surpluses and deficits of domestic units

Latin America points in the same direction, see Kuznesof and Oppenheimer (1985), p. 223.

marry are expected to set up their own household, so those remaining with the parents are usually single. The household, then, is not synonymous with family, but rather smaller in terms of number of kin residing together. This is not to say that only immediate relatives are a part of domestic units, since other relatives, servants and young laborers might be permanent members of rural households.

Domestic units, of course, not only have a certain number of members, but also a certain composition, primarily defined in terms of age and sex, although other characteristics might be relevant, e.g. training and cultural norms affecting economic behavior. Composition of the family decisively influences both consumption needs and labor capacity of the household. Needs include not only biological requirements, but also culturally-defined necessities, such as consumption habits and educational expectations. Regarding labor capacity, it is usually considered minimal for children under twelve and for the elderly, intermediate for adolescents and sometimes, depending on the type of society and task, for adult women, and high for adult men or adults generally. Clearly, there is an economic-demographic family cycle which begins with the establishment of a new household, in societies where young adults leave their parents' homes when they marry. It usually continues with a rise in consumption needs, as children are born, while only the young couple can work. As their children become of age to be economically productive, household labor capacity increases. Finally, in such societies, most sons and daughters leave to establish their own households, and there is a reduction both of consumption needs and of labor capacity. The specific conditions under which the original unit disappears, once the old couple die, are crucial to an understanding of the dynamics of rural households.[13] We will return to this point later, especially with respect to inheritance and the cross-generational viability of domestic units.

Material resources at the disposal of domestic units include land and technological equipment. Land refers not only to a given area, but also to a certain fertility, relief, climate, water availability, potential use, and location. Technological equipment includes tools and other instruments for production, seed and plants, fertilizers, fuel and other inputs, livestock, and technical knowledge. Land and technological equipment are not necessarily a fixed quantum for a given domestic unit over time. As the labor capacity of the household increases, through variations in the number and composition of its members, a quantitative or qualitative change in such resources will be required to productively occupy all family labor and satisfy consumption needs. Either additional land or a more labor-intensive use of the same area might allow the domestic unit to attain a new balance. This would be the case of a society in which land were redistributed according to household requirements, or readily available at low cost. It would also be the case where land use rapidly intensified by a shift from

---

[13] This is a tight, and perhaps oversimplified, summary of the peasant family life-cycle described by Chayanov, "Peasant Farm Organization", in Thorner (1966).

extensive livestock grazing to agriculture proper, or by market-oriented specialization within agriculture. If access to the land were not flexible, and technology unchanging, other outlets for family labor would be necessary for it to be fully occupied and satisfy consumption requirements, e.g. non-agricultural occupations within the household, temporary or permanent emigration, etc.

Output of the domestic unit, resulting from labor capacity applied to material resources, also has quantitative and qualitative aspects which need be mentioned. If the unit were to produce a single good, output could be measured in physical quantities, but that is rarely the case. Usually, domestic units produce several different goods, in variable amounts. In a mercantile economy, total output and the proportion attributable to each type of goods can be associated with a measure of value. However, the total monetary value and the respective proportions vary due to market price fluctuations, an external variable which tends to become especially important as domestic units become more market-oriented. On the other hand, many domestic units also consume part of their output directly, or exchange it with little or no reference to monetary value, so such estimates are to a certain extent arbitrary.

Part of the domestic unit's output may be used to pay debts for products, cash credit, labor, land or any other dues. The remaining output, whether directly as use value or indirectly via monetary exchange, serves two primary purposes from the viewpoint of the household: to satisfy consumption needs of its members, for reinvestment to renew the productive process, whether at the same level or, when unavoidable, at a lower level or, if at all possible, in a cumulative manner.

It is also possible that part of that output be used for other purposes, such as savings, donating, or loaning. In such cases, its role is far from negligible, since it ensures savings for less favorable times, interpersonal relations and social prestige, or future revenues from interest paid. In the first case, this is the equivalent of delaying the decision to consume or invest, as a provision against natural disasters, economic difficulties or simply old age. In the second case, it is another form of consumption, closely linked to the position of individuals or family groups within the community. And in the third case, it is an alternative investment, generating income for the domestic unit.

But the value-equivalent of peasant-farmer households' labor is not always fully available for consumption or investment by members of domestic units once their various market transactions are taken into account. Actually, part of it is transferred to others, through various means of surplus extraction (Figure 2.5). The importance of surplus product or value transfers from domestic units to owners of capital (or to "society") is such that it is a defining characteristic of peasant farming.[14] Although it is

---

14 Alain de Janvry (1981, p. 104) has pointed out, quite rightly, that "what those who argue for the peasant mode posit as a defining behavioral characteristic of the

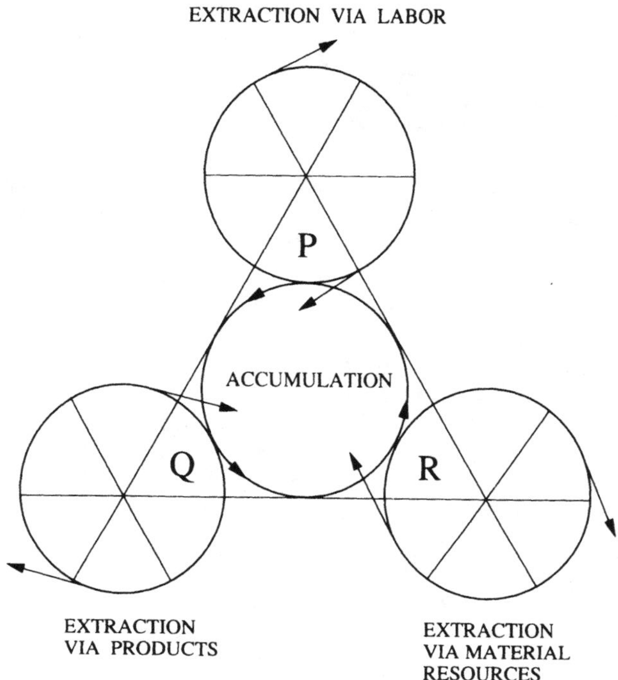

Figure 2.5 Extraction and accumulation via exchanges

empirically difficult to measure such transfers, theoretically there is little doubt about the existence of these mechanisms of exploitation. There is an ongoing debate as to whether they should be characterized as relations of production, of unequal exchange, or otherwise.[15] Despite alternative explanations, the fact is that most peasant-farmers occupy subordinate positions within societies in which the logic of capital prevails and power relations are clearly unequal. The unpaid labor of formally independent producers is appropriated through seemingly egalitarian commercial transactions by merchants, moneylenders, landowners, and others.

The way in which the labor capacity, material resources and output of a domestic unit are to be used involves economic decision-making by its members. This is a process which takes place within the household unit, in accordance with its specific characteristics, but under the influence of external factors. In turn, the aggregate result of decisions adopted by all or many domestic units has an impact, one way or another, on those very same extraneous conditions.

---

peasant (i.e. continued engagement in production without profits) is, in fact, the **result** of a class relation where the peasant's surplus labor is extracted through a variety of channels."

15 Goodman and Redclift (1982, pp. 68-93) provide a critical overview of the various theoretical propositions regarding the nature of such mechanisms.

The process of decision-making by domestic units involves many variables, and household members often face acute dilemmas. There is a need to weigh market-oriented production against self-consumption, and risks accompanying productive specialization against opportunities to obtain greater profits therefrom. They must also decide between continuing intensification of land use to occupy all additional family labor, or seeking solutions outside the domestic unit, e.g. participation in the labor market and emigration. They have to choose between purchasing manufactured goods or carrying out non-agricultural activities within the household, and between cultivation on their own land or obtaining it by rental, sharecropping and other arrangements. In the long run, once the older members of the unit have died or are unable to work, there is also the choice between egalitarian subdivision of household property or avoidance of estate fragmentation which might threaten its viability as a productive unit.[16]

Transmittal of property (or, more properly, of rights associated to land tenure [17]) is essential to the reproduction of social relations through the various "grids of inheritance". In agrarian societies, the legally-sanctioned system of inheritance and the historical variations of inheritance practices can hinder or facilitate the survival of domestic units. In the extremes, absolute partibility would lead to constant fragmentation of peasant holdings among all heirs, while total exclusion of all but one descendant would maintain the integrity of farms but expel population. However, there is usually a much greater degree of flexibility than legal standards suggest, and inheritance practices respond both to the needs of households and to social conditions.[18]

Generally speaking, various systems of inheritance strive to avoid excessive fragmentation while providing as much as possible for the needs of household members, despite the seemingly contraditory nature of these goals.[19] Actual inheritance practices often evolve into some sort of "preferential partition", where all descendants receive some sort of inheritance but with quantitative and/or qualitative differences among them.[20] Inheritance is not, then, a totally independent variable, but rather a component of household strategies, influenced by legal and institutional pressures, but also by socioeconomic and demographic factors, among others.[21] The recurring tension between individual household members'

16 Hymer and Resnick (1969), p. 503; G. Wright (1978), pp. 47 and 62-3; J. de Vries (1978), pp. 4-17.

17 Following E. P. Thompson's discussion of this point in Goody, Thirsk and Thompson (1978), p. 828.

18 J. Yver (1966), pp. 266-7 and 290-299.

19 E. Le Roy Ladurie (1972).

20 Berkner and Mendels, "Inheritance Systems, Family Structure, and Demographic Patterns in Western Europe (1700-1900)", in Tilly (1976), p. 212.

21 *Ibid.*, pp. 216-217.

needs and future viability of domestic units (or, for that matter, of peasant farming[22]) is but one of the dilemmas faced by peasant farmers. Attempted solutions vary in their effectiveness, and of course depend upon specific historical conditions which define the options available.

Clearly, decisions by domestic units regarding inheritance, as well as production and consumption, depend on a variable combination of internal and external factors, and effect modifications on both. With flexible access to the land and other productive resources, as in the case of an open agricultural frontier, options differ significantly from situations where there is little opportunity of acquiring land. But the various peasant strategies lead to very different social outcomes such as a reversion to subsistence-oriented agriculture, or regional specialization in a given product; retaining or expelling population; prevalence of independent or wage labor; multiplication of tiny plots or stability of viable productive units; accelerated or limited social polarization.

Decisions on production and consumption or reinvestment made by individual domestic units are based on each unit's needs for economic reproduction, which include those of its individual members but also those pertaining to renewal of the productive process. These requirements are primarily expressed in a variety of goods, and both material resources and labor must be allocated to obtain them. Within a framework defined by the conditions under which each domestic unit participates in its social environment, such decisions affect the reproductive opportunities of the household unit, either expanding or restricting them.

On the other hand, labor capacity combined with resources provides for a greater or lesser productive potential, which permits a given level of satisfaction of the needs of the economic unit. Equilibrium in terms of the basic components would require that the labor capacity of the domestic unit be precisely that which is appropriate for the material resources available to the household, and that output be just enough for simple reproduction. Actually, this situation is exceptional and unstable. In reality, there tend to be occasional or permanent differences between labor capacities and material resources, as well as between output and reproductive requirements, i.e., basic consumption needs and reinvestment to renew production at a similar level.

Adjustments between production and resources by a given household vary over time, and the same is true for output and reproductive requirements. The same domestic unit may move between situations of deficits and surpluses of labor capacity, material resources, and output. Therefore, typologies based, for example, on family labor versus wage labor, may be analytically useful but do not fully reflect social dynamics,

---

22 Thompson, for example, has pointed out how compensatory outpayments by those who inherit the land to other family members in England may have been "the death-warrant of the yeomanry as a class" in Goody, Thirsk and Thompson (1978), p. 346.

since insufficiencies at one time may be compensated by overabundances at another.

When family labor is in excess of or less than that required by the material resources available to the domestic unit (and either or both situations may occur cyclically, at a given technological level) there is a need to participate in some sort of labor market[23] or to otherwise adjust resources to family-labor capacity. If labor is adjusted, this may mean seeking alternative uses for household members' work, or obtaining additional labor when family work capacity is insufficient. If material resources are adjusted, the unit may temporarily or permanently divest itself of unused land and movables, e.g. by renting out or by sale, and in case of a deficit may instead acquire such resources by similar means, or through credit. The underlying assumption of technological stasis is probably valid only for the short term, since labor/resource adjustments may of course take place through variations in the intensity of land use. Another implicit assumption is that peasant-farmers will, if at all possible, use the domestic unit's labor and land to the fullest, rather than opt for underemployment of family labor capacity or underutilization of material resources. [24]

If output of a given product is below or above the consumption needs of the specific rural household (and very often it is below for one product and above for another), then various exchanges take place to obtain what the domestic unit lacks and dispose of what it cannot or need not consume. As they specialize in the most profitable activities, or those most appropriate for their combination of family labor and material resources, commodity exchanges cease to be occasional and become indispensable.

In rural societies where commercial exchanges are a widespread feature of economic life, domestic units tend to be actively involved not only in product markets, but also in whatever labor market may exist, and in that for material resources. From the viewpoint of the rural households, their primary goal is to attain the most favorable adjustment of labor capacity, material resources and output. If they are lacking in labor, domestic units may rent out land or enter into sharecropping arrangements, sell certain other material resources to obtain cash for wages, exchange products for labor, make loans to be repaid in work, etc. If the domestic units are lacking in material resources, the "surplus" labor can be used in other occupations, thus obtaining income to compensate for insufficient resources. Wage labor by some of its members, like domestic industry, allows the household to purchase goods for consumption or production.

---

23 Here, as with reference to land, credit and product markets, the term includes economic relations which may only be commodified in part, where money does not necessarily change hands, and where local conditions of exchange need not be fully integrated to national and international markets.

24 This assumption, subject to empirical validation, contradicts the notion of negative peasant responsiveness to market incentives, derived from Chayanov's "drudgery of labor" concept.

Credit, too, is a way to obtain resources now, to be paid for with future output.

When a domestic unit adjusts its labor capacity, its material resources and its output, in enters into direct or indirect contact with other productive units and economic forces. Their needs may or may not be complementary, and complementarity in terms of exchanges need not mean equity. Conditions for this interaction are not necessarily egalitarian, but their impact on each unit's opportunities for accumulation varies over time, and cannot be defined a priori. The sale of certain products by peasant-farmers may take place under conditions of unequal exchange; even so, it may (or may not) be advantageous for the direct producers, depending on the other options open to them. In a similar manner, seasonal wage labor by some members of domestic units may involve exploitation by owners of capital, or it may be part of an exchange of labor services among peasant production/consumption units; it may also be a means to productively occupy a temporary surplus of family labor, and allow the domestic unit to atttain a higher level of specialization. In such cases, the domestic unit itself may require additional labor at certain times of year, and its possibilities for accumulation may be increased, rather than reduced, by the fact that some members work for wages periodically. Sharecropping and other arrangements for usufruct of land may or may not involve the transfer of rent; their meaning, too, must be ascertained historically for each case, although it is empirically difficult to do so. Therefore, participation of domestic units in various types of exchanges or "markets", whether of labor, products, or material resources, may be the basis for surplus extraction, but also for accumulation. It is possible, theoretically, to define the nature of such exchanges and to identify conditions which make extraction or accumulation possible, in terms of the overall socioeconomic processes. But the specific question of whether a given domestic unit is in one or the other situation (or perhaps in both?) requires detailed analysis of concrete cases.

A preliminary typology, subject to qualification in the course of empirical analysis, is necessary to roughly categorize the types of units which will be studied in detail throughout the following chapters. Its aim is to allow initially descriptive elements to be discussed in terms of certain basic affinities among such units and of broader analytical issues. Key variables, based on the conceptual framework outlined above, refer primarily to various possible combinations of labor capacity and material resources, which under given technical and social conditions generate a certain output. Production can be compared to consumption/reinvestment requirements, and this in turn defines possibilities of surplus extraction and/or accumulation. Five types of units are proposed:

1. Sub-Family Units

Their land area is so small that even under what at the time was intensive land use, their productive potential would be minimal or insignificant as compared to the family labor capacity and the consumption needs of the household. In more detailed analyses, it would seem appropriate to establish a distinction within this group, between those cases in which the only immovable is a house and the lot it is on, and others in which there is a small plot of land or micro-farm under cultivation. Both subgroups would have chronic insufficiencies of land, livestock and equipment or, in other words, permanent surpluses of household labor as regards the material resources available to such units.

2. Deficit-Yielding Domestic Units

The productive potential of their land and other material resources allows them to use most but not all the households' labor capacity, and to generate an output which, under socially-specific conditions, is sufficient to satisfy a major part of but not all the reproductive requirements of the household. They are domestic production/consumption units in that their own resources (whether directly or through exchanges) are the primary basis for their reproduction as domestic units, though not enough to cover all consumption needs and renew production at exactly the same level. They need to adjust material resources to labor capacity by periodically obtaining additional land under various arrangements, or to supplement household income by regular work at non-agricultural or off-farm tasks.

3. Intermediate Domestic Units

Their land and other material resources usually require all household labor, without there being permanent and significant surpluses of labor capacity. These are domestic units with an overall balance between production and consumption, although they may sell much of their output and buy much of what they consume. Their output, whether directly or most often through exchanges, can satisfy all basic household needs and allows them to make the investments required to continue production at a very similar level. Any seasonal shortage or excess of household labor or of material resources would tend to be compensated during the year.

4. Surplus-Producing Domestic Units

They use family labor on a regular basis, but also have substantial requirements for non-family labor. Income (from sale or direct use of output) is regularly more than household consumption and reinvestment needs, so it is possible to gradually expand production. The disproportion between material resources and labor capacity of the household may be constant or variable, but is a distinctive feature of this type of unit and a potential basis for accumulation.

5. SUPRA-FAMILY UNITS

These are large productive units in which labor is all or almost all by non-relatives, and satisfaction of basic consumption needs of the owner household is a very minor part of total output. They are not domestic production/consumption units, but rather units with significant capital accumulation, in which kinship is irrelevant to labor relations.

Of course, in the past individual households varied in their demographic composition as well as in their material resources, not only in comparison with others but also over time. Therefore, the productive potential and consumption requirements of specific households must be studied in detail to confirm or dismiss preliminary conclusions for larger groups. Furthermore, landless rural families are absent from much of our documentary evidence, and land poor households are not represented as fully as those with larger estates. The typology above cannot provide a quantitatively precise image of social stratification, but rather a means to link the preceding conceptual characterization with the empirical data available for certain types of production/consumption units. Most importantly, changing social relations and overall conditions gave new meanings to such productive potentials, mechanisms of surplus extraction and opportunities for accumulation.

For the purposes of this study, it is especially important to discuss interactions between the various types of productive units and their social environment. This, in turn, is closely linked to historical processes regarding technological change, socioeconomic relations, and relative political power.

Typological construction is only a first step in the design of explanatory models with respect to specific social dynamics, in this case both the transformations which take place within domestic units and their interrelations with other productive units, their participation in various markets, surplus-product extraction and the possibility of accumulation, etc. The following modified version of the schematic model developed by Deere and de Janvry, adapted by Piñeiro and Chapman,[25] places the types of productive units discussed above in the context of such interactions between

---

[25] C. D. Deere and Alain de Janvry, "A Conceptual Framework for the Empirical Analysis of Peasants", in *American Journal of Agricultural Economics*, Vol. 61, No. 4, November, 1979, pp. 601-611; Martín Piñeiro and James Chapman, "Cambio técnico y diferenciación en las economías campesinas: un análisis de seis estudios de caso en América Latina", in *Estudios rurales latinoamericanos*, Vol. 7, January-April, 1984, pp. 27-57.

broader social processes and those taking place within rural domestic units (Figure 2.6).

As shown in Figure 2.6, and already discussed above, domestic units interact with other productive units and with their markets in various ways, which can be related to three major processes: those of production, circulation, and reproduction (which is also one of socioeconomic differentiation). The labor capacity of the family (with its age/sex composition and qualitative characteristics) is applied to the primary material of agriculture, i.e., a given amount of land with its peculiarities in terms of location, fertility, climate, water availability, and so forth.

In transforming nature, members of domestic units use tools and other technological inputs, which change over time. The relationship between household labor capacity and the material resources available to the domestic unit has a major impact on the need to obtain additional workers, under various contractual arrangements, or to find other productive occupations for household labor outside the domestic unit, whether on a permanent or seasonal basis. The specific ways in which different uses of the land and labor are combined, tend to make labor requirements either more or less seasonal. Aside from wage labor, domestic units can carry out direct labor exchanges with other such units, or obtain usufruct of land in exchange for labor obligations, or opt for some of the household members to migrate, e.g. to the frontier or to the city.

Rural domestic production is not restricted to agriculture proper, but can have a non-agricultural component, which includes the processing of agricultural and livestock products, artisan crafts, and perhaps transportation. We know that the decision to specialize in agriculture, or within it, in a specific crop, is partly based on an assessment of risks and advantages of greater commodity specialization by members of the household production and consumption unit.

Total product output is divided into three main components: payment in kind for hired labor and for obligations under sharecropping or other such arrangements; use values consumed directly by household members; and commodities which enter the process of circulation. Although the exchanges can include non-monetary forms, such as product barter, we are referring here to rural societies in which mercantile relations tend to become widespread. When products are sold to buy other goods, terms of trade become an important factor. To a certain extent, this is relevant to exchanges of agricultural products, but primarily to those between agricultural and manufactured products. The trends of such terms of trade reinforce or inhibit specific processes of specialization. And at a more general level, regarding social relations, they are a mechanism of surplus extraction.

Monetary wage payments as well as cash transfers for payment of interest on loans, monetary rent and whatever taxes may exist, are subtracted from the gross income which resulted from sales of household production. Net monetary income of the household unit is based on the remaining cash income from sales, plus wages earned outside the domestic

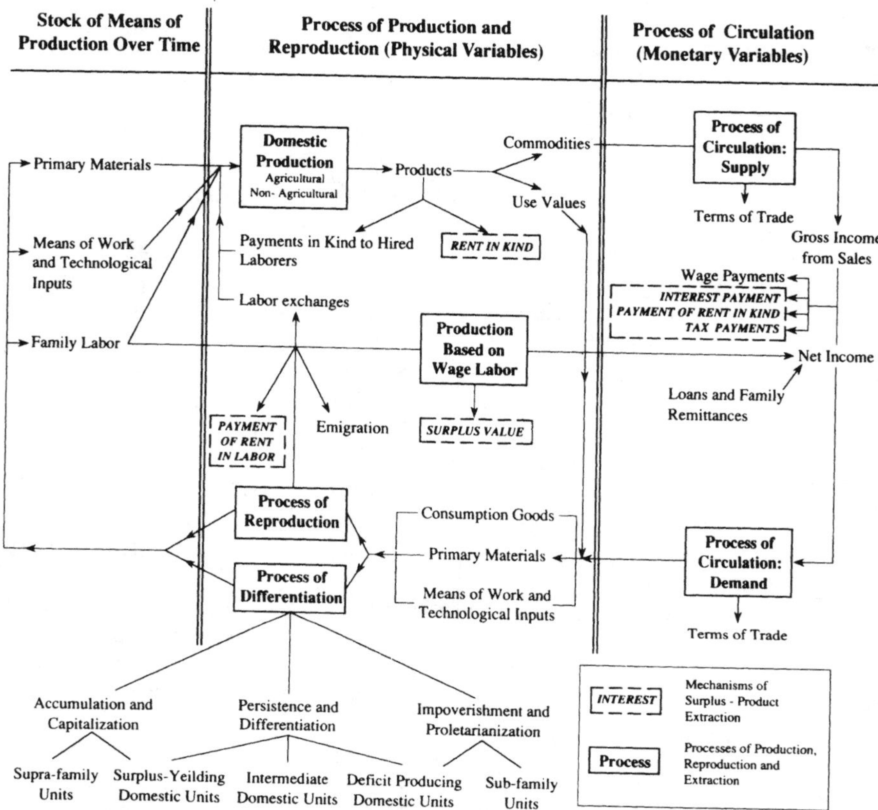

Source: Adapted from Deere and deJanvry (1979) and Piñiero and Chapman (1984)

Figure 2.6 Interactions between domestic units and their socioeconomic environment

unit, new loans obtained and remittances by other members of the family. This net monetary income is used to obtain agricultural and manufactured goods for consumption; primary materials, especially land, but also seed and livestock; as well as tools, equipment and other technological inputs. All of these, together with the constant components of the production/consumption unit, make possible its reproduction as a household, and also renewal of the process of production, whether at a similar, greater or lesser scale than in the preceding cycle.

Socioeconomic differentiation occurs constantly in the course of reproduction of domestic units. The way in which it takes place is a consequence of the interaction between their internal dynamics and the societal environment, but especially their situation regarding disposition of surplus product, i.e. that which is not indispensable for simple reproduction. Just as supra-family units tend to accumulate and capitalize (although that is not always the case), and sub-family units often tend to become more impoverished or their members more proletarianized, domestic units themselves are far from static: surplus-yielding domestic units may tend to capitalize; deficit-yielding domestic units may tend to become impoverished, and intermediate domestic units may move in one or the other direction over time. Of course, under certain conditions domestic units counteract this trend toward differentiation, e.g. through access to the land by some of their members in the course of settlement on the frontier. Supra-family and sub-family units may also become domestic units. The former may be subdivided through inheritance, sale of land or seizures due to heavy indebtedness, or because of acute social conflicts over land tenure and in the context of government-sponsored agrarian reforms, etc. Sub-family units may become domestic units in several ways, for example by rejoining plots of land or introducing technological changes which radically alter productivity.

Aside from the abovementioned socioeconomic factors, other sociopolitical and cultural factors play specific roles in the process of reproduction and differentiation. This applies especially to the cross-generational viability of domestic units and their possibilities for accumulation or impoverishment. Government policies regarding land tenure, prices, credit, taxes and technological inputs are certainly influential in that regard. The same is true for associations and conflicts among organized sociopolitical forces, where the rural population is involved and agrarian issues are at stake. At a more cultural level, decisions made by domestic units regarding the use of their material and human resources undoubtedly have much to do with values and expectations of their members: how they perceive the advantages and risks of productive specialization, wage labor, emigration, and other options. Here we must also take into account inheritance practices of the rural population, which do not always adhere very strictly to the legal and social standards regarding transmittal of property from one generation to the next. Historical analysis must, then, include these and other variables which affect decision-making by members of rural households as well as the concrete social meaning of the options available and the limitations imposed upon them.

The process of decision-making within domestic units has a component of solidarity among their members, but also one of confrontation. Division of labor by age and sex is not merely a technical organization of production; it also brings with it very real inequalities. In other words, the situation of each member of a domestic unit must be understood in the context of a distribution of power within the rural household which is far from equitable. This is reflected in the disposition of the unit's product output, as well as in labor relations within and without the household, in selective emigration, and in the unequal participation of women and children in the process of inheritance.

At another level, each domestic unit as such interacts with other productive units, participates in various markets and in a grid of social relations in which it is, ultimately, in a subordinate position. In doing so, it devises productive and reproductive strategies to attain the most advantageous adjustment of its labor capacity, the consumption needs of its members and the material resources available to it. As an economic unit, it is subject to mechanisms and situations which define and often limit its ability to control the surplus product of the household's labor: rent in cash, products or labor; favorable or unfavorable trends in the terms of trade; wage labor conditions; interest on loans; taxation; etc. However, the rural domestic unit is not a passive entity, whose situation and evolution is defined exclusively by external factors, but rather is characterized by a strongly interactive process. Acute dilemmas are imposed upon it, but each domestic unit tries out responses which reflect its own particularities. The aggregate result is a set of productive and reproductive strategies of domestic units. External conditions establish objective limits, but beyond merely confirming their existence, it is necessary to analyze the effectiveness of peasant-farmer strategies in their respective socio-historical contexts, and more specifically the viability and transformations of household-based commodity production.

The following chapters will discuss these issues historically with respect to agrarian changes in a region where peasant farming was strongly present in market relations and faced increasingly acute dilemmas, from the mid-nineteenth century into the 1930s, and even today.

Chapter 3

THE FIRST MIGRANTS

This chapter focuses on early westward migrations from the previously-settled area within the Meseta Central, during the late colonial period and in the years after Independence from Spain, which was obtained in 1821. Local land settlement was undoubtedly the primary means by which the number and importance of household-based units of production expanded rapidly in nineteenth-century Costa Rica. On the frontier, not only was the landscape transformed, but rural society underwent many changes from initial occupation of formerly uninhabited areas until these, in turn, were the starting point for migrations into other, outlying regions. Yet this process had been ongoing, in a very different societal context, from colonial times, when there was a recurring tension between pressures by Crown and Church for the population to settle in towns, on the one hand, and the existence of abundant, unclaimed lands on the other. We will see, then, how nineteenth-century settlement is both a continuation and a rupture of previous processes associated with the establishment of new towns during the late colonial period.

Each settler had his (or her) own background, like each household group on the frontier had a history of its own, which must be taken into account to understand subsequent developments. The men, women and children who settled the northwestern section of Costa Rica's Central Valley brought with them not only personal items, perhaps some livestock and other movables, but also experiences and expectations. The geographical areas they came from, primarily in the eastward Meseta Central, were also cultural, social and family spaces. We cannot enter into a detailed analysis of the individual and collective roots of these migrants, but we do need to understand the origins of this process of settlement. That is the purpose of this chapter.

Historical-geographic Setting

The Costa Rican case was a specific though not necessarily unique one of nineteenth-century occupation of "empty" areas of the American continent. In the comparative perspective offered by Cardoso and Pérez,[1] we find major similarities and, of course, certain very important differences with colonization in south-central Brazil, in the Argentinian pampa, or in western Colombia. With caution, due to obvious historical specificities, the comparison might even be extended to the midwestern United States or the mountainous inland areas of the Greater Antilles.

In early to mid-nineteenth-century Costa Rica an agricultural frontier, significantly larger than the area of former settlement, was opened to settlers, and a market-oriented rural economy developed at different paces and in different ways. Extremely low population densities of the early nineteenth century gave way to rapid migration to the frontier territory, whether from neighboring regions or more remote lands. The landscape was transformed from forests into pasturelands and fields; infrastructure for transportation was built, and agricultural production reached regional or national markets and ports. There were obvious variations of scale from one case to another, and clearcut differences regarding social relations, the origin and characteristics of migrants, the type of production and other factors. Both the common and differential features are an invitation to approach the Costa Rican case with a broader perspective in mind, to answer questions of a more general nature, and to see it not as a totally unique phenomenon, but as part of a vast process of settlement and agro-export development throughout the continent.

In Costa Rica, the specific region on which this study focuses was, toward the middle of the nineteenth century, the main area where new lands were being opened up by settlers coming from the colonial villages and neighboring countryside. The previously inhabited area, primarily the Meseta Central, was very small in comparison with the territory of the former province of Costa Rica. Indigenous population was by then relatively small, living in certain remote areas toward the Atlantic and Pacific, as well as in hardly a dozen "pueblos de indios", near the main Spanish villages and towns of the Meseta (Figure 3.1).

At the time of Independence, in 1821, the northwestern section of the Central Valley (hereafter the Northwest) was for the most part practically uninhabited, and several centuries of natural growth covered up whatever clearings had been made by itinerant native agriculturalists long before. Only to the east, near the city of Alajuela, were some areas used to raise cattle, which wandered almost wild, or to obtain certain raw materials, especially wood. Almost all the Northwest was a wooded land, with very sparse if any human settlement.

In the late eighteenth and early nineteenth centuries, the Northwest was removed from the colonial transportation routes in Costa Rica, but not at such a great distance that communication with them was extraordinarily difficult. The main road (*camino real*), a mule trail which linked the Meseta Central to Nicaragua and the port of Caldera (as well as southward to Panama), ran some ten to twenty kilometers south of the region we are

---

1 Cardoso and Pérez (1981), vol. II, pp. 63-83.

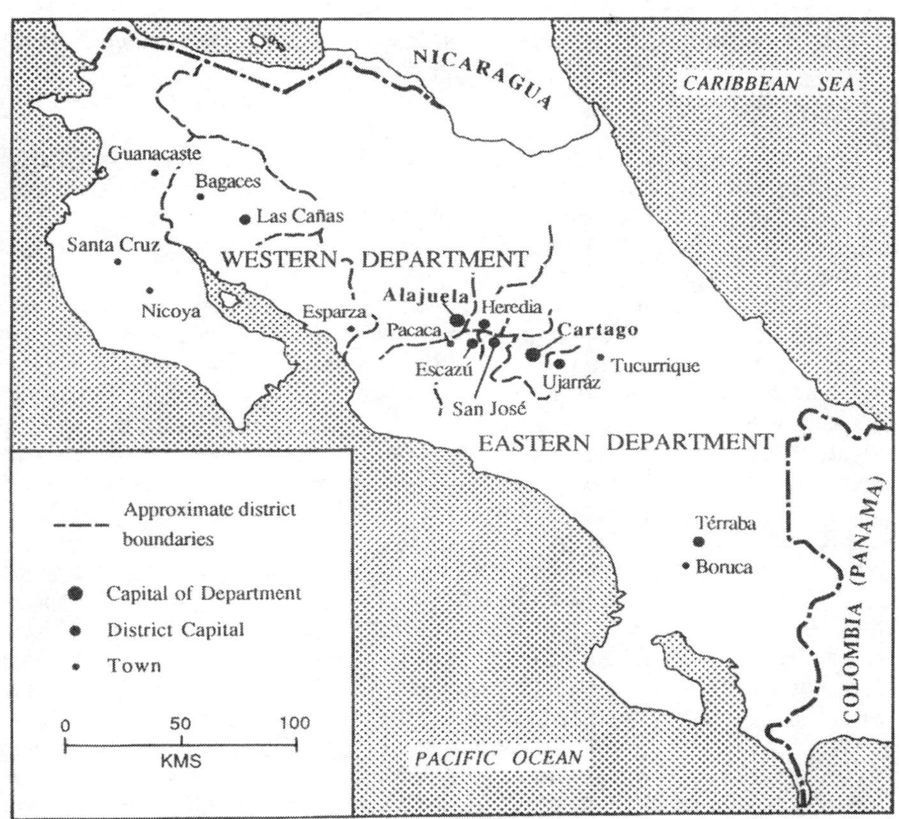

Figure 3.1 Principal settlements and administrative divisions of Costa Rica around 1825

referring to. The same can be said of the major cartroad (*carretera nacional*) built toward the middle of the century (or, for that matter, of the late-nineteenth-century railroad).

In terms of its physical setting, the Central Valley is actually a tectonic depression (*graben*), one hundred kilometers long and fifteen to twenty-five wide, with a roughly east-west orientation. Lined by volcanoes to the north and lower mountains to the south, the Central Valley itself is a counterpoint of hills, gradual slopes and frequent ravines.

West of the Meseta Central, the Central Valley extends for some thirty kilometers before reaching the hills which separate it from the Pacific slope. The Río Grande de Tárcoles runs roughly westward along the southern edge of the Valley, and the land slopes gradually toward the north, up to the mountain range dominated by the Poás volcano.

The natural fertility of the land in this area is greater on the slopes of the Cordillera Central, where soils are mostly of volcanic origin. Toward the south, they are usually poor, lateritic soils, save for those near Palmares and the Tárcoles river, which are of a richer, sedimentary type. The other element of nature which is decisive for agriculture, namely climate, can be described as subtropical and bi-seasonal. Temperatures are in the intermediate range; they vary according to altitude above sea level but much less during the year, in average terms. Rainfall, appropriate for both permanent and seasonal crops, is the main criterion for identifying seasons: there is a well-defined contrast between the nearly dry four-month *verano*, from December to March, and the 2,000 mm. rainfall in *invierno*, the rest of the year, save for a two-week *veranillo* in late July.

There are five main valleys west of Alajuela city and north of the Tárcoles River (Figure 3.2). Four of these valleys are in the Northwest proper, and settlements were established there during the nineteenth century at altitudes of about 1,000 meters above sea level. From east to west, they comprise: Grecia, with several rivers coming down from the slopes of the Poás volcano; Naranjo, which includes several smaller valleys formed by three rivers; Palmares, somewhat to the south; and San Ramón, which several rivers run through. The Valley of Atenas, closer to the Tárcoles river, has less fertile soils and a lower altitude, which historically influenced land use and established differences with the other valleys to the north. All in all, more than thirty rivers and major streams flow from the Cordillera southward through this region, and some of them come together before flowing into the Tárcoles. Between Grecia and San Ramón, there are also a great many smaller streams, but there are few of them toward the south.

Average yearly rainfall in Grecia, Naranjo, Palmares and San Ramón is close to or somewhat higher than 2,000 mm., while in Atenas it is about 1,600 mm. Together with the smaller number of rivers and streams, this indicates somewhat less availabile water for agriculture near the Tárcoles, with more rainfall in the valleys to the north. There are also certain variations among the valleys in connection with the beginning and end of the dry season. This, of course, affects the planting and harvesting periods. In November it is still raining heavily in Palmares, while in Grecia

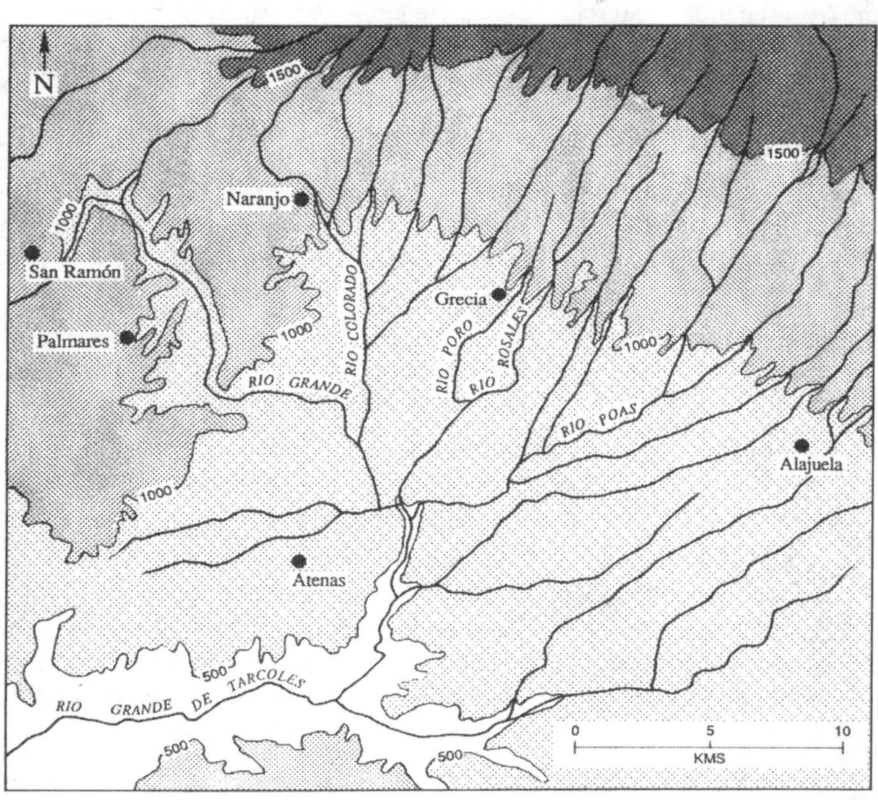

Figure 3.2 Principal rivers, population centers and altitudes of the western Central Valley, Costa Rica

and Naranjo rainfall is diminishing, and in Atenas it is minimal. In April, Palmares is the driest area, and Naranjo the rainiest.

Finally, temperature is a homogeneous factor in all the valleys, since there are no significant variations among them in the various months of the year. Average monthly temperature in the Northwest varies only from 21 to 24°C during the year. The warmest months are March, April and May; the coolest are December and January, as in other parts of the Central Valley.[2] In sum, the Northwest has very favorable conditions for intensive agriculture, and harvesting patterns for certain crops would tend to be quite seasonal, with limited local variations whose significance for rural labor cycles will be discussed later. The area from the valley of Grecia to that of San Ramón had a series of climatic and edaphic similarities with the previously settled region between Alajuela and Cartago. It also was different in several important respects from the dryer, lower altitude lands further south within the Central Valley, through which the main cartroad crossed en route to the Pacific coast. These distinctions become more and more important later on, especially as the diverse economic activities of recently-settled areas gives way to agro-export production. But first, there is need to understand the background for these and other agrarian transformations.

Early Settlement

There is disagreement among historians and other social scientists regarding the simultaneous or successive settlement of the eastern and western parts of the Meseta Central in colonial times.[3] However, recent studies suggest an early settlement of both sections, even though the eastern one was more densely populated during the early and mid-colonial period.[4] The western part of the Meseta, more sparsely settled, received eighteenth-century migrations from the economic and political center of Cartago, to the east.

By the end of the eighteenth century, most of the perhaps 40,000 inhabitants of the Meseta Central lived west of Cartago: Villa Vieja (later Heredia), Villa Nueva (San José), and Villa Hermosa (Alajuela), each had several thousand inhabitants, but smaller, semi-rural *barrios* surrounded each of these towns. Later, when the Northwest was settled, most of the migrants to Grecia, Sarchí, Naranjo, Palmares and San Ramón came precisely from that western section of the Meseta, in what seems to be the continuation of a movement begun more than a century before.

---

2 Sáenz (1966), Table No. 25 and pp. 180-181.

3 See Arguedas and Ramírez (1985), vol. I, p. 11. Aside from Carlos Meléndez and Carlos Monge A., geographers Gerhard Sandner and Carolyn Hall both referred to the characteristics of settlement in the western part of the Central Valley.

4 E. Fonseca (1983), p. 71.

Northwestward migration became significant after 1830, and continued for half a century. Immigrants came, first of all, from the city of Alajuela and nearby areas. The second place of origin was Heredia, both the city and its *barrios*. Fewer people came from San José, and even less from Cartago.[5] We do not know their itinerary and last place of residence, but we do know that this human flow followed two main routes, probably due to geographical factors and the existing roads and settlements:

> This movement was along two routes: one from the city of Alajuela toward Poás, Grecia, Sarchí and Naranjo, and the other, also from Alajuela, toward the Río Grande, through Atenas, and then to the area of Palmares. These routes were separated by the deep canyons of the Grande and Colorado rivers.[6]

Settlement of the Northwest led to a complex process of agrarian changes, involving societal as well as geographical aspects, some of which will be discussed below. But the origins of such transformations are directly related to the origins of the settlers themselves. Who were they? Why did they leave their place of origin? What brought them to the frontier? What did they bring with them, materially and spiritually, what was their technical and cultural equipment? What role did their prior productive experiences, family background, motivations and expectations play? Such questions cannot be answered fully, but a discussion of certain characteristics of this population movement may help us to better understand the people who settled these lands.

We know, of these migrants, that they were generally families and not, for instance, single men. Demographic sources do not indicate a substantial alteration of the sex distribution of the population on the frontier, as compared to previously-settled areas. We know, too, that they were young families, couples with few if any children. Several related families, or groups of neighbors in their place or origin, often moved together, or in a brief period, to the same specific place.[7] Based on their geographic origin and cross-generational migratory linkages, the successive settlement of various areas within the western part of the Central Valley clearly indicates that many of the men and women who occupied new lands between Alajuela and San Ramón were, themselves, the descendants of migrants.

---

5 In the parish of San Anselmo de los Palmares, eleven of the thirty-three married between 1867 and 1871 gave as their place of origin the city of Alajuela. Six mentioned Heredia or Santo Domingo; five Atenas; five -born in the fifties- mentioned San Ramón; four -born in the forties- San José; and two indicated Grecia (Source: Libro de Matrimonios, 1867-1871). Of the probate cases for 1850-1859 which give the place of residence of the father of the deceased, most parents (23) were from Alajuela and nearby "barrios". The second most frequent domicile was Heredia (7), and very few came from other places (Source: Mortuales Independientes, 1850-1859).

6 Fournier (1976), p. 62.

7 Pérez (1983), p. 109; Gudmundson (1982), p. 172; Fournier (1976), p. 62.

There were undoubtedly elements of continuity between the migratory processes before and after Independence. There were also certain important differences in the characteristics of population movement within the Meseta Central, toward the end of the colonial period, and that which took place during the following decades, as settlers spread out beyond the Meseta, especially toward the Northwest. It should be useful to ascertain whether these migrations resulted from the same type of socioeconomic and sociopolitical conditions, and to what extent the colonists themselves were similar in their background and other characteristics.

In terms of the territories successively occupied by migrants, as well as regarding their genealogies, it is quite clear that we are referring to two stages of a single migratory process, which began in the eastern Meseta, specifically the Guarco valley, where the colonial capital of Cartago is located. Migration proceeded toward the western part of the Meseta Central, and then to the valleys of Grecia, Naranjo, Palmares and San Ramón. It must not have been a unidirectional movement, since it also involved outward expansion from the earliest settlements in each subregion. Nevertheless, the migratory flow did have a generally east-west orientation, and those who settled the northwestern part of the Central Valley in the nineteenth century generally came from the area settled several decades before in the Meseta.

As to the characteristics of such internal migrations, a comparison of those which took place in the late eighteenth and early nineteenth centuries, with those half a century later, shows both common and differential features. In one and the other period, migrants were juridically free peasants, mostly either *mestizos* or of Spanish descent. They occupied Crown or government lands individually, even though colonial *composiciones* and Republican land claims were sometimes submitted collectively. In the areas of immigration there were some medium-to-large estates, but also numerous domestic units essentialy based on family labor. In both cases, early migrants raised livestock and planted crops partly to ensure subsistence requirements but also, as soon as possible, for commercial purposes.

On the other hand, while the Northwest had no Indian towns, the western part of the Meseta itself had several, and in the late eighteenth century they had 50% more inhabitants than those around Cartago, in the eastern section of the Meseta Central. Indigenous population seems to have decreased more quickly near Cartago than to the west. At the end of that century, the Indian towns near San José and Heredia had a more restricted "indigenous vital space",[8] and were threatened in their communal land tenure. Interaction between the Indian communities and the mestizo or Spanish newcomers in the western Meseta led to conflicts over landholding, but also regarding competitive land use systems, as between livestock raising and agriculture proper. Instead, settlers beyond the Meseta, in the northwestern part of the Central Valley, found a land which was practically

8 Fonseca (1983), pp. 117 and 126.

uninhabited, though some merchants and livestock raisers had established control over major areas through various legal and extra-legal means. The type of conflicts which could arise, under such conditions, was quite different from those over communal tenures. Conflicts involving settlers in the Northwest encountered specific limits due to real or apparent complementarity, coupled with indirect methods of surplus extraction, in relations between peasant colonists and those speculating in land or merchandise.

Patterns of settlement were also somewhat different in the eighteenth-century Meseta Central, as compared to nineteenth-century colonization beyond the colonial ecumene. There has been substantial debate regarding characteristics of settlement, that is "nucleated" versus "dispersed". Rather extreme positions have been adopted, each emphasizing documentary evidence of either one or the other pattern. It would seem that "nucleated" and "dispersed" settlement were actually combined, in different ways and proportions, in both periods of the migratory process we are discussing here. In the western part of the Meseta Central there is reason to believe that, despite official pressures toward concentration and the existence of town centers, a major part of the population did not live in urban nuclei during the eighteenth century. A report by the Governor, don Diego de la Haya Fernández, on the Valley of Heredia in 1719 describes it as follows:

> The town of Barba, formed by a church and eight straw houses ... all of this in a fertile valley, throughout which there is cattle and numerous homes of Spaniards living in the countryside as miserable as those who came before them...[9]

The description of the area of La Lajuela (in the area of Alajuela city) by the parish priest of Heredia, quoted by Elizabeth Fonseca, is eloquent:

> From the foothills in Quebrada Honda, the ample valley has been settled little by little, so that the people are spread out over the valley, each family occupying the land it needs for its cattle, maize fields, sugarcane mills and other products...[10]

On the other hand, Fonseca recognizes that in the latter half of the eighteenth century, the burning of houses and destruction of crops by colonial authorities forced many people to move into the towns or legalize their tenures.[11] Undoubtedly there was a degree of "nuclearization" in the last few decades of the colonial period, as a direct consequence of such measures and thanks to the more spiritual threat of excommunication, with its probable corollary of social ostracism.

Lowell Gudmundson has presented various propositions in support of his view of highly nucleated colonial settlement:

---

9 Quoted by Yamileth González (1983), p. 142.

10 Quoted by Fonseca (1983), p. 295.

11 *Ibid.*, p. 296.

> Rather than being characterized by dispersed, rancho settlement on isolated farmsteads, precoffee Costa Rica was primarily a series of hamlets and villages of a nucleated household pattern.
> ... as early as 1824 the census specifically mentions the number of 'manzanas', or square blocks, in each settlement in Cartago province, regardless of village size... The only proof of dispersed household settlement offered in the Costa Rican literature is two highly ambiguous documents prohibiting such settlement.
> ... Nucleated settlement amidst near subsistence-level poverty was maintained as the social norm, thanks to both effective hierarchical control and the collective mentality that so prized village life.[12]

In an earlier study on patterns of settlement, Gudmundson had reached the conclusion that:

> ... already in 1838, 74.33% of the inhabitants of Costa Rica lived in typically urban nuclei, while 17.46% followed that trend, living in intermediate nuclei, and only the remaining 8.21% lived in an environment which can be considered rural.[13]

While the specifically "urban" characterization of such nucleated settlements has been qualified by the author, Gudmundson does prove that there were various nucleated settlements other than the main cities and major towns. This contradicts the more simplistic visions of an almost completely dispersed colonial pattern of settlement, and establishes an implicit contrast with the relatively dispersed *rancherías* of eighteenth-century New Spain or certain areas of the midwestern United States in the last century. However, it stretches the point rather too far to state that most of the population of Costa Rica in the late colonial period or shortly after Independence was concentrated in urban centers, even in a broad sense of the term. The very repetitiveness of official provisions to concentrate the population confirms the persistent nature of a problem which the colonial authorities perceived and sought to address, i.e., that part of the inhabitants of the Central Valley resisted their efforts to "civilize" and tax them. Even when they did build houses in town, many of them continued to spend most of their time on their farms. Beyond the discussion of nucleated versus dispersed settlement, there was a third type of settlement which was not quite one or the other, and has received hardly any attention at all: settlement alongside the mule trails which connected towns and villages of the Central Valley with each other and the outside world.

Whatever the specific pattern of settlement, there was undoubtedly an abundance of uncultivated land at the time, even though it was not in the immediate vicinity of the cities and major towns. It was mostly public land (*tierra realenga* or, after Independence, *tierra baldía*), and secondarily

12 Gudmundson (1986a), p. 25 and 31.

13 Gudmundson (1978), p. 132.

communal or privately-owned land not yet under cultivation. With a personally free and mobile population, as well as a relatively weak coercive apparatus, it is doubtful that religious and government pressures alone were very effective in avoiding centrifugal movements. Cultural mechanisms, social cohesion, family ties, neighborly relations and informal mutual support networks certainly operated in nucleated centers during the colonial period. Breaking away from such linkages was surely more difficult than evading the authorities. Insofar as mere subsistence was not the ultimate objective of most rural producers, removal from marketing opportunities was probably another perceived cost of out-migration. Finally, if land-poor or landless people remained in the older settlements, it may have been partly due to their access to communal lands there, or the lack of strong incentives to move out to the existing agricultural frontier.

After Independence, government authorities abandoned restrictive colonial policies regarding out-migration and access to public lands. An early liberalism adopted, instead, legislative and executive policies which promoted agricultural settlement on public lands, especially for market-oriented production. In the 1820s and 1830s, those occupying public lands were given the opportunity to legalize their holdings at a reasonable price. Additional government lands were sold or granted free of cost, the tithe was eliminated for various agricultural products, and prizes were offered to whoever built roads or opened up new agricultural areas. [14]

New population centers were established on the frontier, but their role was primarily one of support to colonization, whether as a starting point for local outward movements, in line with Carolyn Hall's characterization,[15] or resulting from prior occupation of the land, as central places with commercial and service functions. At the same time, increasingly profitable opportunities for agricultural production geared toward markets within the Central Valley and abroad became a strong incentive for a type of settlement which was hardly subsistence-oriented. Colonists sought to become actively involved in commercial production as soon as possible, and self-consumption was merely an expedient to ensure immediate consumption requirements.

In the first half of the nineteenth century there was a counterpoint between forces which might be called centripetal and centrifugal, with the latter tending to prevail. The growing strength of outward population movement had to do with a complete turnabout in government policy toward land settlement, a major change in economic opportunities, and an active role of settler-farmers in taking advantage of favorable conditions. We need to know, then, who these migrants were, what was their social origin and why they migrated, before discussing the type of productive units and socioeconomic relations they established on the frontier.

---

14 J. A. Salas (1984), pp. 20-24.

15 C. Hall (1976), p. 90.

Two clearly contradictory positions have been set forth and debated regarding migration from the Meseta Central toward other areas, and specifically toward the Northwest. On the one hand, there is the "expulsionist" position, according to which impoverished persons, devoid of wordly possessions, were expelled from previously settled areas by processes of landholding concentration, accumulation of wealth and economic expropriation. On the other hand, it has been argued that opportunities to acquire land and become involved in commercial agriculture played a decisive role. While a migratory process such as that described above surely combined "expulsion" and "attraction", there is a need to establish the weight of one or other factor so as to understand the social origin and implications of the migratory process.

Perhaps the best known proponent of the "expulsionist" thesis for Costa Rica is Seligson, whose somewhat idealized vision of Costa Rican society before coffee, borrowed from traditional Costa Rican historiography, has been soundly criticized by Gudmundson.[16] The assumptions underlying Seligson's analysis are a clear statement of this explanatory model:

> Although there is no census information before coffee, all testimonies point to a predominance of small landowners... By 1864 almost half the peasants had ceased to be small landowners ... the process by which the inhabitants were transformed into a proletariat began in the early 19th century with the introduction of coffee, and has continued to increase.
>
> Several factors led peasants to seek new lands. Landholding concentration in the hands of the aristocracy and loss of land by the peasantry... Inflation, mentioned earlier, forced peasants to return to their precapitalist existence... To do this, they needed a place where there was enough arable land for them to be selfsufficient once more. Finally, demographic explosion affected family farms, a situation which could only be alleviated through emigration. The explosion, 34% population increase between 1844 and 1864 ... resulted from lower mortality and the fact that people lived longer than before, because a new source of wealth brought many immigrants to the country, including physicians, medicine, and an improvement in hygiene.
>
> The process of spontaneous settlement began slowly in the 19th century, soon after coffee exports began.[17]

While certain elements of the "expulsion" factors cited by Seligson were to become regionally significant toward the turn of the century, several of his assumptions are not valid for the early stages of migration from the Meseta Central toward the Northwest. In the mid-nineteenth century, for example, there was no unprecedented population pressure to explain out-migration due to purely demographic conditions. Quite the contrary, research has shown that mortality did not decrease substantially in Costa

---

16 Mitchell A. Seligson (1980); Gudmundson, "El campesino y el capitalismo agrario de Costa Rica: Una crítica de ideología como historia" (1979).

17 Seligson (1980), pp. 52-3 and 59-60.

Rica before the late nineteenth and early twentieth centuries, or did so only in a very gradual manner.[18] Furthermore, westward population movement from the Meseta Central, which began before mid-century, may have slowed down somewhat but was far from being halted in the 1850s, when the cholera epidemic killed almost one tenth of the inhabitants of the Central Valley, effectively reducing purely demographic pressures.

Neither has rapid landholding concentration nor a massive expropriation and proletarianization of the Costa Rican peasantry been proven for the early decades of coffee-based agro-export expansion. There may have been a "relative concentration" of well-located land, during the establishment of several coffee estates near San José at the time. Insofar as this ocurred, it was primarily through market transactions, though some of those estates were former livestock-raising areas. On the other hand, the existence of numerous peasant farms in the Meseta Central has been well documented, and was a major obstacle to the formation of very large, continuous holdings as well as a restriction to potential labor supply.[19] Recent contributions by Roger Churnside, Yolanda Baires and Iván Molina to the ongoing debate as to the degree of landholding concentration in the Meseta Central, based on land sales, suggest some accumulation in the coffee-growing area of San José from 1830 to 1850, without a massive dispossession of the peasantry. They also show a lower level of concentration of landed property in the vicinity of Alajuela throughout the first half of the nineteenth century.[20] The re-establishment of many peasant holdings outside the Meseta acted as a compensatory mechanism for whatever pressure may have existed, e.g. for subdivision of holdings by

---

18 H. Pérez (1983), pp. 120-123, shows that there was no mortality decline between 1800 and 1860, that the death rate declined very gradually toward the turn of the century, and that its rapid reduction occured between 1930 and 1950. Recently, Pérez (1987), pp. 7-15, has developed life tables for Costa Rica which show a gradual increase of life expectancy from 1866 to 1927, and one twice as rapid from the latter date to 1950.

19 There is a consensus on the fact that peasants in the Meseta became heavily involved in coffee production and that land tenure patterns strongly influenced the labor scarcity about which estate owners complained during most of the nineteenth century (Cardoso, 1973; Pérez, 1981).

20 Churnside (1985), pp. 141-2; Baires (1986); Molina (1985), pp. 120-128. Churnside was arguing for concentration, but nevertheless found that during the first half of the nineteenth century there was neither "pressure" nor a "crisis" regarding access to the land. Baires emphasizes the predominance of smallholding, in comparison with El Salvador, but reaches the conclusion that twenty-six people concentrated 45% of total value of transactions in San José, from 1831 to 1850, and agrees with Gudmundson that a rural petty bourgeoisie was investing in land given the favorable prospects for coffee cultivation. Molina states that both merchants and peasants were heavily involved in the land market, and that while value of sales does indicate concentration, the low Gini coefficient for Alajuela suggests that it was compensated for by colonization.

inheritance or for sale of land, which was not synonymous to expropriation because it could serve to acquire more land elsewhere.

Another explanation of colonial migrations, put forth by Elizabeth Fonseca, which takes actual historical processes more carefully into account than Seligson and is set in a different time framework, while still attributing a decisive role to expulsion factors. Her explanation refers primarily to the origin of smallholding and the westward population movement within the Meseta Central, although she also suggests possibilities for subsequent stages. First, Fonseca establishes a difference in land-tenure between the eastern section of the Meseta, near Cartago, where there were some large estates in the eighteenth and early nineteenth century, and the western section from San José to Alajuela, where landholding was less concentrated. Subdivision here was due to disintegration of communal holdings and of large estates, and appropriation of Crown lands in the process of "migrations of peasants expelled from areas where the land had been monopolized by a few private owners".[21] Toward the end of the eighteenth century, she states that there was "a segment of landless peasants" working on lands which belonged to large estates.[22] In her opinion, demographic pressure played an important role from the mid-eighteenth century, and generated a growing pressure on the land. Then, in the decades immediately preceding and following Independence from Spain, legislation allowed impoverished farmers and landless people to become small-scale landowners. [23]

In Fonseca's view, lack of opportunities for certain sectors of the population in the eastern valley of El Guarco was a major factor forcing migration toward the western section of the Meseta. This was due to a combination of population growth and landholding concentration. It is essentially an "expulsionist" position, although with a more solid empirical basis. According to Fonseca, the process by which landless peasants were expelled westward would have occured anywhere between fifty to one hundred years before coffee expansion, and in the first half of the nineteenth century peasants actually had readier access to the land than before. Coffee did not, then, cause the demise of a supposedly egalitarian "rural democracy", as in Seligson's view. Although she stresses factors of expulsion (lack of land + population growth), Fonseca offers a more optimistic outlook on the fate of migrants during the early stages of coffee expansion and migration beyond the Meseta Central. [24]

Both authors mentioned above emphasize peasant impoverishment in their place of origin as the main reason for westward migration, whether within or beyond the Meseta. No attention is paid to the positive

---

21 E. Fonseca (1983), p. 295; also p. 290.

22 *Ibid.*, p. 293.

23 *Ibid.*, pp. 299 and 310.

24 Seligson (1980, p. 64) states that "few peasants managed to obtain title to their land" in the process.

motivations for settlers to emigrate to certain specific areas. Migrants are typified as land-poor or landless, and they are envisioned as seeking lands to obtain subsistence for their families. Yet there is no proof that such was the case, nor is there an explanation of what attracted them to the western section of the Meseta during the eighteenth century, or to the northwestern part of the Central Valley during the nineteenth.

Almost as an anecdote, let us note that other "expulsion factors" of a very different nature should also be considered. For example, as Yamileth González points out, some families which the authorities considered unwanted for various reasons were literally expelled from Cartago in 1755, and their descendants appear in land transactions in San José during the years after Independence.[25] In the nineteenth century, a number of people who had committed crimes emigrated (or were forced to emigrate) to the frontier areas, some of which were also for political banishment.[26]

While conflicts of either type with the authorities were an additional "expulsion" factor, far from irrelevant to a history of migrants, opportunities for illegal economic activities on the frontier shed light on the other angle of motivations to migrate. Before and after 1821, government regulations and monopolies indirectly fostered the evasion of such restrictions by persons carrying out the illicit economic activities in relatively remote areas, where the law could rarely be enforced. This is the case of tobacco production, strictly regulated by the state from the 1780s to the mid-nineteenth century. For the colonial period, Acuña states that "tobacco was planted illegally in remote areas, probably on Crown lands... Undoubtedly, the years in which the Renta Real forbade planting of tobacco or decided to reduce the number of cosecheros, were years in which illegal planting increased."[27] The motivations and productive activities of some settlers of the Northwest toward the 1840s are discussed by Hall:

> Once clearings had been opened in the forest and planted in staple food crops, the first commercial crop was tobacco, despite the fact that government regulations restricted its cultivation and sale. The accusation of being involved illegally in tobacco led a farmer in Palmares, don Antonio Alvarez, to abandon his plantations there and seek out a more remote area where he could plant tobacco, on the other side of the hills, in the neighboring valley of San Ramón. Other colonists soon followed Alvarez into this valley.[28]

Illegal tobacco cultivation was only one of the various productive activities through which settlers expected to reach product markets and improve their material living conditions. However, the case of tobacco

25 Y. González (1983), p. 147.

26 Banishment due to criminal or political activities was closely associated to colonization during the nineteenth century, and specifically in the decades immediately after Independence, as explained by M. Granados (1986), chapter I.

27 Acuña (1974), p. 130.

28 Hall (1976), p. 90.

speaks quite clearly of the positive motivations of migrants, for whom self-consumption was not necessarily the ultimate or even the immediate goal.

More than twenty years ago, Gerhard Sandner spoke of the interaction between subjective and objective factors of colonization, i.e. the material living conditions of migrants in their place of origin and their expectations upon becoming settlers. He also established a clear distinction between the motivations of Costa Rican colonists from the mid-nineteenth century to 1880 and after that, when explosive colonization reflected impoverishment of a major sector of the rural population.[29] For Sandner, positive incentives would have played a greater role in the mid-century migrations than "expulsion" factors, which became predominant later on. More recently, Gudmundson has stressed the role of "attraction" in mid-nineteenth century migrations, stating that:

> In addition to expulsion and proletarianization, there exists the obvious and contrary alternative hypothesis that an aggressively mobile, increasingly capitalist peasantry was attracted to new land. The peasants would have migrated with the motive of acquiring larger family plots on the settlement fringe, without any abandonment of market farming but rather based precisely on an expanding market demand. Finally, peasant nonproletarian migrants (the children of peasant smallholders) may have been motivated to move in large part out of a determination not to suffer downward mobility (proletarian status or extreme land poverty) in their home area.[30]

Essentially, my own position coincides with that set forth by Sandner and Gudmundson, for reasons and with certain qualifications which were discussed elsewhere in greater detail.[31] I find "expulsion" to be a weak explanatory factor for early to at least mid-nineteenth century migrations, given the abundance of land and limited labor control. In fact, if colonial population was not almost completely nucleated, nor coercive measures totally effective, then accumulated "pressure" is even less of a key element for migration. Furthermore, westward migration within the Meseta began long before Independence and in spite of restrictive Crown and Church policies, even though it accelerated once government policies changed with respect to land settlement. And in the mid-nineteenth century, whatever population pressure had accumulated was substantially reduced by the cholera epidemic, yet settlers continued to move on to the frontier.

Factors of expulsion, alone, cannot explain sustained out-migration from the eighteenth through the nineteenth century. In other words, from before Independence, probably since the eighteenth century, positive incentives or "attraction" played a role -alongside various "pressures"- in the westward movement of settlers. After Independence, changing socioeconomic and sociopolitical conditions created greater opportunities

---

29 Sandner (1962-4), vol. I, pp. 146-147.

30 Gudmundson (1986a), p. 131.

31 Samper (1983), pp. 28-31.

for migrants. This does not mean that expulsion factors were totally absent at the time, but rather that they are insufficient for a comprehensive understanding of the migratory process. On the other hand, the growing attractiveness of the frontier cannot be seen in isolation from the decreasing opportunities in the settlers' place of origin. Given that "expulsion" and "attraction" always interact, there is a need to integrate both analytical perspectives and establish which type of factor prevailed historically, in a given region and period, and why. During the early stages of settlement in the Northwest, colonists, not necessarily destitute in their place of origin, were attracted by opportunities for access to the land under more favorable conditions, with the ultimate aim of developing commercial agriculture. This leads us to the changing patterns of production and reproduction,[32] which provided the framework for processes such as those discussed above.

Agrarian Changes and Colonization

Production for self-consumption and for exchange were both important, inseparable features of Costa Rica's agrarian economy during the late colonial period and in the early stages of nineteenth-century settlement. Technological, transportation and market limitations restricted the volume of marketable surpluses, but not the widespread, indirect control of formally-independent productive activities by merchant/lenders who often held a considerable measure of political power. While a major part of the Central Valley's agricultural production was not exported regularly until the coffee boom, local commercial activity and external trade were far more significant than the concept of a "closed" or self-subsistent (versus an "open", market-oriented) economy would suggest.[33] Such trade was also more constant than would be derived from the usual references to brief, single-crop export "cycles", separated in time and space but also lacking in continuity with respect to more general changes and to diversified commercial activities.

Recent socioeconomic historiography reflects an ambiguity on this point which the authors themselves seem unaware of, but which is at least partly attributable to a historically ambivalent agrarian economy, compounded by a tendency of retrospective analysts to minimize the role of commercial agriculture before coffee. Roger Churnside, for example, in his

---

32 Reproduction refers here to that of economic units, i.e. household consumption/production units, a concept broader than (but which includes) the reproduction of household members or of rural families per se.

33 I am referring here to the characterization embodied in R. Facio's *Estudio sobre economía costarricense* (1975), but also present in R. Cerdas' (1978) modified version where there is a supposedly "dialectical" but actually dualistic contradiction between a "closed" colonial economy and "pseudo-aristocratic" ruling class in Cartago, and an "open" commercial economy with an "agromercantile bourgeoisie," mainly in San José.

very valuable contribution to the history of labor in Costa Rica, makes two seemingly contradictory characterizations of the eighteenth-century economy: on the one hand, he states that "small, family subsistence units came to characterize the western Meseta, where the availability of Indian labor was less than to the east" in the late colonial period, and that a "dispersed, self-sufficient and independent peasantry" had evolved, with little or no economic contact among peasant units.[34] On the other hand, he tells us that during the latter half of the eighteenth century, tobacco and sugarcane made the local economy much more dynamic than before, and that during that century "wheat cultivation eventually became a family and communal activity for subsistence and for the international market", and that family as well as communal units "produced sugar, tobacco and their end-products for commercial exchange".[35] At this level, there is a recognition of empirical evidence regarding market-oriented peasant production, alongside subsistence agriculture, but the former is omitted upon characterizing the oversimplified agrarian economy which was to be transformed by coffee production.

This ambiguity is found in other studies which refer to a colonial peasant economy where self-consumption was the rule, and at the same time provide evidence indicating a much greater socioeconomic complexity. Yamileth González, for example, states that settlers in the western part of the Central Valley were "dedicated to cultivation of basic consumption products" in a rudimentary "natural economy", with no stable linkages to the international market.[36] However, towns such as Aserrí, Barva and Santa Ana, in the western Meseta, had a great number of *trapiches* or small mills for processing sugarcane to prepare marketable products, and the whole western part of the Central Valley supplied Cartago with meat. In years when there was a scarcity of grain or other foodcrops, no one was allowed to export such products from the region, as was otherwise the case.[37] Furthermore, the petty-merchant (*logreros*) speculated in maize, and according to contemporary testimony the small farmers (*labradores*) would at times "plant less to obtain a profit by selling their crops at exorbitant prices, and necessity forces those who can to buy at whatever price they set".[38] Measures against speculation included price regulation and the obligation to sell at the public *abasto* or marketplace, rather than in private homes.[39] This was certainly not a self-enclosed rural economy of subsistence producers whose production and consumption were essentially the same.

---

34 Churnside (1985), pp. 107-108.

35 *Ibid.*, pp. 71-2 and 80.

36 Y. González (1983), pp. 52, 95 and 151.

37 *Ibid.*, pp. 92, 94 and 119.

38 Quoted by González (1983), p. 120.

39 *Ibid.*, pp. 121-122.

The export "cycles" of the eighteenth century in Costa Rica were, to be sure, on a small scale if compared to other areas of Latin America at the time, or to the nineteenth-century coffee boom. It is also true that peasants produced much of what they consumed, and perhaps highly specialized household production units were infrequent. However, in the late colonial period there was clearly a market-oriented peasant production, not only in tobacco, but also in sugarcane, grain, livestock and others. The Meseta Central, then, can hardly be characterized as a natural self-consumption economy, in which commercial exchanges did not play a significant role. Aside from domestic demand, there was an export trade with neighboring colonies in agricultural commodities such as grain, garlic, sugar, livestock, meat, and tallow, aside from dyewoods and other extractive products.

Money was not always directly involved in commercial exchanges at the time, but this does not mean that barter was the rule in such transactions. This was a commercial system with scarce currency, where credit was essential. Merchants sold their imported goods in exchange for agricultural products, whether previously received or to be delivered, and a monetary calculation was involved. Underlying these commercial exchanges was a subordination of direct producers to commercial capital, which was often linked to political authority. Inegalitarian as this relationship was, it established a degree of economic integration through merchants' indirect control of peasant production.

Rural credit, in its various forms, reflected mercantile relations which would hardly be in accordance with the idea of a "natural" or "closed" economy, nor of "self-sufficiency" and "self-consumption". Even collection of the tithe, primitiae and taxes by merchants, as well as sale by auction of the *tercenas* and *estanquillos* (government-owned rights to sell tobacco and liquor), indicate the existence of a commercial network. In his study of commercial capital in the late colonial period, Iván Molina describes interregional trade within the province of Costa Rica, as well as the various "dependencies" between producers and merchants in the exchange of agricultural products for imported goods.[40] In the late eighteenth to early nineteenth century this included mechanisms such as *habilitaciones* (advance financing of a crop) especially for tobacco, loans and debts in kind, and wholesale/retail commercialization. After Independence, monetary loans became more frequent, as well as *habilitaciones* to coffee growers. Most public and private credit from 1821 to 1850 was concentrated in the area of San José, where the majority of coffee plantations were at the time. [41]

A brief discussion of specific productive activities in the Central Valley is necessary to better understand the socioeconomic processes which were behind colonization in its western section. Livestock raising was, clearly, the productive activity which occupied most land in the Central Valley as a

40 Molina (1984), pp. 87-98.

41 Molina (1986, 1987).

whole during the last decades of the colonial period. Only in a few small areas was a given crop locally predominant over grazing. However, this does not mean that large cattle ranches were the rule in the Central Valley. Here, the average size of herds per *hacienda* was much smaller than in Esparza and Bagaces, toward the Pacific, where much larger ranches belonged to absentee owners.[42] We also know that communal lands were used for grazing, and this was an important economic activity for a major part of the population.

Within the Central Valley, herds and ranches (primarily for meat production) seem to have been larger in the vicinity of Cartago and Heredia than near San José or Alajuela. In 1797, for example, the average size of herds in Villa Vieja (Heredia) was more than twice that in Villa Hermosa (Alajuela).[43] At the time of Independence, despite rising prices of land, the value of livestock in the western Meseta was clearly more than all other property in the probate inventories studied by Molina.[44] Composition of herds was similar throughout the Central Valley: numerically, cattle were two thirds of the total livestock, horses and mules roughly one fourth, and hogs less than one tenth. Sheep were found infrequently. [45]

Regarding crop agriculture proper, we know that in the late colonial period it was quite varied, but also that in terms of land use there was a predominance of staple grain, especially maize and beans, which were usually associated crops. There is little quantitative information, but local censuses of maize farmers indicate that this type of grain was planted almost exclusively on a small and medium scale.[46] Marketable surpluses were small, and natural factors combined with the expansion of other crops to create recurrent grain supply crises, partly buffered by agricultural diversity.[47] Grain production followed the mid-nineteenth century settlers and was an important economic activity on the frontier, but larger and larger quantities had to be imported, partly due to sub-regional specialization in agro-export crops. However, as will be seen in more detail for Heredia, rising prices for grain in certain areas of the Meseta actually favored a

---

42 L. Gudmundson, "La ganadería guanacasteca en la época de la Independencia: La hacienda San Juan de Dios, 1815-1835" (1978), pp. 83-86; Y. González (1983), p. 94.

43 Calculations based on data in González (1983), p. 94.

44 Molina (1985), p. 177. It should be mentioned that in the table there was a much stronger predominance of livestock in Alajuela than in Heredia (44.6% vs. 23.9% of the total value of movables and immovables). These two areas will be discussed in greater detail below.

45 Gudmundson (1985), pp. 183 and 187.

46 Hall (1976), p. 29.

47 González (1983), p. 101 and 109.

degree of peasant specialization in maize, with a concomitant reduction of pastureland at a local level.[48]

Aside from maize and beans, several other agricultural products such as wheat and vegetables were planted on small productive units.[49] These products, like grain, were partly for direct household consumption and partly for sale of surpluses, but were relatively minor in terms of area and value.

Specifically commercial crops, especially sugarcane, tobacco and coffee, were qualitatively important due to their impact on peasant market involvement, even though the area under cultivation with such products in the late eighteenth and early nineteenth century was far smaller than that in pasture and grain. Sugarcane production was widely disseminated on small and medium-sized productive units, on many of which it was the main crop toward the end of the colonial period. Judging by the distribution of *trapiches*, cultivation and processing of sugarcane had become most important in the western section of the Meseta since the eighteenth century.[50]

Preparation and marketing of *dulce* (sugar cakes) were carried out especially by middling peasant farmers,[51] because even though processing technology was relatively simple, it was beyond the possibilities of poorer peasants. Alajuela was already an area where sugarcane was an important crop in 1778, and by the mid-nineteenth century there were sugarcane fields along the *carretera nacional* or main cartroad toward the Pacific. Household production was clearly predominant there, despite the existence of a few larger farms employing wage laborers.[52]

Distilling and sale of sugarcane liquor was subject, before and after Independence, to government monopoly. This led not only to concentration of this type of processing, but also to a strong resistance by sugarcane growers, whose protests were especially frequent in the western Meseta.[53] While they were unable to bring down this profitable state monopoly, they constantly evaded it by bootlegging, an extremely frequent offense throughout the period.

Late in the eighteenth century, tobacco became locally significant, especially among the peasantry near Villa Nueva and Villa Vieja, close to the rivers, but also in other areas of the Meseta. Tobacco production and exports peaked between 1787 and 1792, when some twelve million plants were cultivated, and then decreased significantly, to approximately one

---

48 P. Alvarenga (1986), p. 99.

49 Fonseca (1983), p. 305.

50 *Ibid.* and González (1983), p. 92.

51 That is rural households relying primarily on family labor, as in the case of intermediate and surplus-producing domestic units.

52 Samper (1979), p. 244.

53 Hall (1976), p. 30.

million. With Independence and its sequel of liberalization, tobacco production recovered somewhat, and in the 1840's there were four or five million plants. After mid-century it declined once more, apparently due to the sustained expansion of coffee production in the area.[54]

Tobacco was cultivated on small-scale plantations, basically with household labor, sometimes supplemented by wage labor. The official *Factoría de Tabacos* organized crews of *cosecheros* who were authorized to plant a specific amount of tobacco, usually on land allotted temporarily for this purpose. Their number gives us a rough idea of how many small to medium-sized plantations there were in the "legal" sector: 774 *cosecheros* in 1784, thereafter fluctuating, and a maximum of 1,005 in 1791. After a three year prohibition, the number was most often under two hundred until Independence, and continued to be anywhere between one and two hundred in the 1820s and 1830s.[55] No figures are available for the 1840s, but their number may have increased somewhat. The area planted by each unit expanded in the early nineteenth century, and probably continued to do so after Independence, since tobacco sales grew despite the low number of *cosecheros*.[56] While large plantations did not develop, there may have been a shift from small to medium-sized units, with an associated change in the proportion of family and non-family labor.

The cultivation of tobacco brought with it a degree of productive specialization, though not to the point of excluding other crops. There were tobacco-related tasks during ten months of the year, but the *cosecheros* planted maize and certain other products on their own holdings in April and August. Even before the peak period of tobacco production in Costa Rica, it was said that "many of those who formerly did other work during the day, can now be seen cultivating tobacco".[57] Once it was decreed that tobacco should be planted on specific *tierras de propios*, rather than on peasant farms, specialization undoubtedly increased on such communal plots.

The position of tobacco growers was clearly subordinate, first to commercial capital directly and then via government monopoly, even after Independence. The system of *habilitaciones* (advances in merchandise or money, in exchange for future production) continued throughout, and their value per productive unit tended to increase.[58] Production was regulated from 1784 to 1851, and freedom of cultivation was decreed as of the latter year. Tobacco, then, fostered market-oriented economic activity by a number of small to medium productive units, subject to merchants and government authorities. Production was based on household labor and some wage labor, and constituted a mercantile experience for a segment of

54 Acuña (1974), pp. 58-61; Araya (1981), p. 8-10; González (1983), p. 191.

55 Acuña (1974), pp. 60, 63, 67; Araya (1981), p. 8; González (1983), p. 212.

56 Acuña (1974), p. 71; Araya (1981), p. 19.

57 Quoted by Acuña (1974), p. 65.

58 González (1983), p. 134; Araya (1981), pp. 2 and 4.

the peasantry in Villa Nueva and Villa Vieja, areas where coffee developed in the early to mid-nineteenth century.

The first commercial coffee plantations were established around San José, in the 1810s, and even in the 1840s almost two thirds of Costa Rican coffee was still produced in that area.[59] There were coffee groves further west, near Heredia and Alajuela, but westward expansion of this crop became relevant especially after mid-century. The first authoritative study on coffee, by Carolyn Hall, states that "it was introduced in the Meseta Central mainly on the farms of peasants, who were proud of their landowning tradition. Most of the first properties where coffee was cultivated for export, in the 1840s, were small."[60]

While there is no doubt that peasant coffee production became important in the early stages of its expansion, recent research suggests that even though the initial coffee plantations were small, they frequently belonged to merchants and owners of larger estates.[61] The question, actually, is why coffee production evolved so rapidly into an economic activity with major peasant participation. Apparently, the merchant/planters themselves, both directly and through government, promoted cultivation among small farmers. This was expressed in financing and buying of harvests, free or low-cost distribution of coffee seedlings, granting of property rights on public lands under coffee cultivation, etc. Coffee production was adopted readily by a growing number of peasant-farmers, for whom it was an opportunity to establish stable market ties and seek to obtain a profit. Around mid-century, coffee production in the Meseta Central was an interactive combination of different productive units, many based primarily on household labor, some on permanent and seasonal wage labor.

In terms of land use, despite the rapid expansion of coffee cultivation, it did not totally displace other productive uses on farms within the Meseta before1850. In the 1840s, both peasant coffee farms and larger coffee estates continued to have an area in pastures, whether for a couple of head or a regular herd of cattle. Sugarcane was still present on coffee farms in the mid-nineteenth century, and there were "small maize and bean plantations within many coffee farms, in the 1840s".[62] The agrarian landscape of the western Meseta toward 1850 was, therefore, quite varied both in terms of diversified land use patterns and the heterogeneity of productive units. We shall now focus on the two main areas of out-

59 Hall (1976), pp. 34-35 and 73.

60 Hall (1976), p. 81.

61 The statement may apply to the beginning of coffee cultivation in three different subregions and periods: for San José, we are lacking in detailed studies, but Molina (1985 and 1986) provides some information in support of such a contention; Alvarenga (1986) does so for Heredia, and we shall see in the last section of this chapter that a similar situation occurred in Alajuela.

62 Hall (1976), p. 79 and 81-82.

migration toward the Northwest from the Meseta Central, the vicinities of Heredia and Alajuela, the Villa Vieja and Villa Hermosa of colonial times.

HEREDIA

As mentioned previously, this was the main area of origin for migrants coming from other provinces of Costa Rica to settle in the northwestern section of the Central Valley, around the mid-nineteenth century. Furthermore, many of those who settled in or near Villa Hermosa itself, from the late eighteenth century on, also came from Heredia, and some of them, and especially many of their descendants, were active participants in the colonization of the Northwest.

An understanding of the social origin, productive experiences and cultural equipment of these migrants is necessary to comprehend their future role, closely related to the conditions which generated westward migration. From the late eighteenth to the mid-nineteenth century, the area of Heredia suffered fundamental transformations in its population trends, organization of productive activities, and social relations.

Demographically, Heredia ceased to be an area of immigration, as it had been throughout the colonial period, to become an area of out-migration. Growing numbers of people, themselves the descendants of settlers, moved westward first to Alajuela, then toward the Northwest, and finally to other areas within and beyond the Central Valley.

The productive experience of this new generation of colonists is related to landuse patterns in Heredia. Livestock raising was the predominant activity at the end of the eighteenth century, both on small and large productive units, but by the middle decades of the following century there had been a substantial reduction of herd sizes. There were less cattle, and mules, which had been quite important in the previous century, tended to disappear.[63] There was a process of land use intensification, whereby extensive grazing was displaced by agriculture proper.

According to the census data for 1792 and probate inventories for 1840-1850, studied by Patricia Alvarenga, grain (and especially maize) was the main crop to expand locally during the period. In most units, grain production exceeded subsistence requirements, and producers were at least partly market-oriented.[64] Regarding tobacco and sugarcane, the number of producers declined during the first half of the nineteenth century, and processing of the latter became concentrated on larger farms.[65] Expansion of coffee cultivation in this area was slower and came later than in San José. It began on a few farms of wealthy citizens, whose coffee plantations in the

---

63 Alvarenga (1986), pp. 57-61.

64 *Ibid.*, pp. 75-81.

65 *Ibid.*, pp. 67-74 and 86-87.

1840's were relatively small, usually less than four *manzanas*, with the largest some twenty or thirty *manzanas*.[66]

During the first half of the nineteenth century there was, on variously-sized units in the vicinity of Heredia, a process of agricultural intensification which initially led to partial specialization in grain production, not only for self-consumption but also for commercial exchange, to the detriment of livestock raising and other agricultural commodities. Since this area was only a few miles from San José , where coffee specialization was early and rapid, the abovementioned trend probably was a response to growing demand for grain supplies there. At the same time, a gradual decline of livestock production in Heredia helps to explain its greater development in the vicinity of Alajuela by mid-century. Clearly, sub-regional productive diversification was taking shape.

Conditions for access to the land were also evolving in Heredia. In the late seventeen hundreds, it was not difficult to obtain usufruct rights on communal or Crown lands in Heredia, though absolute private property was another matter. In Alvarenga's view:

> Enclosure was enough to ensure possession of a plot of land, and the peasants' cattle roamed freely about in the unoccupied lands...
>
> Most direct producers used Crown lands for their productive activities, and when market opportunities or an increase in fortune moved them to increase agricultural production, they merely increased the area available to them by enclosing another plot of land.
>
> Crown land which was under possession by direct producers was not assigned any value at all, since it was available to all. Instead, value was assigned to the labor invested in enclosure, which was the mechanism by which possession of the land was ensured. [67]

In actual practice, there may not have been the nearly absolute flexibility in access to the land which one might infer from the quote, but there certainly was an abundance of land and a real possibility of obtaining usufruct. Restrictions probably included, at least, socially differentiated access to the best lands, in terms of quality and location, given the existence of a far from egalitarian social order and vertical power structures. Even so, it would appear that in the late eighteenth century domestic units could, to a certain extent, adjust the amount of agricultural land available to them, in response to changes in their productive capacity.

Over the following decades, difficulties arose for the establishment of new household units with similar productive resources, and overall conditions of access to the land deteriorated for the existing units. Population growth, changes in land tenure and political measures altered the situation for peasant households in the course of a few decades. In the

---

66 Alvarenga (1986), pp. 87-93. A *manzana* is the equivalent of ten thousand square *varas*, or roughly 0.7 hectares (as compared to 0.4 hectares per acre).

67 *Ibid.*, pp. 27-28.

1820's, the *ayuntamiento* or town council of Heredia restricted the use of communal land, for example in maize, and there are references to landless poor, though not in large numbers. From 1830 to 1850, land was rapidly transformed into private property, and its price rose, to the point that it accounted for more than half the estimated value of movables and immovables in probate inventories of the 1840s.[68]

We conclude, then, that during the first half of the nineteenth century access to the land for new households was significantly reduced in Heredia, by comparison to the previous century. The area of land available for domestic units was smaller, due to restricted opportunities on public and communal lands and fragmentation of holdings, partly compensated for by a more intensive use of the land. As unclaimed land became scarcer in the Meseta Central, and private property more expensive, it was increasingly difficult or costly to establish new productive units in the area. Given the availability of lands in neighboring Alajuela, emigration by younger members of peasant households was an attractive option. Under such conditions, out-migration acted as an "escape valve" which, combined with agricultural intensification and specialization, reduced pressures on the existing domestic units in Heredia.

ALAJUELA

In the eighteenth century, productive units in that part of the original jurisdiction of Villa Vieja which would later be called Alajuela combined agriculture and livestock raising, self-consumption and commercial production, household and non-family labor. A century before coffee-based expansion, two rather isolated cases illustrate both social distance and the composition of family fortunes in this recently-settled area. Obviously it is impossible to reach any general conclusion from these two cases, but they do suggest possibilities to be explored.

In 1728, the family of Francisca Arroyo and Juan Venegas, with seven children, had assets estimated to be worth 167 *pesos*. In 1732, Josefa Quesada and José Herra, with six children, had assets worth $400. Given their similar number of children, even though their ages might vary somewhat, these two families were probably in a more or less similar stage of the family life-cycle. While the difference in their total fortunes is not that between the wealthiest and the poorest households, it is sufficient to indicate potential variations within the landholding peasantry. Composition of their fortunes points to certain common features, but also to several differences between one and the other productive unit.

The Venegas/Arroyo family only owned a house with an enclosed plot of land and plantain crop, the barest furniture and household utensils, an ax

68 *Ibid.*, pp. 29-31 and 46.

and a machete, an old horse and 37 head of cattle.[69] The cattle were 55% of the total assets, while the house and enclosure were only 18%. As a productive unit, it combined agriculture and ranching, but cattle was its main economic activity.

The composition of the Herra/Quesada fortune was quite different: While the house was estimated at $20, the *piñuela* enclosure and plantain crop were estimated at $45, and a *sitio de cercado* or enclosed plot another $40.[70] Among the agricultural implements there was a plough, estimated at $20, and the area under cultivation was certainly larger than in the first case. While livestock was a major part of total assets, cattle proper were less significant, with only five head of cattle, including a team of oxen for plowing and transportation. Instead, mules and horses were more than a third of total assets, and several were also owed to the deceased. In the eighteenth century, mule trains were basically for transportation of merchandise, a clear indication that Herra was probably involved in mercantile activities. We also find the type of loans and debts which were associated with merchants at the time; the remaining items were cloth, cotton, tobacco, cacao and other traders' goods.

Both Juan Venegas and José Herra had farming and ranching activities, but their meaning was quite different. For Venegas and his family, agriculture must have been primarily for self-consumption, just as the few head of cattle probably were for the Herras. Instead, cattle was the main productive activity of the Venegas family, and even if on a small scale it must have been their most stable market tie. For the Herra family, it is quite possible that agriculture generated marketable surpluses, but their principal market linkage was through mule trade.

For lack of sufficient cases to make any general comments at this point, let us move on to look at a few other cases which illustrate the situation half a century later.

At the beginning of the 1770s, Juana Oses and Pedro Zúñiga, with five children, had a fortune of close to $400.[71] It included two enclosures and some *tierra compuesta*, land bought from the Crown. Its area was half a *caballería*,[72] or about eleven hectares. These immovables were valued at an estimated $60, the same as a small sugarmill in the inventory. There were

---

69 Mortual Colonial, Heredia, # 1379, year 1728. I thank Patricia Alvarenga for reference to and data from the probate inventories pertaining to Alajuela and classified during the Colonial period under Heredia.

70 Mortual Colonial, Heredia, # 1674, year 1732. At this time, estimates for enclosures often referred only to the fence or wall, but its higher value usually indicated greater enclosed areas, under the assumption of similar fence costs. On the other hand, *sitio de cercado* seems to refer to the land itself.

71 Mortual Colonial, Heredia, # 2969, 1770.

72 A *caballería* was a somewhat imprecise measure for large areas, which in actual practice in Costa Rica was roughly the equivalent of 32 *manzanas*, or some 22 hectares.

several agricultural implements, including a plough, and also a few head of cattle and some horses, but no mules. Neither was there any merchandise, so we conclude that it was essentially an agricultural unit, with livestock raising as a complementary activity, and processing of sugarcane.

Toward the end of that decade, the family of Francisca Villegas and Felipe Morales, with eight children, offers a similar contrast with the Zúñiga/Oses household to that exemplified half a century before, under different circumstances. Their fortune, sizeable for the period, was estimated at over $1,000.[73] They had a medium-sized herd, with 89 head of cattle, and only a few mules. Their land rights included at least five enclosures, mainly sugarcane fields but also a maize field and a plantain one. Their value was twice that of the former case. The sugarcane mill and the agricultural implements were also estimated at twice the cost as the Zúñigas'. There is no mention of merchandise nor of the type of credit relations that merchants usually engaged in.

To avoid generalizing on the basis of these isolated cases, let us merely ask whether productive units in the area were moving toward a market-oriented specialization in sugarcane and cattle, with supplementary crops primarily for consumption.

From 1787 to 1795, we have a small group of cases which allow us to broaden the scope of this initial query, without yet reaching any general conclusions.[74] We can only make qualitative references to certain common features and differences among these cases, because their number is insufficient for any detailed statistical analysis.

Total fortunes in the nine cases for 1787-1795 varied from $190 to $2,286, with an average of $734 which only half the cases were anywhere near to. Immovables were just over one tenth of the assets, and credit was a very minor percentage. Therefore, almost nine tenths of this group's fortunes was in movables. Of these, livestock were undoubtedly the most valuable.

For the group as a whole, with certain variations which will be pointed out, livestock raising was a major economic activity, if we are to judge by the value of livestock. Cattle used for human consumption was numerically predominant, but mules for transportation were also significant. Land, still abundant and only partly enclosed, was not the decisive component of family fortunes in this group of cases. Enclosure was an ongoing process, and the cost of fences or walls was similar to or even higher than that of the land they enclosed. But in seven of the nine cases, there was some sort of possession of land for agriculture. Apparently, private rights over agricultural lands were already in transition from corporate to private ownership, well before legislation which is often said to have effected that change in the nineteenth century.

---

73 Mortual Colonial, Heredia, # 2050, 1779.

74 Mortuales Coloniales, Heredia: #1830, 1787; #1722, 1788; #1547, 1789; #1856, 1789; #1983, 1790; #1438, 1792; #1692, 1794; #1443, 1795; #1986, 1795.

Despite individual variations, a comparison of these cases leads to the conclusion that they were relatively homogeneous with respect to several relevant indicators: In all of them, movables accounted for most of the assets, and livestock was a major component in almost all. Except for two cases, the estimated value of land, crops and fences was less than one fifth of total assets.

There was only one large herd, with 339 head of cattle and 76 mules or horses, and another medium-sized herd, with 73 head of cattle and 13 mules or horses. Their owners were the wealthiest among the nine deceased in 1787-1795. In all the remaining cases, there were less than thirty-five head of cattle, and fifteen or less horses and mules. Livestock raising was an important economic activity, and size of herd was associated with capital wealth. In most of the cases discussed, small-scale ranching took place on what might be considered domestic production/consumption units, with access to untitled land for grazing and a few small, fenced-in plots for specific crops.

Regarding agriculture, the most frequent use of the land in these cases was sugarcane cultivation, followed by staple grain and plantain. In the few cases where the agricultural area was given in the probate documents, it was between one and five *manzanas*. The value of rights to the land, fences and crops was less than $55 in all but one case. Each family had from two to six such rights, but the number was not directly associated with level of fortune. It would not seem that control of specifically agricultural land was extremely unequal, and it was less a criterion for social differentiation than ownership of cattle.

The most important processing equipment was the *trapiche* or small sugarmills. These were clearly concentrated in households of high and intermediate fortunes. It is also quite possible that owners of *trapiches* processed both their own sugarcane as well as that of their neighbors.

Credit balances, on the other hand, did not define greater or lesser wealth in the cases discussed, although use of credit did vary. There were more debts than loans receivable, and while both were especially frequent in one of the higher fortunes, this specific credit balance was only for $7. In other words, debts and credits might be numerous yet balance each other off, and not make a great difference regarding level of fortune.

If the cases discussed are at all representative, livestock was certainly a major economic activity in the late eighteenth century, in combination with sugarcane and grain production. Land was being enclosed, but in small areas, and the value of such rights was not decisive in connection with level of fortune. Clearly, owners of large herds had access to more land for grazing, but this does not seem to have generated well-defined possession rights at the time, which could be transmitted through inheritance. Perhaps the need to legalize such rights had not yet arisen. Movables, especially livestock and processing equipment, were much more important to establish such distinctions.

While these tentative conclusions cannot be proven with just a handful of cases, what we know about early to mid-nineteenth century rural society in the region is quite compatible with these initial findings on the late eighteenth century. Livestock raising continued to be the main activity in terms of land use, while enclosure, the development of absolute private property and a gradual agricultural intensification continued. The productive experience of those who were to settle the Northwest was one in which extensive land use was substantially based on cattle ranching, whether on a small or larger scale. Crop agriculture was a complementary economic activity, partly for self-consumption but also for sale of surpluses. Staple grain and sugarcane were the most widespread crops, with variable market surpluses; tobacco had been a more specialized, commercially-oriented activity for certain groups of peasant farmers, while coffee was a minor crop on larger farms in the areas of out-migration.

The next three chapters will discuss land settlement beyond the town of Alajuela, and especially a fundamental agrarian transformation in the Northwest: from an open agricultural frontier, where access to land (however non-egalitarian) created opportunities for migrants from very diverse social backgrounds, to become an area in which agricultural intensification and specialization on variously-sized productive units delayed but could not avoid the dilemmas which successive generations would have to face.

Chapter 4

A Society of Settlers

This chapter will deal with early to mid-nineteenth-century changes in social relations, settlement patterns and the organization of production in the area from Alajuela city to the western end of the Central Valley. In this period, immigrants to Grecia and other parts of the Northwest came most often from the vicinity of the provincial capital. After a brief overview of macro-societal interactions, our attention will focus on the settlers themselves and on specific productive units in the area, so as to understand the concrete conditions under which members of rural households related among each other and with an increasingly commodified rural society.

Ambivalent Interactions

As the mid-nineteenth century grew near, a gradually expanding area west of Alajuela city was being incorporated not only into the inhabited part of the Central Valley, but also to an economy which was becoming far more dynamic than in colonial times. Linkages with the world market were consolidated as primary exports grew rapidly, imported goods became more readily available, and financial ties were established through mercantile firms as well as governments. The domestic market, still not fully integrated, was nevertheless increasing in terms of consumption, interregional trade and overall cohesion. Transportation and marketing networks evolved accordingly, facilitating the process of regional and subregional specialization begun in the late eighteenth and early nineteenth centuries.

Primary product exports to the foreign markets of the time, especially Europe, were the motive force behind specialization, and not only that geared toward international trade, but also that which was required to supply formerly diversified areas. After Independence, coffee tended to become the most important export crop; however, toward 1850 it was still highly concentrated in the Meseta Central, especially near San José.[1] As mentioned in Chapter 3, Heredia became more of a grain-producing area, with coffee production developing only gradually. Livestock raising was displaced toward Alajuela, with sugarcane and grain production as complementary crops, and a minor amount of coffee:

> In 1824, for example, there were some 5,000 coffee trees in the Legua [community lands] of Alajuela city, on plots which had previously been planted in sugarcane or plantain. For several years, the town council continued to provide land to any citizen wishing to plant coffee.[2]

While coffee production did gradually expand in the vicinity of Alajuela, and then near Grecia, it had not led to any clearly-defined productive specialization in the area by mid-century. Quite the contrary, it was one of several crops which actually diversified a predominantly livestock-raising regional economy. However, this diversification was far from being subsistence-oriented, even if it did satisfy certain local consumption needs. Coffee, grain, sugarcane and other agricultural products, like cattle itself, were also mercantile economic activities, and they responded to the overall monetization and commodity orientation of a booming agro-export economy.

The agricultural frontier we are dealing with was not a remote, isolated area, weakly linked to national and international markets, nor was settlement a flight from the predatory effects of an agrarian capitalism based on primitive accumulation. Just as coffee allowed peasants of the Meseta Central both to prosper and be exploited,[3] settlement on the frontier allowed migrants to obtain access to new lands as independent commodity producers, taking advantage of economic opportunities while at the same time re-establishing market ties which were essential for their indirect subordination to merchants, moneylenders, owners of processing mills, and others. Settlement and local population growth also made it possible for estate owners to obtain at least part of the labor they urgently required, both on a permanent and seasonal basis.

As part of this broader social environment, productive units in the region were involved not only in local exchanges but also in interregional circulation of commodities and in other socioeconomic relations. Members of domestic units, specifically, participated in labor, credit, land and

---

1 Toward mid-century, perhaps two thirds of the country's coffee production still came from San José, where some 7,000 hectares under cultivation reflected increasing specialization by peasant-farmers as well as estate-owners (Hall, 1976, pp. 73-4). *Habilitaciones* or credit advances on coffee were also heavily concentrated in San José (Molina,1986).

2 C. Hall (1976), p. 73. The area planted in coffee at the time, in Alajuela, would therefore have been less than 4 hectares.

3 Samper (1979), pp. 78-79; Gudmundson (1986a), pp. 77-79; Molina (1986).

product markets, within and beyond the region. On the other hand, market integration was still incomplete toward 1850, since there were several very recently-settled areas in the Northwest where infrastructure and mercantile networks were just beginning to develop. Economic relations on the frontier itself were not yet those of a fully mercantile regional economy, but neither were they retrogressive as in a long-term reversion to subsistence agriculture.

During the first half of the nineteenth century, the Northwest was an area with limited access in terms of transportation. It was clearly possible to transport products into or out of the region, but poor roads and trails made their movement difficult, slow and costly. When the *Carretera Nacional* was built in the 1840s, even though it did not run through the Northwest itself but at a relatively short distance, there was a potential for goods to be transported at lower cost to or from the Meseta Central and the Pacific coast (Figure 4.1). But even in the following decades, local road construction was extremely restricted, and ox-cart transportation was not yet possible in several parts of this region. From the 1820s to mid-century, the Northwest was an area where agro-export production could in fact develop, but where highly specialized productive units were still at a disadvantage with respect to those located in the Meseta Central, even if distances to the main port were similar. The location of these new lands relative to transportation routes made them attractive to land speculators and to peasant settlers, but delayed the development of intensive agriculture on the larger estates.

Although many small and medium-sized productive units came to be established on the northwestern settlement frontier, initial land claims in the region from the early to mid-nineteenth century were relatively large. Government-owned lands were sold to individuals or groups of settlers, at low prices often paid later or not at all. As Rosalba Salas' ongoing research clearly shows, extensive land claims often preceded actual colonization: in the 1830s they were especially large, frequently over 1,000 hectares, though less numerous than in the following decades.[4] In the 1840s and 1850s, land claims were somewhat smaller, but many were still several hundred hectares in size, and they accounted for almost half the land claimed during the nineteenth century in this region. Most claims were individual, and those made collectively were generally by close relatives. Subdivision of large claims by sale was quite frequent, allowing those who claimed the land to retain a substantial part for future development, while reaping a profit on the rest as well as attracting settlers and potential laborers, in a process quite similar to the well-known *antioqueño*

---

4 I must express my wholehearted appreciation to Rosalba Salas, who is currently writing up her licenciate thesis on land-tenure in the northwestern part of the Central Valley, at the Universidad Nacional, and was also my research assistant several years ago. We have shared information and ideas, with a common interest in the colonization of this region. The following account of land tenure changes is entirely based on a summary of her findings.

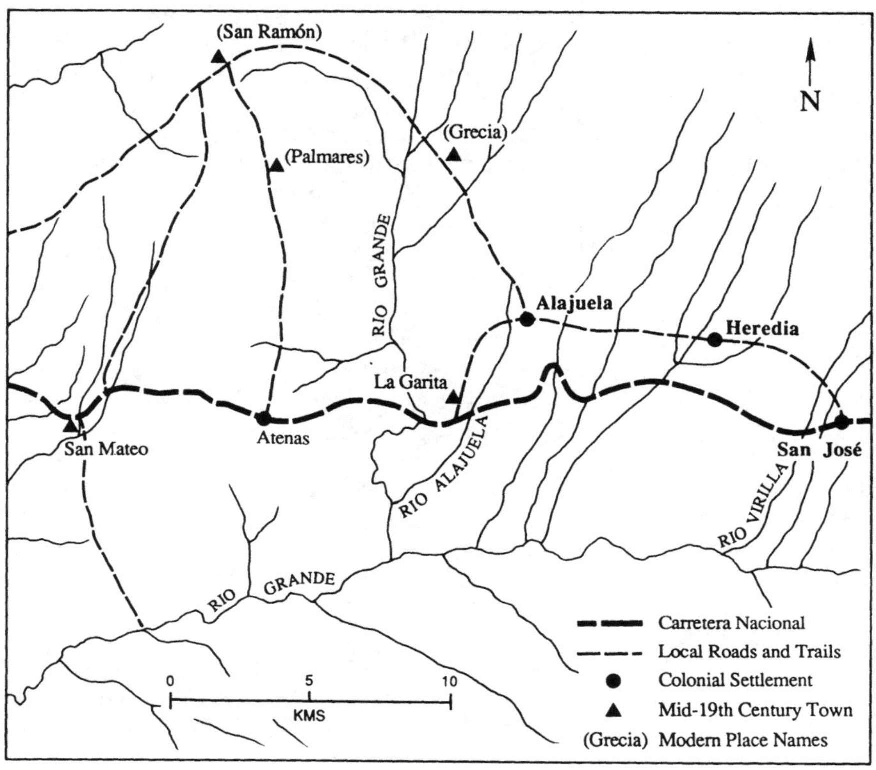

Figure 4.1 Principal roads in the western section of the Central Valley, Costa Rica, mid-nineteenth century

colonization in Colombia. Peasant colonists in Costa Rica's Central Valley had access to the land through purchase, by making small to medium-sized claims either individually or collectively, and via distribution of community lands in the vicinity of the towns founded around mid-century.

Geographic location of land claims indicates a westward movement, somewhat in advance of actual settlement: in the 1820s, near Grecia; in the 1830s toward Naranjo and Palmares; in the 1840s north of these areas and toward SanRamón; and in the 1850s to the northwest and southwest of San Ramón.[5] Apparently, the effective colonization of a neighboring area made the lands just beyond the actual settlement frontier attractive for speculators, while factors such as poor transportation and labor scarcity made it difficult to establish large, labor-intensive estates there.

Initially, land claims were used in a very extensive manner, a major part left uncultivated and the rest for grazing, with extremely limited labor inputs. In the following decades, there is some reference in land claims documents to plantain plots, and later to sugarcane and some coffee, especially near Grecia.[6] Intensification proceeded slowly during the early stages of settlement in this sparsely inhabited and primarily livestock-producing region. Smaller productive units began to invest more labor per area as transportation improved and population density increased. At a household level, it was not yet worthwhile nor necessary to fully specialize in and within agriculture, nor was it yet possible to do so on large estates, given the scarcity of labor and cost of transportation. Labor-intensification occurred gradually, as a response both to population growth and to economic opportunities.

Colonization west of Alajuela was not a retreat from the advance of agrarian capitalism or the expanding "market economy", but rather an attempt to obtain favorable conditions of access to land for commercial production, combined with whatever self-consumption was made necessary by local conditions. There was certainly a rising demand for cattle, which was driven to the main livestock market of the time, the *plaza ganadera* in Alajuela. Sugarcane was another crop with an expanding domestic market, whether for molasses to produce legal and illegal liquor, *dulce* for household consumption, or even to feed livestock. Demand for grain also increased as the Meseta Central shifted toward agro-export production. Coffee, as yet incipient in the Northwest, was nevertheless an attractive potential crop, and while livestock raising was the settlers' present, growing numbers among them saw coffee cultivation as their future.

Insofar as domestic units and their members entered into market exchanges, they were part of a broader network of social relations in which they undoubtedly occupied a subordinate position, but which at least initially offered them the only means to take advantage of existing

5 Based on data provided by Rosalba Salas.

6 Personal communication by Rosalba Salas, based on her study of land claims in the first half of the nineteenth century.

opportunities. Their multiple interactions with merchants, moneylenders and owners of processing mills or of haciendas, were ambivalent in that they involved both exploitation and mutual benefit, just as their sociopolitical relations combined conflict and association. Trade fostered unequal exchange, but was indispensable for traders as well as for peasants. Credit permitted value transfers, but he who lent out money was not always the beneficiary, nor was he who borrowed always the loser in such transactions.[7] Personal relations such as *compadrazgo* (the tie between the father of a child and its godfather) had an element of social verticality, but was equally important to both *compadres*. Among domestic units and within rural households, a complex set of relations also merged seemingly contradictory characteristics. Interwoven with kinship, relations among peasant family members were both reciprocal and authoritarian, and those between neighbors involved cooperation as well as social differentiation. Still, whether at the community or regional level, recent settlement and generally favorable economic trends tended at first to obscure the inegalitarian aspects of frontier society, and enhanced opportunities for many of the settlers not only to obtain land, but also to prosper.

The Settlers

At the start of the nineteenth century, Villahermosa (Alajuela) was a town with 369 households, almost one third of which were headed by women.[8] According to the census taken in 1798, there were also some five to six hundred households in the neighboring *barrios*, especially toward the east, still under the jurisdiction of Heredia.[9] The population of Alajuela was 75% mestizo, there was officially no Indian population at all, and we know there were no Indian communities.[10] The following paragraphs refer to the people who settled the area from Alajuela to San Ramón in the middle decades of the nineteenth century.

In 1829, there were 1,538 households, according to a municipal census count, and slightly under eight thousand inhabitants in what is today the province of Alajuela. Roughly the same situation is found in 1835.[11] The population was still concentrated near the provincial capital, and there

---

7 Molina (1986), presents several cases in which *habilitaciones* permitted borrowers to establish successful coffee enterprises.

8 ANCR, Complementario Colonial, #1303, summarized by Gudmundson (1985), p. 175.

9 ANCR, Complementario Colonial, # 1307, in Gudmundson (1985), p. 176.

10 ANCR, Complementario Colonial, # 5322, in Gudmundson (1985), p. 175; Fonseca (1983), Chapter 3.

11 ANCR, Gobernación, # 9246 and Municipal Alajuela, # 896, summarized in Gudmundson (1985), pp. 197 and 199.

was no evidence of significant settlement in the northwestern part of the Central Valley.

It was not until the 1840s that a census identified settlements in the Northwest, specifically those of Agualote, Sarchí, Calabaza and Santa Gertrudis, in the area which is now known as Grecia (Figure 4.2). Colonization probably had begun in the previous decade, but this is the first administrative recognition of a significant population in the area.[12] Still, more than three fourths of the provincial population was in the vicinity of Alajuela city or the nearby *barrios*, while 15% lived in the Northwest, specifically near Grecia, and less than one tenth lived in Atenas.[13]

Composition of the population in the 1840s, by age and by sex, was similar to that elsewhere in the Central Valley: more than half the population was under twenty, and slightly more than one third was twenty to forty-nine years old. The only difference regarding age was that the percentage of those fifty or more was somewhat lower than in other provinces, something to be expected due to ongoing settlement in the area. As to sex, there was a slightly higher percentage of women than men,[14] which would be inconsistent with immigration of single men from other provinces. Composition of the population points to settlement by relatively young couples and families in Alajuela province, which in turn suggests peasant as opposed to proletarian patterns of migration.

As in the rest of the Central Valley, households headed by women (widows and single women in charge of a family) were a significant proportion, but Alajuela city had the highest percentage of all (39.2%). Instead, as in other provinces, this figure was relatively low (about 21%) in the smaller towns.[15] Very few widowers and hardly any single men headed households; the former tended to remarry rapidly, and the latter were of course in a different situation from that of unwed mothers in the rural society we are discussing. But most significantly, there is no indication that stem families were frequent; instead, nuclear households were clearly predominant. As sons and daughters married, they were expected to form their own households, and in a region where land was accessible on the nearby frontier, this often meant emigrating at the time of family formation.

Average age at marriage in the Alajuela-San Ramón area was similar to that elsewhere in the Central Valley, (i. e. twenty-one or twenty-two for women, and twenty-five or twenty-six for men). According to the 1843-44

---

12 Population of these four settlements in the area of Grecia was 1,357 in 1843, or some 270 households at a ratio of five per household, similar to that in previous censuses. ANCR, Congreso, # 6547.

13 Data from the 1843-1844 census, summarized by Gudmundson (1986a), pp. 243-244.

14 52.8% women, 47.2% men. Data derived from those presented by Gudmundson (1986a), pp. 138-139. These figures are not very different from those for Heredia and Cartago, where out-migration was the rule.

15 *Ibid*, p. 98.

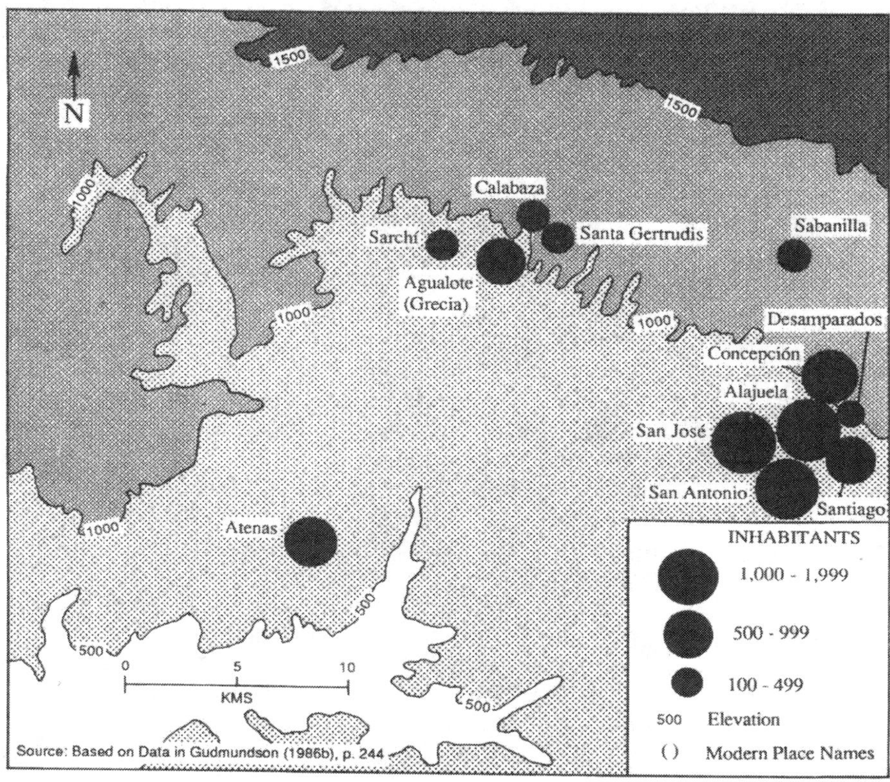

Figure 4.2 Population centers in the western section of the Central Valley, Costa Rica, according to the 1843 census

census, mean size of co-resident family units (those living in the same house) was smaller in the previously settled area of Alajuela province than in the northwestern settlements, where households averaged 5.0 to 5.6 members. In most cases, two to three children lived with the parent or parents. These sons and daughters were almost always under twenty, and one or two of them were usually too young to work at all. The household head was usually under forty at the time, and if it was male-headed household, the spouse was a few years younger.[16] Co-resident households, then, were relatively small, their members young, and consumption needs high vis-à-vis labor capacity.[17] Emigration of young adults allowed household members to obtain new lands on the frontier, and relieved pressure on the original family tenure, but it also meant that older sons who left their parents' home did not contribute labor directly, e.g. to support of their younger brothers and sisters or to further intensify land use.

Westward colonization had a definite impact on the social and specifically occupational characteristics of the population in this region toward mid-century. While Heredia was the province with most *jornaleros* (not necessarily proletarians, but at least part-time wage laborers or very land poor peasants), with over a third of the laboring population thus classified, Alajuela had the lowest such percentage, well under 10%.[18] Instead, *labradores* or independent peasant farmers were by far the predominant category in Alajuela, while they were less frequent in areas of

---

16 Average size of households was 4.3 in the town of Alajuela and even less in some smaller settlements near the provincial capital, but close to five in Sarchí and Agualote, 5.4 in Calabaza and 5.6 in Santa Gertrudis. If there were three children in the co-resident household unit, one was usually under seven years old, another from seven to eleven, and the third from twelve to twenty. There were twenty-five to fifty percent more boys than girls among children in the Northwest, for reasons which are as yet unclear but which may reflect a tendency for some daughters to remain with the grandparents or other relatives. The average age of household heads in the region, according to the 1843-44 census, was 36. Archivo Nacional, Sección Congreso, # 6547; Samper (1985), pp. 65-66; Gudmundson (1986b), pp. 139 and 278-281.

17 For a calculation of hypothetical productive capacity and consumption requirements of an average, five-member co-resident household in Sarchí, for 1843-44, see Samper (1985), p. 85-86, note 18. However, I no longer accept my own assumption (borrowed from Chayanov) regarding relative labor capacities of household members by age and sex. I believe that rural households should be viewed as integrated productive units, where the complementarity of various tasks carried out by individual members is qualitatively much more important than any quantitative measurement of abstract "labor capacity", which assumes that physical strength for certain tasks, usually carried out by adult males, is the parameter by which the labor of other household members should be assessed.

18 Samper (1979), pp. 80-81. Archivo Nacional, Sección Congreso, Documents # 5345, 5424, 5425, 5426, 5428, 5429, 5430, 5431, 6516, 6537, 6545, 6546, 6549, 6550, 6551, 6552, 6555, 6556, 6557, 6564.

out-migration such as Heredia. Within the province of Alajuela, as in other parts of the Central Valley, there was a more diversified occupational structure in the city than in smaller towns, with non-agricultural occupations becoming important in the former, and *labradores* more clearly so in the latter.[19] However, social structure in recently-settled areas was not totally homogeneous, as the four northwestern districts in the area of Grecia exemplify.

In Sarchí, *labradores* were about two thirds of the total laboring population but the rest were considered *jornaleros*. Although two of the latter owned capital, the rest were said to have none at all. More *labradores* had some, usually less than $100, but many were not recorded as having any capital either, and the largest fortune was estimated at $250.[20] It would seem that in Sarchí these occupational categories reflected status, more than major differences in absolute wealth.

In the district of Calabaza, social structure was more diversified, with 22% *agricultores*, 42% *labradores*, 17% *artesanos* and an equal percentage of *jornaleros*. Level of wealth followed that same order, but differences between the first two categories were not great, and probably reflected gradations in terms of land-tenure and social status.[21] Male craftsmen were poor, but *hilanderas* (spinners) were the poorest, whether widows or single women. *Jornaleros* in this area were also quite poor, and usually had no house of their own.

In Santa Gertrudis, almost all the population was classified as *labradores*, with household capital estimates ranging from several thousand *pesos*, in a few cases, to under two hundred in most. The wealthier were akin to the *agricultores* of Calabaza, and tenfold differences in estimated fortune indicate far more social stratification than is suggested by a uniform occupational classification.

In Agualote, too, everyone but a merchant and a carpenter were classified as *labradores*, but there was a tiny rural elite among them, with a maximum fortune estimated, in one case, at $6,000. Most of the population had some capital, but usually no more than $200. Settlers undoubtedly had access to land, but a few had significantly more access than others.

On the whole, the population of Alajuela in the 1840s shared several demographic characteristics with the rest of the inhabitants of the Central Valley, e.g. composition by age and by sex, age at marriage, and approximate size of co-resident nuclear households. Occupational differences between areas of earlier and more recent settlement, notably the strong predominance of *labradores* over *jornaleros*, were clearly related to

---

19 Gudmundson (1986a), p. 37.

20 All figures for this period are in *pesos*. The source for information on the districts of Sarchí, Calabaza, Santa Gertrudis and Agualote is Archivo Nacional, Sección Congreso, # 6547.

21 Average capital for *agricultores* was $191, for *labradores* $134, for *artesanos* $28, and for *jornaleros* only $3.

ease of access to the land on the frontier. While most of the population in the Northwest had some land, colonization did not create a homogeneous rural society but rather one in which gradations of wealth were initially less pronounced than in the previously settled areas.

The outstanding feature of population dynamics during the following decade was the cholera epidemic of 1856, which Costa Rican troops brought back from the war in Nicaragua. It was the greatest demographic crisis of the nineteenth century, and the disease killed off 8% to 10% of the total population. Its socioeconomic consequences were important for the surviving rural population and for the process of settlement. This unusually high mortality certainly relieved population pressure generally, but it had a socially specific impact on the existing and new productive units: difficulties to obtain wage labor increased for owners of large estates and land claims, while domestic units probably were in a better position due to their reliance on family labor and the fact that there were, often, less prospective heirs. Peasant settlement and overall population growth in the region actually continued at a more or less similar rate, while large land claims declined in number and coverage.[22] On the other hand, higher mortality brought with it many more hereditary successions in a region where most of the population was landed.[23] A greater proportion of very diverse productive units was subject to probate procedures and inheritance practices because of the high death rate. This, in turn, had an impact on overall agrarian changes in the context of ongoing settlement.

The deceased of the 1850s with inheritable property can help us look more closely at certain characteristics of the landed population of Alajuela province at the time, many of them settlers or descendants of settlers.[24] On the average, property owners who died between 1850 and 1859 were fifty-one years old, and half of them were forty-six to sixty years of age.[25] Given that life expectancy in Costa Rica at the time was under thirty

---

22 Based on unpublished statistical information provided by Héctor Pérez and Rosalba Salas, which indicate that rapid population growth in the Northwest, substantially due to immigration from the Meseta, was uninterrupted by the1856 demographic crisis even though it may have slowed down somewhat, while size of land grants decreased quite substantially after 1850 and area claimed in the 1860s was only one sixth of that claimed in the 1850s or in the 1840's.

23 All information below in the remainder of this chapter, unless otherwise indicated, is derived from 276 probate records for 1850-1859, listed under primary sources.

24 38.5% of the probate records from this decade in Alajuela province were for 1856, but characteristics such as age, number of heirs, total wealth and others were not significantly different that year from the years before or after. Therefore, higher mortality increased proportional representation of the landed population in probate records, but did not alter distribution under relevant categories within this population.

25 Minimum age at time of death in these probate records was twenty-five, and the oldest deceased was ninety. Only a minor percentage was under thirty or over seventy-five.

years,[26] the landed population was relatively old (Table 4.1). This can be seen in comparison to deaths reported a few years later in the Parish of San Anselmo de los Palmares, where 71% died before their sixteenth birthday, and almost 90% before their forty-sixth.[27] Not only were the landed (i.e., most of those included in probate records) older than the rest of the population, but within the group those with more property also tended to be the eldest (Table 4.2). Both differences are no doubt associated with accumulation of movables and immovables during family life-cycles, but this well-known process does not account for all variations in wealth among the population.

TABLE 4.1 AGE OF DECEASED AT TIME OF DEATH IN PROBATE INVENTORIES, ALAJUELA PROVINCE, 1850-1859

Age	**Frequency**	
	ABSOLUTE	RELATIVE
1 - 15	0	0.0
16 - 30	9	7.0
31 - 45	32	25.0
46 - 60	65	50.8
61 - 75	20	15.6
> 75	2	1.6

Source: All tables in this chapter whose titles refer to probate inventories are based on the probate cases for 1850-1859 listed in the bibliography.

Distribution by sex was also biased, insofar as two thirds of the deceased (mainly property owners) were men, but this in turn was economically differentiated, as the disproportion between sexes was significantly smaller in fortunes under $500 than at higher socioeconomic levels. Since there was legally no such distinction, this would seem to indicate that informal mechanisms transferred control of property from women to men, whether their husbands or brothers, and that such mechanisms were especially strong at intermediate and high levels of wealth.

26 Pérez (1983), p. 123; Robles (1986), p. 41. Infant mortality was twice adult mortality: Tjarks (1976), p. 117.

27 The percentage of deceased persons by age group in the Parish of Palmares, from 1866 to 1868, were: 34.7% up to one year of age; 36.7% between one and fifteen years old; 10.2% from sixteen to thirty; 8.2% from thirty-one to forty-five; 8.2% from forty-six to sixty; and 2.0% from sixty-one to seventy-five years old.

TABLE 4.2 AGE OF DECEASED AT TIME OF DEATH, ACCORDING TO LEVEL OF WEALTH IN PROBATE INVENTORIES, ALAJUELA PROVINCE, 1850-1859

Level of Wealth $	Average Age at Time of Death	Number of Cases with Data
< 500	49.20	24
500 - 1,000	50.12	31
1,000 - 5,000	51.13	60
> 5,000	55.15	13
All	50.93	128

While the geographic distribution of the deceased reflected that of the general population,[28] it varied according to wealth. The main subregional difference was that lower-level fortunes were more frequent than higher-level fortunes in the western frontier of Palmares and San Ramón, while the opposite was the case in previously settled areas such as Alajuela city, Grecia and Naranjo (Table 4.3).[29] This was probably due to the higher price of land, cattle and various movables in the more densely populated part of the province, as well as real capital accumulation over a longer period there.

TABLE 4.3 PLACE OF RESIDENCE OF THE DECEASED ACCORDING TO LEVEL OF WEALTH IN PROBATE INVENTORIES, ALAJUELA PROVINCE, 1850-1859

Residence	Level of Wealth ($)				
	< 500	500 TO < 1,000	1,000 TO < 5,000	≥ 5,000	ALL
Area of Alajuela	50.9	55.7	57.3	55.0	55.5
Grecia - Naranjo	3.8	5.1	6.4	10.0	5.8
San Ramón - Palmares	11.3	5.1	4.1	0.0	5.4
Atenas - San Mateo	3.8	6.3	8.1	5.0	6.5
Other	0.0	1.3	0.8	5.0	1.1
No Data	30.2	26.5	23.3	25.0	25.7

28 Three quarters of the deceased lived in the vicinity of Alajuela town and neighboring rural areas, while 15% lived in the Northwest.

29 While this difference must be qualified by the fact that absolute numbers in the Northwest were small, the distinction is in accordance with the lower price of movables and immovables, and less initial accumulation of wealth by settlers on the frontier.

Socioeconomic differences were also linked to number of heirs, with an average of six per probate case but a gradual increase from less than five in the lower fortunes to slightly under seven in the higher ones (Table 4.4).[30] Sub-regionally, the number of heirs was higher in the Northwest (8.2) than in the vicinity of the provincial capital (5.4).[31] While any firm conclusions on this point will require further diachronic analysis, it may be suggested here that the linkage between number of heirs and time since settlement is probably related not only to household size, but also to land poverty of many households in the previously settled areas, long-standing out-migration from there, and limited exclusion of heirs to counteract extreme subdivision of holdings.

TABLE 4.4 NUMBER OF HEIRS PER PROBATE CASE, ACCORDING TO LEVEL OF WEALTH, ALAJUELA PROVINCE, 1850-1859

Level of Wealth ($)	Average Number of Heirs	Number of Cases with Data
< 500	4.66	50
500 - < 1,000	5.59	76
1,000 - < 5,000	6.90	120
≥ 5,000	6.65	20
All	6.08	266

It should be noted that the *Código General*, enacted by Braulio Carrillo as head of State in 1841, and which was the legal foundation for transmittal of property via inheritance at mid-century, was generally restrictive with respect to parents' rights to freely decide how their properties and other wealth would be distributed among their mandatory or non-mandatory heirs.[32] Undoubtedly, such legislation acquired different concrete meanings in various historical situations, but it does indicate a legal and social pressure toward egalitarian or nearly egalitarian partition among heirs. Given the relative abundance of land at the time and government policies which favored private occupancy of public lands, it seems reasonable that exclusion of heirs should only be significant near the cities and in the more densely settled areas.

30 Since there were also differences in age according to level of wealth, some of this increase in number of heirs could be due to age of the deceased, and in that case greater subdivision of property would have compensated for variations in wealth. However, number of heirs increased fractionally, while levels of fortune increased as multiples, so that "social levelling" did not occur.

31 Given the lower number of cases in the Northwest, the results were checked by eliminating the two with most heirs in this region, and there were still almost two more per case than in or near Alajuela city.

32 See article 31 of the *Código General*, and comments on this article in Badilla (1988), p. 192.

Sub-regional and extra-regional comparison of the characteristics of the population of Alajuela has outlined various linkages between demographic and socioeconomic processes in a context of mid-nineteenth century land settlement. Several of these interwoven variables will now be discussed with specific reference to productive units.

Units of Production in the 1850s

This section will refer to the characteristics of various types of productive units, insofar as they are reflected in the probate inventories for the province of Alajuela, between 1850 and 1859.[33] The deceased whose assets were recorded in such documents cover a broad spectrum of the landholding population, but no general assumption is made here regarding proportional representativeness in terms of social stratification.[34] Instead, cases will be related, insofar as possible, to the initial typology set forth in Chapter 2. Our aim here is to identify characteristics of the various types of productive units at mid-century, as a basis for diachronic analysis in the following chapters.

Generally speaking, immovables (land and buildings of any sort, but especially housing) amounted to 75% or 80% of the total assets of most households, wealthy or poor.[35] Movables used for production (livestock and equipment) were usually about 15% of assets, in terms of value. And non-productive movables, from household goods to clothing, were a very low percentage in all but the poorest, landless or nearly landless households, where, however meager, they became relatively more important among the few worldly possessions of such households (Table 4.5). The overall composition of physical assets (movables and immovables) did not vary significantly according to wealth. This suggests a certain degree of similarity in the make-up of productive units, large and small.

There were, undoubtedly, very major variations in the total value of assets, as well as in their more specific characteristics. Estimates of physical assets ranged from negligible values to over $20,000, quite a fortune in the mid-nineteenth century. Some twenty cases, or about 7%, had more than $5,000 in movables and immovables, and were clearly

---

33 All general references to probate inventories in this section refer to the 276 cases listed in the bibliography.

34 The property-less are absent in documentation regarding inheritance, and the land-poor are probably under-represented to a certain extent. Intermediate and high fortunes are well represented, but some large absentee landowners may have resided outside the province of Alajuela, for example in San José or Heredia.

35 Total assets = $ movables + $ immovables +/- $ credit balance.

TABLE 4.5 CUMULATIVE VALUE OF ASSETS (IN *PESOS*), ACCORDING TO LEVEL OF WEALTH IN PROBATE INVENTORIES, ALAJUELA PROVINCE, 1850-1859

Wealth	**Equipment**[1]		**Livestock**[2] **and Equipment**		**Movables**[3]		**Movables and Immovables**[4]		**Total Fortune**[5]	
	AVERAGE	%	AVERAGE	%	AVERAGE	%	AVERAGE	%	AVERAGE	%
0 - < 500	6.0	1.6	56.8	14.7	103.4	26.8	386.4	100.0	300.4	77.7
500 - < 1,000	13.7	2.0	112.9	16.2	169.8	24.4	695.3	100.0	726.7	104.5
1,000 - < 5,000	39.6	2.0	295.3	15.3	379.6	19.6	1,933.9	100.0	1,993.8	103.1
≥ 5,000	126.5	1.6	1,398.0	17.7	1,691.5	21.5	7,881.0	100.0	8,852.0	112.3
Total	32.0	1.9	277.2	16.2	361.6	21.1	1,713.2	100.0	1,802.9	105.2

[1] Implements, processing equipment and means of transportation.

[2] Cattle, horses and mules, hogs.

[3] Livestock, equipment, buildings, household goods and furniture, other movables.

[4] All movable goods and immovable property.

[5] Movables and immovables plus credit balance.

members of the Alajuelan elite at the time. The origin of such wealth is yet to be established, but since coffee was still a very minor crop in this province, it must be attributed to other economic activities, and may be traced back to colonial times. In Alajuela, where there had been no major export cycles, trade and livestock raising were probably most significant among such activities.

Cattle and other livestock were especially important at higher levels of wealth, not only in absolute monetary value but also, to a certain extent, in relative terms (Table 4.6). Average size of herds owned by the wealthier Alajuelans was sixty-three head of cattle, plus twenty-five mules or horses (Table 4.7). To be sure, such herds were larger than those one would associate with domestic units, but far from the scope of any large Latin American hacienda or, for that matter, the cattle ranches in the province of Guanacaste. Of course, there were a few larger herds in Alajuela, up to four hundred head of cattle, just as there were some wealthy merchants who owned none at all. In domestic units of smaller fortunes, especially below $1,000, the proportional value of livestock tended to be lower, but not unimportant, while housing was usually a somewhat larger part of the whole (Tables 4.6 and 4.8). Relative value of equipment and other components tended to be more or less similar, despite differences in their characteristics.

TABLE 4.6 COMPOSITION OF MOVABLE AND IMMOVABLE ASSETS ACCORDING TO LEVEL OF WEALTH IN PROBATE INVENTORIES, ALAJUELA PROVINCE, 1850-1859

Wealth	**Average Value in Pesos**							
	LAND		LIVESTOCK		MOVABLES OTHER THAN LIVESTOCK		MOVABLES AND IMMOVABLES	
	$	%	$	%	$	%	$	%
0 - < 500	288.5	74.7	50.8	13.1	47.1	12.2	386.4	100.0
500 - < 1,000	525.6	75.6	99.2	143.3	70.5	10.1	695.3	100.0
1,000 - < 5,000	1,554.3	80.4	255.7	13.2	123.9	6.4	1,933.9	100.0
≥ 5,000	6,189.5	78.5	1,271.5	16.2	420.0	5.3	7,881.0	100.0
All	1,356.5	79.2	245.2	14.3	111.5	6.5	1,713.2	100.0

From this initial overview, there appear to be major differences in the scale of productive units in the 1850s, but rather minor ones in their composition. Absolute value of land and livestock, together with ownership of certain processing equipment, established the main socioeconomic distinctions among productive units. Agriculture, broadly speaking, does not seem to have been more technified nor intensive on the larger units. On-farm infrastructure was extremely limited in all types of units, and means of

TABLE 4.7 COMPOSITION OF HERDS BY NUMBER, ACCORDING TO LEVEL OF WEALTH IN PROBATE INVENTORIES, ALAJUELA PROVINCE, 1850-1859

Wealth	**Number**														
	COWS/HEIFERS			OXEN			OTHER CATTLE			HORSES/MULES			HOGS		
	AVG.	MIN.	MAX.	AVG.	MIN.	MAX.	AVG.	MIN.	MAX.	AVG.	MIN.	MAX.	AVG.	MIN.	MAX.
0 - < 500	1.2	0	6	1.1	0	6	0.5	0	3	0.9	0	5	0.2	0	3
500 - < 1,00	3.1	0	19	1.7	0	10	1.2	0	11	2.5	0	10	0.5	0	7
1,000 - < 5,000	9.2	0	77	3.0	0	11	4.1	0	44	5.5	0	40	0.6	0	9
≥ 5,000	44.1	0	367	6.4	0	17	13.1	0	47	25.2	0	85	0.9	0	4
All	8.4	0	367	2.5	0	17	3.2	0	47	5.2	0	85	0.5	0	9

TABLE 4.8 AVERAGE VALUE OF MOVABLES OTHER THAN LIVESTOCK ACCORDING TO LEVEL OF WEALTH IN PROBATE INVENTORIES, ALAJUELA PROVINCE, 1850-1859

Level of Wealth $	Average Value		
	IMPLEMENTS	PROCESSING	TRANSPORTATION
0 - < 500	3.0	0	3.0
500 - < 1,000	2.4	4.7	6.6
1,000 - < 5,000	4.4	24.3	10.9
≥ 5,000	59.5	51.0	16.0
All	7.6	15.9	8.5

Level of Wealth $	Average Value			
	BUILDINGS	HOUSEHOLD	OTHER MOVABLES	TOTAL
0 - < 500	20.0	9.1	17.4	52.7
500 - < 1,000	16.1	11.1	29.6	70.5
1,000 - < 5,000	18.0	20.2	46.1	123.9
≥ 5,000	41.5	67.0	185.0	420.0
All	19.6	18.8	45.9	116.3

transportation were practically identical. Livestock raising, for all its importance, was very extensive, a mere addition of cattle and land at a ratio of no more than two or three head per hectare of pastureland, and often less. Let us now take a closer look at the components of Alajuelan fortunes in the mid-nineteenth century, before returning to a more general characterization.

LIVESTOCK

This was the most valuable of inventoried movables in the majority of cases, increasing in relative importance from the humblest to the wealthiest. Given the small monetary value of equipment for production, as well as the low technological level of agriculture, processing and transportation, livestock was undoubtedly the main movable resource for production. On the average, herds included some fourteen head of cattle, and five mules or horses (Table 4. 7). The vast majority of inventories (85%) included cattle, reflecting its widespread significance for the various types of productive units. Only a few had over one hundred head of cattle, and can be included among the supra-family units. Another half dozen with fifty to a hundred head of cattle might or might not be above the possibilities and requirements of domestic units, depending on their agricultural activities and other assets. One third of all inventories included eleven to fifty head of cattle, and another third itemized from three to ten. These could probably be placed on a continuum from major to lesser domestic units, though again livestock itself is only a partial indicator. Finally, about one fifth of the inventories had less than three head of cattle or none at all, and may be associated with sub-family units in an agrarian economy where ranching was of such widespread importance (Figure 4.3).

Naturally, livestock ownership cannot serve as the sole criterion to classify individual cases, since the meaning of a specific herd size depended on other variables, and some wealthy people owned no cattle at all. Still, the average size of herds increased from each level of wealth to the next, from under three to sixty-three. This increase was especially noticeable regarding cows and heifers, while oxen, horses and mules were less numerous. Nevertheless, seven or eight out of every ten productive units had all these types of livestock, and a major part of the peasantry was involved in small-scale ranching.

When total assets of the deceased were under $500, families generally owned very few livestock: a cow, perhaps with a calf or two; an ox; and a mule or a horse. This was clearly insufficient to satisfy basic needs, and these productive units had to rely very heavily on other sources of income, whether agricultural activities, craft production or wage labor. At the next level of wealth, up to $1,000, households often owned some three cows, a team of oxen, another head of cattle, and two or three horses or mules. In such cases, livestock raising alone could certainly not satisfy all household

Figure 4.3 Head of cattle in probate inventories, Alajuela province, 1850-1859

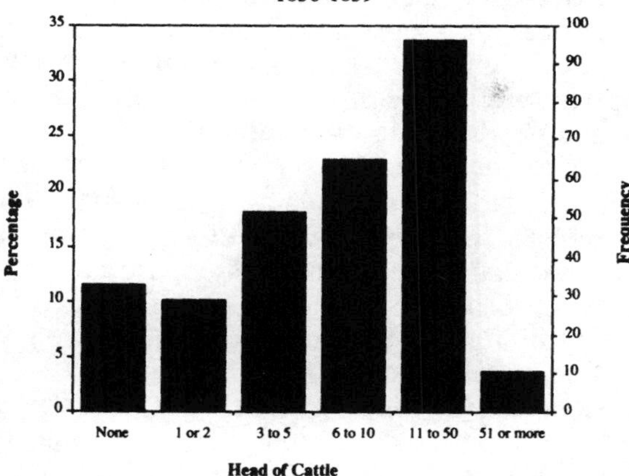

Figure 4.4 Number of individual farms per case in probate inventories, Alajuela province, 1850-1859

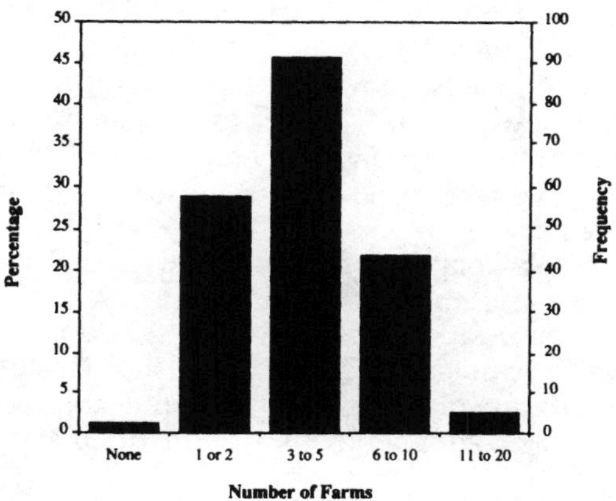

Figure 4.5 Total value per case in probate inventories, Alajuela province, 1850-1859

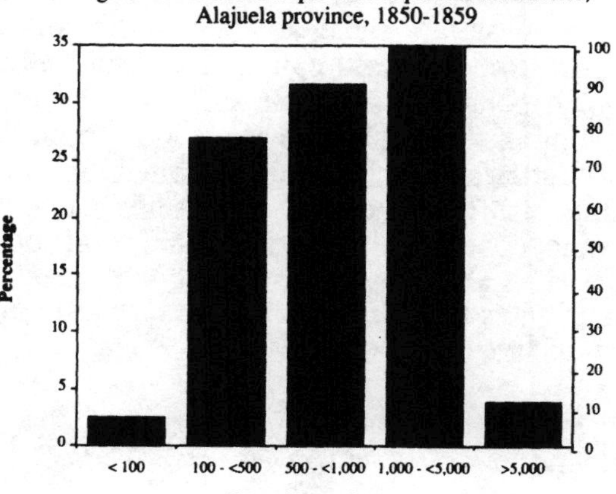

needs nor fully absorb the labor of an average-sized family, but in combination with agriculture proper a major part might be covered. From $1,000 to under $5,000, under the assumption that livestock raising was combined with agriculture, the average herd probably did cover most but perhaps not all these needs: nine cows, three oxen, four other head of cattle, and five or six equines. Since maximum herd size was considerably larger in these intermediate fortunes,[36] a number of such units must have had marketable surpluses. Below-average herds in this group probably did not satisfy domestic needs for direct consumption, use as draft animals, and restocking. Finally, in fortunes above $5,000, the average herd included forty-four cows, four heifers, three teams of oxen, thirteen other head of cattle, and twenty-five mules or horses.

Size of herds, then, was closely related to their composition and economic role. The larger herds were primarily for marketing of beef cattle, and secondarily for local consumption of milk and use as draft animals. Instead, when productive units had fewer livestock, as in fortunes under $1,000, close to two thirds of the value of livestock was neither for consumption nor sale, but rather for transportation and plowing.

Livestock raising was prevalent in the 1850s throughout the inhabited area in the province of Alajuela. However, its importance per productive unit was greater in the newly settled Northwest, where average herd size was 18.6, than near the provincial capital (12.4 head). Colonization was closely associated to livestock production, and to a certain extent the Northwest was a cattle frontier.

Ranching was an appropiate economic activity for a recently settled region with abundance of land and labor scarcity, in the context of subregional specialization in specific crops toward the east, e.g. in San José and Heredia. Settlers did not simply revert to subsistence agriculture, but sought to redevelop commercial ties. Cattle being able to walk to the market, it was clearly an advantageous option on the as yet poorly integrated frontier.

The wealthier colonists, except for a few merchants, certainly did raise cattle as a mercantile activity. An intermediate group of peasant ranchers had enough livestock to satisfy most or all of their consumption and production needs, and probably sold cattle occasionally, although they might buy some too. Among the less fortunate, livestock was mainly for transportation and tilling the land, while an as yet indeterminate population, the poorest, had no cattle at all. Livestock ownership, as reflected in probate inventories, is insufficient to indicate precise social stratification, but it does reflect socioeconomic differences within rural society, more so than other movables. It is also closely associated with level of wealth, in most cases, and contributes to a characterization of sub-family, domestic and supra-family productive units.

---

36 Maximum sizes for intermediate-level fortunes were: 77 cows, 11 oxen, 44 other cattle, 40 equines.

Other Movables and Constructions

These accounted for less than one fourth of total assets in most cases and at various levels of wealth.[37] Productive equipment, specifically, was a minimal part (less than 2%) of physical assets at any level of family fortune. Its absolute value increased more or less proportionally to that of assets, and there does not seem to have been any major technological intensification in the larger productive units of the region at the time (Table 4.5). Agricultural implements, basically simple tools, were the main type of equipment in the highest fortunes. At intermediate levels ($1,000 to under $5,000), it was processing equipment, primarily for sugarcane. Oxcarts were slightly more important than implements or processing equipment on the smaller productive units (Table 4.8). All in all, productive technology was quite rudimentary on the various types of units in mid-century Alajuela.

Regarding non-productive goods, the absolute value of household goods and constructions was quite low in most cases, and did not vary significantly in fortunes under $5,000. It was only among the wealthiest that there was clearly a differentiation in this regard. The same is true for assorted movables, from religious articles to jewelry. A qualitative analysis of the type of goods also reflects the similarity of consumption patterns at lower and intermediate levels of family fortune, and a sharp contrast at the highest levels. Save for a very small but economically powerful elite, most of the population had a rather similar lifestyle, as reflected in durable consumption goods. There were, of course, gradations in the consumption patterns of this majority, but within an austere rural life. The propertied peasantry, on the whole, lacked not only luxuries but also what would later come to be considered basic necessities, such as beds instead of rough boards to sleep on.

Credit

This involves not only a balance of loans minus debts in the probate inventories of the time but also, and most essentially, a socioeconomic as well as personal relationship. Credit relations were quite widespread in the mid-nineteenth century, from Alajuela to San Ramón. Their frequency and characteristics indicate that numerous commercial transactions were backed by credit in this predominantly rural society, with limited currency.

---

[37] Construction (essentially housing and sheds) is discussed here together with movables. At the time, the materials of a house were estimated separately from cost of the land it was on, and in several cases house and land were actually owned by different persons. Movables other than livestock include productive equipment and non-productive goods. The former are agricultural implements, tools and technical equipment for processing or transport of products. The latter include household goods and assorted movables for personal use.

TABLE 4.9 VALUE OF LOANS RECEIVABLE AND PAYABLE, ACCORDING TO LEVEL OF WEALTH IN PROBATE INVENTORIES, ALAJUELA PROVINCE, 1850-1859

Wealth	**Value in $**								
	LOANS RECEIVABLE			LOANS PAYABLE			CREDIT BALANCE		
	AVG.	MIN.	MAX.	AVG.	MIN.	MAX.	AVG.	MIN.	MAX.
0 - < 500	77.2	10	220	179.0	0	182	-101.3	-1,640	160
500 - < 1,000	138.0	0	630	84.8	0	530	40.7	-420	530
1,000 - < 5,000	221.4	0	1,250	196.7	0	1,520	71.4	-1,240	1,070
≥ 5,000	1,948.7	30	10,810	817.5	50	4,480	1,078.6	-4,480	8,200
All	319.6	0	10,810	208.2	0	4,480	108.6	-4,480	8,200

In eight out of every ten probate inventories for 1850-1859, there was a statement of loans, debts, or both. Sixty-six percent of the deceased were debtors, and fifty-eight percent had creditors, but the net credit balance was positive. On the whole, value of loans owed to the families of the deceased was 1.7 times the value of debts pending, and loans receivable averaged $320, while liabilities[38] were $208 per case when at least one or the other is stated. If we take into account those cases with no such indication, the average balance for all inventories was +$90. Indebtedness was usually no more than ten percent of total assets which, together with generally favorable balances, suggests that while credit was important in many ways, liabilities did not threaten the future economic viability of productive units.

On the other hand, we know from the degree of differentiation among fortunes that this was far from being an egalitarian rural society, and inequality was undoubtely reflected in credit relations. There were major variations in individual credit balances, ranging from -$4,500 to +$8,200. However, almost two thirds of all cases varied between +/- $90.

The wealthier not only lent more to others, as a profitable investment, but also borrowed much more for their own productive and commercial activities. The smallest fortunes, under $500, were also those which most often had negative credit balances. At higher levels of wealth, especially above $5,000, the opposite was the case (Table 4.9).

Credit, then, was both a widespread and a socially differentiated economic relation. Although conclusions from probate inventory analysis cannot be applied to the propertyless population, they do point to an economy in which independent rural producers were constantly engaged in credit relations. Naturally, this refers us both to direct financing of productive activities and to exchanges of goods and services, since credit could also have an intermediary function in such exchanges. Individual analysis of credit transactions corroborates case-level findings, but also provides some insight into the nature of these transactions:

Loans receivable were basically advances over inheritance and direct monetary loans. Advances over inheritance usually refer to support provided for the independent establishment of sons and daughters, especially upon marriage or when they became settlers, and were often made in kind. Debts payable were, primarily, for money borowed from others, and secondarily for labor yet to be remunerated. There were also loans and debts for immovables, agricultural products and livestock, but these were less important in terms of total value (Tables 4.10 and 4.11).

38 All debts at the time of death, except for those incurred at that time, e.g. medical expenses, funerary costs and the social event of *velorio* or vigil.

TABLE 4.10 VALUE OF LOANS PAYABLE, ACCORDING TO TYPE OF LOAN IN PROBATE INVENTORIES, ALAJUELA PROVINCE, 1850-1859

Type	Value in $			
	AVERAGE	MINIMUM	MAXIMUM	SUM
1	5.48	0	71	247
2	19.00	0	98	266
3	7.30	0	37	95
4,5,6	2.48	0	15	87
7	6,30	0	25	63
8,9,10	3,79	0	400	2,614
All	4.18	0	400	3,372

1: Money
2: Land
3: Livestock
4: Grain
5: Coffee
6: Other Goods
7: Inheritance
8: Other
9: Unknown
10: Missing

TABLE 4.11 VALUE OF LOANS RECEIVABLE, ACCORDING TO TYPE OF LOAN IN PROBATE INVENTORIES, ALAJUELA PROVINCE, 1850-1859

Type	Value in $			Total	
	AVERAGE	MINIMUM	MAXIMUM	SUM	%
1	36.52	0	193	840	14.4
2	29.11	1	80	262	4.5
3	7.81	1	29	86	1.5
4,5,6	0.68	0	6	26	0.4
7	3.92	0	328	471	8.0
8,9,10	6.38	0	328	4,164	71.2
All	6.85	0	328	5,849	100.0

1: Money
2: Land
3: Livestock
4: Grain
5: Coffee
6: Other Goods
7: Inheritance
8: Other
9: Unknown
10: Missing

Monetary loans had the highest average value, followed by land (mortgages) and livestock. Advances on inheritance were usually small, and loans in merchandise even more so. Composition of debts was different: the largest were amounts owed for land. Debts for livestock, advances on inheritance and money were smaller. Merchandise, especially agricultural products, and unpaid labor were the smallest. Apparently, large sums were lent out in money, and heavy indebtedness was often related to land, while a variety of goods and services were subject to smaller credit transactions. The deceased were very often creditors and debtors at the same time, with a more or less favorable balance depending on, but rarely defining, level of fortune. The characteristics of strong creditors and debtors are relevant to the social role of credit.

There were a few creditors who had many debtors and strongly positive credit balances. For such individual creditors, who were usually merchants, credit transactions were certainly a profit-oriented investment. The Church, too, was a major creditor. However, the vast majority of creditors were not wealthy, did not lend large sums, nor did they have more than two or three debtors. So it is difficult to see credit exclusively as a means of transferring value, through usurious interest rates, to a plutocratic elite.

Large debts, too, were associated with owners of large estates, merchants, or government. Peasants often owed money, but their indebtedness was not heavy with respect to their total assets. Access to borrowing was socially biased, but it was neither an exclusive privilege of the wealthy nor a means for massive expropriation of the poor.

Neither was credit a mechanism systematically applied to any sort of coercive labor control. There is no indication of money or goods being lent to commit future labor, as in "debt peonage". The situation in this regard was quite different from certain other areas of Latin America where agro-export development took place under similar conditions of labor scarcity and abundance of land, but where credit played a very different role in social relations. No doubt other, especially sociopolitical, factors were required for direct, forceful control of workers by plantation owners.

The more frequent debts for unpaid labor were mostly to *jornaleros*, although some were for contract workers in agriculture and transportation. Those owing money for labor generally owned several medium to large farms, a good-sized herd of cattle, and other substantial assets. However, only small amounts were owed to a few workers per case. We can hardly envision a deliberate system of wage retention to tie workers to the estate, in an inverse credit bondage such as that suggested for certain Mexican and South American haciendas. The fact is that workers could move about quite freely in Costa Rica, and sociopolitical conditions were favorable to peasant settlement on the frontier.

Insofar as credit reflected broader societal relations, it speaks of expanding monetary, labor, land and product markets in the mid-nineteenth-century Alajuelan countryside. Even though coffee had not yet become a significant export crop in the region, credit arrangements, mercantile exchanges and the underlying commercial orientation of production were far from any image of a self-contained, subsistence-oriented regional agrarian economy.

IMMOVABLES

These, and specifically land, were the main component of large and small fortunes in the province of Alajuela at the time. Landholding and land use by various productive units in the region were at the base of other transformations associated with westward colonization.

Agricultural production in mid-nineteenth-century Alajuela was organized on units which were quite variable in terms of their landholding characteristics. With reference only to probate inventories, which as stated before did not necessarily reflect the actual proportions of productive units in the countryside, there was a very wide range in number and size of holdings: some had no farm at all, others up to twenty; some had less than a twentieth of a hectare, others one or two thousand hectares.

The average holding per household inventory was approximately seventy-six hectares.[39] This area was usually subdivided, in about four smaller farms. As it turns out, a major segment of the deceased had possessed intermediate-size holdings: one third can be estimated to have had twenty to ninety hectares of land,[40] and 45% of all inventories included three to five properties (Figure 4.4).

Average value of land per case in the inventories for 1850-1859 was $1,356, with a wide variation from negligible values up to $14,000. Distribution of value within this specific population shows that there was some landholding concentration, but also a sizeable middling peasantry which was far from land poor (Figure 4.5). Typically, a rural holding in Alajuela might have three to five individual farms, adding up to several dozen hectares, perhaps even eighty or ninety, and an estimated value of maybe $1,000 to $1,500. The wealthier Alajuelans at mid-century usually had more than ten properties, with an area anywhere up to 2,500 hectares, and immovables worth $5,000 to $10,000 or more. At the other extreme of rural society were those with tiny farms or others who remained totally landless. Their numbers are difficult to determine, but the percentage of *jornaleros* in the economically active population of the province provides a rough indicator: well below one tenth of the population in 1843, and slightly over one fifth twenty years later.[41]

With reference to productive units, despite the existence of a few large estates and of a number of small plots, probate inventories suggest that

---

39 Data were often missing in one or more farms for cases with multiple property rights. Average size of the 448 individual farms whose size is given in the documents was 18.6 hectares, and average number of farms per household, in all cases, was 4.1. The resulting area per case is 76.7% larger than the original average per case (which did not include farms for which information on area was missing).

40 If no adjustment were made for missing data, the areas would be eleven to fifty hectares.

41 Archivo Nacional, Sección Congreso, # 6547; DGEC (1864); Samper (1985), p. 62. The term "economically active" refers here to those identified in the census as having an economic occupation.

middle-sized farms were a major component of this agrarian economy. There is no complete study of land-tenure in the region, to determine the precise representativeness of information derived from probate inventories. However, Rosalba Salas' careful research shows that while early land claims were often large, and some families also concentrated land via purchase, transactions tended to subdivide holdings and many peasants had access to land near the main population centers.[42] Landholding patterns were far from egalitarian, but neither were they as polarized as in areas of Latin America where the concept of a "latifundia-minifundia complex" is applicable. In Alajuela, during the 1850s, many farmer-settlers had enough land to potentially cover domestic production and consumption needs. Of course, the precise meaning of land tenure is dependent upon land use. That is the point we shall turn to next.

In studying the frequency of various types of land use per case, a clear predominance of pasture is apparent. The second most frequent productive use was sugarcane, followed by staple foodcrops (plantain, maize, beans). Use of land for coffee was quantitatively negligible.[43]

At an individual farm level, a very similar pattern is found: pasture is most frequent (on 404 farms), then sugarcane (on180), followed by grain (on 112). Coffee was only reported on seventeen out of 1,130 individual properties (Table 4.12). This was first of all a ranching economy, with sugarcane and foodcrops as associated agricultural activities.

Regarding linkage of specific crops with various farm sizes, it is clear that sugarcane and staple grain crops were generally planted on relatively small farms, averaging six or seven hectares (Table 4.13). Coffee, on the other hand, like pasture and other uses, was located on the larger farms, averaging twenty to fifty hectares but with maximum areas which were sometimes much larger.[44] Coffee, then, while planted initially in small groves, began as an economic activity on medium to large estates rather than on peasant farms. On the latter, sugarcane and foodcrops were much more likely to be found than coffee.

---

42 Rosalba Salas' study of land claims covered the region west of Alajuela to San Ramón, and that of land sales and purchases focused on Grecia and Naranjo, where most of the northwestern settlers were at mid-century. I thank her for allowing me to summarize general conclusions of her forthcoming thesis.

43 In the province of Alajuela, average number of farms with each type of land use, per probate inventory for 1850-1859, was: coffee 0.06; sugarcane 0.65; pasture 1.47; grain 0.40; and uncultivated 1.42.

44 Per value, differences between most uses were smaller than by area because the lower value of lands under extensive use (e.g. pasture and uncultivated) partly compensated for their larger area.

TABLE 4.12 INDIVIDUAL FARMS WITH INDICATION OF LAND USE* IN PROBATE INVENTORIES, ALAJUELA PROVINCE, 1850-1859

Use	#	%
Coffee	17	2.58
Sugarcane	180	25.97
Pasture	404	57.67
Grain	112	16.59
Uncultivated	116	17.18
Dwelling	285	39.29
Other	147	21.60

*Whether or not in association with other uses.

TABLE 4.13 AREA AND VALUE OF FARMS ACCORDING TO LAND USE*, IN PROBATE INVENTORIES, ALAJUELA PROVINCE, 1850-1859

Land Use	Area (hectares)			Value $		
	AVG.	MIN.	MAX.	AVG.	MIN.	MAX.
Coffee	51.58	1.0	186.2	1,038.8	50	8,900
Sugarcane	6.26	0.0	56.0	405.7	0	5,000
Pasture	21.61	0.0	1,202.6	527.4	10	8,900
Grain	7.29	0.0	42.0	384.8	10	1,680
Uncultivated	29.43	0.1	363.8	476.9	0	8,900
Other	39.00	0.0	1,202.6	427.1	10	5,000
All	18.63	0.0	1,202.6	332.1	0	8,900

*Specific agrarian uses of the land, whether or not in association with other uses.

TABLE 4.14 AREA AND VALUE OF INDIVIDUAL FARMS, BY NUMBER OF AGRARIAN USES OF THE LAND, IN PROBATE INVENTORIES, ALAJUELA PROVINCE, 1850-1859

Use	Area (hectares)			Value		
	AVG.	MIN.	MAX.	AVG.	MIN.	MAX.
None	0.12	0.0	0.7	327.0	10	3,000
Single	11.24	0.0	363.8	333.7	0	7,000
Double	42.82	0.0	1,202.6	391.6	20	2,180
Multiple (3-5)	20.32	0.1	186.2	782.2	50	8,900
All	18.63	0.0	1,202.6	332.1	0	8,900

At a case or household level, land use was quite diversified, and usually included pasture, sugarcane, foodcrops, housing and uncultivated areas. On individual farms or properties, the situation was quite different. Though some had up to five distinctive agrarian uses, 60% of them had only one agricultural use, while only 18% had two agrarian uses and 10% had three or more.[45] Productive units therefore included several different, individual farms with more or less specific uses, which together led to a combination of livestock raising, agriculture proper, and others.

Single, double or multiple-use farms were quite variable in terms of area and value (Table 4.14). On all three types of farm, livestock raising was the main economic activity, followed by sugarcane, and thirdly staple foodcrops, especially maize interplanted with beans (Table 4.15). The relative importance of various land uses on very diverse types of productive units, as outlined in preceeding paragraphs, allows us to state that regional land use patterns must not have differed greatly from those derived from probate inventories.

The strongest association among crops on individual farms was, quite clearly, that between sugarcane and pasture. On farms with maizefields, pasture was also the main associated use. The same is true for farms with uncultivated areas. Only on the few farms with coffee was sugarcane slightly more frequent than pasture as an associated crop (Table 4.16). In conclusion, the main binomial linkage on individual farms, as on economic units made up of several farms, was the productive association of livestock raising and sugarcane cultivation. In terms of farm value, a variable related to size, quality and location, the two most frequent agrarian uses in all categories of value were, once again, pasture and secondly sugarcane (Table 4.17).

A brief discussion of the characteristics of single-use farms[46] will allow us to analyze specific crops individually and comparatively. We know that single-use farms were smaller and therefore not fully representative of all properties, so the conclusions on this point are not equally aplicable to all farms in the region. However, as mentioned above, they were the majority of farms, and on them land use can be linked more directly to other variables.

The largest single-use farms were uncultivated, with an average of 26 and a maximum of 363 hectares. The second-largest were pastures, averaging 9.6 hectares (maximum 117). Maize-fields and other grain farms were smaller, with an average size of four hectares, and a maximum of 8.4. The smallest were plots in sugarcane, plantain and minor crops, averaging

---

45 Agrarian uses are all uses other than housing, i.e. whether for agriculture, livestock raising, or uncultivated. The remaining properties had no agricultural use at all, that is, they were exclusively dwellings.

46 Those with only one agrarian use, that is, other than housing. Actually, "single use" does not preclude the possibility of minor supplementary crops, which were probably the rule rather than the exception.

TABLE 4.15 FREQUENCY OF EACH AGRARIAN USE OF THE LAND ON INDIVIDUAL FARMS, ACCORDING TO NUMBER OF USES IN PROBATE INVENTORIES, ALAJUELA PROVINCE, 1850-1859

Use	Coffee		Sugarcane		Pasture		Maize		Uncultivated		Other	
	#	%	#	%	#	%	#	%	#	%	#	%
Single	8	1.8	56	12.6	248	55.7	43	9.7	53	11.9	37	8.3
Double	2	0.7	59	21.7	87	32.0	33	12.1	38	14.0	53	19.5
Multiple	7	2.7	65	24.8	71	27.1	36	13.7	25	9.5	58	22.1

TABLE 4.16 CROP ASSOCIATION ON INDIVIDUAL FARMS, ACCORDING TO SELECTED USE IN PROBATE INVENTORIES, ALAJUELA PROVINCE, 1850-1859

Associated Use	Selected Use									
	COFFEE		SUGARCANE		PASTURE		GRAIN		UNCULTIVATED	
	#	%	#	%	#	%	#	%	#	%
Coffee	-	-	5	3.49	4	1.11	2	2.15	4	4.12
Sugarcane	5	35.71	-	-	82	22.16	30	30.30	21	20.79
Pasture	4	28.57	82	52.90	-	-	48	48.98	49	47.57
Grain	2	14.28	30	20.13	48	13.22	-	-	19	18.62
Uncultivated	4	28.75	21	14.28	49	13.46	19	19.38	-	-

TABLE 4.17 LAND USE ON INDIVIDUAL FARMS, ACCORDING TO VALUE IN PROBATE INVENTORIES, ALAJUELA PROVINCE, 1850-1859

Value	Coffee	Sugarcane	Pasture	Grain	Uncultivated	Dwelling	Other
≥ 1,000	2	15	54	7	12	28	15
500 - < 1,000	2	32	80	26	17	45	25
100 - < 500	9	89	204	64	59	159	69
< 100	4	44	66	15	28	53	38
All	17	180	404	112	116	285	147

less than a hectare (Table 4.18).[47] Pastures were associated with the most valuable such farms, and livestock raising was the main productive use of the land on single-use properties.

TABLE 4.18 AREA AND VALUE OF SINGLE-USE FARMS ACCORDING TO SPECIFIC USE IN PROBATE INVENTORIES, ALAJUELA PROVINCE, 1850-1859

Specific Use	Number of Cases with Data			Area (hectares)			Value ($)		
	USE	AREA	VALUE	AVG.	MIN.	MAX.	AVG.	MIN.	MAX.
Coffee	8	2	8	4.7	1	8.4	298.7	50	640
Sugarcane	56	13	56	0.79	0.3	2.8	126.4	0	480
Pasture	248	93	246	9.59	0	177.7	465.4	10	7,000
Grain	43	21	43	3.97	0	8.4	217.9	10	900
Uncultivated	53	35	53	26.43	0.1	363.8	182.8	0	1,050
Other	37	7	36	0.38	0	0.7	124.7	10	690

Location of single-use farms shows a strong mid-century concentration in areas near the city of Alajuela.[48] However, the situation varied depending on the individual product. Aside from the coffee farms near Alajuela, there were a few other such farms owned by Alajuelans but located in other provinces, especially Heredia where they or their parents often came from.[49] Roughly three out of every four pastures, maize-fields or sugarcane fields were in the sub-region near Alajuela city. The remaining properties under cultivation with one of these crops were mostly located in the Northwest, from Grecia to San Ramón. Very few were in other parts of the province.

Uncultivated farms differed from the distribution described above, as they were less concentrated sub-regionally near the provincial capital, and instead their relative importance increased three to four times in the area of San Ramón and Palmares. In the 1850s, this was the main colonization frontier in the region, so the frequency of uncultivated properties no doubt reflects land claims and other processes of acquiring public lands. Given the much larger average size of these farms, as compared to those under agriculture proper, the amount of land involved was a significant one.

47 There were only two farms exclusively or almost exclusively in coffee (one and four hectares), so an average figure would be meaningless.

48 The area near Alajuela city also includes the administrative units of Concepción, San José, San Antonio, Santiago (este, oeste), San Rafael, Sabanilla and Poás.

49 These farms were excluded from the foregoing discussion due to their location outside the province of Alajuela.

Instead, near or in Alajuela city, uncultivated lands were usually small urban or semi-urban plots.

Association of land use, area and location of single-use farms generally confirms the characterization for all types of farms within the framework of a diversified agrarian economy. However, it also points to specialization on individual farms and to a much more intensive use of the land on smaller farms in the countryside near Alajuela city, while the settlement frontier had larger individual properties with far more extensive land use patterns.

In concluding the separate discussion of land, credit and movable assets, several specific examples may help to illustrate the ways in which components of mid-nineteenth-century fortunes were combined in the Northwest, more specifically near Grecia.

One of the smaller productive units in the vicinity of Grecia and Sarchí during the 1850's belonged to Nicolás Jiménez and his wife, Cecilia Castro.[50] Their 12.5 hectares, worth $545, were divided into two farms. A major part of the land was no doubt used for grazing, as they owned ten cows and the same number both of oxen and of horses or mules. Estimated value of the livestock was $218. The main agricultural activity was sugarcane, supplemented by plantain and other unspecified crops. They had few implements: a plow, an ax, two machetes and a long knife. They also owned an oxcart, but no processing equipment.

Furnishings in the Jiménez/Castro household were poor: a couple of tables, a bench, two stools, an old chest and boards to sleep on. Kitchen utensils were also few and simple: four iron pots, a flat iron dish or *comal* for *tortillas*, and a *piedra de moler* (grinding stone) for maize. Their only other possessions worth including in the inventory were an iron, some rope and a catechism.

The Jiménez family was undoubtedly poor, yet they combined small-scale ranching with small-scale agriculture on a dozen hectares of land. Don Nicolás had contributed $89 to the household when he married doña Cecilia, and her dowry was $55. When the husband died, the widow received $382, and each of their ten children $41. They would also receive a similar amount at the time of her demise. No land, cattle or other advance on inheritance had apparently been given to sons or daughters who married.

In terms of the initial typology set forth in Chapter 2, this particular case would be on or near the limit between a sub-family unit and a deficit-yielding domestic unit. Only a minor part of their sons' and daughters' labor could be productively employed on the parents' farm, and consumption needs of a large family such as this one could probably not be met at the time without additional land or other income. Yet it was an independent, economically viable productive unit, and insofar as older sons and daughters set up their own households on land other than their parents', family labor would be less unbalanced vis-à-vis land. There was a potential for further intensification, but in the context of the regional economy at the

50 Archivo Nacional, Mortual Independiente, #880.

time, the proportion of agricultural, grazing and uncultivated land was probably less extensive than on most larger productive units.

To continue with progressively larger holdings, Ventura Bolaños and his second wife, Juana Hidalgo, were still relatively small landowners for the time in this predominantly ranching economy, with about twenty-eight hectares of land, estimated at $900.[51] The Bolaños/Hidalgo holding was made up of four farms, located at various points in the vicinity of Grecia, but at a distance from each other. Productive use of the land, in terms both of area and of value, was first of all for grazing (about 7 hectares) then sugarcane (slightly under 3 hectares) and thirdly grain cultivation and other annual or semi-annual crops (just over a hectare). They also had some six hectares in uncultivated land, and eleven in *derechos* (hereditary rights) with unspecified use.

The main farm, where the house was located, combined livestock raising and sugarcane, with some uncultivated land, on an area of about twenty hectares. The small herd included ten cows and heifers, seven other cattle and three horses, which together were worth close to $300. The elderly couple had also given their children, as well as two from don Ventura's previous marriage, twelve other head of cattle, usually one to the daughters and three to the sons.

Other movables belonging to the Bolaños family were few and of little value. Implements included only a machete, an ax, and a branding iron. For transportation of products, they owned one oxcart. Household goods were minimal in this case too: five iron pots, a couple of grinding stones, a table, two stools and a bench, a chest, a wooden box and two large boards to sleep on.

They had only one very small debt, and two loans for $35 and $40, aside from advances on inheritance, so their credit balance was clearly favorable. Total wealth of this household was close to $1,500, and when they married, don Ventura had contributed $200 and his wife $110. During their lifetime, they had probably seen some improvement in their material living conditions, but their children would not inherit more than the elderly couple had from their own parents, who lived in Heredia. Emigration had allowed don Ventura and his wife to obtain lands in Grecia, establish a relatively small domestic unit of production there, and give their children a few head of cattle. Yet they remained poor in many ways, and despite the availability of land there was no accumulation of wealth from one generation to the next. At the time, this specific household was probably akin to an intermediate domestic unit, though until most of their children married it may have been a deficit-yielding one.

Santiago Castro and María Mercedes Rojas, residents of Sarchí, owned about one hundred hectares of land, in seven plots one or two hectares in size, and three larger farms. All the land owned by don Santiago and his

---

51 Archivo Nacional, Mortual Independiente, #325.

wife was estimated at approximately $2,500.[52] Three of the parcels, including one planted in coffee and worth $480, were located in the province of San José, where they or their parents must have come from. The main productive use of their land in the province of Alajuela was livestock raising. They also had a few small sugarcane fields, and a parcel in plantain. A couple of small plots were for rustic housing, while uncultivated lands and those with unspecified use accounted for most of the area. The Castro/Rojas family owned a somewhat larger herd than the previous two households: eighteen cows, three oxen, eleven other cattle, sixteen horses and six mules. The value of this livestock was estimated at $382.

On-farm equipment included simple tools (a few more than in the previous case), a plow and, especially, a sugarcane processing mill worth almost one hundred pesos. This productive unit was slightly better equiped regarding implements, but the main difference with the other two households was ownership of the *trapiche*. This allowed them to process sugarcane planted both on the Castro's farms and on those of their neighbors, placing them in an advantageous position within the local economy.

Household goods in the Castro household were, nevertheless, rudimentary, and worth only $5: two tables, a chair, a bench, a cupboard, a wooden box for grain storage, a couple of iron pots and three large bed-boards. Durable consumption patterns do not seem to have varied much between this case and the two previous ones, which had less land and cattle.

Don Santiago and his wife had no debts, but were owed $134 by six people. They had also given two of their daughters an advance on inheritance, probably a dowry since they were the older ones and most likely had married. Each son or daughter inherited $189 at the time of don Santiago's decease, as compared to the $73 contributed by both of their parents when they married. The Castro/Rojas household could probably be characterized as a surplus-producing domestic unit.

Gertrudis Ugalde, a widow whose parents were from Heredia, owned two hundred and ten hectares of land in Grecia, with an estimated value of $2,250.[53] Half the land was uncultivated, and another third in pasture. No agricultural activities were mentioned specifically, though *rastrojo* does allude to previously cultivated land, usually in maize. There is no reference to agricultural implements in the inventory.

Livestock raising had probably been important on her lands, but at the time she died, doña Gertrudis had only ten cows and a few other head of cattle, a couple of horses and two hogs, all worth $120. Since she was quite elderly, we can assume that she had sold or given out additional livestock to her children and grandchildren. Anyhow, her household

---

52 Archivo Nacional, Mortual Independiente, #455.

53 Archivo Nacional, Mortual Independiente, #1696.

goods, worth $28, reflect a standard of living which was neither luxurious nor as modest as in the cases above.

The deceased woman owed no money, but had lent out $205 to relatives, and small amounts in maize to ten other people. These last loans suggest some type of sharecropping or other arrangement by which she provided maize to be planted, probably on her own lands, for repayment at time of harvest.

Doña Gertrudis' fortune ($2,600) was mostly in land, followed by credit and livestock. Since she had outlived two husbands and was eighty-one years old, a major part of her original fortune had probably been passed on through inheritance. Her relatively large holding had been an estate well beyond the characteristics of a domestic unit when her husband was alive, but the small herd and lack of major agricultural activities speak of a decline, and at her age formal ownership was probably disassociated from actual control.

Finally, we can mention Joaquín Méndez and Ramona Rojas, among the wealthier Alajuelans who owned land in Grecia, with a total fortune over $20,000.[54] They owned several hundred hectares in five pastures, some near Alajuela city and others in Grecia. The value of these pasturelands was estimated at $6,770. They also owned a small plot of land in coffee and plantain near the provincial capital, worth $60 in the inventory. They had four fine houses, with an estimated value of $3,710.

The main productive activity on the Méndez/Rojas estate was livestock raising, with a sizeable herd, yet not one of the largest ones in the region: 75 head of cattle, plus 19 horses and mules, altogether worth $1,437. Implements were not very different from those on smaller productive units, and while there were a few more of each kind, their number and value (about $15) do not indicate major agricultural intensification. Means of transportation for products were two oxcarts, and there is no reference to processing equipment other than for homeground coffee.

The Méndez family lived very well, with fine furniture, clothing and decorations, copper kitchen utensils, porcelain plates and silverware. Together with assorted items and cash, non-productive movables were worth more than $700. Their standard of living was well above that which could be financed by a medium-sized herd and minor agricultural activities. This leads us to credit as a source of income.

Debts were numerous but mostly small, fifty-two for a total of about $2,600, while loans were less but much larger: fourteen, adding up to over $10,000. Money owed by the deceased was for labor yet to be paid, cattle and merchandise; loans were mostly for money lent out to receive interest. In this case, credit undoubtedly yielded more economic benefit for the Méndez family than existing livestock or agriculture. On the other hand, given the major amount of pastureland, cattle had probably been of greater importance for this estate in the past. Don Joaquín and his wife had no children, so credit may have become more attractive than expanding

---

54 Archivo Nacional, Mortual Independiente, #1023.

productive activities as they grew older. Furthermore, they seem to have been living in Alajuela city at the time, while some of their land was in Grecia. In any case, this was certainly a supra-family productive unit.

The five examples above provide an idea of various ways in which movables, immovables and credit were combined on specific economic units, in a more concrete and detailed approach than that obtained from the preceding statistical overview of productive units in the 1850's. The individual cases speak of various types of rural households, from the land-poor ones, which combined small-scale livestock-raising and agriculture, to members of the wealthy, landed elite who also engaged in mercantile activities such as money-lending. Yet as productive units, they all had much in common, as was seen with respect to a large number of probate cases.

Cattle was the most widespread type of agrarian production, carried out in a very extensive manner on variously-sized pasturelands. Crop agriculture proper was at a low technical level on large and small farms, and while there were maize-fields and a few coffee groves, the most important crop was sugarcane. Ownership of more or less cattle and land certainly was a basis for socioeconomic differentiation, although the technical organization of agrarian production must not have differed very significantly on larger and smaller units. Social distance in this region, during the mid-nineteenth century, was very real, but could hardly be measured in terms of the type of agrarian production or clear-cut technological distinctions, such as capital intensity in agriculture or livestock raising. Nor were differences in the level of fortune reflected in major variations in the overall composition of family wealth, i.e. in the proportions of various broad categories of assets.

However, there were some identifiable distintions among rural households. Control or processing facilities, however rudimentary (as in the case of sugar mills) was probably a critical factor for differentiation among households relying primarily on family labor. Regular money lending and other commercial activities were certainly among the characteristics which distinguished the local elite from the rest of rural society, especially in connection with greater opportunities for accumulation of capital wealth.

Not all socioeconomic differences were clearly apparent at the time. Insofar as housing and durable consumption goods could indicate material standard of living, only the very wealthy lived in ways which differed substantially at the time. During the early stages of northwestward migration from the vicinity of Heredia or Alajuela cities, the image of rural society which we obtain is one in which, though far from being homogeneous, the stratification which certainly did exist is blurred by the rusticity of a recently-settled frontier. This was neither an egalitarian rural democracy, nor a region where access to land and other opportunities was solely for a priviledged few.

Having outlined the characteristics of rural households as productive units in the context of early settlement in the Northwest, the following chapters will study agrarian changes associated with the later stages of colonization, the shift from a predominantly livestock-raising economy to more intensive agriculture, and the dilemmas faced by the descendants of settlers as initially-favorable conditions gave way to restricted opportunities in the region.

Chapter 5

Sons and Daughters of Settlers

During the latter half of the nineteenth century, those who settled the northwestern part of Costa Rica's Central Valley were active participants in a profound modification of the region's geographic and social environment. While the early- to mid-century landscape was dominated by forests, interspersed with pastures and small maize or sugarcane fields, especially near Grecia, the late nineteenth century witnessed a major process of agricultural intensification in areas of formerly extensive land use. At the same time, effective economic occupation of the land proceeded farther west within the Central Valley and beyond. In addition to previous uses of the land, several of which continued to expand, coffee became a major crop in the region, and former colonists were directly involved in agro-export production. Owners of capital extended credit, and governments facilitated access to land, on an unequal but also non-restrictive basis. Commercial peasant farming in this frontier region was not necessarily an antagonist but rather a component of the specific way in which agrarian capitalism developed there.

Land settlement and the expansion of coffee cultivation were not confined to the northwestern section of the Central Valley, nor to the previously settled Meseta Central where coffee was already the predominant cash crop by mid-century. During the latter half of the nineteenth century, migrants moved up the slopes of the Cordillera Central and farther north, into Guanacaste and the northern plains. They also went into the valleys south of the Meseta, and eastward along the Reventazón river to the other end of the 100-kilometer-long Central Valley and beyond. Ecological conditions for agriculture varied, especially because of altitudinal variations, but wherever coffee could be planted it was, alongside other crops and livestock. Opportunities for peasant-farming also varied, e.g. in the eastern Turrialba-Reventazón Valley where large sugarcane and coffee-producing estates were strongly predominant after railroad construction in the1870s and 1880s. Yet wherever settlers were able to gain access to the land, they sought to develop commercial production, if possible along similar patterns to those of their place of origin.

The inhabitants of the Northwest, specifically, were the individual and collective actors of the region's transformation from an agricultural frontier into an area of intensive settlement. In the course of one or two generations, mid-century immigration gave way to rapidly increasing out-migration. During that time, rural households were confronted with a series of dilemmas in connection with landholding and land use, inheritance and emigration to new lands elsewhere, whether within or without the Central Valley. Their decisions were affected by socioeconomic and sociopolitical processes over which they had little or no immediate control, but the aggregate result of their efforts to ensure the productive and reproductive viability of household units would have a decisive influence on rural society as a whole, not only at the time but also to the present day.

The ways in which domestic units interacted with other types of economic units in the Northwest, as local conditions changed during the latter part of the century, are not only significant for the more recent history of that region itself. They also had a major impact on settlement and agrarian transformations in other parts of the country, then and in the following decades. At a more general level, social relations in the countryside reflected the dynamic, contradictory interrelationship between two fundamental components of this agrarian society: the first, a geographically mobile rural population, primarily formed by peasant-farmer households, with a tradition of land settlement and an active involvement in commodity production and the various factor markets of the time; and the second, a regional elite of wealthy merchants and estate owners, some of whom controlled credit networks and processing facilities, as well as political power.

These were not, of course, the only social actors in this rural area, as prior and ongoing differentiation within the peasantry led to both upward and downward mobility: there were opportunities for accumulation not only by supra-family units but also by certain members of surplus-producing domestic units, as well as the very real prospect of proletarianization for growing numbers of household members in sub-family and deficit-yielding domestic units. Nevertheless, it is of great importance for Costa Rican rural history, then and now, that in the main area of mid-nineteenth century settlement, peasant-farmers continued to be economically (and to some extent politically) significant despite the direct or indirect control of agro-export production and local political power by the regional elite.

This chapter focuses on agrarian changes in the Northwest during this critical period from the mid- to late-nineteenth century, when regional abundance of land gave way to scarcity and wage labor suffered a reverse process. In the course of these decades, the merchant-planter elite strengthened its "triple monopoly" over credit, processing, and foreign trade, while directly controlling a sizeable part of production itself. Domestic units continued to be important in the region and especially in coffee cultivation, but the size of peasant farms declined and the progeny of former settlers faced increasingly limited options within the Northwest.

The first part of this chapter will refer to people and population trends, especially the regional shift from immigration to out-migration; the second will deal with changing regional patterns of land use, especially intensification and what initially was an agricultural diversification rather than specialization. And the third part will discuss the characteristics of and interactions among productive units, diachronically for selected cases and synchronically for 629 turn-of-the-century ones.

Immigrants, Neighbors, Emigrants

In the mid-nineteenth century, Alajuela was the province of the Central Valley with the highest absolute and relative population growth.[1] Given the extremely low initial population, this growth was due primarily to migration from the Meseta Central toward the northwestern part of the Central Valley. For several decades after mid-century, population growth in the Northwest, as reflected in parish-level baptism registration, was well above that in the province as a whole, and especially higher than in the area near Alajuela city (Figure 5.1).[2] This was due to intra-provincial migration from the previously settled area within the Meseta Central, toward Grecia, Sarchí, Naranjo, Palmares and San Ramón, as well as direct migration from other provinces (especially Heredia) to the Northwest (Figure 5.2).

Migration was perhaps slowed somewhat on a very short-term basis by the 1856-1857 demographic crisis, but during the 1860s and 1870s population growth in the Northwest (and especially toward San Ramón) was again well above national and provincial averages. Regional population, according to census counts, increased very rapidly from 1864 to 1883, at a rate well above that elsewhere in the Central Valley or nationwide. Instead, from 1883 to 1892 population growth was similar to the national average in Grecia and Naranjo, and clearly lower in San Ramón

1 DGEC, *Censo de Población, 1864*, p. 3: From 1844 to 1864 the increase (with no adjustment for under-enumeration) was 16,334 inhabitants, or 53.5%.

2 The underlying hypothesis is that differences in the rate of growth of the number of baptisms from one area to another reflect immigration and emigration. Assumptions include cross-regional similarity of: natural growth rates, age structure of the population, distribution by sex, percentage married, and data registration quality. Additional assumptions are the validity of baptism records to indicate births, and that the latter account for population growth. I thank Héctor Pérez and Arodys Robles for clarifying to me the specific assumptions and for corroborating their applicability to the region and period under discussion.

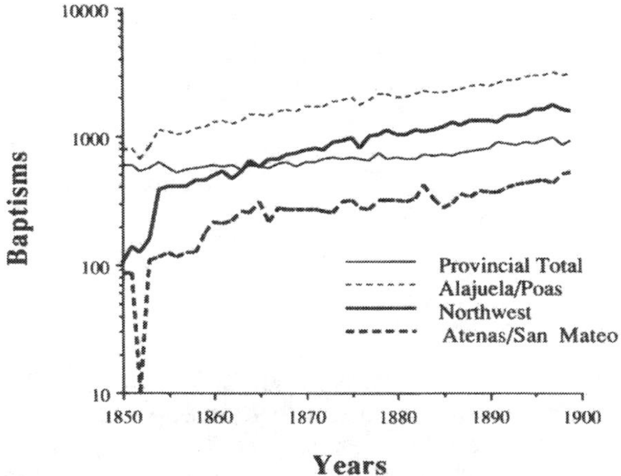

Figure 5.1 Baptisms per year in parishes of Alajuela province, 1850-1899

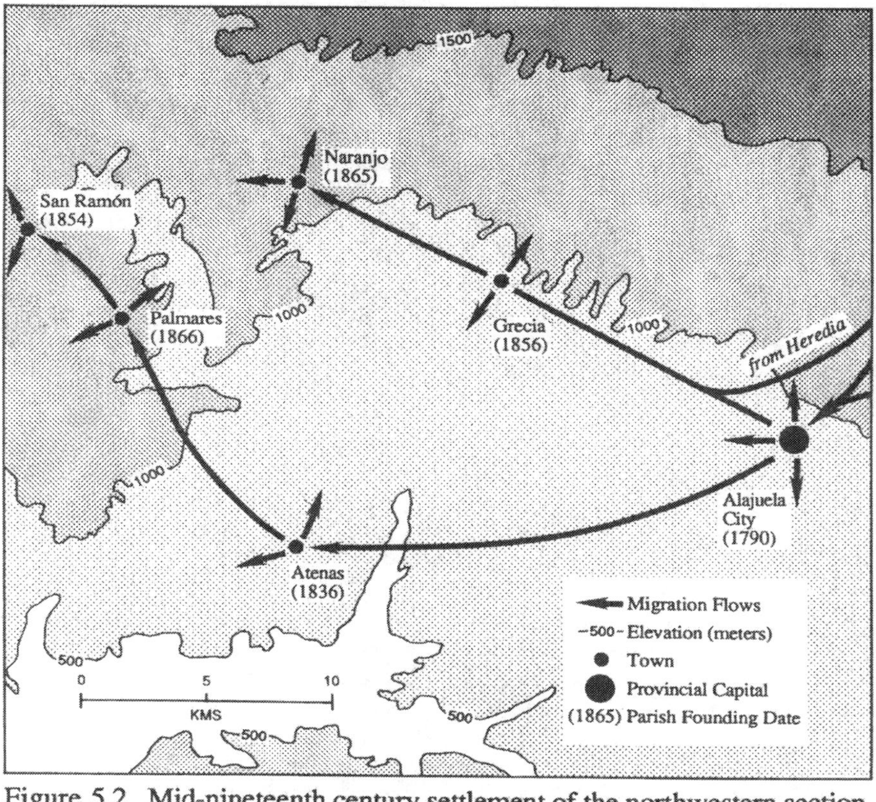

Figure 5.2 Mid-nineteenth century settlement of the northwestern section of the Central Valley, Costa Rica

and Palmares.[3] Thereafter, despite declining mortality, demographic growth in the region fell to even lower levels, as compared to other parts of the country. The Northwest probably was an area of out-migration by the late 1880s, and emigration was certainly the dominant trend by the turn of the century. Regional population increased at a much slower rate in the late nineteenth and early twentieth century, as natural growth and some immigration from the Meseta were counteracted by settlers leaving toward areas such as San Carlos and Tilarán, in the north, or looking for jobs in other areas such as the eastern Turrialba-Reventazón valley and the Atlantic coast. The growth rate based on baptisms for 1855 to 1880 in the Northwest had been twice that of the province or the country, and four times that of the Alajuela-Poás central area. From 1880 to 1900, instead, it was very similar to the provincial and national rates; in other words, immigration into the region was offset by emigration.[4]

TABLE 5.1 POPULATION OF ALAJUELA PROVINCE, 1864 AND 1892, BY DISTRICT

	1864		1892	
	#	%	#	%
Alajuela	11,521	42.40	19,133	33.45
Grecia	3,192	11.75	7,120	12.45
Sarchi	934	3.44	1,590	2.78
Naranjo	1,612	5.93	5,280	9.23
Palmares	758	2.79	2,770	4.84
San Ramón	3,597	13.24	5,924	10.36
Atenas-San Mateo	4,867	17.91	9,561	16.71
Northern Alajuela	690	2.54	5,825	10.18
Province	27,171	100.00	57,203	100.00

Source: Dirección de Estadística y Censos (1864, 1892).

3 Robles (1986), Tables 31 and 15. While absolute rates might be misleading due to greater under-enumeration in 1883, the Alajuela-San Ramón region grew at a rate 8% higher than the national average and 32% higher than the Central region (most of the Meseta) from 1864 to 1883. Instead, it was 23% lower than the national average from 1883 to 1892, and 3% lower than the Central Region. Initially, population growth in the Northwest was much higher than near Alajuela city.

4 A linear regression analysis of the logarithmic transformation of the baptism series for those years gave the following estimates for the country, province, Alajuela-Poás region and the Northwest respectively: 1855-1880: 0.022, 0.028, 0.010, and 0.043; 1880-1900: 0.023, 0.022, 0.018, and 0.023. Results were tested by the Durbin-Watson method, and auto-correlation was not found. Data were provided by Héctor Pérez, the statistical analysis carried out by Arodys Robles, and results discussed in the quantitative history program at the Centro de Investigaciones Históricas, Universidad de Costa Rica.

Population levels, as reflected in the censuses taken in 1864 and 1892, show a decline in the relative importance of Alajuela city and its surrounding districts, directly associated to increases in the Northwest and other parts of the province (Table 5.1). In absolute figures, the northwestern population grew from 10,000 to over 22,000 in that period. Within the Northwest proper, the larger cantones of Grecia, San Ramón and Naranjo clearly absorbed more population growth, while the smaller ones of Palmares and Sarchí were areas of early out-migration.

Relative population growth in Alajuela, toward 1892, was especially strong in frontier areas outside the Central Valley, on the northern and northwestern flank of the Cordillera Central. This settlement was quite recent: in 1864 San Carlos and Sarapiquí were unimportant administrative subdivisions, and even in 1883 San Carlos was only an *aldea* (small village) with 303 inhabitants, under the jurisdiction of Naranjo. Ten years later, the village itself had not grown, and Sarapiquí had only 167 inhabitants, but other areas had already been settled in this outward migration from the Central Valley: Buena Vista and Tapezco, north of Zarcero, and those districts of San Ramón which sloped toward the north and toward the west of the previously inhabited area within the Central Valley.

Population density in the northwestern part of the Central Valley was not very high in 1892. With an area of 429 km^2, the Northwest had an overall density of 53 inhabitants per square kilometer (or 58 with a ten percent upward adjustment for under-enumeration). In certain specific areas, density was higher, as in Palmares, where there were more than one hundred people per km^2.[5] On the average, population density at the time in the Northwest was roughly similar to that estimated for the Meseta Central when westward migration became important. Clearly, there was some demographic pressure, but it does not seem to have been overwhelming. Access to new lands, even if mostly beyond the Central Valley, was undoubtedly an outlet for a new generation of migrants, while agricultural intensification within the region partly compensated for subdivision of holdings. Any analysis of "expulsion" versus "attraction" in out-migration from the Northwest requires a discussion of changing land use patterns, land tenure and inheritance. But first we need to clarify certain other characteristics of this rural population, so as to better understand the linkages between demographic and socioeconomic processes.

Household formation was closely associated with the establishment of independent nuclear families in this predominantly peasant society. Men usually married at age twenty-four or twenty-five in the region at the time, and women most often when they were twenty or twenty-one. These mean ages were very similar to the age at marriage in the Meseta Central during

---

5 DGEC (1892), and IDESPO (n.d.), p. 77.

the late nineteenth century.[6] There is no evidence of a significant reduction of age at marriage during the nineteenth century, which has been associated, in other cases where there has been such a reduction, to earlier household formation among those who fully depend on wage labor, as compared to landholding peasant-farmers.

Child-woman ratios and birthrates were somewhat higher in the Northwest (as in other areas of colonization) than in the previously settled Meseta Central.[7] Together with lower rates of definitive female celibacy in the more recently settled areas, the information points to larger, and probably younger families in these, as compared to the areas of prior settlement.[8] Actually, overall population growth may have accelerated somewhat as a consequence of colonization, precisely in regions such as the Northwest, rather than faster growth rates in the Meseta Central having been the cause of westward migration, which does not seem to be the case in this period.[9]

Mortality declined very slowly toward the turn of the century in Costa Rica as a whole, and the same was true for the specific region under discussion.[10] Life expectancy at time of birth, which was under thirty years in 1865, increased gradually in the nineteenth century, and more rapidly toward the beginning of the twentieth.[11] During the second half of the nineteenth century, mortality was still quite high and most people died relatively young, as compared to the twentieth century. Yet they also had many children, and population grew rapidly.[12] As Héctor Pérez points out, this was not unrelated to socioeconomic processes:

> ...large families were a necessity for the functioning of the coffee economy, and were a basic condition for the geographic expansion of the crop... This is valid at least until the beginning of the twentieth century, and especially for

---

6 Robles (1986), p. 42; Pérez (1983), p. 133; González (1982); Gudmundson (1986a), p. 127.

7 Robles (1986), pp. 16 and 43; Gudmundson (1986a), pp. 128-129.

8 Pérez (1983), p. 124.

9 Gudmundson (1986a), pp. 129-130.

10 Robles (1986), p. 14; Pérez (1983), pp. 115 and 120.

11 Pérez (1983), p. 123, and Pérez (1987), p. 9-10. This author's original estimate was thirty years for 1865-67, revised in the more recent work to 21.56, with the qualification that "mortality was especially high in 1866 and 1867 (4,789 and 4,380 deaths recorded, as opposed to 3,125 in 1865). This is confirmed by death registrations in all parish records, so the Table will show an average mortality situation but at a relatively extreme level." (Pérez, 1987, p. 5).

12 Fertility remained high but constant during the second half of the nineteenth and early twentieth century, with a gross rate of reproduction varying between 3 and 3.5, and a net reproduction rate which rose gradually (due to the slow decline of mortality) from 1.5 to 2.0 between 1864 and 1927 (Pérez, 1983, p. 123).

> the area of expansion from Alajuela to San Ramón, that is, toward the western part of the Central Valley.[13]

The complex interaction of demographic and socioeconomic variables would require further research focusing specifically on that issue, but at this point it can be said that fertility remained high and constant, while mortality declined slowly during the second half of the nineteenth century. There is no evidence of birth control practices. Couples had many children, and people lived somewhat longer toward the turn of the century than in the 1850s or 1860s. Land settlement and perhaps the expansion of coffee cultivation were somehow associated with a moderate increase in birthrates and child/woman ratios, in turn related to lower female celibacy in these recently settled rural areas. If we bear in mind that close to ten percent of the population died in 1856-1857, prior demographic pressure cannot be seen as the main cause of settlement during this period, and indeed population growth may instead have been accelerated by colonization. Of course, higher population densities and gradually restricted access to land in the Northwest did have an effect both on land use patterns and on migration during the latter part of the century, but always in connection with opportunities either for market-oriented production or to obtain new lands elsewhere.

A gradual increase in the rate of demographic growth, due to declining mortality, was not incompatible with the existence of a landholding, mercantile peasant-farmer population in the region. There was less land available, but settler families shifted from extensive livestock raising to intensive agricultural systems, and some descendants of settlers emigrated from the Northwest to San Carlos and other areas from the 1880s. However, population growth and restricted local access to land did increase the availability of labor, and more specifically of part-time wage labor for the harvest and other seasonal tasks on the larger estates. A reference to the socio-occupational characteristics of the inhabitants of the Northwest will allow us to look not only at the landholding peasantry, but also at the growing land poor or landless population, for whom wages became an increasingly important part of household income.

In 1864, the director of the census commented that "there are few, relatively speaking, who are not involved in agricultural activities along with another occupation."[14] Reports in the press and by travelers also speak of part-time wage labor as a frequent occupation of members of peasant families, and estates growing coffee or sugarcane undoubtedly needed to employ seasonal wage labor, especially for harvesting.

From the mid- to late nineteenth century, there was a constant increase in the percentage of *jornaleros* (part- or full-time wage laborers) among the working population: from a very minor percentage in 1844, as mentioned before, jornaleros increased to slightly over one fifth of this population

---

13 Pérez (1983), pp. 114-115 and footnote 15.

14 DGEC (1864), p. XXV.

twenty years later.[15] Within the Northwest, the recently settled area of San Ramón had the lowest percentage of jornaleros, while Grecia had twice as many in absolute and relative terms (Table 5.2).

TABLE 5.2 MAIN OCCUPATIONAL CATEGORIES IN AGRICULTURE, ALAJUELA PROVINCE, 1864

	Jornaleros		Labradores		Agricultores	
	#	%	#	%	#	%
Alajuela	1,259	23.79	1,031	19.48	140	2.65
Grecia	612	21.62	1,106	39.07	101	3.57
San Ramón	305	12.70	875	36.43	64	2.66
Atenas	290	16.77	548	31.69	11	0.64
San Mateo	289	42.50	83	12.12	51	7.50
Province	2,755	21.30	3,643	28.17	367	2.84
Costa Rica	14,333	24.87	9,307	16.15	2,838	4.92

By 1883, *jornaleros* were more than a third of the total working population, and in 1892 they were more than two fifths in the region as a whole, with increases in almost all administrative subdivisions (Table 5.3).[16] Although these *jornaleros* were not necessarily full-time, totally landless wage laborers, there was undoubtedly a major increase in the population for whom wages provided a substantial part of their income.

Labradores (independent farmers) were the largest category of the population toward mid-century in the Northwest, to which we should add most members of specific agricultural groups such as *cafetaleros*, *cañaveraleros* and *ganaderos*, all of which were relatively small as occupational categories in the region.[17] The only occupational group which is more or less comparable to the above in the late nineteenth century censuses (*agricultores*, in this case any type of farmers), had come to be a surprisingly small percentage. According to the 1892 census count, these loosely-defined farmers were ten to fifteen percent of the laboring population in the various subregions of the Northwest (Table 5.3). It must be noted that this last census, like that in 1883, was taken during the coffee

15 DGEC (1864).

16 DGEC (1883, 1892). Information on other occupational categories is also derived from these same censuses.

17 *Cafetaleros* were 2.0 percent of the "economically active" population in Costa Rica, according to the 1864 census; they accounted for 1.5% in Alajuela province, with slightly higher percentages in Grecia (1.9) and San Ramón (1.2). *Cañaveraleros* were 0.8% in Costa Rica, and 2.0% in Alajuela province, with their highest percentage in Grecia (3.9%). *Ganaderos* accounted for 1.1% in Costa Rica and also in Alajuela province, where the highest percentage was in San Ramón (2.1%). (Source: DGEC, *Censo de Poplación*, 1864).

and sugarcane harvest period. Given the expansion of this crop in the region it is quite conceivable that many members of peasant households had recently been or were at the time employed in harvest-related tasks on a seasonal basis. Another reason why members of smallholding domestic units might not have been registered as *agricultores* is the fact that not long before (e. g. in 1864) this term had referred to wealthier peasants and estate owners, both in popular usage and in the census classification: "those who cultivate the land with hired laborers, on a large or small scale."[18] For these reasons, it is quite possible that more part-time wage laborers who were members of smallholder families might have been classified as *jornaleros* in 1883 or 1892 than in 1864. On the other hand, the substantial increase of this category, with a concomitant reduction of that for independent farmers, does suggest a greater role of wage labor in peasant household incomes and in social perceptions, i.e. those of census takers or the surveyed population regarding the meaning and content of such occupational categories.

TABLE 5.3 *JORNALEROS* AND *AGRICULTORES* IN 1883 AND 1892, ALAJUELA PROVINCE

	Jornaleros				**Agricultores**			
	1892		1883		1892		1893	
	#	%	#	%	#	%	#	%
Alajuela	1,859	35.3	2,037	39.9	535	10.1	687	13.5
Grecia	742	40.4	781	39.8	245	13.3	282	14.4
Naranjo	241	33.5	971	62.7	124	17.2	150	9.7
San Ramón	843	37.8	1,219	39.8	192	8.6	342	11.2
Atenas	343	31.2	372	41.5	49	4.5	59	6.6
San Mateo	245	35.5	278	38.2	79	11.4	94	12.9
Province	4,273	36.1	5,658	42.6	1,224	10.3	1,614	12.1
Costa Rica	18,278	33.8	22,190	36.4	6,787	12.5	8,508	14.0

Several simultaneous, inter-related changes took place during the latter part of the nineteenth century, which help to explain the growing importance of wage labor in the region, whether on a part-time or full-time basis. There was a growing need of many domestic units to obtain seasonal income from wage labor by some of their members, as average size of holdings per household diminished. Agricultural intensification, and whatever specialization occurred, made on-farm labor requirements more uneven during the year, generating seasonal family-labor surpluses among smaller productive units and a strong demand for supplementary workers on the larger ones. However, units with diversified land use patterns could even-off seasonal labor requirements to a certain extent. Permanent wage

18 DGEC (1864), p. XXVI.

labor also became more important, as sons of very small landowners sought regular employment, and larger estates required growing numbers of resident workers.

Parish marriage records are a complementary source for occupational analysis. Naturally, they do not conform to census criteria, but rather reflect perceptions of social status. This type of information is valid only for specific periods and places, because criteria for recording occupations of the bridegroom and witnesses varied from one parish priest or secretary to another. Aggregate occupational statistics for a given parish over long periods, as given in most demographic theses to date, are totally misleading.[19] After going back to the original source material for the parish of Palmares, in 1888-1893, the data were compared to those from the 1892 census, and the following results were obtained.[20]

The percentage of *jornaleros* among the bridegrooms in Palmares was 40%, lower but compatible with the census figure for the same area in 1892. However, *agricultores* and *labradores* were a much higher percentage (44%) among bridegrooms in the parish records than among the census population. On the other hand, marriage records report less *jornaleros* (30%) than *labradores* or *agricultores* (52%) among the male witnesses, almost invariably older and often either the father or father-in-law of the bridegroom. Among bridegrooms and witnesses in the parish of Palmares, less day-laborers were reported (and many more independent farmers) than the census figures would suggest. In this local situation, age-specific occupational distinctions are also clear: there were more part- or full-time day-laborers among the relatively young bridegrooms, while there were more independent farmers among the older witnesses. When bridegrooms were entered as *agricultores*, it was often the widowers remarrying. Generally speaking, independent status was acquired (and socially recognized) after marriage rather than before, and probably had to do with dowries, advances on inheritance, actual inheritance, or access to new lands via emigration or other means.

Since Palmares was an area of high population density and land scarcity by the 1890s, access to land must have been at least as difficult here as anywhere else in the Northwest, if not more. Data for other northwestern parishes vary as regards percentages of *jornaleros*, but do indicate a perception of social status according to which there were many more *agricultores* in the region than according to census criteria.[21] The status of *jornaleros*, in this perception, was clearly age-dependent, and sons

---

19 See, for the province of Alajuela, Fallas (1978), Fournier (1976), González (1982), and Vargas (1978). Usually, data from periods in which a careful occupational distinction was made, e.g. between independent farmers and day-laborers, were added indiscriminately to those when all were classified as *agricultores*.

20 Libro de matrimonios, parish of Palmares, 1888-1893; DGEC (1892), pp. LXXXVI to CV.

21 Libros de matrimonios, parishes of Grecia (1894-1898) and Naranjo (1895-1898).

of independent farmers were considered day-laborers at the time of their marriage. Most older men acting as witnesses were not perceived as land-poor or dependent on wages, as might be the case if former smallholders were becoming impoverished. With a settlement frontier to the north and in other parts of the country, regular employment on other farms or the condition of *jornalero* was probably viewed as a provisional status, and emigration of young adult household members as an option to ensure the economic viability of domestic units.

Among the landholding population of the Northwest, demographic characteristics were related to socioeconomic processes in a different way than among the landless, especially regarding the dual role of farm-owning households as productive and reproductive units. The deceased whose probate inventories were studied toward the turn of century,[22] almost all of them proprietors, were older than the average man or woman who died at that time. Among the landowning population represented in probate inventories, despite individual variations, higher levels of wealth tended to be associated with older average ages (Table 5.4). This interlinkage of socioeconomic and demographic variables is suggestive in many ways, though it does not prove any causal relation. Landownership, as the main component of household wealth, seems to have been age-specific, insofar as younger men were less likely to own enough land for inheritance proceedings to be opened by prospective heirs. Of course, there were elderly persons among the land-poor, and relatively young estate owners, but the association between average age and level of fortune is applicable to most, and coincides with the parish-level occupational distinctions discussed above.

TABLE 5.4 AGE OF DECEASED AT TIME OF DEATH, IN PROBATE INVENTORIES, ACCORDING TO LEVEL OF WEALTH, ALAJUELA PROVINCE, 1895-1904

Level of Wealth ($)	Average Age	Number of Cases
Negative	35.9	21
0 - < 100	40.3	66
100 - < 500	45.6	149
500 - < 1,000	45.8	113
1,000 - < 5,000	50.4	196
5,000 - < 10,000	54.6	48
≥ 10,000	50.8	36

Source: Probate Inventories for 1895 - 1904.

Age of the deceased in probate cases of the Northwest (averaging 50 years) was also higher than in the previously settled area near the provincial

22 The following information is based on the 629 probate inventories of Alajuela province for 1895-1904, listed under primary sources.

capital (with an average of 46). This regional variation, which seems to have developed during the latter half of the nineteenth century,[23] also raises questions regarding the geographical and social mobility of population at the time. Perhaps the ongoing emigration of young men and women from the Northwest, sometimes with children, was "aging" the landed population of this region. If so, emigrants were not only members of landless households, but also the sons and daughters of families with sufficient property to merit a probate inventory, which at the time was essential for the transmission of land from one generation to the next.

Emigration toward new agricultural frontiers made population grow much more slowly in the Northwest toward 1900 than half a century before. This out-migration seems to have gone through two stages. First, early emigration from the region toward San Carlos and other parts of the country, around the 1880's, was not only due to "expulsion" factors, nor limited to members of landless or land poor households. The descendants of northwestern settlers were attracted by opportunities to establish independent farms on the frontier beyond the Central Valley. Second, emigration also allowed domestic units to maintain their economic viability despite population growth, land scarcity and subdivision of holdings. At the turn of the century, accumulated pressures made emigration a more urgent necessity for members of peasant households whose holdings could not be subdivided indefinitely. The Northwest was no longer a recently- or sparsely-settled area, and the sons or daughters of settlers faced options which were increasingly limited and less promising than before.

Changing Patterns on the Land

During the second half of the nineteenth century, land use in the Northwest was fundamentally altered by agricultural intensification in response both to market opportunities and to population growth. Various crops intervened in this shift from extensive to semi-intensive uses of the land. Coffee played a very important role, and expanded rapidly throughout the region after initial settlement. Sugarcane had already been planted there before, but it became significant as a commercial crop during this period, especially near Grecia. Grain production was not necessarily displaced nor confined to subsistence agriculture, and in the vicinity of Alajuela city it was primarily a commercial crop. Agriculture proper may have pushed livestock raising into less accessible areas within the region, but even grazing became more intensive as new grasses were introduced. Given the amount of uncultivated land available at mid-century, the early stages of agricultural intensification proceeded to a large extent on virgin forests and in long-

---

23 In the 1850s, ages of the deceased in probate cases were only slightly higher in the Northwest than in Alajuela city and neighboring counties (49.8 vs. 50.4), and quite similar in both cases to the provincial average.

fallow areas. Specific forms of land use in the region during the latter part of the nineteenth century must now be examined.

LIVESTOCK RAISING

As shown in the previous chapter, this was the main economic activity in the region toward 1850. Even in 1888, Alajuela still had the second largest amount of cattle per province in Costa Rica, after Guanacaste. In Grecia, Naranjo, Palmares and San Ramón there were at least 24,000 head of cattle and over 5,500 mules or horses, or about half the total herd of the province.[24] The 1888 livestock census does not provide information on area in pastures, but with a similar ratio of land per head of livestock as in 1905,[25] these four cantones had approximately 31,200 hectares of pasturelands in 1888. Some of this land may have been outside the Central Valley, but since land claims and settlement in the northern part of the province were still quite recent, it is safe to assume that most pastureland was still within the Northwest.

In 1905, according to the agricultural census,[26] these same cantones had 31,500 hectares of pasturelands, four fifths of which were classifified as improved or "artificial" (as opposed to "natural") pastures. The numbers and proportions of adult livestock were very similar to those registered seventeen years before, i.e. 24,123 head of cattle and 5,405 horses or mules (Table 5.5). Even though livestock raising was still significant in the previously settled area, as exemplified by the small canton of Palmares, there was probably more cattle than before on lands outside the Central Valley in San Ramón, Grecia and Naranjo, which had districts north or west of the Central Valley.

Generally speaking, data available for the period speak of an average of one head of adult livestock per hectare in the Northwest toward the turn of the century. Imported pastures and a regional context of agricultural intensification suggest that livestock raising was somewhat more intensive within the Central Valley than in the late-nineteenth-century settlement frontiers. While still an extensive form of land use, grazing probably occupied less land in the Northwest around 1900 than fifty years earlier.

---

24 "Ganado vacuno, caballar y lanar existente en la República", in DGEC (1888b).

25 1.06 hectares per head of adult livestock, according to the 1905 agricultural census.

26 DGEC (1905).

TABLE 5.5 HEAD OF BOVINE, EQUINE AND PORCINE LIVESTOCK, BY CANTON IN THE NORTHWEST, 1905

Cantón	**Head of Livestock**		
	BOVINE*	EQUINE	PORCINE
San Ramón	8,238	2,674	7,605
Grecia	6,539	2,080	3,037
Naranjo	8,158	1,444	2,011
Palmares	1,188	207	424
Total	24,123	5,450	13,077

*Excluding calves.

Source: DGEC (1905).

Even though cattle comprised the predominant type of livestock in the area, hogs seem to have acquired some importance toward the turn of the century. Although there are no details in agricultural statistics of previous years, 16,185 swine were enumerated in Alajuela province in 1892, and according to the agricultural census published in 1905 there were 13,077 only in the Northwest.[27] Of course, due to their manner of feeding, swine were irrelevant to land use proper, but they appear to have become a complement to the predominant form of livestock raising on certain economic units in the region.

COFFEE

In contrast to its quantitative unimportance half a century earlier, coffee was undoubtedly the main agricultural activity in the Northwest by the end of the nineteenth century. In 1878, according to the detailed provincial coffee census[28] whose very existence reflects contemporary recognition of the regional importance of this crop, there were 2,121,986 coffee trees in the area from Grecia to San Ramón. According to the relatively high average of 1,704 coffee trees per hectare in that census[29], there were approximately 1,245 hectares planted in coffee at the time, in Grecia, Naranjo, Palmares and San Ramón. Ten years later, agricultural statistics record 3,013,277

27 "Estadística del ganado," in DGEC (1892), p. CLXIX, and DGEC (1905).

28 Archivo Nacional, Serie Gobernación, doc. # 7319.

29 Or 1,200 coffee trees per *manzana*. See Samper (1985), notes 11 and 24, pp. 84 and 86. Carolyn Hall (1976) gives a somewhat lower figure, 1,000 per *manzana*, while Molina (1987) gives a higher one, up to 2,000 trees per *manzana*.

coffee trees in the four cantones of the Northwest.[30] By 1892, the number of coffee trees had risen to 3,301,311, or 1,937 hectares according to the previously mentioned density.[31] In 1905, although there is no indication of the number of trees, the agricultural census records an area of 3,188 hectares in the four northwestern cantones. It must be noted that in the case of coffee, hardly any was planted outside the Central Valley at the time, as shall be seen below in connection with productive units. Coffee was a major crop in all four cantones, but relative to their area within the Central Valley, the coffee-growing area was more important in Palmares and Naranjo.[32] We conclude, then, that in the quarter of a century after1880 there was a considerable expansion of the area planted in coffee within the Northwest.

SUGARCANE

As has been noted, sugarcane was a small-scale but rather disseminated crop at mid-century. In the 1880's, the sugarcane area in the four cantones of the Northwest was about 1,200 hectares, and it increased slightly over 50% by 1905, when it included some 1,915 hectares.[33] Certainly, as will be seen in the discussion of specific productive units, there were sugarcane plantations outside the Central Valley. However, most commercial production of sugarcane in Grecia, Naranjo and San Ramón -as well as all that in Palmares- was located primarily within the Northwest, and especially in Grecia.[34]

---

30 "Cuadro que manifiesta la producción de café en la República, correspondiente a la cosecha que comenzó en noviembre de 1887 y concluyó en abril de 1888", in DGEC (1888a).

31 "Estadística del café en 1892", in DGEC (1892), p. CLXV.

32 According to the 1905 agricultural census (DGEC, 1905), Grecia had the largest area in coffee of the four Northwestern cantons: 1,248 hectares, or 39.2%. Naranjo had 869 hectares (27.3%), San Ramón 659 (20.7%), and Palmares 412 (12.9%).

33 "Cuadro que manifiesta la producción de café en la República, correspondiente a la cosecha que comenzó en noviembre de 1887 y concluyó en abril de 1888", in DGEC (1888a).

34 By 1905, Grecia had approximately 960 hectares planted in sugarcane, followed by San Ramón with 607, Naranjo with 293 and Palmares with 55 ha. By comparison with data available for 1884, the increase was greatest in Grecia, which then had 593 ha. in sugarcane, and in Naranjo, where there were 105 ha. of this crop in 1884. Growth of sugarcane production in San Ramón, instead, was relatively small, as there were 582 ha. in that county, which in 1884 included Palmares too. (Sources: DGEC, 1884, 1905).

STAPLE GRAIN

The staple crops in the region were primarily maize, the main foodcrop, and black beans which were usually planted in association with maize. Rice and wheat were minimal. Therefore, the area planted in maize was, essentially, the area in staple grain. Although there is no statistical information on agriculture for the mid-nineteenth century, probate inventories suggest that maize was planted in small plots throughout the inhabited area in Alajuela. Between 1883 and 1892, agricultural statistics indicate an increase of maizefields in the four northwestern cantones, but especially in San Ramón.[35] Given the need to make conversions of volumes harvested into areas, and to compensate for possible variations due to yields and other factors from year to year, an average was calculated which would indicate the area constantly under cultivation with maize during the 1880's. A comparison of these figures with those of the 1905 census showed that in the four cantones as a whole there was neither a major increase nor a very major reduction of maize cultivation during that quarter of a century in which coffee production expanded rapidly there. The area harvested in maize would, then, have been about 4,000 hectares, even though there may have been regional and sub-regional variations, and we know that maize production was not restricted to the Central Valley.[36]

In the case of maize, as well as black beans associated with it, spatial distribution within Grecia, Naranjo and San Ramón must have varied with agricultural settlement, but it is difficult to establish the precise proportions with such sources. In Palmares, our test case due to the its lack of lands outside the Central Valley, there was in fact a strong reduction of the maize-producing area during this period.[37] It is probably safe to assume that maize production within the Central Valley proper may have declined somewhat in the other three Northwestern cantones, while it must have increased in recently settled areas of these same cantones, north of the Central Valley.

35 "Estadística agrícola, año de 1884", in Meléndez (1978); DGEC (1888a, 1905, 1955). The agricultural census taken in 1955, though beyond our period, provided the basis for an approximate conversion of area harvested and corn production, in *fanegas*, at a rate of 2.64 per hectare. In 1905, the area was given by the census. In the nineteenth century sources, liters per *fanega* were converted at 399.8, rounded off to 400.

36 The average number of *fanegas* of corn production in 1884/1888 was 11,497, and 10,649 in 1905. Average area planted in corn during the former years can be estimated at 4,354, and in 1905 was about 4,034.

37 Area planted in corn declined from some 284 to 152 hectares in Palmares between the 1884/1888 average and the 1905 census. Proportional reductions were smaller in Grecia (971 to 899 ha.) and San Ramón (1,743 to 1,166 ha.), while the corn-farming area in Naranjo increased from 1,356 to 1,817 ha. between the two estimates. Clearly, these figures must be considered only approximations, due to the rudimentary nature of agricultural statistics at the time and variations between 1884 and 1888 in the estimates for grain production.

OTHER LAND USES

In agricultural estimates of the time these were mainly, plantain and fruit trees. They were widely disseminated on farms throughout the region, both for self-consumption and for sale. However, the way in which they were usually planted, in association with other major crops such as coffee or in tiny plots, meant that the areas exclusively in plantain or fruit trees were quite small. Plantain, for example, was often found as a shade for coffee, and references to plantain plots were always very small.

Only uncultivated lands covered more area than pasturelands in the four northwestern cantones. We have no appropriate data before 1905, but in that year there were still more than 50,000 hectares of uncultivated lands, according to the agricultural census. These were located, especially, in the cantones of San Ramón and Naranjo, major parts of which were outside the Central Valley. Grecia had relatively little uncultivated land, and Palmares an extremely small amount.[38] It is doubtful that the uncultivated areas were accurately estimated, but the figures give a rough idea of the order of importance of such lands. As data for Palmares show, the uncultivated area within the Northwest was much smaller than on the settlement frontier to the north and elsewhere.

The picture we obtain from the approximate data discussed above is one of a region in which uncultivated land had declined significantly within the Central Valley, but was still of major importance in the territories immediately north of the Cordillera. Pastureland was the main productive use of the land in the four Northwestern cantones, although it was probably somewhat more important on the turn-of-the-century frontier than in areas of earlier settlement. Maize production was widespread, still the main specifically agricultural land use, even though it may have declined somewhat within the Central Valley. In terms of area, it was followed by coffee production, which had expanded rapidly in the Northwestern section of the Central Valley during the latter part of the century. Sugarcane, even if on a smaller scale, had also increased significantly in the late nineteenth century.

Given the imprecise and aggregate nature of the statistical information discussed above, there is a need to establish the types of changes in land use which took place on specific units of production over time. For this, twenty-two northwestern farms (mostly from Grecia and Palmares, but also from Naranjo and San Ramón) were traced retrospectively. A selection of

---

38 According to the 1905 agricultural census estimate, uncultivated land was especially important in San Ramón (24,121 ha.) and Naranjo (22,060 ha.). It was less significant in Grecia (4,426 ha.), and minimal in Palmares (132 ha.). Once again, the information must be dealt with only as a rough approximation, given the difficulty of accurately estimating uncultivated areas at the time. However, it is consistent with qualitative information, e.g. the fact that Palmares, a small canton, was totally within the Central Valley and fully settled at the time, while the other three cantons had major areas north of the Central Valley, where settlement was an ongoing process at the turn of the century.

cases from the probate inventories of 1895-1904 was followed through the real estate registry back to the 1870's. The main objective of this procedure was to establish to what extent coffee had displaced other crops, and whether or not it had led to specialization. Despite the inevitable time-lag in such records, the crop sequence can be roughly reconstructed in this way.

On most of these farms, coffee and sugarcane expanded on lands which had formerly been uncultivated or in pastures. Only on some farms in Palmares did coffee displace grain production. In other cases it was sugarcane that had expanded to the detriment of grain, pastures, or uncultivated lands. And on several other farms, it was actually grain cultivation that took over pasturelands, forests or long-fallow areas.

The process on individual farms over time corroborates the impression derived from statistical information: coffee did not expand in this region primarily by substituting grain production, as has sometimes been generalized from what seems to have been the case in parts of the Meseta Central. Nor did the expansion of coffee lead to a high degree of specialization, save for certain small farms in Palmares where coffee was the most intensive land use option in a context of dense settlement and subdivision of holdings. In most cases, coffee and other crops tended to diversify (at the same time that they intensified) a formerly extensive pattern of land use based on grazing, isolated agricultural plots and much uncultivated land.

Toward 1900, we find that after half a century of colonization in the Northwest and beyond, there were still unsettled areas but most were in the northern part of the province. Each of the three larger cantones of the Northwest had an "internal frontier", which by the turn of the century was located outside the Central Valley, but rather than being remote hinterlands they were more or less accesible in terms of distance and rudimentary transportation. Even within the Northwest there were lands yet to be cultivated, although it is quite probable that they had already been claimed or were part of existing properties.

Land for livestock raising was still, at the turn of the century, roughly twice the area under agriculture proper. The more extensive use predominated clearly in San Carlos and other areas of settlement, while semi-intensive agriculture had acquired greater importance in the Northwest, without completely displacing cattle. Once again, the cantón of Palmares is a good example of the situation in the more densely populated areas of the northwestern Central Valley: with about a thousand head of cattle and a couple hundred horses or mules, pastures occupied four times the uncultivated lands, and slightly less than crop agriculture proper in 1905.

Coffee cultivation expanded rapidly in the Northwest during the latter half of the nineteenth century, but it would be a mistake to characterize this region as a single-crop economy. Even though livestock raising was less significant than fifty years before, it was far from unimportant as an economic activity. And there were several other crops which, rather than disappearing had expanded and occupied a larger farm area than coffee.

Cornfields, for example, trebled the area in coffee groves in the four northwestern cantones. Since the agricultural statistics provide no district-level data, we can only assume that for ecological reasons, among others, maize, like cattle, had accompanied the new generation of settlers after 1880, while coffee was largely confined to the Central Valley despite experiments in its cultivation elsewhere. Therefore, the difference between the area in maizefields and in coffee groves must have been much smaller within the Northwest. In Palmares, which had no territory in the northern part of the province, the area planted in maize was quite similar to that in coffee. In most other parts of the Northwest, ideal for coffee cultivation, its area was probably not much smaller than that in grain, but neither could it have been much larger if we are to judge by the example of Palmares.

Sugarcane, too, occupied a significant area within the Central Valley and especially near Grecia. Generally speaking, sugarcane fields accounted for about two thirds of the coffee-plantation area. If we add to this the existence of other, secondary crops, even if on a small scale, the resulting land use patterns are very different from a single-crop economy. Instead, the turn-of-the-century landscape was that of a highly diversified agrarian economy, though a mercantile rather than a subsistence-oriented one.

The main changes during the late nineteenth and the early twentieth century had been a significant reduction of the uncultivated area, while pasturelands had declined slightly in the Northwest. Regarding agriculture proper, the three main crops had expanded, to occupy more land than before and contribute to an overall intensification of land use. Together, coffee, sugarcane and maize added 4,200 new hectares between the early 1880's and 1905. Coffee was doubtless the most dynamic crop in terms of land use: it contributed more than the others to this increase of the cultivated area, and the yearly growth rate of the area in coffee groves was much higher than that of any other use of the land (Table 5.6).

TABLE 5.6 EXPANSION OF FARM AREA IN COFFEE, SUGARCANE AND MAIZE IN CANTONES OF THE NORTHWEST, 1878/1884 TO 1905

Crop	**Period**	**Increase**		
		HECTARES	PERCENTAGE	
			TOTAL	ANNUAL
Coffee	1878 - 1905	1,943	156.0	5.8
Sugarcane	1884 - 1905	635	49.6	2.4
Maize	1884 - 1905	1,711	19.1	0.9

Sources: Archivo Nacional, Gobernación, Doc. # 7319;
DGEC (1884, 1905).

By the end of the nineteenth century, the Northwest was fully incorporated into agricultural production with a mixed technological level. It combined what were at the time relatively extensive and intensive land use patterns, in terms of labor per area.[39] There had clearly been a process of agricultural intensification, but as of 1900 it had not yet reached the levels of intensity achieved long before in the Meseta Central. Furthermore, while coffee cultivation played a major role in the market-oriented dynamics of the northwestern regional economy, its development was far from single-crop specialization. Rather than displacing other agricultural activities, coffee was associated with a slower but significant increase of sugarcane cultivation, while maize production increased slightly and livestock raising declined without, however, becoming a minor economic activity. The outcome, at that point, was a highly diversified agricultural production system of unequal labor intensity, with a potential for greater intensification and for specialization.

Regarding a question raised in the first section of this chapter, pertaining to the connections between migratory and socioeconomic processes, it would seem that at least in the 1880s and to a certain extent toward 1900, the region could still absorb more population and more agricultural labor, although this would require greater intensification together with specialization, both in and within agriculture. The fact that emigration had begun before the area reached a technological "point of saturation" suggests the existence of multiple strategies by members of productive units. Perhaps unwittingly, rural households maintained a certain balance between gradual labor-intensification and out-migration. The turn-of-the-century Northwest was still reminiscent of mid-century diversity of options for rural households, yet also the harbinger to pressing dilemmas which would become unavoidable for many of them two or three decades later.

Domestic Units and Estates

In the mid-nineteenth century, as demonstrated in Chapter 4, the main economic activity on most productive units in Alajuela was ranching, and especially in the recently settled Northwest land use was quite extensive. Variations between the larger and smaller units were primarily a matter of scale, rather than type of production or technological level. While there had been some relatively large land claims, labor scarcity and transportation difficulties together with other factors had limited the establishment of vast productive estates in the region.

Fifty years later, there were many more productive units in the region, and agricultural intensification together with subdivision of holdings had substantially reduced the area of what might be considered a domestic unit of production. Several large agro-industrial firms controlled processing of the main commercial crops, labor was no longer as scarce as before, and

---

39 Labor rather than capital-intensity is used here as the criterion for distinguishing between more extensive or intensive uses of the land, because technological inputs were minimal for the various uses on large and small farms.

real wages tended to decline. The situation of rural households in the region was less promising than half a century earlier in many respects. Their options were limited; they depended more than ever on the various markets in which their members were participants, without obtaining the same benefits as before; further fragmentation of tenures would tend to produce economically non-viable units, while sale of small holdings or modification of inheritance practices involved difficult decisions. There was always the frontier, though less accessible than before and perhaps offering fewer opportunities for social advancement to members of peasant families.

Despite late-nineteenth-century emigration, many descendants of settlers remained in the northwestern part of the Central Valley, and additional immigrants arrived there from the Meseta, so that local population continued to increase. The number of productive units also grew, despite the fact that there was little unclaimed land in the Northwest, and average size of holdings decreased. Coffee and other semi-intensive crops expanded on previously uncultivated or extensively used areas of many farms in the region. Let us briefly follow this process on specific productive units during the latter part of the century, before discussing the situation of domestic units and estates toward 1900.

As was shown in the previous chapter, mid-century coffee plantations in Alajuela were quite small, only a few hectares, but the first ones were quite often on *haciendas* or estates. Carolyn Hall points out that coffee occupied only a minor part of the area on most properties, large or small, and provides several cases for the area of Grecia:

> An eighteen manzana farm near Grecia, for example, which had first been for pastures, already had five thousand new coffee trees when it was put up for sale in 1862... In 1853, for example, also near Grecia, a new hacienda with a total area of four hundred manzanas had fifty in coffee, fifty in sugarcane, and had its own beneficio [processing facility] for coffee; the rest of the farm must have been forests,or at the most land cleared for pastures... In the cantón of Grecia, for example, almost half the coffee plantations in the real estate registry, from 1867 to 1872, were plots under one manzana, at distances of no more than half a kilometer from the town square. Most of these properties included small plots in sugarcane as well as pastures, and a house for the farmer and his family. .. a coffee hacienda, El Tacacal, in Grecia, had an area of 577 manzanas in 1868. This area was divided into twenty-two parts, ranging from 129 to 3/4 manzana. This was the largest area of land probably held at that time by one of the most powerful coffeegrowers in the Meseta Central. However, the total area in coffee, 102 manzanas, was not larger than the area planted in the main haciendas near San José. Although some basic foodcrops were planted on El Tacacal, together with sugarcane for the preparation of dulce [unrefined sugar cakes] on the farm's trapiche [small processing mill], there were still large pastures for fattening of beef cattle.[40]

Coffee, then, was gradually introduced on variously-sized farms on which land use had previously been quite extensive, and it did not

40 Hall (1976), pp. 91-94.

necessarily lead to rapid specialization at the level of productive units in the Northwest. Instead, it was often associated with other crops, e.g. sugarcane and grain. Usually, a more intensive use replaced a less intensive one, rather than one semi-intensive crop displacing another, less profitable one, as may have been the case in parts of the Meseta Central. Coffee production (and in Grecia sugarcane too) was the basis for a substantial intensification of landuse patterns, both in terms of labor inputs and of value output per area. This was a response to economic opportunities and also an alternative in face of gradually restricted access to land in the region, which made it difficult to expand farm area locally given relatively high prices.

This process can be exemplified with a specific mid-century livestock-producing domestic unit in the Northwest. Let us take the case of Fernando Molina, who died in San Ramón at the age of fifty, in 1855.[41] His properties included just over fifty *manzanas* (about thirty-five hectares) of pastures, non-cultivated land and a part with unspecified use, plus a small maizefield and a sugarcane plot. In his pastureland, Molina had only ten head of cattle and two horses, according to the inventory, but even with a herd twice or three times that size, it would still have been essentially a domestic unit, in terms of livestock production. Instead, the same area in coffee, according to the 1878 densities, would contain some sixty thousand coffee trees, and require about twelve permanent workers, aside from seasonal harvesters.[42] A hypothetically complete shift from pasture to coffee would have turned an intermediate or deficit-yielding domestic unit into either a surplus-producing one, or an enterprise which might depend more on non-family than on household labor. Of course, we know that intensification was gradual and specialization incomplete during the nineteenth century, but the example gives us an idea of the potential impact of coffee on a given area of pastureland.

In actual fact, when Molina died, his properties were divided equally among the four sons, so each received an area which, in pasture, was clearly insufficient for household labor and consumption requirements. If land use were thereafter intensified substantially, these smaller farms might absorb a major part of each new household's labor and satisfy most of its needs, though hardly all of them. In such cases, assuming there was no access to additional land, intensification and specialization could not lead to any long-term accumulation of wealth, given the subdivision of property from one generation to the next. However, more intensive or specialized land use would counteract the smaller size of holdings and avoid rapid impoverishment as they were subdivided.

41 Archivo Nacional, Mortual Independiente, Doc. #1018.

42 According to the 1878 document "Café en Alajuela" (Archivo Nacional, Serie Gobernación, Doc. #7319), there were some 1,200 coffee trees per *manzana*. Toward the mid-nineteenth century, Wagner and Scherzer (1944, p. 197) reported that a permanent worker could care for about 5,000 coffee trees.

Intensification and specialization were in part a response to local population growth, but also to other, positive incentives. Furthermore, both processes took place despite land availability first within the region and later on elsewhere. Gradual intensification and incomplete specialization, together with subdivision of holdings through inheritance, suggest a changing yet enduring balance between demographic pressures and opportunities on the frontier, as well as between subsistence requirements and market incentives.

In another case for this period, it is possible to follow the changes in land use and land tenure over several generations. Ramón Carvajal Bogantes, a *labrador*, was living in Sarchí in 1844.[43] He was forty years old, and the other members of this family were his wife, an eight-year-old girl, and three other children under seven. Their capital wealth was estimated at $50, roughly that of a smallholder family at the time.

The parents of both Ramón and his wife were from Heredia, though his parents already lived in Sarchí in the 1840s. It seems that Ramón's father had been a *jornalero*, and in any case he only contributed a few head of cattle to his own marriage. However, when the father died in 1856, his capital was $535, including some forty to forty-five *manzanas* of land, thirty head of cattle, and a house, albeit with no luxuries. He was no longer poor, but neither was he a wealthy man.

Ramón, himself, contributed no land to his marriage, and only four head of cattle, although his wife did contribute a plot of land. When Ramón also died in 1856, the couple owned capital wealth estimated at $835, somewhat more than his parents. We do not know the exact area of his properties, but based on their value they were probably larger than his father's. At the time of his death, Ramón owned twenty-three head of cattle, a *trapiche*, an ox-cart and a house, with no luxuries either. He was still a *labrador*, but he was apparently better-off than his father in 1856, when the two died during the plague. Both households reflect a degree of upward socioeconomic mobility, in connection with access to land during settlement of the Northwest, and before coffee expanded significantly in the area.

In 1856, the widow of Ramón Carvajal received $355, for her own contribution to the marriage and her share of *gananciales* (joint property acquired after marriage). Each son received $61 as inheritance from their father, including landrights on two farms and one head of cattle for each of them. When the widow died in 1873, her capital wealth was estimated to be $395, and once the cost of legal procedures had been deducted, each of the three surviving sons received $100 as inheritance from their mother, in rights to two plots of land. They also received $18 as inheritance from the fourth son, already deceased. Ultimately, each of the three surviving sons received $180 as inheritance from both parents, while at the time their

---

43 Archivo Nacional, Congreso, Doc. #6547, for the 1844 census, and Mortual Independiente, Docs. #463, 532 and 1620, for follow-up of three generations in probate cases.

father's father died, inheritance was only $74. The monetary increase probably did not correspond to a very major increase in real value,[44] but neither was there a strong reduction in real terms. In any case, each individual heir in 1883 received considerably less land than their parents had toward mid-century.[45] Yet these were not land-poor, sub-family units, although subdivision among one more generation of heirs could easily lead to that result.

After 1856, land use on the property belonging to this family was gradually intensified. In 1873, even though there was still a major area in pastures and uncultivated land, there were also coffee, plantains and staple grain. While coffee would later become the main crop, agricultural intensification was first associated to productive diversification, and only later to specialization.

In the course of several generations from the mid- to late-nineteenth century, domestic units such as those described above devised flexible strategies to take advantage of initial opportunities and counteract growing difficulties. At first, immigrants from the Meseta had access to land on the northwestern frontier; holdings could be expanded by land claims, purchases or other means, and land use patterns were extensive, mainly geared toward livestock raising. Thereafter, agricultural intensification proceeded gradually at first, diversifying land use patterns and compensating for subdivision of holdings and increased difficulties of access to land within the region. Finally, fragmentation of tenure among successive generations of heirs was associated with further intensification, specialization, a greater reliance on wage labor, and emigration. In discussing the characteristics of productive units in 1895-1904, we will seek to ascertain to what extent these processes had been completed in the region by the end of the century.

HOUSEHOLD WEALTH

In turn-of-the-century probate inventories household wealth averaged close to $3,300 in Alajuela province, about twice the mid-century average. This level was somewhat higher in the town of Alajuela and its neighboring cantones, lower in the Northwest. Variability of family fortunes near and in the provincial capital was far greater than in the Northwest or elsewhere, suggesting that social distances may have been especially great in the former, previously settled area.

---

44 As an example, rather than a precise indicator, cows were estimated at $9 to $12 in the region in 1856, and $30 to $35 in 1883. Of course, there was more livestock production at mid-century, while the agrarian system was more diversified toward the latter date. Unfortunately, a valid price series has not yet been developed for the period and region, whether for cattle or any basic foodcrop.

45 The widow's assets in the probate inventory were only 12 *manzanas* ($300), even though in 1873 she had another farm, 16 *manzanas* in size.

The land-poor population of the province seems to have been concentrated near the capital, if we are to judge by their relative geographic representation in probate inventories (Table 5.7). At intermediate levels of fortune, there was an approximate balance between this area and the Northwest, while the latter region had a rather wealthy local elite by this time. Apparently, intra-provincial migration had not curbed relative impoverishment of the petty landowning population in the various cantones near Alajuela,[46] while in the Northwest there was still a sizeable middling peasantry despite the growth of a land-poor and perhaps a landless population there too.

TABLE 5.7 LEVEL OF FORTUNE AND RESIDENCE OF DECEASED BY REGION IN PROBATE INVENTORIES, ALAJUELA PROVINCE, 1895-1904

Level of Provincial Fortune ($ or ¢)	Capital*		Northwest		Other Alajuela		Other Province	
	#	%	#	%	#	%	#	%
Negative	9	69.2	2	15.4	1	7.7	1	7.7
0 - < 100	38	67.9	13	23.2	2	3.6	3	5.4
100 - < 500	68	60.7	28	25.0	15	13.4	1	0.9
500 - < 1,000	43	46.2	35	37.6	14	15.1	1	1.1
1,000 - < 5,000	65	39.6	65	39.6	31	18.9	3	1.8
5,000 - < 10,000	16	37.2	31	48.8	6	14.0	0	0
≥ 10,000	9	33.3	13	48.2	5	18.5	0	0

Source: Probate inventories for 1895 - 1904.

* Alajuela city and surrounding cantons.

In comparison to the mid-nineteenth century, land was an even greater component of wealth estimates in 1895-1904. Value of livestock, equipment and other goods was usually quite low, and was not decisive in defining level of wealth despite a positive association between these values and wealth.[47] In the province as a whole and in its main regions there were negative average credit balances, which reduced household wealth

46 Elimination of the urban core (to avoid a bias due to small plots for housing) reduced this difference but did not make it disappear.

47 There is less detail on movables in most cases for 1895-1904 than in the 1850s, and transmission of legal rights to the land was clearly the main reason for probate procedures to take place. Costly delays, taxation and the more or less recent establishment of the Registro de la Propiedad (Real Estate Registry) are some explanatory factors explaining the less detailed inventories. Yet ownership of cattle, equipment and other movables did tend to be associated with level of wealth, so we cannot dismiss this reduction of movable productive assets.

(Table 5.8). All this speaks of socioeconomic pressures on the smaller productive units, especially in and around the provincial capital.

TABLE 5.8 VALUE OF VARIOUS ASSETS PER CASE, BY PLACE OF RESIDENCE OF DECEASED IN PROBATE INVENTORIES, ALAJUELA PROVINCE, 1895-1904

	Average Value ($ or ¢)		
ITEMS	CAPITAL AND SURROUNDINGS	NORTHWEST	ALAJUELA PROVINCE
Land	3,148.15	3,170.79	3,030.27
Livestock	76.33	155.93	113.77
Equipment	13.63	31.30	21.64
Other Movables*	139.80	200.28	143.85
Total Fortune	3,341.78	3,394.56	3,249.53

* Buildings, household goods, assorted movables.

Source: Probate inventories for 1895 - 1904.

TABLE 5.9 VALUE OF VARIOUS ASSETS PER CASE, BY LEVEL OF WEALTH OF DECEASED IN PROBATE INVENTORIES, ALAJUELA PROVINCE, 1895-1904

Level of Wealth ($ or ¢)	Land	Livestock	Equipment	Other Movables	Credit Balance
Negative	1,083.33	54.29	0	125.71	-2,386.67
0 - < 100	286.36	1.82	0	3.94	-18.64
100 - < 500	289.99	12.89	0.54	10.74	-62.08
500 - < 1,000	839.20	46.19	5.40	34.96	-231.86
1,000 - < 5,000	2,308.11	113.06	23.83	82.76	-145.31
5,000 - < 10,000	5,787.92	291.46	69.38	372.08	600.21
≥10,000	28,140.83	750.28	136.67	1,331.94	1,318.61

Source: Probate inventories for 1895 - 1904.

Value of physical assets increased at higher levels of wealth, but land was clearly predominant in all cases. Negative fortunes, however, were asociated with a combination of intermediate-level landownership and heavy debts. On the other hand, small landowners were often indebted for relatively small amounts, and only the wealthier Alajuelans had positive average credit balances (Table 5.9). Livestock and all types of productive equipment were negligible in estates under $1,000, and modest in intermediate ones.[48] Once again, it was only in fortunes of $5,000 or more that either of these movables was noteworthy at all, with the possible exception of cattle in the case of heavily indebted, and usually young, landowners (Tables 5.9 and 5.10).

Credit was reported less frequently in 1895-1904 than in mid-century probate inventories, but was proportionally more important at the turn of the century.[49] Indebtedness could often threaten the viability of economic units, in contrast to the situation half a century earlier, when debts were small though frequent, and credit balances were mostly favorable.

Individual credits and debts averaged about $500, but varied greatly from numerous very small ones to others for several thousand *pesos* or *colones*.[50] Individual credits were most often amounts owed for land (32%), followed by cash loans (23%). Debts were usually for monetary loans (37%), as well as assorted merchandise (23%). By comparison with the mid-nineteenth-century probate inventories, monetary loans had become more important vis-à-vis advances on inheritance or debts for unpaid labor and various non-monetary transactions. If mid-century credit reflected the development of mercantile relations in an economic environment with scarce currency, turn-of-the-century credit indicated monetization of the rural economy.

At higher levels of wealth, assets tended to be subdivided among a larger number of heirs, actually about twice as many in estates of $10,000 or more than in those under $1,000.[51] This did not necessarily mean larger families, as non-children inherited more frequently at higher levels of wealth. However, since wealth was also associated with age, it is possible

---

48 There was clearly a positive association between herd size, value and level of fortune, but under $5,000 household wealth included, on the average, less than three head of cattle or than $90 worth of same in any category. From $5,000 to under $10,000 fortune, average herds were 7 head, or $240, and from $10,000 on, the averages were 17 head of cattle and $592.

49 Ninety cases out of 629 had credits, and 140 had debts in 1895-1904, as opposed to eight out of ten cases having credits, debts or both in 1850-1859. Average credit per case in 1895-1904, excluding those without loans, was $2,060, and average debt $1,602, or about half of average fortunes. If we include cases without loans, average credit was still $356 and average debt $295. Given the greater frequency of such passive loans, total debt in probate inventories of Alajuela was $224,220, vs. $185,420 total credit.

50 ndividual credits averaged $464, and debts $534, but maxima were $9,020 and $18,750 respectively, with minima of a few *pesos* or *colones*. The name of local currency changed together with the monetary system at the turn of the century, but *pesos* and *colones* were equivalent monetary units, so all prices will be given in the former.

51 Fortunes from negligible values to under $100 had 3.55 heirs; those from $100 up to less than $500 had 3.76; $500 to under $1,000, 4.94; from $1,000 to under $5,000, they averaged 5.68; $5,000 to under $10,000, 6.85, and from $10,000 on the number of heirs averaged 7.22.

TABLE 5.10 AVERAGE VALUE OF MOVABLES OTHER THAN LIVESTOCK, BY LEVEL OF WEALTH IN PROBATE INVENTORIES, ALAJUELA PROVINCE, 1895-1904

Level of Fortune ($ or ¢)	**Value ($ or ¢)**					
	IMPLEMENTS	PROCESSING	TRANSPORTATION	CONSTRUCTION	HOUSEHOLD GOODS	OTHER MOVABLES
Negative	0.0	0.0	0.0	72.9	1.4	51.4
0 - < 100	0.0	0.0	0.0	3.3	0.6	0.0
100 - < 5000	0.1	0.0	0.5	5.0	2.0	3.9
500 - < 1,000	0.2	2.5	2.7	11.5	7.4	16.8
1,000 - < 5,000	4.3	12.8	6.7	37.5	11.9	34.4
5,000 - < 10,000	0.2	49.4	19.8	88.3	34.2	266.2
≥ 10,000	93.3	19.4	23.9	109.7	96.4	1,192.1

Source: Probate inventories for 1895 - 1904.

that family size did vary in this regard, even if actual co-resident households of the elderly were usually smaller than those of younger couples.

It is possible that preferential inheritance and exclusion of one or more heirs were significant among the land-poor and in areas where fragmentation of tenures threatened their viability. Certainly, liberal legislation of the previous decade allowed greater freedom to parents regarding testamentary provisions on distribution of wealth among mandadory and non-mandatory heirs. This was reflected in the *Ley de sucesiones*, enacted in 1881, and the *Código Civil* of 1888, which gave owners greater leeway for testamentary disposition of their property, save for religious donations which were restricted by the liberals.[52]

However, in contrast with areas where land had become scarce and household tenures insufficient, the need for a generalization of such mechanisms to limit fragmentation of holdings was still not very strong in the recently settled areas, where intensification of land use partly compensated for subdivision of property. As will be seen in the following chapter, this need for compensatory mechanisms arose throughout the region, even if unequally, in the course of the following decades.

Landholding

In probate inventories from 1895-1904 landholdings varied quite significantly, including sizes from minimal amounts to over 1,400 hectares. An "average" unit in Alajuela province had four individual properties, with some forty hectares of land worth approximately $3,000.[53] While this value acounted for more than double the mid-century estimates, the average area in 1895-1904 was just over half that for 1850-1859. Furthermore, while in the 1850s there were quite a number of cases with holdings similar to the provincial averages, this can only be said for a few actual cases in the late nineteenth century, as we shall see below.

Regarding the number of individual properties, even though the nature of the source precluded any large number of landless households, most cases (51%) had only one or two properties; another twenty-five percent had three to five properties; slightly over one tenth had six to ten; and 8% had eleven or more. Within the landholding population represented (to a greater or lesser extent) in probate inventories, there were many cases with

---

52 Badilla (1988), p. 192.

53 Even though area per case was 29.4 for properties with data in probate inventories, an adjustment is necessary because 27% of the individual properties had no indication of the exact area. For this reason, the average area per case was established by multiplying the number of properties per case (3.83) by the average area of properties for which area is indicated (10.62 hectares). Value is indicated for almost all cases, averaging $796.57. This information, like other data in this section unless otherwise stated, is derived from statistical analysis of the 629 probate cases for this period, listed under primary sources.

only one or two properties, and few with more than five. Of course, this would not indicate a similar degree of landholding concentration, unless it were associated with a comparable inequality in the distribution of area and value of the land, but this does seem to be the case here.[54]

In almost two thirds of the cases, households had less than ten hectares, and often tiny plots of land. About 15% owned ten to less than twenty-five hectares, only 8% were close to the average, and just over one tenth had fifty hectares or more. About half of these last cases included less than a hundred hectares, and almost all the rest owned less than five hundred. The largest total property in the province was 1,500 hectares.[55] We know, too, that very small farms were almost certainly under-represented in probate inventories. A vast majority of units, then, owned less than the average, and only a few had relatively large estates. Even these were usually not much larger than coffee-producing estates in the Meseta Central at the time, and they were much smaller than many Brazilian *fazendas* or their Mexican, Andean and Central American equivalents.

Regarding value of property per case there was an acute polarization within the landholding population. In most instances (54.5%), land was estimated at less than $1,000, with a predominance of values under $500, certainly a modest sum at the turn of the century. One third of all cases included intermediate estimates of $1,000 to less than $5,000. A few had land estimated at much higher values, up to $147,000, quite a sizeable fortune at the time in terms of land ownership.

With the exception of negative fortunes, where indebtedness cancelled out sizeable holdings, there was a generally positive association between level of wealth, on the one hand, and number of properties and area on the other (Table 5.11). Fortunes under $1,000 usually had one to three properties, with a total area no larger than ten hectares. At higher levels of wealth, individual properties were more numerous and also larger.

---

54 The following analysis refers only to private property, not to other forms of land tenure. Nor was it possible, for lack of appropriate sources, to study the various types of usufruct, such as land rental and sharecropping, or de facto occupation of the land, later legalized by *información posesoria* (a legal procedure involving witnesses, to claim possession) or other means.

55 As mentioned in a note above, area was not stated for all individual properties. Yet even if we increase areas by 25% for all cases, two thirds of them had less than thirteen hectares, and the largest was under 1,900 hectares.

TABLE 5.11 AVERAGE NUMBER, AREA AND VALUE OF PROPERTIES PER CASE, BY LEVEL OF WEALTH IN PROBATE INVENTORIES, ALAJUELA PROVINCE, 1895-1904

Level of Fortune ($ or ¢)	**Average**		
	NUMBER OF PROPERTIES	TOTAL AREA (HAS.)	TOTAL VALUE ($ OR ¢)
Negative	4.1	79.3	265
0 - < 100	1.0	8.4	295
100 - < 5000	1.8	3.6	167
500 - < 1,000	2.8	10.0	299
1,000 - < 5,000	4.6	23.5	506
5,000 - < 10,000	7.0	65.4	832
≥ 10,000	12.5	190.6	2,257

Source: Probate inventories for 1895 - 1904.

Household units in Alajuela province, insofar as they were represented in probate inventories, were far from homogeneous regarding any of the abovementioned variables. In fact, one fifth of them were actually not domestic units proper, but rather sub-family economic units, since their holding was basically the site of a house and, sometimes, a tiny plot of land, uncultivated or for marginal economic activities. There was, as discussed previously, a growing landless population, absent from probate inventories. At the other extreme of Alajuelan society, there were cases such as that of José Luis Vasco y Garita, the owner of thirty properties, estimated at close to 140,000 *colones*, with an area of about two hundred and fifty rather intensively-cultivated hectares in the vicinity of the provincial capital.[56]

There were also several regional differences regarding these variables within the province of Alajuela. There were more individual farms per case in the Northwest than near the town of Alajuela (4.1 vs. 3.5); the total area per case was also greater in the northwestern cases (39.5 vs. 24.8 hectares), and average value was also higher ($809 vs. $577). In the area of late-nineteenth-century settlement beyond the Central Valley, in the northern part of the province, farms were usually larger, but the price of land was lower, so that average values were similar to those in the Northwest.

What has been said about landownership in the three regions is an indication of variations associated with successive stages and changing local conditions during the process of colonization. At mid-century, this movement was from the Meseta Central toward the Northwest, and by the turn of the century had begun to open up new areas beyond the Central

56 Archivo Nacional, Juzgado Civil, Doc. #803.

Valley, as in San Carlos. Of course, emigration from the vicinity of Alajuela and other parts of the Meseta was not only toward the Northwest, nor did emigrants from the latter area settle only in the northern part of Alajuela province. Nevertheless, spatial and generational continuities allow us to consider the movement of settlers along this route as part of an ongoing process which began in Colonial times and would continue well into the twentieth century. In the late nineteenth century, the Northwest was clearly in an intermediate situation, historically and geographically, between late Colonial patterns of migration within the Meseta, and settlement on the periphery of Costa Rica, typical of more recent times.

Productive Units

These may now be discussed in terms of an initial distinction by area of landholding per case, subject to certain qualifications which will be explained where relevant. First and foremost among these is the obvious insufficiency of a single variable to appropriately classify economic units with respect to a more complex typology such as that set forth in Chapter 2. However, just as level of wealth was more appropriate than farm area for the mid-nineteenth century, primarily due to relative quality of the information, landholding was the most adequate variable for a preliminary categorization of probate cases in 1895-1904, when value of immovables as well as movables was reported much less accurately than area.[57] Landownership was not necessarily the equivalent of total land available to household members (which could vary with temporary arrangements), but it did establish the stable, inheritable basis of household access to land.

As a starting point for the comparative characterization of productive units, the following breakpoints were defined regarding total farm area per case: one, five, twenty-five and fifty hectares. Criteria for these dividers was potential labor absorption of land under intensive use, with respect to an average household during the latter part of the nineteenth century.[58]

57 As probate proceedings became lengthier and more costly for the prospective heirs, agreements with the appraisers to lower the estimates became more frequent. On the other hand, establishment of the *Registro de la Propiedad*, together with the smaller size of holdings and the fact that most farms were no longer in areas of recent settlement, resulted in the area being reported much more frequently and accurately. The above distinction was confirmed by extensive follow-up of specific probate cases in the real estate registry.

58 Household size and composition have already been outlined in a previous section. Regarding productive potential of the land, intensive use was defined as specialized coffee production, with a relatively high density (1,704 coffee trees per hectare). According to contemporary testimony and more recent studies of untechnified farms (Fernández, 1984, p. 142) one man could care for 5,000 coffee trees or 2.93 hectares during the year, except for harvest time. A household with labor capacity of 1.9 adults (Samper, 1985, pp. 65 and 85-86) could care for 5.57 hectares of coffee trees. Under one hectare, less than a third of the labor capacity of such a household could

While the five resulting categories were conceived in terms of the proposed typology, three additional breakpoints were required to facilitate statistical analysis: one tenth of a hectare, ten hectares, and one hundred hectares.

As a working hypothesis, holdings under one hectare were associated, in a preliminary manner, to sub-family units and those under five to deficit-yielding domestic units. When properties added up to fifty hectares or more, the unit was hypothetically considered a supra-family one, and down to twenty-five hectares a surplus-yielding domestic unit. By elimination, those from five to under twenty-five hectares might be classified preliminarily as intermediate domestic units, but actual land use would no doubt introduce major variations: specialized coffee farms over ten hectares would probably be surplus-producing units, while more extensive uses on smaller areas could mean that they were deficit-yielding domestic units.

While a number of individual cases would undoubtably differ from any such classification, due to household size and composition as well as specific forms of land tenure and land use, farm area does provide a useful preliminary classification for relatively large groups. Detailed case analysis and the discussion of other variables will help to overcome some of the inherent limitations of this approach. At this point, a descriptive characterization of units falling within each area category will show both the usefulness and the shortcomings of our initial criterion.

TABLE 5.12 NUMBER OF INDIVIDUAL PROPERTIES PER CASE IN PROBATE INVENTORIES, BY TOTAL AREA OF HOLDINGS, ALAJUELA PROVINCE, 1895-1904

Area (Has.)	Number of Properties	Number of Cases		
	AVERAGE	MINIMUM	MAXIMUM	
< 1	1.6	0	16	219
1 - < 5	2.5	1	11	113
5 - < 10	3.9	1	36	76
10 - < 25	4.7	1	22	96
25 - < 50	6.6	1	19	52
50 - < 100	7.6	1	48	35
≥ 100	11.0	1	30	38

Source: Probate inventories for 1895 - 1904.

be employed in intensive agriculture. From twenty-two to twenty-eight hectares in coffee, the same amount of family labor would be only one fourth to one fifth of total labor required for permanent care of a coffee plantation that size. And a fifty or fifty-five hectare coffee farm would need ten times more regular labor than the previously defined household labor. For a more detailed discussion of these points, see Samper (1987).

TABLE 5.13 TOTAL VALUE OF PROPERTIES PER CASE, BY AREA IN PROBATE INVENTORIES, ALAJUELA PROVINCE, 1895-1904

Area (Has.)	Value ($ or ¢)			Number of Cases
	AVERAGE	MINIMUM	MAXIMUM	
<1	536	0	4,800	219
1 - < 5	1,042	0	10,750	113
5 - < 10	2,358	0	18,950	76
10 - < 25	2,786	0	38,700	96
25 - < 50	4,36	0	48,020	52
50 - < 100	4,703	450	30,250	35
≥ 100	21,849	0	147,500	38

Source: Probate inventories for 1895 - 1904.

TABLE 5.14 FREQUENCY OF LAND USE PER CASE, BY TOTAL AREA IN PROBATE INVENTORIES, ALAJUELA PROVINCE, 1895-1904

Area (Has.)	Average Frequency of Each Use						
	COFFEE	SUGAR-CANE	PASTURE	GRAIN	UNCULTIVATED	HOUSE	OTHER
< 1	0.4	0.2	0.3	0.3	0.3	0.6	0.1
1 < 5	0.8	0.7	0.8	0.6	0.5	0.7	0.2
5 - < 10	0.9	0.8	1.4	1.1	0.9	0.8	0.3
10 - < 25	1.0	1.0	2.0	1.2	1.4	0.8	0.2
25 - < 50	1.4	1.2	2.1	1.4	1.9	1.2	0.5
50 - < 100	1.9	1.2	3.1	1.7	2.3	1.4	0.7
≥ 100	2.3	1.6	4.8	1.6	3.3	2.1	0.6

Source: Probate inventories for 1895 - 1904.

In cases with less than one hectare (219 cases, or just under a third) there were usually one or two properties, with total value averaging about $500, though it could vary from minimal amounts to almost ten times more, primarily due to cost of buildings on small plots of land. The main productive use of these parcels was no doubt coffee, followed by pasture, grain and sugarcane, in that order (Tables 5.12 to 5.14, which provide data for the other four main categories too). Households in slightly over half the cases included in this category owned less than one tenth of a hectare, and productive use of such tiny lots was minimal or nonexistent. In the remaining cases, specialization in coffee can be related to intensification of land use on micro-farms, but also to a tendency toward greater fragmentation of coffee plantations than, for example, pastures.

TABLE 5.15 PERSONAL DATA AND ASSETS PER CASE, BY AREA OF LANDHOLDING IN PROBATE INVENTORIES, ALAJUELA PROVINCE, 1895-1904

Personal Data

Area (Has.)	Avg. Age	% Male	Place of Residence		# of Heirs	# of Cases
			CAPITAL*	NORTHWEST		
<.1	39.9	48.1	57.0	25.8	3.5	126
.1 - < 1	47.1	48.4	69.4	20.8	4.1	93
1 < 5	47.8	49.6	56.3	25.3	4.9	113
5 - < 10	48.9	67.1	42.2	40.6	5.0	76
10 - < 25	49.1	60.4	43.9	42.6	5.3	96
25 - < 50	51.0	61.5	29.2	47.9	6.3	52
50 - < 100	50.7	68.6	26.7	43.3	7.9	35
≥ 100	53.9	73.7	34.4	50.0	7.3	38

Assets

Area (Has.)	# of Properties	Value ($ or ¢)			
		PROPERTIES	MOVABLES	CREDIT	FORTUNE
<.1	1.5	466	63	91	621
.1 - < 1	1.8	631	63	115	809
1 < 5	2.5	1,042	80	-44	1,077
5 - < 10	4.0	2,358	188	-148	2,399
10 - < 25	4.7	2,758	448	-346	2,888
25 - < 50	6.6	4,435	550	-172	4,813
50 - < 100	7.6	4,703	757	108	6,535
≥ 100	11.0	21,850	1,061	-106	21,847

* Alajuela city and surrounding cantones.

Source: Probate inventories for 1895 - 1904.

Households with plots under one hectare also had little movable wealth, though usually they had more credits than debts. Micro-farms were strongly concentrated in the vicinity of the provincial capital, and there were few such units in the Northwest. In terms of distribution by sex, there was a balance between men and women among the deceased with small properties, although a slight predominance of the latter might be related to their receiving inheritance rights to houses more often than their brothers and husbands. The deceased in this category, and especially those owning less than a tenth of a hectare, were younger than those whose properties fell under other categories (Table 5.15). Households owning under one hectare tended to have less heirs than households with more land, but they usually had four to five members. Despite intensive land use, their tiny plot could absorb only a minimal part of family labor, and satisfy only a fraction of the household's consumption needs, while in cases with less than a tenth of a hectare their agricultural activities were insignificant or non-existent. Specific examples of each of these two situations may now be examined.

Narcisa Morera Gutiérrez, a forty-year-old widow, died in Concepción, near Alajuela city, in 1893. She owned three tiny plots in the same area, described as follows in the probate inventory:[59] a house and lot with some coffee and other trees, on an area six by forty-one meters, estimated at $150; another parcel with coffee, eight by forty-one meters, worth $90; and a strip of uncultivated land, one by forty-one meters, $10. Clearly, these were the minute remnants of a larger holding, fragmented by inheritance over successive generations. Doña Narcisa's movables, according to the inventory, included some humble furniture and household goods, estimated at $21. Her property was auctioned off, as it would have been absurd to subdivide it further among her six children, and the $300 product was used to cover expenses. The holding, with less than five hundred square meters in coffee, was certainly not a viable, household productive unit.

Margarita Hernández Acuña, also a widow, died at the age of sixty in Desamparados de Alajuela, near the provincial capital, in 1885, although this probate case was dated ten years later. Her six children were to receive inheritance rights on a one-hectare plot and house, estimated at $720.[60] According to the inventory, the land was uncultivated, but one of the prospective heirs claims that it was cultivated in sugarcane, maize, beans and pasture (all of this in one hectare!). Part of the land had been rented out for others to plant grain, and there were bitter complaints that the executor was receiving undeclared income from such rentals and from sugarcane harvests. The lawyer was also accused of delaying the legal process to make prospective heirs sell him their inheritance rights. The son who filed this complaint, in turn, acquired the rights of two of his brothers, while another two sold theirs to a third party. Apparently, there was ongoing conflict over control of inheritance rights and an attempt to bring several of these together, given the prospect of extreme fragmentation of an already minute productive unit.

In the following category (i.e. cases with areas from one to under five hectares; 113 cases, or 18%), households usually owned two or three properties, with an average value of some $1,000, although this figure too could be minimal or tenfold. Coffee and livestock raising were the most frequent uses of the land in such cases. There were also sugarcane and maize fields. Land use was often diversified, and less intensive than on the the micro-farms described above.

---

59 Archivo Nacional, Alcaldía Segunda, Alajuela, Doc. #932.

60 Archivo Nacional, Alcaldía Primera, Alajuela, Doc. #450.

Movables were a very modest part of these relatively small household units, which like the sub-family farms above tended to be in the vicinity of Alajuela city. Credit balances were usually negative, though for small amounts. There were almost exactly the same number of men and women among the deceased in this category, and they tended to be rather young. Families in this category had, on the average, about five prospective heirs. The following examples will give an idea of why these are considered, with some possible exceptions, deficit-yielding domestic units.

Feliciana Alvarez Solórzano, dead at age 45 in San José de Alajuela, was survived by her husband and four children. They owned two small, adjacent farms, estimated together at $325.[61] Each was two hectares in size. One had coffee, pasture and a house, the other mostly sugarcane. The couple also owned two cows, but no other goods were included in the inventory. On a very small scale, this was a diversified productive unit, and judging by land use, production must have been partly for direct consumption, partly for sale. Yet the labor of such a household could hardly be occupied completely on their farm, nor would output fully satisfy family consumption requirements.

Simona Sanabria Herrera, a resident of Sarchí Sur, was fifty years old when she died at the turn of the century, and she left seven children.[62] She and her late husband had owned three small farms: one just under a hectare, with pasture, coffee and sugarcane, was worth $200 in the inventory; another was 1.2 hectares in size, with coffee and a house, estimated at $400; the third one was 4.8 hectares, with sugarcane, pasture and an uncultivated area, worth $1,200 in the original estimate. Part of this land was sold during the probate process, at less than the original value, perhaps due to the economic crisis of the time which depressed the land market.[63] Doña Simona and her husband owed $67 for merchandise, but no movables were included in the inventory. Each descendant received $78 inheritance, but at least one of them had sold her rights to a third party before the legal procedure was completed. Sale of property and hereditary rights would seem to indicate that actual subdivision of the land among all heirs was not necessarily perceived as the unavoidable or even the desirable outcome of inheritance procedures.

While many cases were similar to the example above, those with just over a hectare or with non-intensive land use on larger areas within this category were probably closer to being sub-family units, while highly specialized coffee farms near the upper limit were akin to intermediate domestic units, which will be discussed below.

---

61 Archivo Nacional, Alcaldía Primera, Alajuela, Doc. #300.

62 Archivo Nacional, Alcaldía Unica, Grecia, Doc. #825.

63 The turn-of-the-century crisis, which began, for coffee-producing nations, in 1896 with massive over-production by Brazil, was compounded by the international economic crisis, which became acute and widespread as of 1900.

In cases with declared areas from five to twenty-five hectares (172, or 27%), there were usually four to five properties, although their number might reach up to thirty-six very small plots of land. Their total value varied quite significantly, depending on exact area, location, quality of soil, type of land use and other factors. Average value was about $2,500, but uncultivated lands could have minimal values, while a well-developed, intensive-use farm was worth $38,000, not a modest amount at the time. The most frequent use of the land was pasture, followed by grain, coffee and sugarcane, in that order. Uncultivated areas were more frequent in the larger units within this category, but the proportions of other uses were quite similar in those above or below ten hectares. The basic difference, which made overall land use more intensive on the smaller units of this category, was the fact that they had less uncultivated land. Many of the individual cases had similar uses, and can be characterized as intermediate domestic units. Some small units with extensive land use patterns might have been deficit-yielding, while a few larger units with rather intensive land use should probably be considered surplus-producing domestic units or supra-family units.[64] In any case, intermediate domestic units tended to be relatively unstable as such, and were affected not only by market factors and technological transformations, but also by the changing mix of material resources, labor capacity and consumption requirements during the household life-cycle.

Owners of more than ten hectares within this category usually had more movable assets, yet they also had more debts. Cases above and below the ten-hectare subdivider were almost equally distributed in the Northwest and near the provincial capital, reflecting the importance of medium-sized units in the more recently settled area. Age and number of heirs were also somewhat higher than in the previous categories, yet the increase in probable household size was far from compensating for larger average tenure.[65] Distribution by sex was heavily weighted toward males in both categories, suggesting some type of exclusion of women from substantial property ownership. We see, then, that whatever legal or extra-legal mechanisms tended to compensate for subdivision of holdings, their effect was biased against female ownership and inheritance of land. Let us

---

64 A 25-hectare coffee farm would use four times the average labor capacity of households in the region. In cases with relatively intensive land use on farms estimated at 20 to 25 hectares, but with unrecorded areas for one or more properties, actual size may have been larger and they would certainly fit into the upper category. However, in most cases there was more uncultivated land on the larger properties. When landuse was very extensive or property belonged to very large families, even areas greater than 25 hectares may have been intermediate domestic units.

65 Furthermore, number of children only indicated maximum household size when they were of age, since they usually established their own independent households upon marriage.

now give a couple of examples of actual productive units in the intermediate landholding category we referred to above.

In Santa Gertrudis de Grecia, also in the Northwest, Jacinto Araya Avendaño and his wife owned two seven-hectare farms, estimated at just under $2,000.[66] The first farm was divided into five plots: one with the house and a small pasture; the second planted in sugarcane, coffee and pasture; the third only in coffee, the fourth only in sugarcane, and the fifth in pasture and sugarcane. All five were sold to third parties during the probate process. The second farm included pasture and uncultivated land, and was said to have been sold several years after don Jacinto's demise, but before the probate case was opened upon the death of his widow. No movables were inventoried, but there was a $36 credit as well as five debts, for a sum of $144. Two of the four children had also received advances on inheritance, and one of these, apparently the older son, received $200 preferential inheritance. In this case, the elderly widow apparently began to reduce the size of the holding, both by sale and donation, perhaps to ensure her own care in coming years. In any case, it probably had been a rather typical intermediate domestic unit some time before.

Josefa Soto Madrigal, dead at age thirty-five, owned six separate farms together with her husband in the area of Naranjo, adding up to seven hectares and an estimated value just over $300.[67] Three of the plots had coffee, but pasture was equally frequent, and there was also a maizefield and some uncultivated land. They owned some livestock: three cows, an ox, four other head of cattle and a colt, altogether worth $94. Their movables were very few, an oxcart and some humble furniture, estimated at only $5. The couple had one child, a young girl, and the holding was probably more than sufficient for such a small household, though as more children were born their consumption needs would have increased, and later on the family's labor capacity.

Clearly, the opportunities for either simple or expanded reproduction of economic units in this specific category, as well as the risk of downward social mobility for their members, were strongly associated to ongoing processes of socioeconomic differentiation, in turn related to changing internal conditions (e.g. household size and composition vis-a-vis material resources) and external factors, such as the price of various commodities.

In somewhat larger units with twenty-five to under fifty hectares (52 cases, or 8%), there were often six or seven individual properties, and in one case up to nineteen. Their total estimated value averaged some $4,500, though it could be ten times more, or considerably less. Regarding land use, there was a predominance of pasture, followed by grain and coffee, with sugarcane being somewhat less frequent. Uncultivated lands were clearly more important than in the previous category. Specific cases with high values, large areas and intensive land use were not domestic units at

66 Archivo Nacional, Alcaldía Unica, Grecia, Doc. #4.

67 Archivo Nacional, Alcaldía Unica, Naranjo, Doc. #532.

all, but they were exceptional due to the more extensive use of land on most holdings in the 25 to 50 hectare range.

Average value of movables in this category was somewhat higher than in units with 10 to under 25 hectares, while indebtedness tended to be lower. The difference in total wealth was, therefore, greater than that in value of immovables. These larger landholding units (25 to 50 ha.) were concentrated in the Northwest, and as in the previous category there was a strong predominance of men among the deceased in these cases. They were also older than the average case, and had more heirs, though not all were their children. Again, household size had something to do with landownership, but average area of holdings grew much more rapidly than the number of heirs from one category to the next. The two cases below illustrate the situation on some of the smaller and larger property units within the category we are dealing with here.

José Alfaro Hidalgo and his wife died in their seventies, and their heirs were four children, two grandchildren and two other persons specified in the will.[68] They owned four variously-sized farms: two small plots planted to coffee, adding up to less than two hectares and $650, house included; a five-hectare pasture, worth $450, and a twenty-two-hectare land claim, part of a larger one made some time before together with other relatives. No use is specified for this land, but we can assume that it was uncultivated or, anyhow, quite extensive in terms of land use. The deceased couple had three debts, for a sum of $890, and movables worth almost $400. These included a few head of cattle, agricultural implements, construction materials, household goods, clothing and assorted items. The description of durable consumption goods in the inventory establishes, on the one hand, that the elderly couple had a higher standard of living than most peasant households but, on the other hand, it was well below the consumption patterns of the wealthy elite.

Mercedes Castro Arrostigui and her husband owned four farms in Concepción del Naranjo, when she died at age 45 in 1899.[69] Only the smallest one, 2.7 hectares, was planted in coffee, estimated at $600. A 5.8 hectare farm was in sugarcane and pasture, worth $1,000 in the inventory. The two larger farms, 17.8 and 22 hectares in size, combined pasture and uncultivated land, but one of them was in San Mateo, a cantón which is not part of the Northwest proper. The couple owed $1,800 to several creditors, and owned three houses, as well as some furniture and probably other household goods, which added up to $192. They had eight children, most of whom still lived with their parents. Since several were of working age, labor capacity of this household was above average, but was still insufficient to satisfy all labor and consumption requirements of the household units described above. Some wage labor or other working arrangement was certainly necessary, though only a more intensive use of

68 Archivo Nacional, Alcaldía Unica, Grecia, Doc. #201.

69 Archivo Nacional, Alcaldía Unica, Naranjo, Doc. #498.

the land would have made a large number of regular employees indispensable. It would probably be safe to consider this economic unit, as well as the previous one, a surplus-producing domestic unit, yet one with a potential to become a supra-family unit through more labor-intensive land use patterns.

In unit sizes above 50 hectares, the number of properties as well as their area and average value grew rapidly in the seventy-three cases thus classified (11.6% of all cases). To avoid fictitious averages within this broad category, a 100-hectare subdivider was applied to establish two subgroups. From fifty to under one hundred hectares, there were usually seven to eight properties, with an average value of some $4,700. Larger units often had about eleven individual farms, with an average total value of over $21,000.[70]

As far as land use is concerned, there was a very strong predominance of pasture, followed by uncultivated land, in both subgroups. Coffee was the most frequent crop in both, while grain gave way to sugarcane at larger areas. Except for a few cases with very extensive uses on property just above the fifty-hectare divider, most units falling in this category can be considered supra-family ones. It would seem convenient to distinguish between medium-sized enterprises (mostly from 50 to under one hundred hectares), in which household labor might yet be present despite a clear predominance of non-family workers, and the larger enterprises, often belonging to absentee landowners with hired administrators and no productive family labor in most cases.

The value of movables was notably higher in cases with more than fifty and, especially, one hundred hectares, as compared to units with less land. As in the previous two categories, there was strong regional concentration in the Northwest, and an even stronger predominance of men among the deceased, reflecting systematic exclusion of women from large-scale landownership in wealthy Alajuelan families. Age at time of death was especially high among those owning more than one hundred hectares, a feature associated with accumulation of property during their lifetimes. There were more heirs in probate cases with over fifty hectares of land, but this was only partly due to family size, as non-children inherited more often than in land-poor families. Our last two examples are of landholding units in the lower and upper subgroups of this category.

Aurora Rodríguez Rodríguez and her husband owned nine farms in San Ramón, for a total area of approximately sixty-eight hectares.[71] The value of these properties totalled $5,680. References to land use were quite varied. Almost all the smaller properties had coffee, but some of them also had grain and sugarcane; the larger farms were either pastures or

70 In the second subgroup there was one case with an unrealistic, minimal estimated value for large holdings, so the true average must have been even higher.

71 Archivo Nacional, Juzgado Civil, San Ramón, Doc. #194. A relatively small but undefined area would have to be added, for an inheritance right worth $147.

uncultivated. The couple also owned a *trapiche* for processing sugarcane, 19 head of cattle, three horses, and four oxcarts, altogether worth $442. While most domestic units did not have such equipment, the combination of extensive and intensive land use places this unit close to the limit between supra-family and surplus-producing domestic units. The widow received under forty hectares, and each child one fifth that amount. In this case, unless household members had access to lands elsewhere, inheritance broke down a larger productive unit into several medium-sized farms which might be considered domestic units.

A second case is that of Isidoro Soto Ramírez, who died in Paris, at age forty-eight. At that time, he was the absentee owner of close to eight hundred hectares in Alajuela province, with an estimated value of $70,000.[72] His sixteen properties, including six houses, were located mostly in or near the city, although the largest farm (678 hectares) was in Buena Vista de Naranjo. Only two very small properties had coffee, and pasture was clearly the main productive use of the land. There were also several uncultivated properties. Movables were estimated at $1,732. Household goods, including fine dinnerware, jewelry, a piano and even two spittoons, were those of the wealthiest among the local elite, and his European demise, itself, sets don Isidoro in the uppermost stratum of Alajuelan society.

The foregoing statistical and case analysis generally confirms both the validity and the limitations of land tenure as a criterion to typify productive units in the region at the turn of the century. Clear associations were found between area, value and land use, despite some overlapping of categories especially at the higher levels. A more general analysis allows us to say that grazing was the most frequent type of land use on productive units in Alajuela, followed by uncultivated land, coffee, grain and sugarcane in that order.[73] So, actually, land use was diversified rather than specialized in the province as a whole.

By region, pasture was predominant both in the Northwest and near the capital, though less strongly than half a century before (Table 5.16). On productive units with cattle, herd size was almost three times larger in the former region than in the latter, though generally smaller than in the mid-nineteenth century.[74] Regarding agriculture proper, grain production was more frequent than coffee or any other use near Alajuela city, while coffee was the most important agricultural activity in the Northwest. Outside the

---

72 Archivo Nacional, Juzgado Civil, Alajuela, Doc. #904.

73 The average number of properties with each type of landuse per case, in the 1895-1904 probate inventories, was: coffee 0.9; sugarcane 0.7; pasture 1.4; grain 0.8; and uncultivated 1.0. This information can be compared to that in note 43 of Chapter 4.

74 Herd size in the Northwest was 2.8 times that near Alajuela city. Average size of cattle herds per case was only 1.7, with a maximum of 78 head of cattle (1.63 near the provincial capital, 4.72 in the Northwest).

Central Valley, on the agricultural frontier, there was doubtless a predominance of uncultivated land, livestock raising and small-scale grain production.

TABLE 5.16 FREQUENCY OF EACH TYPE OF LAND USE, BY PLACE OF RESIDENCE OF DECEASED, ALAJUELA PROVINCE, 1895-1904

Land Use	Average per Case		Total Frequency	
	CAPITAL*	NORTHWEST**	CAPITAL*	NORTHWEST**
Coffee	0.75	1.29	188	230
Sugarcane	0.57	0.91	142	162
Pasture	1.27	1.53	316	272
Grain	0.99	0.62	247	111
Uncultivated	0.77	1.28	192	228
Dwelling	0.83	0.78	207	139
Other	0.19	0.32	48	57

* Alajuela city and surrounding cantones.
** Cantones of the northwestern Central Valley.

Source: Probate inventories for 1895 - 1904.

TABLE 5.17 INDIVIDUAL FARMS WITH INDICATION OF LAND USE* IN PROBATE INVENTORIES, ALAJUELA PROVINCE, 1895-1904

Land Use	Affirmative Indication		Negative Indication	
	#	%	#	%
Coffee	575	30.5	1,313	69.5
Sugarcane	442	23.5	1,441	76.5
Pasture	978	50.8	947	49.2
Grain	520	25.8	1,494	74.2
Uncultivated	623	32.4	1,298	67.6
Dwelling	533	26.5	1,479	73.5
Other	169	9.0	1,717	91.0

*Whether or not in association with other uses of the land.

Source: Probate inventories for 1895 - 1904.

At an individual property level, we find that there were pastures on more than half the farms in probate cases for 1895-1904, and that pastures were much more frequent than any other use of the land (Table 5.17). The number of pastures had more than doubled as compared to the mid-nineteenth century, even though in relative terms there was a slight reduction. In contrast to the situation half a century before, coffee cultivation had become the main agricultural use of the land on individual farms, followed by grain, whose absolute and relative importance also increased considerably with respect to the 1850s. Sugarcane continued to be a significant crop, on one out of every four properties, and a third of all individual farms had uncultivated land. While agro-export expansion had undoubtedly affected many farms, Alajuela was a long distance from single-crop specialization.

TABLE 5.18 AREA AND VALUE OF HOLDINGS ACCORDING TO AGRARIAN LAND USE* IN PROBATE INVENTORIES, ALAJUELA PROVINCE, 1895-1904

Land Use	Area (Has.)		Value ($ or ¢)		Indications of		
	AVG.	MAX.	AVG.	MAX.	USE	AREA	VALUE
Coffee	4.5	140	1,249	75,500	575	454	569
Sugarcane	5.4	90	1,066	30,000	442	344	435
Pasture	11.8	406	1,156	75,500	978	764	964
Grain	9.9	400	691	20,000	520	401	514
Uncultivated	20.1	409	992	26,800	623	473	618
Other	9.5	80	1,542	28,920	169	116	165
All	10.6	1,500	797	75,500	2,417	1,743	2,396

*Whether or not in association with other uses of the land.

Source: Probate inventories for 1895 - 1904.

Generally speaking, farms were smaller in 1895-1904 than half a century earlier, but this reduction did not affect all uses of the land equally. By size and value of properties, sugarcane continued to be associated with relatively small farms. Grain, pasture and secondary uses were often on farms with intermediate areas. Only uncultivated land was most frequently found on relatively large farms (Table 5.18). The most interesting change was on farms with coffee, a crop which had been associated to the largest farms in the 1850's, and at the turn of the century was on the smallest ones instead, averaging 4.5 hectares. This is not to say that there were no intermediate-to-large cofee farms, but even maximum areas of farms with coffee were significantly lower than most other uses. Participation of smallholders in the regional expansion of coffee after mid-century and greater fragmentation of coffee farms are among the explanatory factors which need be considered.

However, the smaller average size of farms with coffee groves was more than compensated for by the high price of such lands. In 1895-1904, small farms with coffee plantations were the most valuable properties.[75] On farms with sugarcane, pasture and non-cultivated parts, area and intensity of land use balanced-off to produce roughly similar values. Grain, instead, was associated with the least valuable farms (Table 5.18).

75 In "other uses", infrastructure and installations altered land value, and in all uses there were greater variations in value than in area.

TABLE 5.19 FREQUENCY OF AGRARIAN LAND USE ON INDIVIDUAL FARMS, BY NUMBER OF USES IN PROBATE INVENTORIES, ALAJUELA PROVINCE, 1895-1904

# of Cases	Coffee		Sugarcane		Pasture		Grain		Uncultivated		Other		Total
	#	%	#	%	#	%	#	%	#	%	#	%	#
1	244	21.7	86	7.7	323	28.7	245	21.7	218	19.4	10	0.9	1,126
2	171	13.8	159	12.8	409	33.0	156	12.6	277	22.4	66	5.3	1,238
3 +	160	17.0	197	20.9	246	26.1	119	12.6	128	13.6	93	9.9	943

Source: Probate inventories for 1895 - 1904.

Certainly, coffee plantations required a greater investment than other crops, but this was compounded by an objective and subjective valuation of coffee as probably the most profitable economic activity. The question remains as to why land use patterns remained more diverse in the Northwest than the Meseta Central, and whether specialization in coffee production would continue in the following decades.

Whatever the reason, landscape in Alajuela province, and specifically in the Northwest, was far from homogeneous, and individual farms reflected this diversity. Pasture predominated on single, double and multiple-use farms, but in combination with various agricultural uses. Coffee was quite important all three types of farms, but grain was more frequent on single-use properties, and sugarcane on multiple-use ones (Table 5.19). In terms of crop combinations, pasture was associated either to coffee and sugarcane, on the more intensive and market-oriented farms, or to uncultivated land and maize on the more extensive ones (Table 5.20). Both triads were present in the main regions of the province, even though coffee cultivation was of course less frequent outside the Central Valley.[76] Overall land use patterns on individual farms situate the local expansion of coffee cultivation in the context of a highly diversified agrarian economy, where livestock raising and other crops were far from disappearing.

TABLE 5.20 CROP ASSOCIATION ON INDIVIDUAL PROPERTIES, ACCORDING TO SELECTED LAND USE, PROBATE INVENTORIES OF ALAJUELA PROVINCE, 1895-1904

Associated Uses	Selected Uses									
	COFFEE		SUGARCANE		PASTURE		GRAIN		UNCULTIVATED	
	#	%	#	%	#	%	#	%	#	%
Coffee	-	-	176	40.1	185	19.7	55	14.2	61	10.5
Sugarcane	176	31.0	-	-	253	27.0	62	16.1	67	11.5
Pasture	185	32.5	253	57.4	-	-	173	41.9	301	50.7
Grain	55	9.7	62	14.2	173	18.0	-	-	131	21.4
Uncultivated	61	10.8	67	15.3	301	31.8	131	31.5	-	-

Source: Probate inventories for 1895 - 1904.

76 In the cantons near Alajuela, coffee was associated most often with pasture (on 77 individual properties) and sugarcane (on 70 such properties), but much less frequently with grain (on 22 individual farms) and uncultivated land (on 17). The situation was similar in the Northwestern section of the Central Valley: coffee was associated on 78 farms with sugarcane and on 74 with pasture, and only on 21 with grain and on 29 with uncultivated land). Instead, coffee in other parts of the province (Atenas, San Mateo, Zarcero, San Carlos and Upala) was associated with pasture on 22 farms, sugarcane on 15, grain on 5, and uncultivated land on 7.

Regionally, coffee production was most frequent in the Northwest, where it was planted on 40% of the properties, though most often in association with other uses.[77] Maize production, instead, was especially important in the cantones near Alajuela, where there were more grain farms than coffee groves, and twice as many maizefields as in the Northwest.[78] This clearly invalidates the usual image of coffee displacing maize, e.g. from the area of Alajuela within the Meseta toward the western end of the Central Valley. It also points to the commercial nature of much grain production, in a similar process to that which had taken place half a century before in Heredia, when, so to speak, "the maize ate up the cows" to supply a growing demand in more specialized agro-export areas.[79] Finally, it indicates that land use patterns were diverse not only at a case level, but also geographically and on individual farms.

Regarding on-farm productive diversity, the number of agrarian uses of the land per individual farm in 1895-1904 was linked to larger areas and higher values.[80] Paradoxically, agricultural diversification during the latter part of the nineteenth century was parallel to a considerable reduction of farm size. In the province as a whole, area of individual properties in probate inventories suffered a substantial decline, especially on single- and double-use farms. Value, instead, doubled in each category (Table 5.21).[81] Sub-regionally, smaller farms tended to be closer to the provincial capital, intermediate-sized ones in the Northwest, and the largest individual properties were more frequent on the turn-of-the-century settlement frontier, e.g. toward San Carlos, in the northern part of the province.[82] Given the association between farm size and number of uses of the land, productive diversity in areas of smallholding must be related to specialization of individual single-use farms in different crops.

---

77 In the Northwest, in 1895-1904, there was coffee on 39.3% of all individual properties in probate inventories; sugarcane on 35.8%, uncultivated land on 35.3%, pasture on 32.8% and grain on 22.6%. Two hundred and thirty properties had coffee in the Northwest, versus 188 in the area near the provincial capital.

78 In the cantons near the town of Alajuela, there was an average of one property per case with grain, versus .75 in coffee and .57 in sugarcane. Only pasture was more frequent, with 1.27 per case. Two hundred and forty-seven properties had grain in this area, versus one hundred and eleven in the Northwest.

79 See Alvarenga (1986), pp. 84-86.

80 Properties with no agrarian use, i.e. housing plots, broke this pattern due to the relatively high value of buildings.

81 See Chapter 4.

82 63.2% of properties under one hectare and 50.7% of those from one to less than five were in the counties of the area near Alajuela. These percentages declined to 45.1% of farms under 10 hectares, and 38.6% of those under 50 hectares, increasing proportionally in the Northwest. And only 28% of properties with an area of fifty hectares or larger were near the provincial capital, while they were especially important in other parts of the province.

TABLE 5.21 AREA AND VALUE OF INDIVIDUAL FARMS BY NUMBER OF AGRARIAN LAND USES IN PROBATE INVENTORIES, ALAJUELA PROVINCE, 1895-1904

Number of Uses	Area (Has.)		Value		Number of Cases
	AVG.	MAX.	AVG.	MAX.	
None	0.7	4	1,158	5,000	20
Single	6.1	409	509	10,000	1,126
Double	11.8	406	950	75,500	619
Multiple	14.8	400	1,822	30,000	282

Source: Probate inventories for 1895 - 1904.

Toward 1900, as in the mid-nineteenth century, most individual farms had only one type of agrarian use. Of these single-use properties, leaving aside the uncultivated ones, 37% were in pasture, one out of every four in grain, the same number in coffee, and one out of every ten in sugarcane (Table 5.22). Despite the predominance of pasture, the various agricultural activities corroborate the tendency toward parallel specializations on individual, single-use farms, rather than a strong dominance of coffee or any other crop.

Regionally, single-use maize and sugarcane farms tended to be near the provincial capital, while there was less such concentration in coffee, pasture and uncultivated farms.[83] Pasture was the most frequent use on single-use farms throughout the province, followed by grain in the vicinity of the capital, coffee in the Northwest, and uncultivated land elsewhere. These dyadic regional associations between pasture and one or another specific crop are the concise expression of interrelated agrarian transformations in each area from the time of initial settlement to the turn of the century.

At a more general level, the spatial distribution of land use patterns on all types of farms, in the context of a highly diversified agrarian economy, indicates certain important regional variations: there was maize production in all parts of the province, but it was especially important near the provincial capital as a market-oriented activity; coffee was most significant in the Northwest, though in combination with other crops; and uncultivated lands were found especially on the settlement frontier beyond the Central Valley. The common denominator and most extensive form of land use in all regions was livestock raising, but its relative importance had declined by comparison with the mid-nineteenth century.

83 The counties near Alajuela city included 71.5% of the single-use properties in grain, 68.3% of those in sugarcane, 55.9% of coffee farms, 51.9% of pasturelands, and 46.3% of uncultivated single-use farms. It should be noted that the term "single-use" excludes constructions.

TABLE 5.22 AREA AND VALUE OF SINGLE-USE FARMS, BY TYPE OF LAND USE IN PROBATE INVENTORIES, ALAJUELA PROVINCE, 1895-1904

Land Use	**Area (Has.)**		**Value ($ or ¢)**		**Indications of**		
	AVG.	MAX.	AVG.	MAX.	USE	AREA	VALUE
Coffee	0.8	34	581	10,000	244	184	244
Sugarcane	0.5	2	250	3,000	86	69	84
Pasture	4.8	125	578	7,800	323	266	320
Grain	2.7	36	285	2,400	245	192	244
Uncultivated	10.3	409	649	6,000	218	162	217
Other	7.5	45	1,074	5,790	10	7	10
All	6.1	409	509	10,000	1,126	880	1,119

Source: Probate inventories for 1895 - 1904.

The Northwest, specifically, was undergoing agrarian changes which involved a rapid intensification of land use, primarily through an expansion of coffee cultivation. However, this process in reality diversified local production during the latter part of the nineteenth century, rather than leading to specialization by the turn of the century.

Household Strategies

The organization of production on specific units was affected by macrosocial variables over which the individual households had no control, although the aggregate result of their decisions did affect the socioeconomic -and also sociopolitical- environment in many ways. The previous sections have portrayed demographic, economic and social transformations which are related to the development of a specific type of agrarian change or "transition" toward a fully commodified rural economy, in which owners of capital constitute a well-defined, dominant class and wage-labor becomes important, but a landholding, mercantile peasantry is actively involved in agro-export production and other market-oriented activities. In this, we find affinities with other Latin American cases which do not fill well into a "latifundia-minifundia" model, which leaves little room for smallholder entrepreneurship and is therefore useless to explain both the success of commercial peasant-farmers in establishing a hold on the lands and markets, and the dilemmas which they had to face.

In the Costa Rican case discussed here to 1900, agricultural settlement on a receding frontier and changes in both land tenure and land use were essential components of the broader social processes in which individual fortunes were made and lost, and in which rural households sought to adapt their productive and reproductive strategies to gradually deteriorating conditions for most of the population.

In the middle decades of the nineteenth century, as discussed earlier in this chapter, migration from the Meseta Central toward the Northwest was combined with natural population growth in the region to rapidly increase local population density. Even though immigration continued, there was (at least after 1880) a growing emigration from the Northwest toward other areas of settlement in the northern part of the country, in the highlands of Guanacaste, and elsewhere. At first, many members of this new generation of migrants were probably the descendants of successful settlers, seeking new opportunities to develop commercial agriculture in the newly-opened frontiers, rather than an impoverished rural population expelled by landlessness and in search of mere subsistence. The decision of certain household members to emigrate helped maintain the economic viability of domestic units in the region, though it could not avoid the gradual accumulation of social pressures in the region.

Toward the turn of the century, there was little unclaimed land in the Northwest, and local population growth had only been slowed down somewhat by emigration. While availability of labor allowed some large estates to become firmly established in the region, the landholding area of most productive units declined significantly. Land use was intensified, with greater investment of labor per surface area. Three interrelated processes defined the situation for rural households in the Northwest: fragmentation of property, primarily due to partible inheritance; gradual intensification of land use in terms of labor input; and emigration of certain members of domestic and sub-family units.

On the other hand, despite a more intensive use of the land which reduced the uncultivated areas and increased the relative participation of agriculture in total output, the Northwest and Alajuela province as a whole maintained a diversified agrarian economy. Both at a regional level and on most productive units, there was a combination of intensive, semi-intensive and extensive land use patterns. Proportions varied depending on specific local and on-farm conditions, especially more or less recent settlement; labor capacity vis-a-vis material resources; consumption requirements; and market ties.

Well-defined associations were found among a set of relevant variables: distance from the provincial capital and transportation routes; time of settlement; local population density; type and number of agrarian uses of the land; total area per productive unit; average size and number of properties per case; and characteristics of individual farms. The specific associations have already been described, but certain general conclusions and possible explanations may be stated here regarding the various types of productive units:

Even though all types of economic units were represented throughout the province, sub-family units were especially frequent in the area of earlier settlement near the provincial capital. To a somewhat lesser extent, the same can be said of deficit-yielding domestic units. Supra-family units, instead, were especially important outside the Central Valley, in areas of ongoing settlement and other 'peripheral' (i.e. less integrated) parts of the province. Intermediate domestic units, and even more so the surplus-producing ones, were most frequent in the northwestern section of the Central Valley. While exact proportions in probate cases were not necessarily the precise image of social stratification, there is no reason to assume that significant differences among regions or sub-regions were unrelated to socioeconomic processes. Furthermore, demographic and occupational data, as well as information on land claims and transactions, tend to confirm these regional variations in the importance of each type of productive unit.

Land use patterns on such units (with a common denominator of diversity, predominance of pasture despite its relative decline, and expansion of coffee in combination with other crops) also varied regionally and by type of unit. Maize and bean production was especially important on small to medium-sized farms in the cantones near the provincial capital, as a commercial activity, even though it accompanied the settlers wherever they went as a staple crop for local consumption. Although coffee was present in other parts of the Central Valley and on a wide range of productive units, it was most significant in the Northwest, often on intermediate-sized productive units and in association with sugarcane as well as pasture, even if coffee groves tended to be subdivided more than other individual properties. Extensive land use patterns, i.e. grazing and uncultivated areas, were found on the larger individual farms and productive units in the various regions, but more frequently in outlying regions such as the settlement frontier of the late nineteenth and early twentieth century in San Carlos.

With reference to the Northwest, specifically, diversified economic activities on intermediate and surplus-producing domestic units (both in terms of the crop mix and the various labor-intensities) were an integral part of the household production and reproduction strategies of the middling peasantry. Whereas complete specialization would increase seasonal labor peaks, diversity evened out labor requirements somewhat during the year, and therefore reduced the need for these domestic units to hire harvest workers or to work for wages in the off-seasons. Diversified yet market-oriented agricultural production also made it possible for rural households to purchase non-agricultural goods, rather than manufacture them artisanally. This was important due to the lower cost of imported textiles and other industrial products during the latter part of the nineteenth century.

The productive and reproductive strategy of domestic units sought to maintain a balance between the labor capacity and the material resources available to each household. Adjustments were not made by a modification of sexual conduct, e.g. to restrict births, nor by subsistence-oriented economic behavior, with negative responses to market stimuli. Neither were partible inheritance patterns altered sufficiently to avoid fragmentation of holdings. Quite the contrary, population grew even more rapidly, rural households were more and more actively involved in commercial production, and property became increasingly subdivided. How, then, did these units adapt to less favorable conditions relative to local availability of land, population densities, socioeconomic relations and other factors?

Strategies of domestic units involved several complementary components. Gradual intensification of land use partly counteracted the reduction of holdings, while emigration of certain household members reduced consumption requirements and adjusted family labor to material resources. Diversified agricultural production allowed domestic units to combine direct consumption with market-oriented activities, and made it possible for the latter to expand despite the costs associated with cultivation of the main agro-export crop of the time (which involved direct investments, perhaps a temporary reduction of income and certainly a permanent one of foodcrops, as well as greater risks due to market or harvest fluctuations).

Most domestic units in the region were not highly specialized at the turn of the century, yet they were firmly integrated to their various markets, and self-consumption was in no way their primary goal. There was still room for agricultural intensification and, especially, for productive specialization. If members of these households emigrated early on, it was not necessarily due to the absolute impossibility of absorbing additional labor on the family holding, but rather to the existence of opportunities on the new frontier, and to anticipate future subdivision of household property by supporting the establishment of new domestic units through advances on inheritance. However, pressures were accumulating, and local options were becoming limited toward the turn of the century. The following chapter will focus on the increasingly acute dilemmas faced by rural households during the following decades.

Chapter 6

A New Generation of Migrants

This chapter focuses on changes in the Alajuelan countryside from early to mid-twentieth century, as land scarcity became acute in the North-west his chapter focuses on changes in the Alajuelan countryside from early to mid-twentieth century, as land scarcity became acute in the Northwest and as the agricultural frontiers beyond the Central Valley received a growing influx of emigrants from the region. Our discusion here will proceed from the overall interaction of demographic and socioeconomic factors, through transformations in land-tenure and land use, both regionally and at the level of productive units, to the dilemmas faced by rural households in face of multiple threats to the viability of domestic units, and the means by which they attempted to counteract such pressures.

The profound modifications which took place during the first half of the twentieth century, regarding the situation of former settlers and their descendants in the Northwest, were part of agrarian changes throughout the Central Valley, but also in the outlying areas of the country. By the turn of the century, colonization had reached the eastern end of the Central Valley, and migrants had already begun to move beyond. During the early decades of the twentieth century, land became scarce in the previously settled territories, and colonization proceeded essentially in areas outside the tectonic depression. Ecological conditions, land tenure and social relations evolved very differently there, and the children or grandchildren of many Central Valley farmers encountered less favorable prospects for independent access to the land and for commercial peasant farming. The options imposed upon rural households of the Northwest and the multiple strategies by which they sought to survive and, if possible, prosper, were a part of society-wide processes which, to a certain extent, are both explained by, and explanatory of, regional transformations such as those discussed below.

Limited Options

After the turn of the century, accumulated population growth and restricted access to land in the Northwest, in a social context of decreasing or stagnant real income for direct producers,[1] led to a situation in which the establishment of additional domestic units of production in the region could only take place under increasingly difficult conditions. While there was still some leeway for agricultural intensification and, primarily, specialization, local population growth in the Northwest together with continued immigration from the Meseta would lead to a potentially untenable situation for a major sector of the rural population. Fragmentation of holdings would threaten the economic viability of many smallholder farms, unless counteracted by inheritance mechanisms or access to new lands.

Impoverishment and proletarianization were the very real prospects faced by young adult members of relatively land-poor households in the region. For them, emigration was to become an almost inevitable option, if they were to reestablish viable domestic units of production. At the same time, the wealthier farmers also sought to expand their holdings and productive units, whether by gradually acquiring more land in the Northwest or in the areas of ongoing settlement, especially in nearby San Carlos. In this section the demographic evolution of Alajuela during the first half of the twentieth century will be traced, before discussing other socioeconomic changes in the region.

Although the population of Alajuela province increased 68% between 1892 and 1927, the relative decline with respect to national population during that same period was only greater in Heredia, which had long been an area of emigration toward the Northwest and other parts of the country. The yearly growth rate of population in Alajuela, for this period, was well below the national average, and was just over half the provincial average for the latter part of the nineteenth century.[2] Furthermore, despite the fact that immigrants continued to arrive from Heredia and other densely settled areas, and that many emigrants from the Alajuela city to San Ramón area remained within the province, Alajuela was in 1927 the province with the highest negative net migration, in absolute terms.[3]

---

1 This decline or low level of real income was partly due to the fact that formerly scarce labor was becoming more abundant, which led to stagnant real wages, at the same time that small-scale coffee and sugarcane farmers confronted a "buyers' market" situation vis-à-vis the owners of processing mills. Short or medium-term rises in the export price of coffee and sugar were not proportionally transferred to smallholder producers, while down-trends of the international market were, due to the level of concentration of these agro-industries and lack of government regulation or effective organization of direct agricultural producers before the 1930's. Cf. Ramírez and Solís (1979), vol. 1, pp. 48-67.

2 DGEC (1864, 1883, 1892, 1927); Robles (1986), Tables 12 and 13, p. 29.

3 Robles (1986), Table 25, p. 40.

We may thus conclude that in the early twentieth century there was already a steady flow of emigrants leaving the province, at a faster rate than those arriving from other places. Many of those who left in these years went to Tilarán, in the highlands of Guanacaste, where Alajuelans, mostly from San Ramón and Palmares, were prominent among the settlers.[4] Almost one out of every ten inhabitants of Guanacaste in 1927 had been born in Alajuela, and there were numerous Alajuelans in the coastal provinces of Puntarenas and Limón.[5] Emigration from Alajuela province continued to increase after 1927, reaching a high of 16.6% in 1950.[6]

Despite net emigration and the fact that 93% of the population of the province in 1927 had been born there, Alajuela continued to receive immigrants from other provinces, especially Heredia.[7] More importantly, there was major intraprovincial migration, from the cantones within the Central Valley to those without, primarily located on the northern settlement frontier of the time.

While the relative decline of population was concentrated in the cantones from Alajuela to San Ramón (down from 18.7% to 15.1% of national population between 1892 and 1927), population in the northern part of the country (mainly San Carlos and Sarapiquí, in terms of actual settlement) trebled during that same period.[8] After 1927, the population of San Carlos continued to grow very rapidly, with a 183% increase between that date and the following census.[9]

The annual population growth rate declined more acutely in the Northwest than in the province as a whole. While growth in the region had been rapid up to the 1880s (with an annual rate of 2.7 in 1883-1892), it slowed down to 1.3 between 1892 and 1927. At the same time, population growth in the northern part of the province and of the country, already high in the late nineteenth century, was also quite rapid (above 3% p. a.) in the early decades of the twentieth.[10]

---

4 Sandner (1962-1964), Vol. 1, p. 114. Brunilda Hilje (1987) demonstrates the major role of settlers from Palmares and San Ramón in the agricultural development of this area, where they sought to reestablish a rural economy similar to that of the Central Valley. In his incisive comparative discussion of agrarian conflict in highland and lowland Guanacaste, Gudmundson (1983) stresses the smallholder heritage of inhabitants from the Central Valley who settled the area of Tilarán.

5 DGEC (1927), Table XVIII, p. 94.

6 DGEC (1950), p. 69.

7 DGEC (1927), p. 94.

8 Robles (1986), p. 30.

9 DGEC (1950), p. 50.

10 Robles (1986), p. 30.

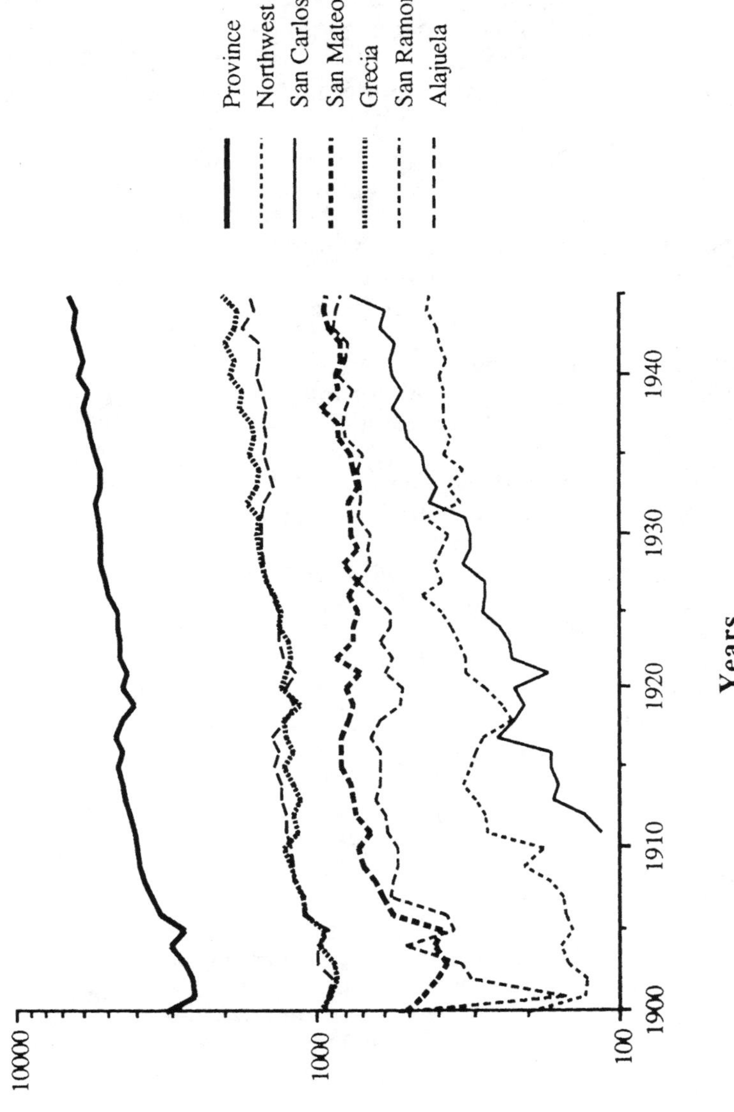

Figure 6.1 Births per year in Alajuela province, by region, 1900-1945

Insofar as the growth rate of births per year in specific subregions reflects permanent migration,[11] the low rates in areas other than San Carlos reflect a sustained out-migration from the previously settled areas of Alajuela, within the Central Valley (Figure 6.1). Within the Northwest, only Grecia had net immigration in the early twentieth century, but this canton still included northern territories where settlement was underway.

The establishment of new towns, parishes and cantones depicts this northward movement of population, which had already begun on a very small scale in the mid- to late-nineteenth century, but became significant after the turn of the century. From San Ramón, Palmares, Grecia, Naranjo, and Zarcero (founded as a parish in 1895, northward and at a higher altitude), the settlers moved toward San Carlos. They remained primarily on the northern foothills of the Cordillera Central, in several settlements from Florencia to Venecia.[12] Villa Quesada became the head of the new cantón of San Carlos, established in 1911, with less than the usually required three thousand inhabitants. By 1927, the population of this canton had doubled, and in 1950 there were almost three times as many inhabitants as in the previous census (Figure 6. 2).

TABLE 6.1 POPULATION OF ALAJUELA PROVINCE, 1927 AND 1950, BY CANTON

Canton	1927		1950	
	#	%	#	%
Alajuela/Poás	29,226	29.95	42,511	28.56
Grecia/ValverdeVega	16,130	16.53	27,884	18.73
Naranjo	7,910	8.11	10,839	7.28
Palmares	6,683	6.85	7,934	5.33
San Ramón	13,805	14.15	19,951	13.40
Atenas/San Mateo/Oroteo	15,016	15.39	18,875	12.68
Alfaro Ruíz	3,088	3.16	4,676	3.14
San Carlos	5,719	5.86	16,180	10.87
Province	97,577	100.00	148,850	100.00

Source: DGEC (1927), p. 34; (1950), pp. 110-111.

Expanding settlement on the twentieth-century frontiers, within and without the province, did not preclude population growth in previously-settled areas. Population density in the province as a whole, still only 5.8 inhabitants per square kilometer in 1892, had nearly doubled by 1927 and trebled by 1950. While this increase was especially rapid in the northern

11 Underlying assumptions were discussed in the previous chapter. For the twentieth century, baptisms are no longer as representative as in the ninteenth, so the analysis was based on birth records of the civil registry, provided by Arodys Robles.

12 Sandner (1962), pp. 102-103.

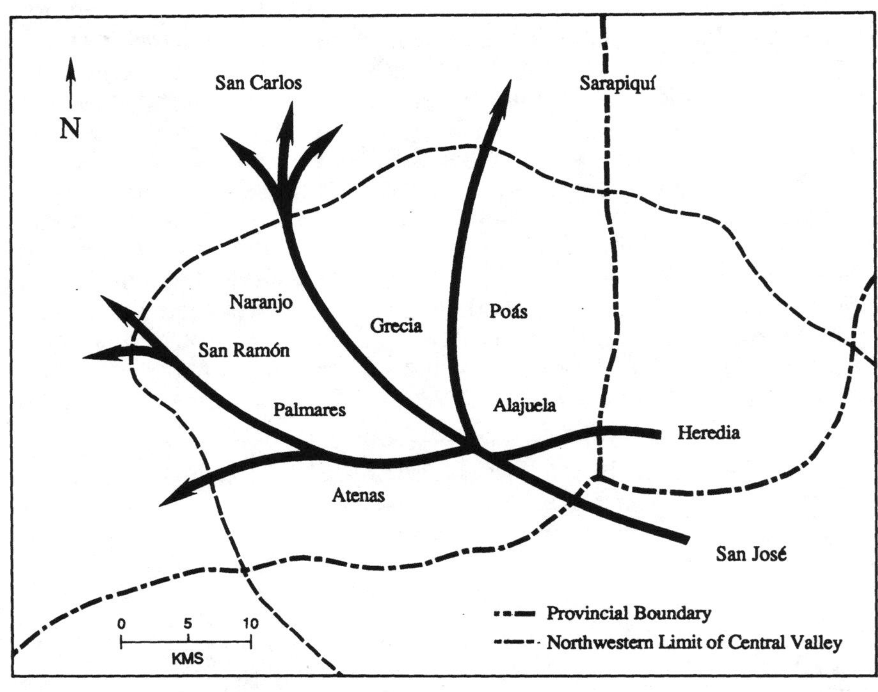

Figure 6.2 Turn-of-the-century migrations beyond the Central Valley in Alajuela province, Costa Rica

part of the province during the early twentieth century, there was also substantial population growth in what were already more densely populated areas in the late nineteenth century (Table 6.1). Palmares, for example, had a population density of 107 in 1892, 176 in 1927, and 209 in 1950.[13] Clearly, emigration did not fully counteract local population growth, and lacking alternative sources of employment, major changes were inevitable in rural labor, land-tenure and land use. Yet the way in which domestic units, specifically, responded to imbalances between household resources, family labor capacity and consumption needs varied over time and subregionally.

Before proceeding with an analysis of socioeconomic interactions during these yars, let us briefly characterize the landowners of Alajuela, insofar as they are represented in probate inventories for 1926-1935.[14]

Regarding age of the deceased, there was a substantial increase in the probate cases of this period, in comparison to age in the turn-of-the-century cases. Average age of the deceased with property to be inherited by their descendants increased ten years during the first three decades of the twentieth century. The older age of the deceased in probate inventories toward 1930 cannot be explained exclusively by the gradual decline in mortality. Since there were also less probate cases available in 1926-1935 than in 1895-1904, the higher age might reflect a stronger bias toward intermediate and upper levels of wealth.

At fifty-seven, the age of the deceased in probate inventories was notably higher than nationwide life expectancy, still under forty years at the time [15] The rapid decline of death rates would only occur in the thirties and forties, when life expectancy rose steeply to reach fifty-five toward 1950.[16] The older age of property-owners at time of death is in accordance with the minimal representation of minors, household accumulation of wealth over the years, and the far greater probability of probate proceedings being initiated and completed for those at intermediate and high levels of fortune, than among the land-poor or landless population. By age groups, almost sixty percent of the deceased in probate inventories were 31 to 60 years old, while less than 25% of the general population alive in 1927 (and also in 1950 in Alajuela) was between those same ages.[17]

---

13 Based on data from DGEC (1892, 1927, 1950).

14 Unless otherwise indicated, data for the remainder of this section are derived from a 50% sample of probate cases for the years 1926-1935 in Alajuela province, listed under primary sources. General cautions regarding representativeness of probate inventories have already been stated. Additionally, in 1926-1935 the total number of probate inventories from which the sample was taken were only two thirds the number for 1895-1904, while the population had increased 70% between 1892 and 1927.

15 Pérez (1987), Table 2, p. 9.

16 Pérez (1983), pp. 123, 129 and 131, (1987) p. 10.

17 DGEC (1927), pp. 37-8, (1950), p. 56.

Place of residence of the deceased property-owners also varied with respect to the probate inventories discussed in the previous chapter. While in 1895-1904 they were strongly concentrated near the provincial capital, in 1926-1935 more than half were residents of the Northwest, especially Grecia, Naranjo and Sarchí. As this area ceased to be one of settlement, local population density increased, as mentioned above, but landholding by local residents also became more stable and valuable, which led to initiating more probate proceedings. On the other hand, there were only a few cases of residents in the northern part of the province, even though there had been a major migration to the area since the late nineteenth century, and medium-to-large landowners often had farms in San Carlos. Although it is possible that some probate cases are yet to be found for this region, land titling by settlers took place later and more slowly than that by residents of the Central Valley who established farms in San Carlos without changing their own place of residence, even if perhaps they themselves or their sons spent part of the year there. Furthermore, the population of San Carlos was probably younger and less wealthy than those who owned land there but lived elsewhere. Our cases for 1926-1935, however, are almost all of residents within the Central Valley, even if they had property in other areas.

Analysed by sex, we find that the bias toward men in probate inventories was greater in 1926-1935 than it was thirty years before, since women (who tended to live longer) were only 38% of the deceased property-owners for whom such proceedings were opened. We will return to the issue of under-representation of women in the last section of this chapter, in dealing with inheritance.

In sum, Alajuelan property-owners represented in probate inventories toward 1930 were predominantly male, residents of the Central Valley, with an average age of 57 at time of death, and with a bias toward intermediate-to-high levels of wealth. In the following section we discuss the socioeconomic characteristics of the propertied and general population.

Landowners and Day-laborers

In a context of increasingly limited access to land in the Northwest, with partible inheritance practices and local population growth despite emigration, many peasant households in the region went through a process of fragmentation of family holdings from one generation to the next. In association with changes in labor requirements due to greater productive specialization, this smaller size of holdings led to an increased reliance on wage labor, not only by a landless population, but also by members of smallholder families.

During the first half of the twentieth century, there was a sustained growth of the wage-earning rural population. This was reflected in a substantial growth of the *jornalero* category nationwide toward 1927, a process significant in Alajuela province.[18] By 1950, there were close to eighteen thousand agricultural wage-laborers in the province, and at 38% their percentage with respect to all occupational categories was well above the national average.[19]

The growing number of daylaborers did not, however, amount to a disappearance of domestic productive units in the Northwest. The very real reduction in size of most holdings was partly counteracted by additional intensification and by a greater reliance on one main commercial crop, which in turn made domestic units have more seasonal surpluses and/or deficits of household labor. At this point the issue of land tenure in the region during this period needs to be considered, as it relates to agricultural intensification, specialization and labor.

There has been considerable debate on the extent of landholding concentration in the coffee-producing areas of the Central Valley toward 1935, when a detailed census of coffee farms was taken. At the time, economist Carlos Merz wrote in the journal of the Instituto de Defensa del Café that coffee production was substantially based on smallholding, and considerably less centralized than other crops in the country as a whole.[20] Subsequently, various scholars have either shared his viewpoints or criticized them, with a gradually more refined statistical analysis in this unending debate.[21] It does seem clear that concentration of land cultivated in coffee was far lower than that of other types of land, whether on coffee farms themselves or on other types of holdings.[22] On the other hand, while there were many small coffee farms in the Central Valley, there were quite a few large ones, and land tenure was far from egalitarian even if there was a much larger middling coffee-farmer population than in several other, but not all, Latin American cases.

In the province of Alajuela, whose coffee-producing area in 1935 was essentially that from Alajuela city to San Ramón, it was undoubtedly the province of the Central Valley with the lowest level of concentration of coffee production. In terms of number of trees per producer, control of a small minority over large areas of coffee farms was less pronounced in the province of Alajuela than in other provinces.[23] Average coffee-farm size per owner was seven to ten hectares in all cantones of Alajuela province (Table 6.2).

---

18 Samper (1979), 143, 146, 281-284.

19 DGEC (1950), pp. 296-297 and 308-309.

20 Mertz (1937), p. 293, commented on in Churnside (1985), p. 201.

21 For two opposite viewpoints on landholding concentration in the 1935 coffee-farm census, see Hall (1976), p. 106, and Churnside (1985), pp. 201-204. While the former views coffee as a predominantly (but not exclusively) small to middling farmer crop, the latter coincides with Rodrigo Facio's 1941 critique of the "democratic" view of coffee cultivation (see Facio, 1975).

22 Churnside (1978), p. 13.

23 Churnside (1985), Table 4.4 (n.p.n.).

TABLE 6.2 COFFEE PRODUCING FARM AREA AND PROPERTIES IN ALAJUELA PROVINCE, BY CANTON, 1935

Cantón	Farm Area (Has.)	Number of Farms	Avg. Farm Area (Has.)	Number of Owners	Avg. Property Area (Has.)
Central	10,605	1,766	6.0	1,619	6.5
San Ramón	7,322	922	7.9	835	8.8
Grecia	10,011	1,312	7.6	1,006	9.9
Atenas	2,201	363	6.0	326	6.7
Naranjo	5,181	1,097	4.7	674	7.6
Palmares	2,657	457	5.8	375	7.1
Poás	2,734	319	8.5	261	10.4
Province	40,712	6,245	6.5	5,096	8.0

Source: IDC (1935).

However, there were substantial differences in landholding concentration, at least with respect to coffee production, among the various cantones of Alajuela province. Insofar as the number of coffee trees per farm indirectly reflects land-tenure patterns (Table 6.3), extremely small farms were almost three quarters of all farms in the vicinity of the town of Alajuela, where fragmentation of holdings had begun earlier and proceeded further. Palmares, instead, was the canton where peasant holdings (as opposed to sub-family or supra-family ones) were by far the predominant sector of coffee production. The proportion of small to medium-sized farms was greater throughout the Northwest than in the districts near Alajuela city. In all the province, there were only eight estates with one or two hundred thousand coffee trees, or some 67 to 134 hectares planted in coffee.[24]

In the northwestern part of the Central Valley, there were close to 3,800 coffee farms, with 2,890 owners. Four out of every five owners in 1935 lived on their farms, while others probably lived in towns nearby.[25] Less than five percent of the farms were administrated by resident

24 Assumptions for the foregoing analysis are: 1,500 coffee trees per hectare, based on the national density of planting in 1935, and that farms with 1,000 to 20,000 coffee trees were small to medium-sized, ranging from sub-family to surplus-yielding domestic units. Since total area of coffee-producing farms was, on the average, 2.7 times that planted in coffee, such farms could have roughly 2 to 36 hectares of land.

25 Housing on coffee farms was predominantly occupied by their owners in the various cantons of Alajuela province in 1935 (percentages ranged from 51% to 87.6%). Rental was only significant, and on a small scale (5.6%), in the central canton. Occupance by day laborers was under thirty percent in all cantons except Poás (46.3%), Naranjo (39.0%) and Grecia (33.5%), but it was minimal only in San Ramón (8.5%).

TABLE 6.3 OWNERSHIP OF COFFEE-PRODUCING LAND IN ALAJUELA PROVINCE, BY CANTON, 1935

Coffee Trees	Area (Has.)	Percent of Farms							
		PROVINCE	CENTRAL	SAN RAMON	GRECIA	ATENAS	NARANJO	PALMARES	POAS
1 - 1,000	≤0.66	59.64	72.27	62.23	57.55	63.80	47.48	25.07	53.64
1,001 - 3,000	0.67 - 2.00	22.71	15.19	25.99	25.84	24.20	23.60	33.60	26.8
3,001 - 5,000	2.01 - 3.33	6.77	4.32	5.51	5.86	4.91	10.20	16.27	9.2
5,001 - 20,000	3.34 - 13.33	8.82	6.36	5.03	8.95	6.44	13.80	21.33	8.05
20,001 - 60,000	13.34 - 40.00	1.58	1.42	0.12	1.09	0.61	4.01	3.20	1.92
60,001 - 100,000	40.01 - 66.66	0.32	0.31	0.12	0.40	0.00	0.59	0.27	0.38
≥100,001	≥66.67	0.16	0.12	0.00	0.30	0.00	0.30	0.27	0.00

TABLE 6.4 ADULT POPULATION LIVING AND WORKING ON COFFEE FARMS IN ALAJUELA PROVINCE, 1935

Cantón	Adults Living on Farm	Total Workers	Adminis-trators	Day Laborers	Ox-cart Drivers	Servants and Chauffeurs
Central	5,261	1,860	436	1,105	179	140
San Ramón	2,868	1,291	101	1,088	66	36
Grecia	4,054	1,998	96	1,660	190	52
Atenas	1,296	102	11	72	17	2
Naranjo	2,254	1,092	178	842	44	28
Palmares	1,261	1,119	38	1,054	24	3
Poás	1,085	534	12	483	34	5

Source: DCEG (1950b).

TABLE 6.5 HOUSEHOLD AND WAGE-LABOR ON FARMS IN THE NORTHWESTERN CANTONES, 1950

Cantón	Household Labor			Wage Labor			Total # of Farms
	PERSONS	FARMS REPORTED	AVG. PER FARM	PERSONS	FARMS REPORTED	AVG. PER FARM	
San Ramón	2,729	1,207	2.3	1,097	160	6.9	1,617
Grecia	2,967	1,132	2.6	2,884	263	11.0	1,882
Naranjo	963	379	2.5	1,102	131	8.4	662
Palmares	744	357	2.1	326	50	6.5	494
Valverde Vega	295	184	1.6	523	29	18.0	252
Northwest	7,698	3,259	2.4	5,932	633	9.4	4,907

Source: IDC (1935).

mandadores on behalf of absentee owners (Table 6.4). With few exceptions, coffee farms in the Northwest toward 1935 were under the direct administration of their resident owners. Family labor was important on most productive units. Some of them, due to specialization, were domestic units with variable labor requirements, while others had definitely become sub-family units or micro-plots, even if intensively cultivated.

On the other hand, permanent wage labor was also becoming significant in the region at the time the coffee-farm census was taken. Except for San Ramón, housing for resident *peones* was a significant proportion of all dwellings on coffee farms in the various northwestern cantones. In the Northwest, without including other employees such as ox-team and truck drivers or servants, there were 60% more permanent daylaborers than resident farm owners among the persons working on coffee farms. Of course, the former were concentrated on a smaller number of farms, so that most productive units did not have permanent hired hands, although some certainly required seasonal wage labor.

In 1950, when the first modern agricultural census was taken, Alajuela was still -in spite of the growing number of daylaborers- the province with most household labor and least regular employees, after Guanacaste.[26] Five times as many farms of all types (i. e. not only coffee-producing farms) in the Northwest reported family labor as those which hired wage laborers in mid-May, 1950 (Table 6.5). In other words, at least four out of every five farms used only family labor at the time, and a significant percentage of those employing daylaborers probably also occupied family labor to some extent. Widespread reliance on household members for agricultural tasks was associated with the existence of a large number of medium-to-small holdings, i.e. domestic and sub-family units of production.

Within the Northwest, wage labor in 1950 was more frequent in Grecia, Naranjo and Valverde Vega (Sarchí, formerly a part of Grecia). In San Ramón and Palmares, instead, household labor more than doubled wage labor on farms. The difference is due to the existence of several large agricultural enterprises in the former area, where there was also more fragmentation of small farms, while domestic units of production were relatively more important toward the western end of the Central Valley at the time.

Wage labor was in no way restricted to large or even middle-sized farms in Alajuela toward the mid-twentieth century. The number of daylaborers was of course much higher on farms larger than 500 *manzanas* (about 350 hectares). However, even quite small farms could have one or two hired hands. More than 8,000 farms under 35 hectares in size had daylaborers, with average numbers increasing gradually from 1.6 to 2.7 hired workers according to farm size (Table 6.6).

---

26 DGEC (1950), p. 105.

TABLE 6.6 WAGE-LABOR ON FARMS IN ALAJUELA PROVINCE, BY SIZE OF FARMS, MAY 1950

Area of Farms (Has.)	Wage Labor				
	WORKERS		FARMS		AVERAGE
	#	%	#	%	#
0.7 - < 3.5	4,654	16.3	2,923	28.2	1.6
3.5 - < 7.0	3,588	12.6	1,805	17.4	1.9
7.0 - < 10.5	2,498	8.8	1,068	10.3	2.3
10.5 - < 21.0	3,853	13.5	1,547	14.9	2.5
21.0 - < 35.0	3,100	10.9	1,128	10.9	2.7
35.0 - < 70.0	3,444	12.1	1,063	10.2	3.2
70.0 - < 350.0	4,439	15.5	734	7.1	6.0
≥ 350	2,947	10.3	109	1.0	27.0
Total	28,523	100.0	10,377	100.0	2.8

Source: DCEG (1950b), p.122.

Household labor was, of course, especially frequent on these same small- to medium-sized farms, aside from an even larger number which hired no day-laborers at all or did so only at harvest time. A lower yet substantial number of small- to medium-scale agricultural producers in Alajuela province also worked off-farm during the year (Table 6.7). Many of them were owners of some land, although others were tenant farmers. By type of tenure, 18.5% of farm-owners of Alajuela province in 1950 worked off-farm 24 weeks or more per year. Of those whose land was obtained through rental and sharecropping arrangements, 29% also worked elsewhere in that same year.

TABLE 6.7 OFF-FARM LABOR OF AGRICULTURAL PRODUCERS IN ALAJUELA PROVINCE, BY SIZE OF FARMS, 1950

Weeks	Area (Hectares)					
	0.7 - < 7		7 - < 35		≥ 35	
	#	%	#	%	#	%
≥ 24	820	17.3	596	15.9	473	24.9
4 - 23	164	3.5	73	2.0	24	1.2
< 4	99	2.1	84	2.2	91	4.8
Non-reported	3,645	77.1	2,990	79.9	1,315	69.1
Total	4,728	100.0	3,743	100.0	1,903	100.0

Source: DGEC (1950b), p.24.

From the above, we conclude that numerous farms in the region, many of which could be characterized as domestic units, combined family and non-family labor. Others employed daylaborers who worked there on a regular basis, though some of these workers were also the owners of tiny, highly specialized sub-family holdings. Labor relations were, quite often, only one aspect of multi-level socioeconomic interactions among productive units.

HOUSEHOLD WEALTH

Information from probate inventories for the period 1926 to 1935 allows one to compare the composition of assets associated with the types of units discussed in previous chapters, even though less details are available on movables than on real estate for this period. A follow-up of specific cases through oral history and other sources will provide the opportunity to look beyond the official, legal documentation at more concrete social relations.

Total assets of the deceased in these years averaged ¢3,800 (*colones*), and value of the land per case ¢5,009.[27] In comparing this last figure with that for 1895-1904, and both to the monetary data available,[28] we find that the increase in nominal value of immovable property per case was slightly lower than the devaluation of local currency. One may thus assume that the increase in nominal value of the land was at least compensated for by devaluation, and that a two-thirds increase in value estimates for the land over this period did not amount to higher real values.

Given the great variability of levels of wealth and value of real estate in these years,[29] general averages need give way to analysis by categories. These, in turn, were not directly representative of social strata, but rather biased toward intermediate and higher levels.[30] Not even one third of the cases were within a range from half to twice the average fortunes, and most

27 Since the value of movables was minimal, the surplus of land value over total wealth is essentially due to negative credit balances, discussed in the following subsection. All data in the remainder of this section, unless specified otherwise, are from the probate cases listed under primary sources for 1926-1935.

28 From 1907 to 1926, the exchange rate in Costa Rican *colones* per U.S. dollar increased from 2.12 to 4.00 (Albarracín and Pérez, 1977, p. 26). At the same time, the average value of properties per case increased from $/¢3,033 in 1895-1904 to ¢5,009 in 1926-1935.

29 Level of wealth ranged from - ¢27,684 to + ¢80,000, and real estate from negligible values up to ¢193,640.

30 Only 8% of fortunes were below ¢100, and 24% were from ¢100 to under ¢500. Intermediate fortunes (¢500 to < ¢5,000) were 49%, and the remaining 19% were relatively high fortunes. Value of immovable property per case, though higher, followed a very similar pattern.

were well below the average (four out of every five cases had less real estate than the average estimate). There was, undoubtedly, a strong socioeconomic differentiation among the deceased whose probate inventories were studied.

By geographical areas, wealth tended to be higher among those residing in or near the provincial capital; they were lower in Grecia-Naranjo, and intermediate in Palmares-San Ramón.[31] The provincial capital was the place of residence for absentee landowners with relatively large estates in other parts of the province, while the low level of average wealth near Grecia resulted to a large extent from indebtedness of certain residents in the area. Instead, the landed population of Palmares and San Ramón seems to have had more intermediate fortunes due to a closer balance between real estate and credit. It will be necessary to discuss this further upon dealing with the specifics of the regional distribution of productive units.

Those who had died from 45 to 60 years of age generally had much higher than average total wealth, while those who died when they were 31 to 45 years old tended to have not only much lower levels,[32] but often more liabilities than assets, as will be discussed in the following subsection.

It should be noted here that the economic crisis which struck Costa Rica after 1930 did not reduce the value of probate fortunes generally, although reassessments of property were requested more often as of that date and were invariably lower. The average values in probate inventories actually increased from $3,252 in 1926-1929 to ¢4,300 in 1930-1935. A possible explanation is that fewer low-fortune probate cases were initiated in the latter subperiod due to economic difficulties of smallholders, but further research would be required. All that can be said at this point is that while the crisis did depress the land market, it did not reduce the average value of assets in probate inventories.

From the above, we can conclude that the landholding population represented (unequally) in probate proceedings was highly differentiated in terms of overall wealth and real estate ownership, and by age groups or regions.

---

31 Average fortunes were ¢5,999 near Alajuela, ¢1,921 in Grecia-Naranjo, and ¢3,673 for Palmares-San Ramón.

32 Average wealth of those 45 to 60 years old was ¢5,693, and for those 31 to 45 it was - ¢552.

Credit Relations

These were recorded only for a small minority of the deceased in 1926-1935, and two or three large debts weighed heavily on average values.[33] If all cases with or without credit are included, value of debts in Alajuela province was twelve times that of loans receivable. Individual debts, more numerous than loans, were also eight times larger in monetary terms. Aside from the fact that some of the creditors for large amounts were almost certainly from other provinces, it is quite possible that the combination of apparent prosperity in the late twenties and economic crisis in the early thirties led to greater indebtedness in some cases.

Descendants of several of the deceased corroborated that there were neither loans receivable nor debts at the time of his or her demise,[34] and they stressed the concept of *cabalidad* (honorability), according to which their forebears could not have left any debts: "father was an honorable man, he owed no one", or "father was very responsible...he did not owe anyone money, nor did anyone owe him".[35] This concept was derived from an implicit cultural norm that a person who died should leave no unsettled accounts. When this was inevitable, they sought to clearly state both debts and loans receivable, for example in a will. Yet when a person died relatively young, or unexpectedly, there were sometimes amounts due or to be collected from others. In any case, the desire to settle accounts before dying indicates that credit was not an infrequent social relation in the area at this time.

We know, from our interviews for this period and from the frequency of loans in earlier probate inventories, that credit relations must have been more important in this rural society than is suggested by the few cases with debts or credits in 1926-1935. It seems that occasional loans were usually not recorded in writing:

> ...before it was done this way: the money was lent and there were no promissory notes... nor anything at all, just a person's word... someone came and said: do me the favor of lending me some money, and you gave it to them; when my father had the money, he went and paid it... yes, they lent money to each other, but not very often... everyone had at home what they

---

33 By eliminating the most negative credit balance (-¢ 208,104), the average credit balance did not become positive, but it was reduced to - ¢510, less than a third of the original average.

34 Deceased: María Alvarado Rodríguez; interviewed: Isabelina Alvarez Alvarado. Deceased: Tranquilino Avila Oviedo; interviewed: Orfilia Avila Ballestero. Deceased: Santana Arias Guzmán; interviewed: Cristina Arias Espinoza. Deceased: Angelina Herrera Rodríguez; interviewed: Félix Herrera Corrales. Deceased: Abelardo González Murillo; interviewed: Julia González Alfaro.

35 Interviews: Isabelina Alvarez Alvarado and Bernardo Barahona Campos.

> needed, yes... maybe if a person was very poor, and... neeeded some money for the family...[36]

Credit relations, like other aspects of household economic life, were often handled exclusively by the husband, who did not consult his wife:

> My father was one who did not communicate anything... like now, to the wife: let us do this, or that. Those persons back then kept things to themselves, only did what they wanted to do and nothing else...[37]

Under such conditions, death of a substantial creditor could leave payment of debts to the conscience of debtors, or to a moral and social pressure which tended to weaken:

> [my father] lent out a great amount of money, and when he died, as there was no document of anything, nor any witness of anything, all that money was lost.[38]

It might also be that money was deposited in the hands of others, for them to keep safely or manage, but that certain amounts were also borrowed from the same person, and upon the demise of the depositor/debtor the actual credit balance could not be established:

> Father sold the harvests and cows, and gave the money to certain persons, his friends, to keep for him...he gave money to [...], who was also his friend, I don't know if he was a moneylender, but he would give him money to keep. When he died, mother sent for the money, but he said that there was none, that father owed him money instead... who knows, one cannot say anything about these things, because only they could know how things were.[39]

In some cases, it could be established that even though no credits were recorded in the probate inventory, certain amounts were either owed to the deceased or by him. Usually these were small amounts, and some were paid while others were not:

> ... a little that he owed, mother paid his debts.[he owed no one anything but] other people, also very poor, did owe him... they didn't pay...My father... had been offered the money but they didn't pay it, though it wasn't much...he didn't like to owe anyone money.[40]

---

36 Interview: Belarmina Ramírez.

37 Interview: María Ignacia Bogantes Zamora.

38 Interview: Esperanza Arias Vargas.

39 Interviews: Angela and María Ignacia Bogantes Zamora.

40 Interviews: Rosa Fernández Araya, Mery Vega Bolaños, Maximina Ballestero Boza.

Loans and debts were most often monetary (seven and six, respectively, out of every ten). There were also debts for coffee, as well as other goods and services. Monetary debts were the largest ones, followed by those for coffee. However, monetary credit was sometimes related to real estate transactions: "Father...would perhaps borrow some money to buy a farm".[41] Or a person who needed to sell land might request someone "to lend him while he sold, to get by meanwhile".[42]

Whether in money or in kind, loans for household sustenance were often obtained during the year and paid back at the following harvest: "There were stores where you could buy on credit, and when the harvest came around you went and paid everything", or "when the coffee harvest came, you paid what you owed".[43]

There were, then, short-term loans which were relatively small and paid back in less than a year, but larger ones were for several years. In the case of domestic units, as more children came of age to work, there was often a need to purchase more land, and debts were a means to this end. The young adults of wealthier families also became indebted, sometimes heavily, to establish their own enterprises. In either case, when these debtors died relatively young, such debts were often unpaid, and could be quite substantial with respect to household assets. It has already been pointed out that credit balances tended to be negative among those in their thirties and early forties, and positive among older persons.[44] Heavy debtors were usually young adults, while moneylenders tended to be relatively old. Two specific cases illustrate the extreme situations, but also allow us to focus on the connection between level of indebtedness and composition of houshold assets.

The strongest positive credit balance was that of Bartola Chávez and Rafael Arias.[45] They lived in Santiago Oeste, in the area of the provincial capital. When she died at age 76, leaving six children, they owned eighteen properties, with a total area of about one hundred and fifty hectares, estimated at ¢29,000. The main use of the land on these properties was livestock raising, and there were some farms partly in grain or sugarcane. There was only one small coffee grove according to the inventory. The Arias Chávez family had no debts, or they were paid directly through sale of unregistered movables or by other means. They did have twenty-one loans receivable, for a total of ¢4,930. Almost all were for sums under ¢300, and probably for money lent out at a given interest rate, as was frequent among elderly persons.

---

41 Interview: José Herrera Rodríguez.

42 Interview: Rosa Fernández Araya.

43 Interviews: Raimundo Salazar Ulate and María Ignacia Bogantes Zamora.

44 Elimination of the strongest negative credit balance only reduced the average balance to -¢2,900.

45 Archivo Nacional, Juzgado Civil de Alajuela, Doc. #6230, 930.

At the other end of the credit line, we may cite the example of thirty-six-year-old Guillermo Matamoros and his wife Julia Alvarado, who lived in Naranjo.[46] Guillermo shared a 50% right to twenty-seven farms with his brother; we do not know the exact area, but the value of these properties was ¢193,615, a very significant amount. Twenty-three were located in Naranjo, and almost all of these were coffee farms, with a few pastures and a grain plot. There was also a modern coffee processing mill, and housing for resident daylaborers. The four other properties were in San Carlos, and included cattle, sugarcane cultivation and processing, production of wood, bananas and grain. The oldest daughter of the deceased states that the coffee farms in Naranjo were several hundred hectares, and his properties in San Carlos were at least 1,400 hectares. Regarding the twenty-three debts of the Matamoros brothers' estate, she explains that several large ones were to bankers who regularly funded their enterprises, whether for purchasing land, equipment or operating expenses, at a time when they were making substantial investments both in Naranjo and in San Carlos.[47] While the larger debts were either for monetary loans or mortgages, there were more small debts due to unpaid coffee received at the processing mill. Some of these were "difficult to verify, since they came from coffee delivered by small farmers, where receipts are destroyed".[48] The Matamoros estate was indebted but in the process of expanding, and the early demise of one of the associates explains this highly negative credit balance.

These two extreme cases of credit balances exemplify, for relatively large productive units, the close relationship between age at time of death and highly favorable or unfavorable balances. At intermediate levels, assets and liabilities were better balanced. In some cases, judiciary execution of debts or imminent death of the owner might lead to sale of properties so as to cancel debts or guaranties. In such cases, the outcome could be the disappearance of household patrimony:

> [he sold the farms] because he said that he owed money... once he told me that for signing guaranties for inconsiderate people, he had lost everything in life...On my father's side, everything disappeared, because he signed guaranties for anyone, and I didn't want him to, but he felt sorry for them, and that he should. Then it turned out that the farm was going to be taken away...[49]

If guaranties could ruin some farmers, the combination of indebtedness and unfavorable economic conditions led to loss of lands by others, and bankruptcies among some of the larger landowners. This process, which had already begun to happen in the late nineteenth century, became more

---

46 Archivo Nacional, Juzgado Civil de Alajuela, Doc. #8500, 1934.

47 Interview: Julia Matamoros Alvarado.

48 Archivo Nacional, Juzgado Civil de Alajuela, Doc. #6230.

49 Interviews: María Ignacia Bogantes Zamora and Andrés Lobo González.

frequent in the early 1930's.[50] But its immediate origin could be traced to the previous period of apparent prosperity, during the 1920's, and more specifically to heavy indebtedness not only of the country as a whole but also of individual producers. As former President Alfredo González Flores stated at the time:

> ...credit facilities and the false prosperity resulting from foreign loans led people to buy farms whose value had been inflated artificially -by devaluation of the colón-, which in turn created the problem of debtors. During the depression, they had to face an exaggerated value of mortgaged properties due to revaluation of the colón...[51]

The moratorium on debts in 1932 certainly alleviated the situation for the owners of larger units with bank loans, but its effect on peasant-farmers subject to informal credit ties still requires further study.

MOVABLES

These were only recorded in twenty-nine probate inventories for 1926-1935, and will be discussed only on an individual case level. While during most of the nineteenth century, movables had been carefully recorded, they were less frequent toward the turn of the century and tended to disappear from probate proceedings towards the 1920s and 1930s. Instead, land which had been less precisely recorded in terms of area during the late colonial and early republican period, became the primary component of probate inventories. Cattle and certain capital goods or valuable items were sometimes recorded, but probate proceedings tended to be essentially a means of transmitting legal property of the land to heirs or third parties. There were several reasons for this, including: the rising cost of land; the need to record ownership in the Real Estate Registry; variations in the ways in which land and other assests were perceived and assessed; the necessity to reduce the cost of proceedings; and changes in legislation.

Two cases with movable assets estimated at more than the ¢3,447 average are summarized below to exemplify situations in which movables were recorded, and then several smallholder households with few or no such indications in the probate inventory will be traced through oral historical evidence.

Julio Herra, an Alajuelan merchant who died at age fifty, in 1933,[52] had a trading partnership with his brother. According to the inventory, don Julio's assets were a house, estimated at ¢5,000, and fifteen ¢5,000 shares

---

50 Cf., for example, Cortés (1981), pp. 73 and 85.

51 González (1936), pp. 87-88.

52 Archivo Nacional, Juzgado Civil de Alajuela, Remesa 1330, #361, 1933.

in the partnership. These were essentially trading goods, and perhaps a store. No cash nor any durable consumption goods were included in the inventory, although a well established businessman like don Julio undoubtedly had both. His fortune was therefore larger than was reflected in the proceedings, and if the shares were included it was probably because of the need to ensure their legal transfer to his heirs.

Bruno Maroto Salas, a farmer from Puente de Piedra, in Grecia, was sixty-three years old when he died in 1935.[53] He owned seventeen properties, with a total area above 134 hectares. Productive activities included livestock raising, especially on the larger farms, as well as grain, sugarcane and coffee on the smaller ones. According to the probate inventory, don Bruno had a pair of oxen worth ¢300 and forty other head of cattle estimated at ¢3,000. The remaining movables were three ox-carts (¢300), sixty *cajuelas* of black beans (¢480), and ¢707 in cash. Although this is one of the most complete inventories for the period, no durable consumption goods were included, nor the implements required by a medium-sized productive unit such as this one.

In these and other cases, movables included were primarily those requiring legal transfer, such as shares, contracts and trading goods of a partnership, or a sizeable herd of cattle as in the previous case. No durable consumption goods were listed, as had been the case during the nineteenth century. Such movables were probably distributed directly among heirs or disposed of out of court, perhaps to pay unlisted creditors.

Livestock merits an additional reference, despite limited information for these years. We know there were many pastures, yet cattle was rarely included in the inventories. Its value with respect to total fortune of the whole population was insignificant. Even if we take only the cases in which livestock is mentioned, average herd size was just seven head of cattle. The largest herd was that mentioned above, with forty-two head, all the rest possessing just a few head of cattle. Since large ranches in San Carlos were nevertheless included in inventories with no cattle, we must conclude that livestock was unfortunately left out of inventories in many cases, even if coffee did reduce its importance within the Central Valley. Yet we can follow up on some of these cases through interviews with descendents of the deceased.

The probate inventory of Higinio Gonzålez, a wealthy man with several hundred hectares of land, a major part in pastures, included as movables only two horses, a pair of oxen and an ox-cart. However, we know that he was "one of the main cattle traders", that he regularly sent cattle from Río Cuarto, in northern Grecia, to the cattle fair in Alajuela, and that he had "a lot of cattle, and quite a few ox-carts". He also "had a lot of hogs... up to twenty hogs", and other movables, both for production and durable consumption: a water-powered *trapiche*; equipment for processing coffee; and "the first car which arrived in Grecia". However, despite his fortune, he did not have any luxury items, only "simple clothes to wear...

53 Archivo Nacional, Remesa 1330, #445, 1935.

and strong but rustic furniture".[54] Most of the movables left out of the inventory were for production, although processing equipment may have been included in the value of farms. Livestock was perhaps distributed by don Higinio before dying, or in an out of court settlement by his heirs, to pay off debts or avoid higher legal costs. We will return to this point in the last section, in discussing inheritance.

Generally speaking, descendants of the deceased in cases with no inventoried movables state that such assets did exist, although they were not very valuable. A few examples will suffice to give an idea of the type of movables left out of the inventories. Juan Bogantes had a small coffee farm in San Ramón, his only property in the inventory, but he also owned a horse which he used to take coffee to the local *beneficio*, and "right there [on his coffee farm] there was a plot for the cows, milk for the home..." [55] Miguel Fernández, in Palmares, also owned a small coffee grove. Although no movables were included in the inventory, he did in fact have some: two cows and a few other movables, inherited by the unmarried sons. The family led a poor and austere life, with no comforts at all, and "always slept on the boards with an *estera* (straw mat)".[56]

When María Alvarado died in Grecia, no movables were recorded, only a right to one tiny plot. Her husband was a *jornalero* (day-laborer), and she supplemented household income by washing clothes for other families and working in the coffee harvests. Despite their poverty, they had a few cows, which they later traded for a pair of oxen and an ox-cart.[57]

Tranquilino Avila's heirs initiated probate proceedings exclusively to ratify a sale of property made during his lifetime, and no assets at all were listed. Even so, he did have certain movables, which must have passed on to his heirs: "a cow...to provide milk for household consumption... a shovel and a machete", and some furniture, "just the kitchen cupboard, and the iron stove and stools and a table, and nothing else at all." [58]

Finally, there were times when unlisted movables were hidden by various means to avoid payment of debts:

> ...then they began to take things away, first of all livestock... they were sold to pay guaranties... When I saw how things were, the ox-cart was a very good one... I said to my brother-in-law, what shall we do with the oxcart, I would not want to lose it, and he said, 'if you sell it to me I'll save it'; I sold it to him for fifty pesos, and he took it and hid it. They asked for the oxcart, what had I done with the oxcart, well it left before that... He took it to [...] When it came back, no one could recognize it, the oxcart was different.[59]

---

54 Interviews: Guillermo González Brenes and Saturnino González Vargas.

55 Interview: María Ignacia Bogantes Zamora.

56 Interview: Rosa Fernández Araya.

57 Interview: Isabelina Alvarez Alvarado.

58 Interview: Orfilia Avila Ballestero.

59 Interview: L. G. A.

Livestock also tended to vanish, as did almost all durable consumption goods. There were usually several unlisted movables, and even when there was only a tiny plot of land or none at all, households usually had a few head of cattle, some furniture, household goods and sometimes tools. Among the wealthier of the deceased, omission of cattle was patent, given both the description of land use and oral testimony. On the other hand, even among merchants and relatively large farmers, life was generally austere, with no great conforts or luxuries. Socioeconomic differentiation was quite pronounced regarding land tenure, yet it was expressed only to a limited extent in durable consumption and lifestyle.

IMMOVABLES

These were the main object of probate proceedings, and quality of information on land-tenure in 1926-1935 was adequate, especially with respect to area. Even so, there were cases in which a farm was not included in the inventory because the real estate transaction by which it was acquired had not been legally formalized:

> Father sold some land, and the way land was sold was, as they say, by the hair of their whiskers. No deeds, no papers, nothing... The man who bought the land came to buy it and he said yes, because in those times a person's word was binding, and the deal was made, and then each pulled out a whisker and that was a sign that they had made a deal.[60]

In this way, properties changed hands several times, until one of the buyers required a deed, and then the transaction might end up being recorded as a sale from one of the previous owners to the last buyer. This system was made possible by kinship and neighborly relations, but transmittal of property via inheritance required that ownership be legally established.

Value of immovable property per case increased with area, but at gradually slower rates given the lower intensity of land use on most large farms than on smaller ones, and the fact that they were usually at greater distances from the main population centers and transportation routes.[61] By geographical areas within the Central Valley, average values of holdings per case was highest in Grecia and Naranjo.[62] However, mortgages in this

---

60 Interview: Rosa Fernández Araya.

61 Average values increased gradually from ¢1,229 for holdings under one hectare and ¢1,542 for those under five, through ¢4,371 and $5,720 for holdings under ten and twenty-five hectares, to ¢7,912 for those from twenty-five to under one hundred hectares, and ¢22,968 for the largest ones.

62 Average value of holdings per case in Grecia-Naranjo was ¢7,147, versus ¢4,200 near Alajuela city and ¢3,438 in Palmares-San Ramón.

area were especially high, so that the actual value of immovable assets per case may not have been much higher here than elsewhere in the Central Valley.

Area of holdings per case averaged twenty-four hectares in 1926-1935, a 20% reduction with respect to 1895-1904. In the 1920s and 1930s there were a few cases with no real estate, and others with several hundred hectares. Frequency of cases by area does not faithfully reflect actual proportions of holdings in rural Alajuela, and is useful basically to evaluate the meaning of data from probate inventories.[63] On the other hand, even if area of holdings must be related to land use patterns to be meaningful for the analysis of specific productive units, it does allow for comparisons with landholding in probate inventories at the turn of the century. Proportions among the five main categories of holdings by area were actually quite similar in 1926-1935 and at the turn of the century, with some variation at the extremes: a relative increase of the smallest holdings, and a reduction of the largest ones toward the late twenties and early thirties. While intermediate units were relatively stable, if somewhat smaller, it is possible that there had been some fragmentation of smallholdings, together with subdivision of certain large estates.

By level of fortune, average area per case was approximately four hectares in fortunes under ¢1,000, fourteen in the following category, and eighty hectares in fortunes from ¢5,000 on. Classification by value of the land followed a similar pattern,[64] while geographical distribution by place of residence showed sub-regional differences in land tenure per household: holdings were about twice as large in the Northwest as in cantones around Alajuela city, and somewhat larger at the western end of the Valley than near Grecia.[65]

The number of individual properties per case, averaging 2.8 in 1926-1935, had declined 25% with respect to 1895-1904. The number of cases with one or two properties increased significantly, while there were less multiple properties. Number of farms was usually associated with area of holdings: cases with less than five hectares often had only one or two properties; those from five to under twenty-five hectares usually had three or four, and larger holdings were formed by numerous properties (Table

63 38% of holdings were under one hectare, and would classify as sub-family units according to area. 19% were one to under five hectares, or hypothetically deficit-yielding domestic units. 25% were potentially intermediate domestic units, with areas from five to under twenty-five hectares. There were only a few cases in the following category, but 14% were fifty hectares or more. As discussed in previous chapters, the actual classification of specific cases with respect to the typology requires consideration of land use and other factors.

64 When land value was either under ¢500 or ¢500 to less than ¢1,000, average area was 2.5 to 3.8 hectares; in the following two categories it was 15.9 and 17.5 hectares, and 123 when holdings per case were estimated at ¢10,000 or more.

65 Average sizes were 11.5 hectares near the provincial capital, 21.5 in Grecia-Naranjo, and 25.7 in Palmares-San Ramón.

6.8). Together with a similar but less pronounced association between number of farms and value,[66] as well as a general reduction in area per case, this would seem to indicate a deterioration of the landholding basis of many rural households during the first third of the twentieth century.

TABLE 6.8 NUMBER OF INDIVIDUAL PROPERTIES PER CASE IN PROBATE INVENTORIES, BY TOTAL AREA OF HOLDINGS, ALAJUELA PROVINCE, 1926-1935

Area (Has.)	Number of Individual Properties			Cases
	AVERAGE	MINIMUM	MAXIMUM	
< 1	1.3	0	4	50
1 - < 5	2.1	1	5	25
5 - < 10	3.9	1	14	15
10 - < 25	3.5	1	9	17
25 - < 100	5.8	1	19	16
≥ 100	8.0	1	23	7

Source: Probate inventories for 1926-1935.

This descriptive characterization can now be related to the typology of rural economic units. Pending a discussion of land use in the following section, and given that household composition and access to land by other means varied from case to case, this is only a preliminary approximation. However, it will allow us to compare similarly-sized holdings over time, and serve as a starting point for further analysis.

Those holdings which by their area (less than one hectare) may be considered sub-family units in 1926-1935, were usually constituted by a single property, worth ¢500 to ¢1,000. Potentially deficit-yielding domestic units, according to the initial criterion of area per case, were more often formed by two properties, with values ranging from about ¢1,000 to ¢3,000. Holdings which were intermediate in terms of area usually included three to four farms, with a value which fluctuated above and below an average value of some ¢5,000. Units with areas from twenty-five to under fifty hectares were most often made up of five or six properties, with value varying well beyond or under the average of ¢10,000. Finally, the larger productive units might have anywhere between seven and twenty-seven farms, with estimated value averaging some ¢30,000, although it could be considerably less or up to ¢190,000.

In comparing the characteristics of Alajuelan holdings in these years with the situation in 1895-1904, we find that there was a significant increase in the nominal value of each type of landholding unit, while the

66 Average number of individual properties per case in 1926-1935 did not grow significantly for holdings under ¢500, ¢1,000 and ¢5,000, but it did increase from 2.1 to 6.8 per case as value of all holdings surpassed ¢5,000.

number of properties tended to decline somewhat. As shown above, average size of holdings also declined significantly, together with average number of farms per case. Sub-family-sized units increased in relative number, while the three types hypothetically characterized as domestic units were a constant proportion, and the larger units lost ground numerically. Flexible access to land, in the nineteenth century, had given way to subdivision of holdings, especially within the Central Valley, although intermediate-sized units did not tend to disappear. Together with persistence of market-oriented domestic units whose members were active participants in multiple commodity exchanges, there certainly was an ongoing process of socioeconomic differentiation, as reflected in labor and credit relations, household fortunes, and landholding in this mercantile rural society. Yet the meaning of land-tenure also changed, as agricultural intensification and productive specialization proceeded further, and in various ways, during the early decades of the twentieth century.

Labors of the Land

During the first half of the twentieth century, there were major changes in land use patterns in the Northwest, specifically, and the province of Alajuela as a whole. Agricultural intensification resulted both from the investment of additional labor in previously uncultivated or very extensively-used lands, and from a trend toward productive specialization in certain areas and types of productive units. This section will deal with transformations in regional uses of the land, in the organization of labor, and in production on various economic units.

Semi-perennial crops, primarily coffee and sugarcane, more than doubled the area under cultivation from Alajuela to San Ramón in the half-century after 1905, while grain production seems to have declined, especially in the Northwest.[67] Toward 1935, coffee was clearly the predominant crop in the Northwest, but there was a significant subregional variation in its association with other crops. In the easternmost cantones, and most strongly in Grecia, coffee was combined with sugarcane, locally and at the level of productive units. Instead, further westward, San Ramón, Palmares, and to a certain extent Naranjo, were areas in which coffee was most often combined with grain crops, even if these were planted on a small scale.[68] By the mid-twentieth century, coffee had almost completed its occupation of the intermediate altitudes, while sugarcane became more important at lower altitudes within the Northwest, and staples were mostly in the periphery of the Central Valley and beyond.[69]

67 DGEC (1905,1955).

68 IDC (1935).

69 DGEC (1950b, 1955).

Livestock raising shifted outward once again in the twentieth century. Beef cattle became especially important in the recently settled northern part of the province, and retained its importance in the southwestern section of the Central Valley. Dairy production expanded at higher altitudes on the Cordillera, but from Alajuela to San Ramón cattle was gradually reduced to that necessary for direct consumption of milk and meat, and to the use of oxen as draft animals.[70]

A closer look at the subregional distribution of agricultural activities in the agricultural censuses of these years will allow comparison with previous land use patterns and with other regions.

With some 10,000 hectares of coffee plantations in Alajuela, on 6,245 farms covering three and a half times that area, Alajuela was second only to San José in area under coffee production. For ecological reasons, coffee was highly concentrated in the Central Valley, so data on the province refer almost exclusively to the region from Alajuela city to San Ramón, even after a century of agro-export development.[71] While many farms in the area from Alajuela city to San Ramón had coffee groves by 1935, Alajuela was still the province in which coffee was combined -on those same farms- with the largest area in other crops (62%, vs. 30% to 32% in Heredia, San José and Cartago). On the other hand, Alajuela was, after Heredia, the province with least uncultivated area per coffee farm (one third the amount in San José and Cartago). From the above, we conclude that the expansion of coffee production in Alajuela was a major component of a broader process of agricultural intensification. However, this was still not a single-crop regional economy, nor were productive units totally specialized in coffee to the exclusion of other economic activities.

Sub-regionally, Naranjo and Palmares were the cantones where coffee farms had become most specialized by 1935 (Table 6.9). In Grecia there was still more pastureland than area in coffee on those farms, and there was almost as much sugarcane as coffee in terms of area. Pasture was also predominant on coffee farms in San Ramón, where grain production, too, covered a slightly larger area than coffee. Taken as a regional economy, the Northwest was still a diversified one, even if specific areas did tend to concentrate more in certain types of production.

While Grecia was the area with most sugarcane production on coffee farms in 1935 (and there were also a few large, specialized sugarcane plantations there), it was also the one with proportionally less *trapiches* for small-scale processing of the cane. This is directly related to the establishment of large *ingenios* or modern sugarmills in Grecia. Instead, areas such as Palmares and San Ramón, where peasant farming was most important in the 1930's, as it is today, had more *trapiches* per area planted in sugarcane on such farms. Small-scale, independent sugarcane production and processing were associated, to some extent, with coffee and other

---

70 DGEC (1905, 1950b, 1955).

71 All data for this year are based on IDC (1935).

TABLE 6.9 LAND USE ON COFFEE-PRODUCING FARMS IN ALAJUELA PROVINCE, 1935

Cantón	Area in Farms									
	COFFEE		SUGARCANE		GRAIN		PASTURE		UNCULTIVATED	
	HAS.	%	HAS.	%	HAS.	%	HAS.	%	HAS.	%
Central	3,151	34.3	1,168	12.7	851	9.2	3,617	39.4	1,443	13.6
San Ramón	788	12.7	253	4.0	950	15.3	4,094	66.2	1,142	15.5
Grecia	1,807	21.1	1,694	19.7	150	1.7	4,849	56.6	1,456	14.5
Atenas	333	15.4	107	4.9	388	17.9	1,287	59.7	45	2.0
Naranjo	2,292	52.1	202	4.6	505	11.4	1,357	30.8	795	15.3
Palmares	1,149	46.4	104	4.1	283	11.4	739	29.8	181	6.8
Poás	441	18.5	441	18.5	106	4.4	1,370	57.5	356	13.0

Source: IDC (1935).

economic activities by peasant farmers in this area. Large-scale planting and processing of both crops was the equivalent economic strategy of estate-owners especially in the vicinity of Grecia, as was also the case in Juan Viñas, toward the other end of the Central Valley.

In 1948, the first study focusing specifically on sugarcane found 5,764 hectares (almost half the area for all Costa Rica) in the 2,500 sugarcane fields of Alajuela province.[72] Grecia was clearly the main sugar-producing area, with the largest average size of plantations. The other northwestern cantones were minor sugarcane producers, and plantations were relatively small there. Sugarcane production was, however, widespread throughout the province, from the densely settled rural areas near Alajuela city to the more recently and sparsely settled ones beyond the Central Valley, e.g. in San Carlos.

In 1950, when the first comprehensive agricultural census was taken, coffee groves covered over 9,000 hectares in the province, and sugarcane half that area (Table 6.10). Sub-regional specialization within the Northwest had become quite pronounced, with Grecia occupying much more land for sugarcane than for coffee. Palmares and Naranjo, in turn, had a much larger area in the latter crop. Two thirds of coffee production in the province came from the Northwest and over half that of sugarcane. The area planted in both crops had approximately doubled there since 1905.

TABLE 6.10 COFFEE AND SUGARCANE ON FARMS IN THE NORTHWEST, 1950

Canton	Type of Use							
	COFFEE				SUGARCANE			
	FARMS		AREA		FARMS		AREA	
	#	%	HAS.	%	#	%	HAS.	%
San Ramón	634	18.5	1,001	10.9	613	17.3	725	8.7
Grecia	459	13.4	1,160	12.6	700	19.8	3,032	36.4
Naranjo	480	14.0	2,316	25.1	238	6.7	390	4.7
Palmares	376	10.9	1,043	11.3	97	2.7	64	0.7
Valverde Vega	153	4.5	631	6.8	168	4.7	332	4.0
Northwest	2,102	61.3	6,151	66.7	1,816	51.2	4,542	54.5
Alajuela	3,431	100.0	9,228	100.0	3,545	100.0	8,328	100

Source DGEC (1950b), pp. 64 and 74.

Grain production was not itemized by cantons in the 1950 census, but there were just over two thousand farms in the Northwest in1955, with some 2,800 hectares of cornfields in the first harvest.[73] This was a thirty-

72 DGEC (1948).

73 DGEC (1955), Table 16, p. 30.

percent reduction with respect to 1905. Naranjo and Palmares had the smallest area in cornfields, while Grecia and San Ramón (both of which had territories outside the Central Valley) accounted for over 75% of regional production. Elsewhere in the province, grain cultivation was still important near Alajuela city, and was becoming significant in San Carlos.

Grazing was still the main form of productive use of the land in mid-century Grecia and San Ramón, although not necessarily within the Central Valley (Table 6.11). It was less significant in Naranjo, and minimal in Palmares. Beyond the Central Valley, it had become especially important in San Carlos, where there were 34,000 hectares of pastureland. Livestock raising, with an average of two head of adult cattle per hectare, was somewhat less extensive than in the late nineteenth century.[74]

TABLE 6.11 PASTURE AND CATTLE IN THE NORTHWEST, 1950

Canton	**Pasture**				**Cattle** *		
	FARMS		AREA (HAS.)				
	#	%	#	%	#	%	AVG./HA.
San Ramón	1,132	16.3	21,374	16.4	14,711	13.1	1.5
Grecia	1,147	16.5	19,179	14.7	16,745	14.9	1.2
Naranjo	416	6.0	3,999	3.1	2,888	2.6	1.4
Palmares	245	3.5	1,132	0.9	1,491	1.3	0.8
Valverde Vega	176	2.5	2,712	2.1	1,925	1.7	1.4
Northwest	3,116	44.8	48,396	37.2	37,760	33.6	1.3
Alajuela	6,943	100.0	130,084	100.0	112,349	100.0	1.2

* More than one year old.

Source: DGEC (1950b), p. 57.

AGRICULTURAL LABOR

This undoubtedly was affected by changing crop mixes and agricultural intensification. More labor was invested per unit area, yet there were no deep technological transformations. Agricultural implements remained more or less the same as in the nineteenth century, and if anything coffee tended to substitute draft animals with manual labor. Only a few hundred ploughs were found in the mid-twentieth century in the Northwest, primarily for the reduced area in semi-annual crops, or to prepare the land for planting new coffee groves or sugarcane fields. Nine tenths of coffee groves used only shovels, and two thirds of 371 intensively-cultivated

74 DGEC (1950), p. 57. As mentioned in the previous chapter, maximum carrying capacity of pastureland at the turn of the century was about one head of cattle per hectare.

farms farms used only of a *macana* (a type of planting stick with a flat metal end) and a hoe.[75] Clearly, tools were not the means by which formerly more extensive agriculture was intensified.

Fertilizer was of very limited importance on most farms. Hardly any was used then, or is used today for maize cultivation, whether alone or associated with beans. In 1935 only 2.5% of the farms producing coffee in this part of the Central Valley used fertilizers, and less than one sixth of the coffee acreage was fertilized. In the following years, such practices spread slowly. In 1950, fertilizers were applied on 5.6% of all farms. Use of manure, imported *guano* and artificial fertilizers probably began on the larger farms, although it gradually was adopted by smaller ones where it offered a possibility of obtaining high yields to counteract landholding fragmentation. Grecia, an area of larger farms, was the cantón with most coffee groves fertilized in 1935, but smallholder Palmares accounted for over half the farms using fertilizers in 1950.[76]

Intensification of land use was essentially the result of more labor inputs per unit area through changes in the crop mixes. As coffee became the predominant crop, labor requirement peaks became more prononunced. In contrast to the situation at the eastern end of the Central Valley, where less-defined seasons prolongued flowering and harvest time, which lasted several months more,[77] the coffee harvest was gathered from late November to early February in the western part of the Central Valley, with slight subregional variations. Sugarcane also required most labor for the harvest, which tended to concentrate in the dry season; however, even at mid-century, sugarcane was cut almost year round in several cantones of the region (Figure 6.3). Monthly distribution of sugarcane production also varied significantly from year to year, sometimes peaking in January-February, others in September, and being extremely even in other years.[78] While in some years there was a clear overlap with the coffee harvest, in others there was less of an overlap. Generally speaking, and partly due to the limited milling capacity of small *trapiches* and even of the medium-sized sugarmills, the sugarcane harvest tended to last very long, up to 200 days, including part of the rainy season, which meant higher transportation costs and lowered sugar or syrup yields.[79] The two main semi-perennial crops were, then, competitive in terms of labor requirements during the dry season in the region, but while the coffee harvest was highly concentrated between late November and early February, sugarcane was cut at other times of the year even at mid-century, thus evening out its labor requirements somewhat.

---

75 O. Benavides, quoted in Sandner (1962-1964), Vol. II, pp. 79-80.

76 DGEC (1935, 1950b).

77 Hall (1976), p. 21.

78 Ortiz (1949), pp. 324-329).

79 Revilla (1948), pp. 110-113.

MONTHLY AGRICULTURAL ACTIVITIES BY CANTON IN WESTERN CENTRAL VALLEY, 1948-49

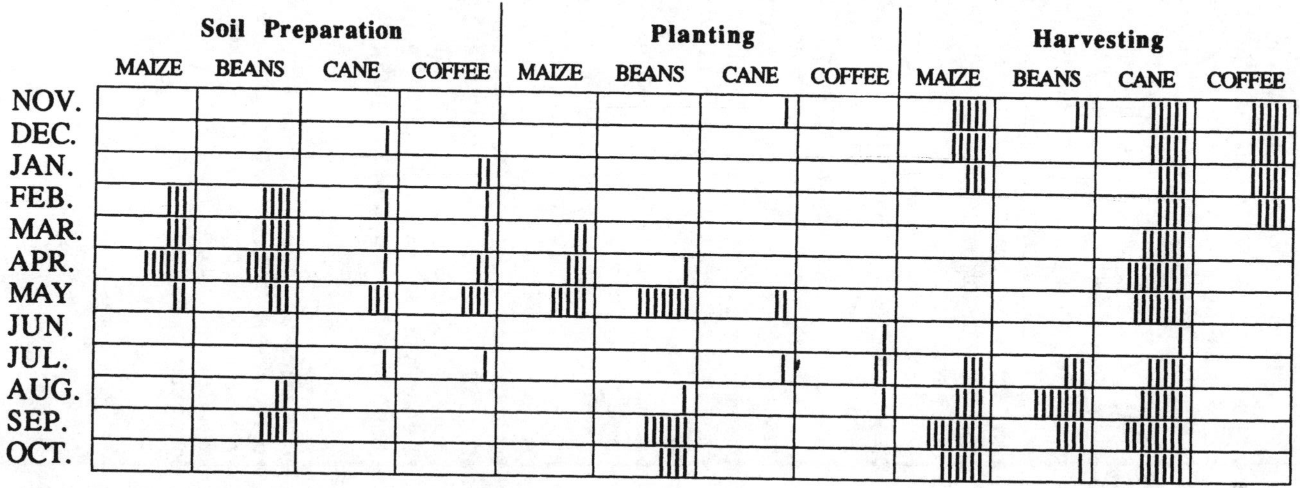

	Soil Preparation				Planting				Harvesting			
	MAIZE	BEANS	CANE	COFFEE	MAIZE	BEANS	CANE	COFFEE	MAIZE	BEANS	CANE	COFFEE
NOV.							1		5	2	5	5
DEC.			1						5		5	5
JAN.				2					3		4	5
FEB.	3	4	1	1							4	4
MAR.	3	4	1	1	2						6	
APR.	6	6	1	2	3	1					8	
MAY	2	3	3	4	5	7	2				7	
JUN.								1			1	
JUL.			1	1			1	2	3	3	5	
AUG.		2				1		1	4	7	6	
SEP.		4				6			8	4	8	
OCT.						4			6	1	6	

Source: *Suelo Tico*, Dec. 1948 to Nov. 1949

Figure 6.3

Semi-annual crops, especially grain, did not openly compete with the semiperennials for seasonal labor. Maize, for example, was planted twice a year, the first usually in May, to be harvested four or five months later. A second, smaller planting took place in some areas toward September. In Grecia and San Ramón, the first planting was approximately four times larger than the second one, while in Naranjo and Palmares the latter was minimal. Instead, the second planting of maize was relatively large in other parts of the province, such as Atenas, as it probably had been during the nineteenth century in the Northwest.[80] Other cultural practices in maize and coffee did not compete much for labor during the first half of the twentieth century:[81] pruning of coffee trees in late January; clearing of the land for planting, usually by *quema*, in March and ploughing in April, for maize; cleaning and shoveling (*raspa y palea*) in coffee groves from March to July, but not in April; preparation of the soil for a second planting of maize, from the short *veranillo* in July, to September. Several varieties of beans complemented maize, not only for nitrogen fixation in the soil, but also because they were associated crops in the first planting. *Vainicas* (green beans) were harvested in August, and the second planting took place in the late rainy season, for harvesting in the summer as black beans. In San Ramón, the second planting of beans was larger than the first, probably on the same lands on which maize had been harvested before.[82]

Monthly labor requirements by all crops in Alajuela province, but especially in the area from Alajuela to San Ramón, were far from even in 1950.[83] December was the month in which most coffee farms had more laborers, although they also had many in November and January. May, June and September were months with especially high labor requirements on grain-producing farms, for planting and harvesting of maize.

Additionally, while crops were combined on many farms, they tended to specialize more in one or the other, and there were also differences between the large estates and small farms. As was clearly stated during a congressional discussion of taxes on imported grain in 1930, the production of maize and beans was an endeavor of peasant-farmers, whose grain output responded positively to price trends of grain, and not to the decline of coffee prices and of wages:

> ...it is not the daylaborer on the haciendas who plants grain. It is the small farmer, who has a manzana or two of land, and at least a pair of oxen, who is not a wage laborer but rather takes care of the plot of land which he owns or that which he rents in exchange for a part of the harvest, doing his work and exchanging jornales (daylabor) with his neighbors.

---

80 DGEC (1955), p. 30.

81 *La Gaceta*, June 11th, 1930, p. 894.

82 DGEC (1955), p. 30.

83 DGEC (1950), p. XXIX and 129; Oficina de Censos (1950).

> When the price of maize and of beans has been good, our man plants more the following year, or at least the same amount as the previous year; when the price is bad, he plants less.[84]

If we add to the above the sub-regional variations in land use, previously mentioned, we conclude that labor requirements varied not only seasonally, but also by geographic areas and types of economic units. It is time now to discuss the latter.

PRODUCTIVE UNITS

In Alajuela province, as a whole, the productive units were not much more specialized in 1926-1935 than they had been at the turn of the century. There was only a slight increase in the frequency of coffee cultivation per case, and a similar reduction of other productive uses of the land.[85] Even though area under cultivation per crop can only be analyzed for single-use farms, productive diversity per economic unit was actually more than would be suggested by frequency of land use: documents from probate inventories and from the real estate registry often left out secondary crops, which were not commercially important but did play a significant role in the domestic economy of Alajuelan peasants, then as in the previous century. Furthermore, oral testimony in various cases shows how coffee cultivation, specifically, was very different on large estates than on domestic and subfamily units in the twentieth century. In the latter, it was associated much more frequently with subsistence crops, interplanted in the coffee groves, and even density of planting differed:

> In those days, work was so different that you can hardly compare; on the same little plot of land you would find coffee, tiquisque [malanga or spoonflower], and yuca plants [cassava], everything planted on the same piece of land... [the coffee trees] were not planted very thickly, no, because they used to plant things in between. Not very thickly, but not too far, either... in between they would plant some yuca, and people before would not waste anything; at the beginning of each row, they planted yuca, and in the middle, or where they thought best, the tiquisque, or a chayote, and let it spread out.[86]

Grain and various crops for self-consumption were also planted on small-to-medium-sized holdings which, according to the inventories, were in pasture or sugarcane. For example, Domingo Lobo had eight uncultivated

---

84 *La Gaceta*, July 11th, 1930, p. 893.

85 The number of properties per case with each type of land use, in probate inventories for 1926-1935, was: coffee 1.0; sugarcane 0.5; pasture 1.2; grain 0.6; and uncultivated 0.9.

86 Interview: Rosa Fernández Araya.

hectares and a similiar or slightly smaller area in pasture and sugarcane, but his descendants claim that he also "cultivated black beans and maize".[87] In other cases, "there was pasture... and some coffee trees, just for the household... [and also] *chayote, yuca,* and *tiquisque*".[88]

Sub-regionally, coffee was the most frequent type of land use on productive units in Grecia and Naranjo, although pasture and uncultivated land were also found often in the inventories for 1926-1935 (Table 6.12). Sugarcane was the next most frequent agricultural use of the land, while staple grain and other crops such as plantain were not recorded often in probate cases for this region. In Palmares and San Ramón, instead, there were more uncultivated lands, while pasture was the most frequent type of productive use, followed by coffee. When the deceased lived near Alajuela city, grain-production and pasture was still frequent on their holdings, although some of the latter were located eslewhere, especially in San Carlos. Coffee production is found less frequently in such cases, and sugarcane even less. As the most urbanized area, there were of course many plots used exclusively for housing. Production was diversified throughout the province, though coffee specialization was stronger on productive units in the Northwest, primarily near Grecia and Naranjo.

TABLE 6.12 FREQUENCY OF EACH TYPE OF LAND USE PER CASE, BY PLACE OF RESIDENCE OF DECEASED, ALAJUELA PROVINCE, 1926-1935

Land Use	Average per Case			Maximum		
	CAPITAL*	G-N-VV**	SR-P***	CAPITAL*	G-N-VV**	SR-P***
Coffee	0.6	1.5	1.1	4	15	7
Sugarcane	0.4	0.6	0.5	5	3	2
Pasture	1.2	1.3	1.3	13	12	11
Grain	1.1	0.3	0.3	10	3	2
Uncultivated	0.6	1.0	1.2	7	9	8
Dwelling	0.1	0.2	0.1	4	5	5
Other	0.1	0.2	0.1	1	3	1

* Alajuela city and surrounding cantónes.

** Grecia, Naranjo, Valverde Vega.

*** San Ramón and Palmares

By level of wealth, coffee cultivation was definitely the most frequent productive use in wealth under ¢1,000, followed by pasture (Table 6.13). Pasture predominated slightly over coffee at intermediate levels of fortune,

87 Interview: Andrés Lobo González.

88 Interview: Orifilia Avila Ballestero.

TABLE 6.13 FREQUENCY OF EACH TYPE OF LAND USE PER CASE, BY LEVEL OF WEALTH IN PROBATE INVENTORIES, ALAJUELA PROVINCE, 1926-1935

Level of Wealth	Land Use							Number of Cases
	COFFEE	SUGARCANE	PASTURE	GRAIN	UNCULTIVATED	DWELLING	OTHER	
< 500	0.9	0.4	0.7	0.2	0.4	0.9	0.2	54
500 - < 1,000	0.6	0.2	0.5	0.4	0.4	0.6	0.1	30
1,000 - < 5,000	0.7	0.4	0.8	0.6	0.6	0.8	0.1	54
≥ 5,000	2.0	1.1	3.4	1.5	2.5	1.6	0.5	33

Source: Probate cases for 1926-1935.

TABLE 6.14 FREQUENCY OF EACH TYPE OF LAND USE, BY TOTAL AREA PER CASE, 1926-1935

Area (Has.)	Land Use (Average Frequency per Case)							Number of Cases
	COFFEE	SUGARCANE	PASTURE	GRAIN	UNCULTIVATED	DWELLING	OTHER	
0 - < 0.7	0.6	0.3	0.3	0.2	0.3	0.7	0.1	50
0.7 - < 3.5	0.9	0.5	0.6	0.5	0.6	0.6	0.1	25
3.5 - < 7.0	1.0	0.9	2.1	1.2	1.0	0.9	0.1	15
7.0 - < 17.5	0.8	0.5	1.6	1.3	1.0	0.9	0.2	17
17.5 - < 70.0	1.6	0.8	3.4	1.1	2.8	1.0	0.3	16
≥ 70.0	1.7	1.3	3.9	1.6	3.1	2.0	0.9	7

Source: Probate inventories for 1926-1935.

and strongly at higher levels.[89] By size of holdings, coffee was the most frequent agrarian use of the land on those under five hectares, and pasture on the larger ones (Table 6.14). Grain production was important on small to medium-sized holdings, but especially on those from five to under ten hectares. While the various uses of the land were often combined on very diverse holdings, coffee was especially frequent on the smaller ones, together with grain and sugarcane, while grazing was the main form of land use on larger holdings, followed by coffee.

TABLE 6.15 AREA AND VALUE OF FARMS ACCORDING TO LAND USE IN PROBATE INVENTORIES OF ALAJUELA PROVINCE, 1926-1935

Land Use	**Area (Has.)**			**Value ($ or ¢)**			**Cases with Data**		
	AVG.	MIN.	MAX.	AVG.	MIN.	MAX.	USE	AREA	VALUE
Coffee	5.6	0.1	196	1,748	20	25,000	171	90	168
Sugarcane	10.5	0.2	196	2,314	50	30,000	84	53	83
Pasture	15.1	0.1	271	2,020	25	30,000	210	126	206
Grain	11.8	0.2	200	1,737	50	30,000	108	73	107
Uncultivated	24.3	0.1	417	2,273	50	30,000	151	95	148
Other	33.8	0.7	196	4,219	50	30,000	32	16	29

Source: Probate inventories for 1926-1935.

Individual properties, averaging 10.8 hectares and ¢1,583, were mostly single-use farms. Close to thirty percent had two agrarian uses, and relatively few were multiple-use properties. However, secondary uses were also more frequent on individual farms than is reflected in probate inventories:

> ... he planted maize, beans...plantain, yuca, things to eat, tiquisque, sweet potato...In that time there was uncultivated land, small pastures for a cow or two, and they also planted maize, beans...and a little coffee, but it wasn't for profit...just for the household....they said that in the plot of land they had cleared, they should plant a little of everything.[90]

While pasture continued to be the most frequent use of the land on individual properties of Alajuela province in the cases for 1926-1935, its relative importance had diminished with respect to the turn of the century. At that time, coffee growing had already been the main crop, and its importance increased during the early decades of the twentieth century, becoming almost as frequent as grazing. Grain cultivation, sugarcane and uncultivated lands had declined only slightly in their relative frequency,

89 A similar association was found with value of properties, which as stated before were the main component of fortunes. Coffee was the predominant use in 82 properties estimated at less than ¢1,000, and pasture in 87 properties worth more than that, but especially in those from ¢10,000 on.

90 Interview: Rosa Fernández Araya.

TABLE 6.16 LAND USE ON INDIVIDUAL FARMS IN PROBATE INVENTORIES OF ALAJUELA PROVINCE, BY AREA, 1926-1935

Area (Has.)	Type of Land Use													
	COFFEE		SUGARCANE		PASTURE		GRAIN		UNCULTURED		DWELLING		OTHER	
	#	%	#	%	#	%	#	%	#	%	#	%	#	%
≥ 25	3	13.6	4	18.2	15	68.2	5	22.7	17	77.3	8	36.4	4	18.2
10 - < 25	1	4.3	4	17.4	15	65.2	10	43.5	11	47.8	7	30.4	3	13.0
5 - < 10	8	25.0	5	15.6	25	78.1	11	34.4	15	46.9	4	12.5	3	9.4
1 - < 5	35	33.0	25	23.6	51	48.1	31	29.2	29	27.4	22	20.8	3	2.8
< 1	43	40.6	15	14.2	20	18.9	16	15.1	23	21.7	48	45.3	3	2.8

Source: Probate inventories for 1926-1935.

partly due to the incorporation of new lands outside the Central Valley.[91] Coffee specialization must therefore have been especially frequent on individual properties in the Northwest, while cattle predominated in San Carlos and other recently settled areas.

As in 1895-1904, farms on which coffee was cultivated, whether alone or in association with other crops, were the smallest, averaging some five hectares, although their value was similar to that of other farms. Grain and sugarcane farms were usually of intermediate sizes, while those with pastures or uncultivated areas tended to be the largest (Table 6.15). When farms are classified by area for 1926-1935, coffee was clearly predominant in the smallest farms, grain was especially frequent on those in the five- to ten-hectare range, and pasture on the larger ones (Table 6.16).

As in 1895-1904, average areas and values of individual farms increased with the number of agrarian uses (Table 6.17). On single-use farms, it was no longer pasture but coffee that predominated in 1926-1935. Livestock production was still more frequent on double- and multiple-use farms (Table 6.18). Coffee-producing farms, then, were relatively more specialized than those with pastures or other crops.

TABLE 6.17 AREA AND VALUE OF INDIVIDUAL FARMS, BY NUMBER OF AGRARIAN USES IN PROBATE INVENTORIES, ALAJUELA PROVINCE, 1926-1935

Number of Uses	**Area (Has.)**		**Value ($ or ¢)**		**Number of Farms**
	AVERAGE	MAXIMUM	AVERAGE	MAXIMUM	
None	11.6	91.1	1,462	5,025	35
Single	6.2	417.0	1,124	23,000	248
Double	12.7	271.0	1,744	25,000	134
Multiple	23.9	200.0	2,933	30,000	72

Source: Probate inventories for 1926-1935.

The same land-use triads were found in 1926-1935 as a third of a century before: coffee-sugarcane-pasture, and pasture-grain-uncultivated land. The difference was that toward 1930 coffee was associated more often to sugarcane than to livestock on individual farms, while the association between grain and uncultivated lands had weakened somewhat (Table 6.19). These same crop associations were present in the subregions within the Central Valley. Within the Northwest, coffee was strongly associated with sugarcane in Grecia-Naranjo, and with pasture in Palmares-

91 Relative frequency of pasture on individual properties in probate inventories of Alajuela province for 1926-1935 was 42.9%; there was coffee on 35.0% of such properties; uncultivated land on 30.9%; grain on 22.1%; sugarcane on 17.2%; dwellings on 28.8%; and other uses on 6.5%.

TABLE 6.18 FREQUENCY OF AGRARIAN USE OF THE LAND ON INDIVIDUAL FARMS, BY NUMBER OF USES IN PROBATE INVENTORIES, ALAJUELA PROVINCE, 1926-1935

Number of Uses	Coffee		Sugar-cane		Pasture		Grain		Uncultivated		Other	
	#	%	#	%	#	%	#	%	#	%	#	%
1	92	37.2	9	3.6	56	22.6	44	17.7	44	17.7	3	1.2
2	37	13.8	29	10.8	95	35.4	37	13.8	61	22.8	9	3.4
3 +	42	17.5	46	19.2	59	24.6	27	11.2	46	19.2	20	8.3

Source: Probate inventories for 1926-1935.

San Ramón. As in the late nineteenth century, grain-producing farms concentrated near the provincial capital. There was also grain in Atenas and San Mateo, but there are fewer references to maize production in probate inventories in the Northwest.[92]

TABLE 6.19 CROP ASSOCIATION ON INDIVIDUAL PROPERTIES, ACCORDING TO SELECTED LAND USE, PROBATE INVENTORIES OF ALAJUELA PROVINCE, 1926-1935

Associated Uses	Selected Uses									
	COFFEE		SUGAR-CANE		PASTURE		GRAIN		UNCULTIVATED	
	#	%	#	%	#	%	#	%	#	%
Coffee	-	-	44	52.4	39	18.6	16	14.8	26	17.2
Sugarcane	44	25.7	-	-	46	21.9	14	13.0	24	15.9
Pasture	39	22.8	46	54.8	-	-	46	42.6	86	57.0
Grain	16	9.4	14	16.7	46	21.9	-	-	20	13.2
Uncultivated	26	15.2	24	28.6	86	41.0	20	18.5	-	-

Source: Probate inventories for 1926-1935.

By 1926-1935, half the coffee farms were concentrated in the area of Grecia and Naranjo, and the Northwest contained seventy percent of all coffee farms in the province. To a lesser extent, sugarcane plantations similarly concentrated in this region. While pastures were important in the Northwest, they were also becoming frequent in the northern part of the province.[93] In the context of a gradual yet incomplete specialization in coffee production from Alajuela city to San Ramón, this crop seems to have been especially significant on productive units in Grecia and Naranjo, where single-use properties were also most frequent.

Area and value of individual properties were closely associated to each other, especially for sizes between one and twenty-five hectares or values

92 In the cantons near the town ofAlajuela, according to the sample of 1926-1935 probate records, coffee was associated with sugarcane on eleven individual farms, with grain on nine, pasture on eight, and uncultivated land on one. In that part of Grecia and Naranjo within the Central Valley, coffee was found on twenty-three individual properties together with sugarcane, on fourteen with pasture, and on one with grain. In Palmares and the part of San Ramón which is inside the Central Valley, association of coffee with other crops was primarily with pasture (on thirteen such farms) and sugarcane (on seven), in contrast with only two associations with grain, and eight with uncultivated land.

93 50% of coffee farms and 38% of sugarcane fields were in Grecia-Naranjo, while 43% of grain-producing farms were in the vicinity of the provincial capital, and pasture was more evenly distributed.

from ¢500 to ¢10,000. The smallest farms, under five hectares, were most often near Grecia or Alajuela city. Medium-sized farms were important in the Northwest as a whole, but especially toward San Ramón, while the larger individual farms were frequent in San Carlos.[94] Roughly the same pattern was found in terms of values, except that Grecia-Naranjo not only had most of the properties under ¢1,000, but also of those worth ¢5,000 or more. At an individual-farm level, there was more fragmentation in the vicinity of Grecia and Alajuela city, while intermediate farms were still important at the western end of the Valley, and the largest ones were on the northern frontier or other recently settled areas.

TABLE 6.20 AREA AND VALUE OF SINGLE-USE FARMS, BY LAND USE IN PROBATE INVENTORIES, ALAJUELA PROVINCE, 1926-1935

Land Use	Area (Has.)		Value ($ or ¢)		Indications of		
	AVG.	MAX.	AVG.	MAX.	USE	AREA	VALUE
Coffee	0.9	4.9	1,331	23,000	92	44	91
Sugarcane	0.4	0.7	406	900	9	6	9
Pasture	5.2	45.0	940	5,200	56	35	56
Grain	2.2	19.6	876	7,900	44	31	43
Uncultivated	18.8	417.0	1,238	5,000	44	33	43
Other	10.5	14.0	3,000	3,000	3	2	2

Source: Probate inventories for 1926-1935.

Regarding single-use farms, their area was very similar for each type of productive use in 1926-1935 as in the late nineteenth century, although maximum sizes had declined (Table 6.20). It would seem that the size of many already-small farms could not be reduced further, and tended to stabilize at a given level. Individual sugarcane fields were especially minute and few, but coffee groves and cornfields not associated with other crops were quite small too. On the other hand, as in 1895-1904, coffee was the most valuable crop (¢1,478 per hectare on single-use farms). Geographically, such coffee plots as well as the sugarcane fields were concentrated in Grecia and Naranjo, while cornfields were near the capital.[95] Generally speaking, the use of the land on these specialized farms confirms our previous findings, and identifies the limits of physical subdivision of viable individual farms for each productive activity.

94 In the probate inventories for 1926-1935, 58% of individual properties under one hectare and 54% of those from one to under five hectares were in Grecia-Naranjo and the area near Alajuela. 31% of 5<10 hectare farms were in San Ramón-Palmares, and 28% in Grecia-Naranjo. San Carlos was the region with most large individual farms (28%).

95 58% of single-use coffee farms were in Grecia-Naranjo, while 56% of cornfields were near Alajuela city.

In conclusion, while livestock raising was still the predominant use of the land on individual farms in the province as a whole, coffee cultivation had increased significantly in the Northwest during the first third of the twentieth century. This was not a single-crop local economy, not only because coffee farms were often part of productive units with other economic activities, but also because on many individual properties, coffee was associated with sugarcane, cattle or grain. Furthermore, oral testimony indicates that coffee was interplanted, on peasant holdings, with secondary crops for direct consumption.

Within the Northwest, Grecia and Naranjo were the areas with more coffee farms, although there was also a strong association with sugarcane in this specific subregion. On farms near the provincial capital, staple grain crops retained their importance as market-oriented activities, together with coffee, while at the western end of the Central Valley coffee was more often combined with grazing. In San Carlos, to the north, pastureland and uncultivated areas were associated, to a lesser extent, with local grain production.

Coffee farms were clearly the most valuable ones per area, although together with sugarcane fields they were the smallest farms. Coffee was the predominant crop on highly specialized and small single-use farms (which might nevertheless include subsistence crops), from Alajuela to San Ramón but even more so near Grecia and Naranjo. Instead, livestock raising was more frequent on the larger, double or multiple-use farms, both in the vicinity of San Ramón and in the northern part of the province.

Land use patterns on productive units near the provincial capital were geared toward more diversified commercial activities which included coffee, maize, beans, livestock and other products, on small to medium-sized holdings. In Grecia and Naranjo, grain was less important as a commercial crop, and instead the many small farms as well as several large estates were substantially based on coffee, often associated with sugarcane in this sub-region. Toward San Ramón, coffee and cattle were the prevalent uses of the land on units of intermediate size and value. Within this subregion, Palmares was probably more specialized in coffee production, judging by the census data on land use and the fact that San Ramón had major territories outside the Central Valley. In the northern part of the province, livestock raising was the predominant productive use of the land on relatively large farms, which also included significant uncultivated areas.

In each of the abovementioned areas, the crop mixes and degree of specialization of productive units responded to multiple factors, in view of which households and enterprises made decisions regarding production. Some of these factors were geographical (e.g. location and means of transportation) which affected costs and therefore the decision to produce certain crops for sale or for direct consumption. We have seen, also, that coffee could be a subsistence crop under certain conditions, and grain was often a mercantile one. On the other hand, demographic processes, changes in land tenure and socioeconomic relations affected labor availability, which in turn had a different meaning for units which relied to a greater or lesser extent on daylabor. Changing crop mixes, which could themselves be more competitive or complementary in terms of their labor cycles, altered labor requirements on productive units, large and small. Market-oriented production of certain crops and direct consumption of others resulted more from the units' assessment of such factors, than from an inherent predisposition, e. g. of peasant farmers toward self-consumption and of owners of large estates toward commercial production. Even if risk-avoidance was a consideration for domestic units, they could and often did specialize more than the larger estates in coffee production or other crops, and smallholder grain production was certainly responsive to market incentives. On the other hand, while estate-owners did seek to develop commercial agriculture and to specialize insofar as possible and profitable, factors such as labor availability and the remoteness of regions in which large landholding units could be established at the time, often forced them to maintain a more diversified pattern of land use. Thus, maize production was a viable agricultural commodity for peasant-farmers near the provincial capital; coffee and sugarcane were attractive both for large and small productive units in the area of Grecia and Naranjo; coffee and livestock toward San Ramón, and grazing in the recently settled and relatively remote northern part of the province, ecologically inappropriate for coffee. In all these areas, specific land use systems on the various types of productive units are essential to understand the meaning of landholding characteristics; of commodity production by sub-family, domestic and supra-family units; and of the increasingly complex situations which household production/consumption units faced in this region at the time.

Dilemmas

This last section will focus on linkages between the various options and/or constraints faced by members of rural households, and the transmittal of property from one generation to the next. After a general discussion of the implications of twentieth-century agrarian changes on inheritance, specific mechanisms by which peasant households sought to avoid extreme fragmentation of holdings will be examined. This, in turn, will lead us to consider the impact of inheritance practices on the viability of domestic units, and their connections with other components of peasant economic strategies under increasingly adverse social conditions.

Given the trends in land use and landholding outlined in previous sections, clearly the Northwest underwent a process of agricultural intensification, together with an increased importance of coffee in the regional economy and a reduction in the size of many holdings. One of the responses to population growth, once there were hardly any agricultural lands to be claimed in the region, was the investment of greater amounts of labor per unit area, and a gradual productive specialization, to allow domestic (and perhaps some sub-family) units to survive despite the reduced availability of land per household. This, in turn, was substantially due to fragmentation of property in successive generations, through inheritance. Social norms in this regard were fundamentally egalitarian, and there was undoubtedly a strong pressure toward fragmentation, which led to the formation of smaller and smaller holdings. Specialization in coffee, itself, probably facilitated this subdivision or property, partly due to its greater labor intensity and profitability, partly due to its responsiveness to intensive cultural practices, minimal investments in equipment or other technical inputs, and its economic viability on extremely small plots.

On the other hand, subdivision by inheritance was partly counteracted by other means, whether or not those involved were aware of this. Such mechanisms, one of which was emigration, reduced the pressure toward fragmentation to a certain extent, and when subdivision surpassed the limits of economic viability other mechanisms sometimes led to a reversal of the process of dismemberment, re-establishing larger holdings or productive units. In 1930, the possibilities of claiming government lands in the western part of the Central Valley were practically non-existent, and would-be settlers had to travel relatively long distances and face much less favorable conditions than those under which their forebears had come to the Northwest from the Meseta Central. Even so, emigration was a frequently-chosen or perhaps imposed option for young adult members of rural households in the region. As shown in the first section of this chapter, many left permanently towards San Carlos, Guanacaste and the Atlantic region, while a certain number went to the cities. Under conditions of land scarcity, emigration had a major impact on inheritance.

In the cases which were followed up through interviews (as in many in which it was impossible to find heirs residing in the Northwest) relatives and neighbors speak often of descendants of the deceased in 1926-1935 who left precisely for those regions outside the Central Valley. Such cases were usually families whose minimal holdings in 1926-1935, often in the category of sub-family units, would in no way allow the heirs to obtain a living on the parental household lands. For example, after the demise of Modesta Blanco, the only property, half a hectare of sugarcane, was sold out of court. Her son Pablo emigrated first to La Línea, on the way to the Atlantic port of Limón, and then to Hojancha, in Guanacaste, but he was also in San Carlos at one point in time.[96]

In those cases in which heirs were found still living in the Northwest, they were often women, while men frequently emigrated, whether before or after the death of their parents. To cite only one example, Santana Arias was a daylaborer who had sold the few things the family owned upon the death of his wife. Of his two sons, one emigrated toward San Carlos and the other toward San José, while the daughter remained in Grecia.[97]

---

96 Interviews: Raimundo and Asdrúbal Salazar Ulate.

97 Interview: Cristina Arias Espinoza.

Beyond such individual cases, the general effect of emigration from the Northwest toward the outlying areas of the country was to reduce pressure toward fragmentation of the landholding base of small and perhaps medium-sized productive units in the region. It remains to be seen whether their inheritance rights were respected by their siblings, despite physical absence of these prospective heirs, and what arrangements were made among those who inherited or with third parties during the probate proceedings or after legal division of property.

Another difficulty faced by members of a growing number of rural households in the Northwest was the fact that remaining in their place of origin amounted to extreme land-poverty or landlessness, and therefore the need to obtain family sustenance by other means. One of these, in the peasant-farmer tradition, was to obtain lands through rental, sharecropping or association. Thus, when land was insufficient for household needs, it might be obtained to cultivate tobacco, grain or other products, sometimes sharing the work and product with other peasant-farmers.[98] However, the problem was not always that of a surplus of family labor with respect to material resources at their disposal. Sometimes, emigration of young adults or the old age of owners created the opposite situation, with domestic units being circumstantially transformed into units with more material resources than the household labor could utilize fully. The solutions, in such cases, included sale of lands and various contractual arrangements with other peasants needing land. Tranquilino Avila, for example, died at age seventy with only three children, and had sold his properties before dying, but prior to that he had rented out lands for other peasants' cattle to graze.[99]

Domestic piecework and permanent, seasonal or occasional wage labor were certainly another of the imposed options faced by members of sub-family units and deficit-yielding domestic units in the twentieth century. Piecework at home and domestically-related wage labor were quite frequent among female members of impoverished rural households, as among widows. They often carried out tasks similar to the traditional household chores, e.g. washing other people's clothes, cooking for the daylaborers on a farm, or preparing pastries and other edibles for sale.[100] Rural society undoubtedly had a negative valuation of permanent wage labor by adult women, although if necessary the daughters might work outside to help at home:

> Oh, no! After he died, she [the widow] did not work ouside, but at home... She ground other people's maize, and washed their clothes, and made tamales to sell... We also went out to work, to help her... She made toffee this way,

98 Interview: Ramona Lobo González; interview: Bernardo Barahona Campos.

99 Interview: Orfilia Avila Ballestero.

100 A specific example is to be found in the interview with: Isabelina Alvarez Alvarado, and the probate case of her deceased relative.

> by hand... they paid her sixty cents the dozen for the clothes she washed, and if she ironed, one-fifty [colones] the dozen.[101]

Women in families where holdings were insufficient to satisfy basic domestic needs also worked in the artisanal processing of agricultural products. In Palmares, where property was fragmented and there was tobacco production, "my sister, she worked, she made cigars, made tobacco into cigars... at that time they were one thousand for five *colones*...[and I] made cigars too."[102]

Seasonally, women, children and youths in many deficit-yielding and sub-family units worked outside their homes, in the coffee harvest.[103] Permanent wage labor within the region was, apparently, a last resort for members of intermediate and even deficit-yielding domestic units. Those who defined themselves or were defined in interviews and probate proceedings as *jornaleros* were, almost invariably, members of sub-family units with a minute plot of land, usually a house and garden.[104] Of course, there was a landless day-laborer population, often working on the large estates in the region, but given the nature of probate inventories there are very few cases of landlessness in this source.[105] In other cases, the single sons of smallholders with permanent surpluses of household labor did work for wages on a regular basis.[106]

However, occasional work on others' lands was not necessarily associated with a constant lack or surplus of household labor, nor was its content always that of wage relations proper. It was, sometimes, a way to compensate for seasonal variations in labor requirements, without resorting to direct wage labor. Labor exchanges (here called *manos cambiadas*) were mostly between domestic units whose members did not work as daylaborers:

> He only worked at home, although sometimes a friend would ask him to help weed some land that he needed to do quickly... then he would say, all right, I'll go and help you, and then you come and help me clean a little coffee grove with a shovel, or something, 'manos cambiadas', as they say. He would go and help for the other person to come later and help him, but when he was

101 Interview: María Ignacia Bogantes Zamora.

102 Interview: Rosa Fernández Araya.

103 Two examples are the interviews: Lucila Vega Bolaños and Isabelina Alvarez Alvarado, together with the probate cases of their deceased relatives.

104 This is the case of Raimundo Salazar Muñoz and Manuel Alvarez Matamoros.

105 For example Santana Arias Guzmán and Tranquilino Avila Oviedo. In other such cases in which there were no immovables in the inventory, interviews confirmed that there had been some during the lifetime of the deceased, although their value was quite low.

106 Interview: Rosa Fernández Araya.

going to help, he was going to help the other person, it was not that they paid him.[107]

On the other hand, there was a degree of flexibility in the interaction between labor capacity and household consumption needs, not only during the chayanovian 'lifecycle' of the domestic unit, but also during the year: exploitation of unpaid labor of sons and daughters could be intensified at certain times of the year, while in others it was difficult to fully occupy the household's labor capacity on the farm. Consumption, too, could increase or diminish somewhat during the year, especially in connection with the harvest:

> [in the rainy seasons] there was less work and then you had to buy very little of everything... then, well, you had to spare things more because you knew there was no money to go and buy the following day... [in the dry season] you ate better. It's not that food was lacking at any time, but you ate more and better... in the dry season... you sold the maize, if you had maize, and the sugarcane was taken to market in the dry season... all the things you sold were better in the dry season.[108]

It should also be mentioned that despite their longstanding commodity orientation, economic relations within this rural society, towards the end of our period, were still not totally limited to monetary forms or to the dictates of an all-embracing 'invisible hand'. The members of various domestic units exchanged products with no monetary calculation involved; the labor of children and women was sometimes paid in kind with no equivalence to salaries; and the local sale of agricultural products did not necessarily respond exclusively to mercantile criteria:

> ... for example, maybe that neighbor had chayotes and you had squash, he could give you and you could give them, that's how we got along, that's the way it was...I used to work, say, washing other people's clothes or grinding their maize... as was usual then in payment, they paid with a tapa de dulce [sugarcake], or some maize, or some beans, anything; they never paid with money...The maize was gathered... and then a neighbor would come for a cuartillo [unit of measure], and another neighbor would come for some more, and that's how it was sold, and depending on how poor the person who came to buy it was... then you sold it at a lower price, in other words, there was no fixed price...[109]

Regarding certain types of labor, then, there was sometimes an avoidance of monetary payment, perhaps due to shortage of money or social perceptions of such labor relations. In the case of agricultural products sold to or exchanged with neighbors, there was still something

---

107 Interview: María Ignacia Bogantes Zamora.

108 Interview: Rosa Fernández Araya.

109 Interview: Rosa Fernández Araya.

akin to 'moral economy' concepts, despite the generally mercantile mentality of these very same peasant farmers.

Labor and consumption requirements of the various domestic and other units were balanced-off by various means, some of which have been mentioned above. These mechanisms, together with emigration and intensification/specialization, were partly responses to the pressures derived from difficulty of access to land within the region, population growth, landholding concentration and subdivision, and other factors. Another option which rural households came up against was to adjust the system of inheritance so as to limit fragmentation of holdings due to partibility. Efforts in this direction, and their relative success or failure, are discussed below.

Inheritance and Household Strategies

Transmittal of household wealth (or poverty) from the deceased to his or her heirs raised the dilemma of whether to subdivide holdings on an equal basis, in accordance with social norms, or to limit subdivision in some way, so as to maintain somewhat larger and more viable productive units. We will first look at certain specific cases in a broader time frame, before mentioning certain data for 1926-1935 and possible interpretations.

The early settlers of each area within the northwestern Central Valley, especially during the latter half of the nineteenth century, undoubtedly had more opportunities of acquiring land than those who came later. In the following generation, many such holdings were still sufficient to provide each son or daughter with a smaller yet sufficient area for the establishment of a domestic unit, given a gradual process of agricultural intensification. In the third generation, unless there had been accumulation of new lands to multiply the size of the previously inherited holding, fragmentation would reach a point where intensification and specialization could hardly compensate for reduction of size, and the reproduction of domestic units was threatened. The following case illustrates the tension between subdivision of holdings and the economic viability of such units over several generations. The father of one of the deceased from the 1926-1936 probate cases:

> .. was one of the first to come here, when this was still a wooded area... he had his little farm... well, not so little, it was actually large enough; he had about six sons and six daughters, and gave each of them a plot of land.[110]

---

110 Interview: F.A.R. All data regarding this case are from the same interview, or from the probate proceedings. Order of initials has been altered and place names eliminated in certain cases regarding inheritance, for obvious reasons.

The distribution may not have been totally egalitarian, as one of them "got the best inheritance... because in those times, as I say, they did what they liked..." One of the heirs, Miguel, married the daughter of another middling farmer whose heirs each received ten *manzanas* of land, even though it is not quite clear what happened with a considerable amount of cash. When Miguel and his wife were elderly, they sold part of their land: when he "could not work, then they would sell plots of land to live", and "she sold some lands to get better" from a disease. In this way, "by the time she died, she only had a very small plot, perhaps not even half a *manzana*..."

In the inventory of don Miguel's property in 1933, when he died at age sixty-six, there were three plots of land: one fifth of a hectare in coffee, worth ¢200; another piece of land in coffee, ¢50; and a third one in pasture and coffee, with a house, estimated at ¢250. The last one had, apparently, been sold by the widow to a daughter, and when the widow died, each of the three heirs received ¢66 in rights to the other two properties. The husband of the daughter who had bought the third plot of land also bought the inheritance rights of his brother- and sister-in-law, thus re-establishing a small but less fragmented productive unit. In the following generation, subdivision is once again threatening it with disintegration, but steps have been taken to avoid that: "my husband said: well, we are old now, let us give each of the children their little piece of land..., but they all have it in a single farm... only one of them is in charge", while the others have their own jobs.

In the case outlined above, there was landholding subdivision over several generations, but also a sustained effort to curb partibility, starting out with a less than egalitarian distribution and ending up in an agreement to avoid further fragmentation of an already small productive unit.

Between the late nineteenth century and the 1930s there were several cases of downward social mobility due to a combination of unfavorable economic conditions and the abovementioned tension between absolute partibility and the economic viability of productive units. The case of two coffee-growers from Heredia, don Canuto Vega and don Agapito Bolaños, is a good example of this, and speaks of a hidden aspect of a booming agro-export economy. Both were relatively wealthy, but were ruined during the turn-of-the-century crisis: "my grandparents were ruined because the price of coffee plummeted to very low levels. They had a lot of coffee... that was about fifteen years before I was born."[111]

A son of don Canuto, Guillermo, married don Agapito's daughter Rosa. They emigrated to Palmares, with no wealth at all, and even though he became involved in commercial activities, in agriculture on the northern frontier, and even in a mining project, Guillermo died young and his widow and small children inherited only a few worldly goods which she had to

111 Interview: Mery Vega Bolaños, born in 1915.

sell, little by little.[112] When the widow died some time later, in 1933, they only had half a *manzana* of land, with a house and some coffee, estimated at ¢300. Seven of the nine heirs sold their inheritance rights to an in-law, for ¢70. At this point, further fragmentation was no longer feasible.

Not all settlers in a given area, who were often relatives, obtained similar benefits during the early stages of colonization, nor did their heirs receive comparable amounts of land. Relations between descendants of settlers reflect very real inequalities and sometimes violent antagonisms, as well as reciprocities. For them, such daily relations were highly personalized, and both kinship and personal animosity obscured their social content. Yet these interactions were a part of ongoing, if ambivalent, socioeconomic processes: on the one hand, socioeconomic differentiation within this rural population was becoming well-defined by this time; on the other hand, relations between specific people, even if on an unequal basis, were filtered by kinship and personal ties. Antagonisms as well as reciprocities are reflected both in historical documentation and in current perceptions of descendants. Let us discuss one last case in this connection.

Don Pedro was a rather well-to-do farmer, who "had forty day-laborers in [...] who came to pick coffee... he had a lot of cattle, and several farms".[113] He had come from the Meseta Central, emigrating to the Northwest with his wife, who was from a town in this region. At least one of his brothers came, and there were already material differences in the family, as "at home we were surrounded by poor people, his nephews and relatives". There were violent personal conflicts, at least one of them due a confrontation over ownership of some land: "they tried to kill him once, crossing a fence... another time because [a relative] was envious; the farm was ours, but they were fighting for it, I don't know why..." At the same time that there was personalized social conflict, social inequality was also reflected in paternalistic attitudes toward the poorer relatives:

> ...they came and said, please give me some dulce... and one old lady would take a sugarcake, and then another would come, and another... and a pitcher full of buttermilk to make biscuits, and they would be told, come for a cuartillo of maize to make biscuits. Now no one will even give you a cup of coffee...[114]

When don Pedro died, at a very old age, his capital had diminished. Perhaps there was some distribution of property beforehand, but there were also legal problems and seizures which forced him to sell. He had also lent out a considerable amount of money, which was difficult to recover after his demise because these were not documented loans. Whatever land was left, was distributed among the sons and daughters "on an equal basis... a *manzana*" for each. The sons had probably received some cattle before, as

---

112 Interviews: Lila and Mery Vega Bolaños.

113 Interview: A.E.E. All quotes for this case are from the same interview.

114 Interview: A.E.E.

each had his own oxen for transportation of coffee when they were still working on their father's farm. The youngest daughter also received a cow and calf. She and her brothers also received a small inheritance from a single relative, and all their inheritance rights on this farm, which added up to two *manzanas* in coffee and uncultivated land, were sold to one of the brothers for a small sum. A point was reached where further subdivision would create what were perceived as excessively small units, and sale of inheritance rights was an outcome of the growing tension between partible inheritance and economic viability.

Inheritance patterns in the probate cases of Alajuela for 1926-1935 were similar in some respects to those from the turn of the century: number of heirs per case only increased slightly, to 5.2, and a similar sub-regional variation was found. In the area near the capital, number of heirs tended to be lower (4.6), while in San Ramón-Palmares it was higher (6.3). These figures are not very different from those for 1895-1904, except that Grecia-Naranjo was in an intermediate position (5.2 heirs per case) in the second period. The number of heirs was somehow linked to factors such as time since settlement, population trends and changes in local landholding and production. Actual household size was also smaller in Alajuela city than in the rural areas of the province, even though the differences in number of heirs were greater than those between size of households.[115] There may have been less heirs in the city due to smaller family size associated with urban life, but also due to emigration. In any case, such differences suggest the exclusion of certain resident and non-resident heirs, especially in areas of earlier settlement.

Even though age at time of death and level of wealth were correlated, and in certain cases both variables were associated with number of heirs, there was no clear correlation for all cases between either of those variables and number of heirs.[116] Neither was sex the explanatory factor, as men and women had similar numbers of heirs.[117] Yet exclusion did occur among various types of rural households.

---

115 Families were defined in the 1927 census as "a person or group of persons who live in the same house, where some depend economically on the others, or, as the saying goes, sit at the same table." Such co-resident households averaged 5.0 members in Alajuela city and 5.4 in the province as a whole. Alajuela city included just under 7% of the population of the province, so households in the rural areas were only slightly larger. DGEC (1927), pp.34, 36 and 88-89.

116 Correlation level between level of fortune and heirs, for all cases in 1926-1935, was 0.12, and that between age of the deceased and number of heirs was 0.13.

117 5.16 heirs per male deceased person, and 5.06 per woman.

Property Rights and Dispossession

When holdings were very small, e.g. those associated with sub-family and deficit-yielding domestic units, there was a tendency to exclude more heirs, or for some of them to sell their inheritance rights to other heirs and to third parties. While preserving minute productive units from extreme fragmentation, this also involved the expulsion of household members from the parental holding. In such cases, young adult sons whose labor could not be employed on such units and who had no hope of inheriting more than a microscopic parcel could work for wages or sharecrop locally, but they could also, and often did, become part of the growing number of impoverished emigrants.

When landholding was substantial, subdivision of farms already under intensive cultivation could still threaten household members with downward mobility, as in the case of intermediate and surplus-yielding domestic units. In such cases, total exclusion of heirs seems to have been less frequent than giving some of them advances on inheritance, often in cash or cattle rather than land. This was for them to start a new farm elsewhere, perhaps on the frontier, and was later carefully deducted from their share in the property retained by their parents. Migration under such circumstances was probably less frequent than during the nineteenth century, and chances of success were also lower.

The avoidance of subdivision on variously-sized holdings was reflected in agreements to maintain them undivided despite legal partition, and in the sale of inheritance rights among heirs. There were more inheritance rights (those on undivided land, as opposed to individualized properties) in 1926-1935 than during the nineteenth century. Approximately one out of every five properties in the inventories was an inheritance right, still undefined in terms of specific area and location.[118] This in itself points to shared rights on specific farms, rather than physical subdivision of plots. And inheritance rights were twice or three times as frequent in low-level fortunes with little land as in the intermediate-to-high fortunes.[119] In other words, when holdings were very small, inheritance rights from a previous probate proceeding were retained more often and longer, thus avoiding actual fragmentation of such productive units, even if legal property was subdivided.

By geographical areas, we find that individualized properties were much more frequent in the vicinity of San Ramón, where farm size tended

118 On the average, there were 0.54 such rights per case and 2.26 individualized properties in 1926-1935.

119 Probate fortunes under ¢500, for 1926-1935, averaged 1.3 individual properties and 0.7 inheritance rights; those from ¢500 to under ¢1,000 had 1.2 individual properties and 0.2 inheritance rights; the following level of fortune had 1.8 individual properties and 0.2 inheritance rights; and those fortunes estimated at ¢5,000 or more included 5.5 individual properties as opposed to 1.1 inheritance rights.

to be larger, than near Grecia or Alajuela city, where landholding fragmentation (and perhaps concentration) had proceeded further.[120] Finally, by type of land use, inheritance rights were most frequent in pastureland and uncultivated land, while individualized properties were more often under intensive agriculture or used for housing (Table 6.21). In the case of pastures, subdivision would tend to make them less viable as livestock-producing units, and if subdivided beyond a certain point, the need would arise to intensify land use on the smaller individual areas. Permanent agriculture, and especially the more intensive commercial crops such as coffee and sugarcane, were more readily subdivided and retained their economic viability in small plots.

TABLE 6.21 TYPE OF LANDOWNERSHIP IN PROBATE INVENTORIES OF ALAJUELA PROVINCE, BY LAND USE, 1926-1935

Land Use	Individual Properties		Inheritance Rights	
	#	%	#	%
Coffee	136	81.4	31	18.6
Sugarcane	69	83.1	14	16.9
Pasture	156	76.5	48	23.5
Grain	87	82.9	18	17.1
Uncultivated	118	78.7	32	21.3
Dwelling	122	87.8	17	12.2
Other	23	74.2	8	25.8

Source: Probate inventories for 1926-1935.

Generally speaking, those inheritance rights which were maintained over time were usually on units whose physical subdivision would negatively affect production. On the other hand, inheritance rights were sometimes a legal fiction, disguising the actual exclusion of certain heirs, especially women. One or several of them might retain their parents' house and some nearby plot, but control of productive activities on more distant farms often ended up in the hands of one of the male heirs. Whatever the legal provisions, such arrangements were frequent, in exchange for some sort of repayment then or at a future time, a commitment which might or might not be fully honored.

Toward the 1920s and 1930s, another mechanism was becoming significant in the alteration of formally partible inheritance practices, i.e. the *cesión* (legal granting or sale) of inheritance rights. Such cessions were either to third parties, who bought these rights during the probate

120 By place of residence according to probate inventories for 1926-1935, the area near Alajuela city averaged 2.0 individual properties and 0.6 inheritance rights; Grecia/Naranjo had 2.4 and 0.8 respectively, and Palmares/San Ramón had 2.4 individual properties and 0.2 inheritance rights.

proceedings, or among close relatives.[121] When sale of one or more properties out of court was legally authorized, this was sometimes to pay debts but usually because they were properties which would be difficult to subdivide due to their small area. For example, when Modesta Blanco died in 1927, she and her husband only had a half-hectare sugarcane field, according to the probate inventory. It was located in Santa Gertrudis, near Grecia, and although no estimate was included in the inventory, its value in the Real Estate Registry was ¢250.[122] The sugarcane field was sold out of court in 1937. If the sons and daughters received any inheritance, it was not distributed through the probate process, and must have been a small amount of money from the sale. We know of the case of one of Modesta's five children, Pablo Salazar. Soon after his mother died, Pablo left Grecia with his wife and children, to work as a plantation day-laborer in the Atlantic region of Costa Rica; then he travelled to the northern part of the country, and at one point had a small farm in Guanacaste.[123] There is no indication that he received any property as inheritance, so at least in his case, sale of the land by heirs led to emigration, initially as a day-laborer.

Cessions were often made in cases when land owned by the household was less than ten hectares, and they were much less frequent when holdings were twenty-five hectares or more.[124] Fortunes with no cessions at all were usually much larger than those in which one or more heirs sold their rights. Additionally, cession of inheritance rights among relatives was common at intermediate levels of fortune, where other members of the family or in-laws had the possibility of acquiring them. Instead, cessions to third parties were usually associated with lower levels of wealth.[125]

Geographical distribution of cessions was not uniform, since they were more frequent in the Northwest (and especially in San Ramón) than near the provincial capital.[126] This, together with the avoidance of physical subdivision especially near Alajuela city, would seem to indicate that there were different sub-regional strategies regarding inheritance, although they shared a common goal, to curb fragmentation.

---

121 44% of all probate cases studied for 1926-1935 had at least one cession of inheritance rights. Just over half were to third parties, more than a third to relatives, and one twentieth to both.

122 Registro de la Propiedad, Partido de Alajuela, Vol. 135, folio 357, asiento #2.

123 Interview: Raimundo and Asdrúbal Salazar Ulate.

124 Average frequency of cessions per probate case in 1926-1935 was 0.5 in those with holdings under one, five, or ten hectares; 0.4 in cases from 10<25 hectares, 0.26 in those from 25<75 hectares, and 0.13 when holdings were 75 hectares or more.

125 Average fortunes according to type of cession were: no cession, ¢5,306; to relatives, ¢2,398; to third parties, ¢1,498; and both to relatives and third parties, ¢2,080.

126 Average frequency for the population studied through probate inventories was 0.44. Near Alajuela city, it was 0.3, while in Grecia-Naranjo it was 0.48 and in San Ramón-Palmares 0.53.

Those who received cessions were almost invariably male, whether the father, brother or uncle of the person selling his or her rights. The same was true for third parties receiving the cessions. Among relatives, the legally-appointed executor was in a privileged position during probate proceedings, both with respect to administration and distribution of property. On the other hand, legal expenses and ecclesiastical bequests could amount to a considerable part of household assets. In these ways, property was also transferred to third parties. Lawyers, especially, were in an advantageous situation with respect to often poor, illiterate potential heirs. Some may have been quite honest, but others made their clients bitterly aware of the distance between formal equality in the eyes of the law and actual access to the legal means for defense of rights denied:

> My father's property was grabbed by the lawyers, we didn't get anything at all... before they used to prepare false documents and have them registered, the lawyers did so many things, that the registration of the farm could not be found, and to find out what happened you would need a lot of time, and money to investigate the properties, that one took them away from another, and sold them to another, and another... already, perhaps, with a legal deed.[127]

In some cases, certain heirs were dispossessed through legal and extra-legal tricks. Sometimes the lawyer would get together with the executor against one or more heirs; other times several heirs would connive against others; or movables and unregistered properties would be omitted, the former even stolen; or a very unequal distribution was made to seem egalitarian, in collusion with those in charge of assessing property. This sordid struggle pitted relatives against each other and tore families apart, but it was only one of the multiple ways in which partible inheritance practices were altered.

In other cases, for example, probate proceedings opened exclusively to "ratify sales made during the lifetime" of the deceased, the holding sometimes remained in the family, one way or another. One may cite, for example, the case of Tranquilino Avila, who had been a day-laborer and upon his death in 1929, at age seventy, in fact had no land at all.[128] However, his mother had owned an eight *manzana* farm, and he inherited half of it. He later sold that property, and purchased another. Finally, don Tranquilino sold the property, some eight *manzanas* of land, to his son-in-law for ¢900. This same in-law bought the inheritance rights of his wife Orfilia and her brother and sister, for about two *manzanas*, in their mother's property. Apparently, these were the sales to be ratified. After these sales, brother and sister emigrated. The outcome was that an in-law re-established the family holding, reverting the process of fragmentation which had already taken place legally (by buying the three rights), and avoiding potential subdivision (by purchasing the eight *manzana* farm during the

---

[127] Interview: S. Ch. I.

[128] Interview: Orfilia Avila Ballestero.

lifetime of the deceased). It was, then, a mechanism which re-established a domestic unit through direct sale of a farm and several rights to a single relative.

We should add to the above that in many of the incomplete probate proceedings (that is, without an inventory and assessment of property) there was an authorization to sell out of court. Most of these were undoubtedly very small properties, difficult to subdivide unless they were to be used for housing. While fragmentation of holdings was widespread, it had clear limits with respect to productive units, even if under intensive cultivation. Various mechanisms evolved to counteract it, whether legally or not. They were geographically and socially diverse, yet they responded to the same essential contradiction between egalitarianism and the need to restrict subdivision of property.

Absolute primogeniture was non-existent, and even disinheriting one or more children was rare. When a son or daughter was disowned, as stated in wills, it was due to personal confrontations with the parents, while approximate partibility was maintained for the other brothers and sisters. Male adults were sometimes privileged in the distribution of farmland, though not necessarily of the parents' home and adjoining lands.[129] Young children, especially, often received a minimal share despite apparent legal equality. Other times, nominal rights of women and children were recognized, but the productive unit maintained its operational integrity under the administration of an older son. The memory of inequality in the distribution of inheritance has been transmitted from generation to generation, and is expressed in complaints that the grandparents did not distribute property on an equal basis, because some of their sons took advantage of the rest.[130]

Descendants of certain families are well aware of inequality in distribution of property between the sexes, because "they gave more to the men, and less to the women... [since it was] a very large family, thirteen or fourteen, and [they said that] the women had done no work at all".[131] Inequality between the sexes was also reflected in legal cessions by one or more heirs to an adult male in the family, whether of the same generation or not.[132] They often received some sort of payment or compensation for their inheritance rights, but the the transfer of real estate through cessions was clearly male-oriented.

Young children often received less inheritance, in the long run, than their older brothers. In one case, the only farm (some four *manzanas* of

---

129 I thank Lowell Gudmundson for pointing this out to me, based on his ongoing research for the Meseta Central. There were cases in the Northwest, too, where daughters retained control of their parents' residence and some land nearby, while sons received land at much greater distances, e.g. in San Carlos.

130 Interview: M. B. G.

131 Interview: H. C. F.

132 Registro de la Propiedad, Partido de Alajuela, Vol. 836, f. 260, asiento 1, #39527.

sugarcane, coffee, and a house) was "almost all in J.'s hands, who ended up with a lot of money after all... he left little for my father [his brother], because he was the youngest, and like anyone who was the youngest..."[133] Sometimes the legal documentation gives no indication of the way inheritance rights were distributed, but oral testimony shows that it could be far from egalitarian, and that age of heirs was definitely a factor:

> When they made the distribution, poor D., the youngest, got almost nothing at all... down there where that bouganvillea is, they gave him a tiny little piece, and the others kept everything else for themselves... the old lady was left alone with the boys, and they fooled her and made her sign...[134]

When the only real estate owned by a family was so small that it was not feasible to subdivide it further without its losing all economic viability, there was the problem of deciding who would inherit it, and ways were found to transmit it undivided over several generations. In one case, the deceased had inherited a plot of land worth two hundred *colones*, and since it was "a very small piece of land" it was not divided among all her brothers and sisters.[135] When she died in 1933, the only property was an inheritance right worth three hundred colones in an area less than a tenth of a hectare, with a hut built by the deceased and her husband. The right was transmitted to the widower, who later passed it on to a son-in-law, because "since he has feeling ill and could not work..., and was also nervous, R. took advantage of him and said that he should give him ownership of the plot, and he would look after us [the children]."[136] In this case, the plot was not the basis for family sustenance, and wage labor was an important component of household income. On the other hand, six of the seven children were women, and the only boy was the youngest, unable to take charge of the household's plot. Property rights were transmitted in this case during the lifetime of the deceased, in exchange for an offer to care for the minors.

When fortunes were more or less large, complete exclusion of any heir was extremely difficult, but there were cases of inequality, as well as struggles between heirs. Differences regarding inheritance went back, in some families, to advances on inheritance. In one such case, the direct heirs of a wealthy settler received ¢935 each, from a ¢7,500 capital, although family fortune was greater. There were sales and distributions before the father's demise, "because he suffered a long time, and perhaps had distributed all that before, because when he died, my father only received a relatively small amount".[137] Aside from the sales and

---

[133] Interview: G. A. J.

[134] Interview: R. B.

[135] Interview: A. A. I.

[136] Interview: A. A. A.

[137] Interview: G. B. G.

distributions made by the deceased when he fell ill, several of his sons and daughters had received farms, livestock or money as advances on inheritance. Women were not excluded in this case, as "the oldest daughter got the farm first...about forty *manzanas*", when she married.[138]

In certain cases, agreements were reached by the heirs to avoid fragmentation of holdings and at the same time ensure sustenance and care of the elderly: "They [sons and daughters] signed an authorization to sell, because the old ones were very old... they all gave it to one, for her to care for the old ones".[139]

Even though subdivision of coffee plots was often extreme, it too had a limit: if the transmission of plots from one generation to the next created plots under one hectare, subdivision usually stopped, and was later reverted. A deceased person in 1933, at age sixty, left nine children and a plot of land with coffee trees and a house, estimated at ¢400. Most of the land ended up in the hands of one daughter, and was passed on to her son. Other heirs received about one quarter of a *manzana*. Carpentry tools were inherited by one son of the deceased, while several daughters received no dowry at all upon marrying. There was undoubtedly an effort made to avoid dismemberment of a very small holding by exclusion of potential heirs.[140]

EGALITARIANISM AND VIABILITY

The examples mentioned above basically question the apparent equality of inheritance practices, and represent systematic attempts to counteract the effects of partibility in the Northwest, given limited access to land by the early twentieth century. Mechanisms devised include: advances on inheritance for certain household members to establish new holdings; maintaining inheritance rights to avoid physical subdivision of farms; agreements to operate the legally-divided holding as a single economic unit; cession of rights among heirs; unequal distribution of property; exclusion of one or more potential heirs; sale to third parties, and other means.

When fragmentation of holdings had reached a point where non-viable economic units were being created, inheritance rights were maintained or prolonged by an almost imperative need, and even so did not avoid impoverishment, or the complete holding was sold, usually to a third party. When subdivision had not yet reached that point and other options were open to household members (for example settlement on an accessible frontier or alternative occupations) preventive mechanisms operated to avoid further fragmentation, such as advances on inheritance and sale of rights among relatives to preserve domestic units.

---

138 Interview: G. V. S.

139 Interview: S. Ch. G.

140 Interview: C. S. A.

Thus, two basic inheritance strategies to attain these goals can be identified, which were applied by economically diverse rural households in various parts of the province, but were more strongly associated with specific areas and types of units. The first, by surplus-yielding and intermediate domestic units, especially toward the western end of the Central Valley, where there was still a strong middling peasanty, was based essentially on sale of rights among relatives, in combination with substantial advances on inheritance to young adults and, in some cases, preferential treatment of certain heirs. The second, by sub-family and deficit-yielding domestic units, most often in the area of fragmented land tenure near Alajuela city and Grecia, was based on maintaining inheritance rights without physical subdivision of plots, as well as agreeing on unified administration, or selling the whole plot to a third party.

Such mechanisms sometimes managed to reduce partition of small holdings, or even to revert extreme fragmentation, but they could not prevent the subdivision of property in the region as a whole. Even when they were successful to a certain extent, they generated out-migration of those who did not inherit or were given advances on inheritance. A study of inheritance in Atenas, in the southwestern part of the province within the Central Valley, concluded that "emigration was more frequent among members of landholding families... which seems to indicate that the emigrants had more economic means which allowed them a certain type of mobility."[141] Even though longstanding emigration of impoverished persons might not be as well documented locally as that of members of rural households whose holdings remained within the family, both types of out-migration were clearly important in the western part of the Central Valley during the first half of the twentieth century.

Advances on inheritance played a role in allowing certain members of domestic units to reestablish holdings elsewhere or, as settlement frontiers became inaccessible toward mid-century, to seek occupational mobility by other means, such as independent non-agricultural activities or professional education. This allowed certain household members or relatives to preserve the economic integrity or viability of peasant farming, despite strong social norms regarding partible inheritance.

In land-poor households, on the other hand, transmittal of property rights to one more generation of descendants would dismember already minute holdings, and effective partition would create non-viable units. Through various means, from the avoidance of physical division of plots among heirs to the sale of inheritance rights to third parties, these micro-farms tended to persist over time, at minimum sizes which were dependent, to a certain extent, on specific land use patterns. For most members of such households, however, the outcome was in fact landlessness, and they often sought employment on the larger productive units within the region or moved to other parts of the country.

---

141 Montoya and Reuss (1960), p. 7. This document was kindly brought to my attention by Lowell Gudmundson.

Inheritance practices, then, were intertwined with processes outlined in previous sections of this chapter for the early to mid-twentieth century: the growing number of emigrants from the Northwest, especially, to San Carlos and to other provinces, while local population continued to grow; a gradual increase in relative importance of wage labor, while household labor continued to be predominant on most farms in the region; subdivision of large and small holdings, yet without widespread fragmentation beyond the limits of economic viability; and an intensification of land use patterns and a trend toward productive specialization, especially on the smaller units, even if there was still a degree of diversified production in the region. All these were components of multi-pronged strategies through which rural households reacted to changing social conditions and options imposed upon them during the first half of the twentieth century. Some were more successful, others less so: the dilemmas remain even today.

Chapter 7

EPILOGUE: UNIQUENESS AND CONVERGENT PATHS

From initial settlement to continuous emigration, the preceding chapters have followed the routes opened by several generations of colonists and their descendants through a region of Costa Rica in which land use and social relations underwent major changes between the mid-nineteenth and the mid-twentieth century. Most of the early settlers came from the Meseta Central, inhabited from colonial times, and brought with them a tradition of extensive livestock raising supplemented by sugarcane and grain cultivation on variously-sized and not necessarily titled holdings. From the mid- to late-nineteenth century, the settlement frontier moved westward from Alajuela city to San Ramón, but also in other directions within and without the Central Valley. Especially after the turn of the century, more and more second- or third-generation inhabitants of the Northwest moved on to the new lands in San Carlos, Tilarán and other parts of the country.

The regional process of agrarian transformation discussed in the preceding chapters was critical to Costa Rican history, despite the relatively small size of the northwestern section of the Central Valley. It was the first economically-significant area of outward migration from the Meseta Central, where most of the population had lived during colonial times. The fact that peasants obtained access to the land and came to account for a major part of regional coffee production during the latter part of the nineteenth century is not only relevant to understanding rural society in this specific region, but in Costa Rica as a whole. In combination with market-oriented peasant farming in the Meseta and the existence of other agricultural frontiers where the descendants of settlers could migrate to, it contributed to the strengthening of a middling peasantry which has been a decisive factor in the economic, social and political development of the country. Peasant-farmers were in no way peripheral to, but rather essential components of a historically-specific path to agrarian capitalism, one which is both singular and has much in common with other Latin American experiences. The following sections will refer, first of all, to conclusions reached regarding the regional case-study, then to the Costa Rican context, and finally to comparable experiences and certain issues of interpretation.

The Northwest

In this region population grew rapidly during most of that century, as natural population growth was compounded by immigration from the previously settled areas. In the late nineteenth and early twentieth century, despite a gradual decline in mortality and some additional immigration, population growth slowed down in the region, primarily due to net emigration as the sons and grandchildren of settlers moved beyond the Central Valley, especially toward the northern territories.

As regional population grew and the area was effectively occupied by settlers, land use patterns were transformed in the Northwest and in most of Alajuela province. Agricultural intensification was made possible, and partly stimulated, by settlement itself, but interlinkages between the regional and national economy played a major role: improved transportation routes, specific types of productive specialization in the previously settled areas, a growing demand for certain commodities, and overall economic growth. Greater labor inputs per unit area were, then, a response both to market and demographic factors.

Initially extensive uses of the land, with a predominance of pasture and forest, gave way to a more intensive yet diversified crop mix. Several traditional and non-traditional agricultural commodities expanded simultaneously during the latter part of the nineteenth century. Grain production, essentially that of maize, was widespread throughout the province but commercially important near the provincial capital. Sugarcane became most significant in the vicinity of Grecia, while livestock raising retained its importance longer toward the western end of the Central Valley, and accompanied the new generation of settlers beyond. Coffee gradually became the predominant crop from Alajuela to San Ramón, but always in association with other uses of the land, which together accounted for a larger area. Until 1900, the territorial expansion of coffee took place most often on formerly uncultivated or grazing lands, rather than to the detriment of other crops.

Only in the twentieth century was there a clearly defined trend toward specialization within agriculture, as coffee displaced other economic activities in the Northwest. Even toward mid-century, however, this was far from being a single-crop regional economy, nor did most coffee farms here specialize to the same extent as those in the Meseta Central.

In the early stages of settlement, in the mid-nineteenth century, units of production varied significantly in their scale, but far less in their productive orientation. In most cases, ranching was the main economic activity, and very diverse family fortunes had similar relative values in land, herds and other assets.

Over time, extensive land use patterns continued to be important on the larger, supra-family units, which devoted only part of their land to commercial agriculture. Intermediate and surplus-producing domestic units shifted more into agriculture yet they tended to retain a diversified product mix, even if coffee did gain ground on such units from the late-nineteenth to the mid-twentieth century. The smaller productive units (essentially the deficit yielding and sub-family ones) were not only the most labor intensive of all, but also those with the highest levels of productive specialization. These were often minute coffee farms, even if that crop was interplanted with others, but in certain cases such micro-farms were either maize or sugarcane fields.

As agricultural intensification proceeded and land became scarce within the Northwest for a growing population, average size of holdings per household diminished quite significantly in the century after initial settlement. If we are to judge by probate inventories, households at the end of the period held only about one third of the land owned by the average household of the 1850's. Despite additional labor inputs and yields per area, many rural households faced a series of dilemmas which were not easily solved.

Local access to land became increasingly difficult and costly, but also a necessity for large families with reduced holdings. Credit relations were perhaps less frequent from the turn of the century, but debts weighed more heavily on the viability of economic units than in the middle decades of the nineteenth century. Involvement in the labor market, which at first had allowed households to specialize more than would otherwise have been the case, came to be an indispensable supplementary income. Seasonal wage labor continued to be important, but permanent employment was becoming widespread among the rural population. In spite of stagnant or declining real wages, supra-family units had much less difficulty than before in obtaining the labor force they required, partly from land-poor households.

Emigration, which for many of their nineteenth century forebears was an opportunity for upward socioeconomic mobility, was an imposed option for more and more young adult members of rural households in the early- to mid-twentieth century, as they sought to avoid proletarianization. Some of these emigrants still received advances on inheritance, but these were less frequent and usually for smaller amounts. Furthermore, conditions on the twentieth-century settlement frontier were less propitious for the sons of peasant farmers, as relatively large holdings and productive units were rapidly established by members of the wealthier families and by foreign interests.

Modification of socially-sanctioned partible inheritance practices was a means to the end of counteracting extreme fragmentation of holdings. Of little urgency in the previous century, when agricultural intensification compensated for reduced tenures, it became a necessity in the twentieth century, as the viability of small productive units was seriously threatened. Mechanisms such as sale of inheritance rights to relatives or third parties, unequal distribution, partial exclusion of heirs, and agreements to avoid actual subdivision of holdings were sometimes effective in avoiding further fragmentation, or even in reestablishing viable economic units. However, the overall trend toward subdivision could not be reverted by such means, and in those cases in which rural households established stable tenures, most members had to seek other occupational alternatives.

Peasant-farmer strategies and, more specifically, those of rural domestic units in the area, involved multiple interacting components and constant decisionmaking about land tenure and land use, labor intensity and employment of family labor, disposition of products for sale and consumption, credit relations, inheritance, emigration, etc. Such decisions took into account the potential combinations of material resources, labor capacity and consumption requirements of the rural household, but were highly responsive to the changing conditions under which domestic units interacted with other productive units, with their markets and with the broader social environment. They took advantage of initially favorable conditions to establish a strong foothold in the nineteenth-century agro-export economy, and as conditions imposed upon them became far more harsh and exploitative, they devised numerous ways to counteract the external and internal pressures. The enforced dilemmas could not be avoided nor overcome, and there was landholding concentration as well as impoverishment. Yet peasant farming has survived in the region, not so much in spite of, but rather due to, emigration and reliance on wage labor by household members, together with market-oriented agricultural intensification and specialization.

Rather than recapitulating the more specific conclusions reached in each chapter, the following pages will attempt to place the agrarian changes, here observed at a regional level, within a broader context. First, that of ongoing settlement elsewhere in Costa Rica and certain societal transformations; then, however briefly, with respect to Colombia and other comparable cases in Latin America and the Caribbean, and also to selected issues which are relevant to the conceptual framework set forth in the opening chapter.

Costa Rica

While the main thrust of colonization in the Central Valley during the middle decades of the nineteenth century was certainly toward the Northwest, there were also numerous landclaims and some population movement in other directions. Toward the relatively remote eastern end of the Central Valley, for example, there were at least ninety-six successful landclaims between 1830 and 1870, most of them relatively large.[1] During the last three decades of the nineteenth century, primarily due to construction of the railroad to the Atlantic, land claims became even more frequent in the Turrialba-Reventazón area, and actual settlement was associated primarily with the establishment of medium-to-large estates. Some of these estates availed themselves of peasant farmers, through formal or informal contractual arrangements, to clear the wooded areas which would later become coffee groves. At the same time, vast banana plantations beyond the ecological limits of coffee, on the Atlantic coastal

---

1 Based on Table No. 1 in Salas (1985), pp. 42-43.

plain, were a byproduct of the railroad project and brought large-scale immigration of foreign workers, mostly of Jamaican origin, to that coastal region.

Within the Central Valley, the 227-hectare Cóncavas estate studied by Carolyn Hall near Paraíso, east of Cartago, illustrates both the similarities and major differences between comparable productive units in this area and the Northwest.[2] Originally an extensive cattle ranch with a minor area in coffee and sugarcane, and very little infrastructure, it was transformed during the late nineteenth century into an estate which relied heavily on coffee as a commercial activity. However, livestock raising continued to be important, and at the turn of the century improved pastures still occupied almost twice the area in coffee groves. Furthermore, coffee was interplanted with maize and other foodcrops, and there were small sugarcane fields and grain plots in various parts of the farm. In this regard, Cóncavas was similar to many supra-family units in the Northwest. In some areas east of Cartago, such as Juan Viñas, coffee cultivation on haciendas was combined with large-scale sugarcane plantations, which led to a subregional pattern of land use which was much like that found near Grecia at the other end of the Central Valley.

Coffee-producing units in the eastern section of the Central Valley tended to have a more even distribution of labor requirements over the year, and while day-labor was not necessarily abundant, haciendas in this region had a more stable contingent of resident *peones*. Given the lack of a clearly-defined dry season in the eastern part of the Central Valley, there were several flowerings and the coffee harvest took much longer than in the Northwest, from four to eight months. Estates such as Cóncavas, which had processing facilities, also purchased almost as much coffee from neighboring farms as they harvested directly. There was in this region, as in the Northwest, a combination of relatively large estates and smaller farms, but the former weighed far more heavily in local land-tenure and social relations.

Land claims and settlement also occupied other parts in the periphery of the Central Valley, such as the higher altitudes on the slopes of the Cordillera Central, which flanks the Northwest and the Meseta along their northern edge. From Heredia and Santo Domingo, for example, there was intra-provincial migration toward Santa Bárbara, and from Naranjo toward Zarcero. Despite the relatively short distances involved, climatic changes led to very different land use patterns, with a limited amount of coffee and more dairy cattle, plus diversified agricultural intensification and, eventually, local productive specialization in ecological niches (Figure 7.1).

Southward from the Central Valley, inhabitants of the Meseta moved into the valleys of Candelaria and Puriscal during the nineteenth century,[3] as well as to the area known as Los Santos, on what was to become the

---

2 Hall (1978), especially pp. 8-38.

3 Salas (n.d.), pp. 52-81.

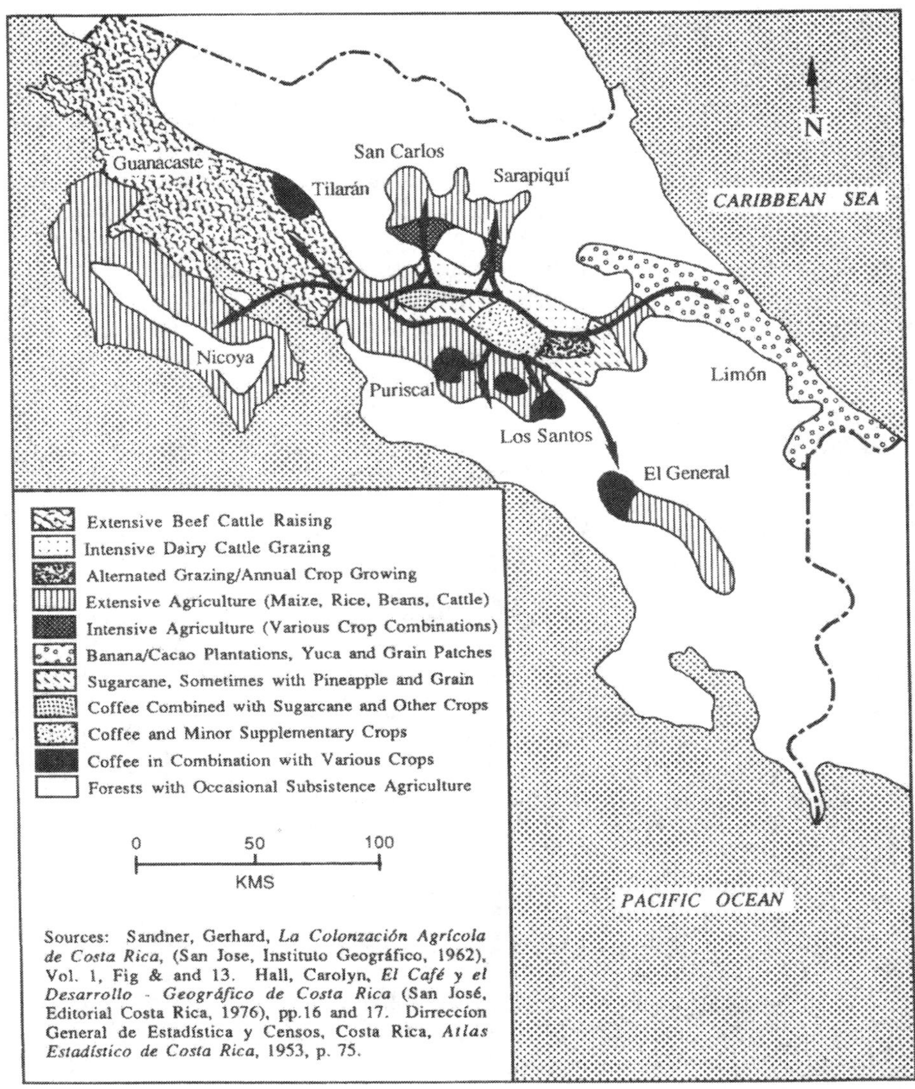

Figure 7.1 Out-migration and land use in Costa Rica c. 1935

route toward the valley of San Isidro del General, settled in the early twentieth century. Whenever possible, settlers in these areas sought to develop coffee cultivation, but land use usually was quite diversified. In some of these areas, climate and soil were not appropriate for coffee at all. Further south, vast lowland territories were settled around 1940, when the banana plantations were transferred from the Atlantic toward the south Pacific. Soon after that, Italian and Costa Rican settlers in San Vito de Java developed coffee production, in association with cattle and other crops on medium-sized farms, at intermediate altitudes on the southern end of the Cordillera de Talamanca.[4]

Settlement in these areas, together with that already discussed in the northern part of the country, presents us with a picture of a century-long outward movement in almost all directions from the colonial core area in the Meseta. Early land claims and actual colonization were mostly within the Central Valley, longitudinally but also up the slope of the mountain ranges which define the limits of this tectonic depression. As these areas were claimed and occupied, settlement proceeded beyond, to the intermediate-altitude lands outside the Central Valley, where peasant-farmers often sought to reproduce the agrarian economy of previously settled areas, and to the lowlands of the periphery, where large-scale ranching and tropical plantations were the rule.

The first generations of settlers, especially in the Northwest, had little difficulty in securing land-tenure, despite the parallel establishment of larger land claims and productive units in the region. Land grant policies, scarcity of labor, initial transportation difficulties, concentration of capital investments in the Meseta, successful market-oriented peasant farming and the precedence of "attraction" over "expulsion" in the decision to settle in the Northwest are among the factors which help explain peasant access to the land in this region during the nineteenth century. The complex, multi-pronged strategies of domestic units were essential to the survival of commercial peasant farming into the twentieth century, in face of deteriorating conditions, both in terms of their internal organization and their multiple insertions in the various markets and in other societal processes.

There was, and still is, little explicit conflict over landholding in the Northwest, and social confrontation in the region has expressed itself in other ways. During the early twentieth century, small and middling peasant-farmers began to unite against the processing firms which often joined together to pay low prices for their coffee and sugarcane.[5] In the 1920's, smallholders in certain coffee-producing areas of the western Central Valley were among the main rural supporters of movements for advanced social reform via governmental intervention, although in other cases they were in alliance with the regional elite to promote specific

---

4 Bariatti (1987), pp. 273-276,

5 Hall (1976), p. 47; Samper (1979), p. 150-159.

interests, from road construction to local and national politics.[6] In the early thirties, the economic depression caused much less unemployment in the Northwest than in the Meseta Central or Turrialba-Reventazón area, but low prices of coffee and unequal assimilation of the effects of the economic crisis did accentuate conflicts between domestic units and processing firms. The government intervened, declaring a moratorium on debts and finally regulating their relations through the Instituto de Defensa del Café. Thereafter, peasant-farmers in the region, especially those specializing in coffee production, have organized in various ways to further their interests vis-à-vis government and *beneficiadores*.

Social confrontation has reflected contradictory economic interests of these two groups and a perception of the latter (at least until the establishment of cooperatives with processing plants) as an exploitative "trust".[7] But struggles have almost invariably been non-violent, usually within a framework of legality, and conflicts have been solved through negotiation. Government arbitration was been sought since the early twentieth century, and institutionalized since the 1930s. Currently, the largest and most influential agrarian union, *Upanacional*, is substantially based on small and middling farmers of this region, and its efforts are geared toward influencing government policy in the agricultural sector, rather than any clearly defined social confrontation.

It is also striking that despite the growing number of rural wage laborers in the Northwest since the late nineteenth century, there have been few significant attempts at labor unionization or even isolated labor conflicts, other than a sugarcane plantation workers' strike in the seventies. This must somehow be related to the survival of smallholder agriculture in the region, with multiple linkages between *hacendados, peones* and *campesinos*. In the eastern part of the Central Valley, instead, where large coffee and sugarcane estates occupy a larger and more permanent labor force, there have been more labor conflicts since the early twentieth century.

As new generations of settlers left the Central Valley to pursue their goal of re-establishing independent farms on the late-nineteenth and early-twentieth-century frontiers, they found that much of the uncultivated land had already been claimed by members of the Costa Rican elite and by foreign companies, and open confrontation became inevitable.[8] Brothers, sons and grandchildren of the inhabitants of the Northwest, for example, were involved in often violent conflicts with the authorities and with groups representing the interests of individual or corporate owners of large tracts of land in Guanacaste and other outlying territories.[9]

---

6 Samper (1987a).

7 Acuña (1985 and 1986).

8 Salas (1984?), especially pp. 62-63, 100-106, and 113-125.

9 Gudmundson, "Las luchas agrarias en Guanacaste...", in *Hacendados, políticos y precaristas* (1983).

Under the rather indirect influence of the Mexican revolution, the cry of "*la tierra para el que la trabaja*" became a popular political slogan in Costa Rica toward the 1920s. Many Congressional discussions of that and the following decades centered on the issue of squatters, first labeled *parásitos* and then, more respectfully, *precaristas*. Successive governments carried out land redistribution plans, but were unable to stem the flow of landless migrants. As the remaining agricultural frontier became almost inaccessible toward the mid-twentieth century,[10] conflicts over privately-owned lands became even more frequent, and there were organized occupations of uncultivated areas, with sometimes tragic outcomes. Growing numbers of landless emigrants from the Central Valley were also becoming wage laborers on ranches and lowland plantations in the outlying areas of Costa Rica, given the difficulty of titling agricultural lands. Emigrant members of land poor households in the Northwest, specifically, were less and less successful in obtaining land on the receding frontier during the twentieth century, and were faced with the prospect of landlessness or direct social confrontation. But this process can best be understood in a comparative perspective.

Latin America and the Caribbean

In Latin America and the Caribbean, where agro-export development in the nineteenth and early twentieth century followed many different paths, the Costa Rican experience was far from unique, despite its undeniable specificities. Recent discussion of the history of coffee cultivation in Costa Rica and other areas has pointed to the need for a systematic comparison of such agrarian transformations, especially with respect to the role of peasant farmers in export agriculture.[11]

A comprehensive comparative analysis is obviously beyond the scope of this work, and should probably result from a collective effort. Yet the Costa Rican case-study does make it possible to raise certain questions with respect to comparable Latin American processes. The more specific ones will be stated in connection with the well-known Colombian case, actually a set of very different regional transformations associated with coffee, land settlement, or both. More general issues will thereafter be raised in connection with a broader comparative framework.

First of all, why did peasant farmers gain access to major amounts of land and become successfully involved in agro-export production in certain regions, and not in others within each country? Even in such a small area as the Central Valley of Costa Rica, we find that while domestic units were very important in the western section, supra-family units were clearly predominant in the East. Yet initial land claims were large throughout the

---

10 Augelli (1987), p. 14.

11 Gudmundson (1986b), Kuznesof (1986), LeGrand (1986), Roseberry (1986).

Central Valley, and coffee production started on haciendas in both areas. In other Latin American cases, such as Colombia, there were similar regional and subregional variations in composition of productive units, despite very inegalitarian legal access to the land.

Cundinamarca and part of Tolima, in central Colombia, are described as areas where large coffee estates were strongly predominant during the late nineteenth and early twentieth centuries.[12] Even though landholding concentration in the highland *sabana* was substantially based on the expansion of colonial haciendas to the detriment of peasant holdings, "latifundia on the temperate slopes and torrid mountainous areas seem to have been established on 'new lands'."[13] Yet the outcome in terms of productive units would be quite different. Many of the coffee-producing haciendas in central Colombia were broken apart after 1920, by a combination of internal and external economic conditions, organized social pressure and government policies.[14]

The areas of Antioqueño settlement toward the west, where there were vast colonial and Republican land grants, have been typified -and to a certain extent idealized- as a "democratic society of smallholders, in a continent dominated by traditional Latin latifundia".[15] Rural society there was undoubtedly more complex and stratified, as Colombian scholarship over the last decade has shown,[16] and there were areas (e.g. southwest of Medellín) where haciendas rather than domestic units were clearly predominant.[17] The effort to counteract what was perceived as a *leyenda rosa*, even though early scholarship on Antioquia recognized the importance of latifundia, has sometimes minimized the significance of peasant settlers' access to the land.[18] The fact remains that Antioqueño settlement led to a variegated pattern of land tenure in which many small to medium-sized productive units came to control most coffee production, even in areas where initial landholding was quite concentrated.

Peasant farming was probably in a better position than estates during the 1920s and 1930s, but relatively large coffee haciendas in southwestern Antioquia proper not only survived the difficulties of those years, but were actually quite profitable.[19]

---

12 Palacios (1983), pp. 189-194.

13 *Ibid.*, p. 147.

14 Palacios (1983), pp. 362-375.

15 Parsons (1979), p. 134; also pp. 17-18 and 97-124.

16 Palacios (1983), pp. 295-296, 313.

17 Arango (1981), p. 90.

18 Arango (1981), p. 69, states that "contrary to what has been thought, Antioqueño settlement did not lead to a democratization of landownership in Antioquia and Caldas".

19 Arango (1982), pp. 19, 33, 90.

Further north and east of Antioquia, Santander had been the main coffee-producing area during the third quarter of the nineteenth century, with almost nine tenths of Colombian production in 1874.[20] In some respects, the Santanderes were similar to Costa Rica's Meseta Central, given their background as areas where export activities had been relatively weak during most of the colonial period, and there were few Indians or slaves. D. C. Johnson's characterization of rural Santander in colonial times, as an independent freeholder economy with few latifundia, brings to mind the part-mythical, part-real Costa Rican vision of a "rural democracy", and one may wonder how egalitarian it actually was. Nevertheless, smallholders were certainly more important there than, for example, in Cundinamarca. On the other hand, artisan industries, especially urban textile crafts and hatmaking, seem to have been rather more important in Santander than in the Costa Rican case, where such activities were less widespread and tended to disappear after the mid-nineteenth century.[21]

As in Costa Rica, the introduction of coffee in Santander apparently strengthened both smallholder production and larger estates. Smallholding was significant enough in the area for Johnson to affirm that "coffee in Santander tended to reinforce the pattern of small holdings which was already prevalent".[22] However, there were other medium-to-large properties, and an active land market in which transactions led both to subdivision and concentration of holdings.[23] Toward 1930, Machado finds that coffee production was actually as concentrated in Santander as in Cundinamarca, despite a very different history of land tenure and social relations.[24]

The Colombian experience, like that of Costa Rica, suggests that early legal landholding patterns, which often preceded settlement, were not decisive regarding the outcome in terms of actual peasant access to the land. Furthermore, the fact that coffee cultivation usually started on relatively large estates, frequently owned by merchants, did not preclude the later predominance of peasant farming in the same or neighboring areas, even if undoubtedly subject to merchant capital.

The question remains as to why domestic units came to be of major importance in certain regions where agricultural exports were the main economic activity. Explanations often refer to lack of profit-orientation, that peasant households produce only to satisfy domestic consumption needs and not to maximize profits.[25] Peasant farming certainly has certain

---

20 Machado (1977), p. 36.

21 Johnson (1975), p. 166.

22 Johnson (1975), p. 186.

23 Johnson (1975), pp. 347-358.

24 Machado (1977), pp. 97-98.

25 This viewpoint is typical of the Chayanovian tradition, but is also frequent in the anthropological literature on peasant societies. Colombian scholars interested in the

"comparative advantages" with respect to capitalist farms under adverse economic and environmental conditions. However, domestic units in the areas we are referring to were hardly self-contained or subsistence-oriented. Peasant-farmers tended to shift from extensive, traditional uses of the land into agricultural export crops not only due to population pressure (since land was still abundant in the areas and periods we are dealing with), but also due to the greater profitability of the latter.

As we have seen in Costa Rica, and LeGrand has shown for Colombia,[26] settlers were not fleeing from the market economy, but rather seeking to redevelop independent commercial production under more favorable landholding conditions. At first, land use patterns were extensive due to abundance of land and transport difficulties, which were even greater in late-nineteenth-century Colombia than in mid-nineteenth-century Costa Rica. Livestock was at first the most promising commodity under such conditions, given the specific combination of material resources, labor capacity and access to markets. As local population grew and communications were improved, agricultural intensification became possible, and eventually led to gradual specialization in the most lucrative crop at the time.

The efforts and attitudes of settlers were essential to their successful re-insertion into a commercial economy, of which these frontiers were most definitely a part. Had they not sought to redevelop market ties and improve transportation, they might have ended up reverting to subsistence-oriented rather than commercial agriculture. However, this does not suffice to explain their substantial access to the land nor their successful involvement in agro-export production. In other words, these results were not merely the natural outcome of spontaneous peasant settlement and self-determined agrarian transformations.

In certain areas where labor was scarce and personally free, land abundant and transportation costly, peasant settlement was actually promoted, rather than opposed, by those holding large land grants in the regions where colonization took place. Antioqueño settlement, like that of the Northwestern section of Costa Rica's Central Valley, resulted partly from private sales or donations of land to settlers. Even though conflicts might later become violent, squatters were initially tolerated by large landowners in need of laborers.

Moderately conservative policies in Antioquia, or moderately liberal ones in Costa Rica, both expressing the interests of a merchant-planter elite, actively promoted peasant access to the land and agro-export production. Additionally, the very same merchants who established the first major plantations in each of these regions lent money to and bought coffee from numerous smallholders. In Costa Rica, merchant-planters had the advantage of control over processing of coffee after the mid-nineteenth

---

resilience of peasant farming have adopted similar positions, e.g. Palacios (1983), p. 444, and Arango (1982), pp. 33-35.

26 LeGrand (1984), pp. 31-33.

century. There was no such centralization in Colombia, where pulp removal was a peasant endeavor, but the purchasing firms established sophisticated networks in the coffee-producing regions to ensure not only supply, but also low prices, and merchants did control *trillado*, the last phase of processing for export.[27]

Merchant-planters in Costa Rica or Colombia, and especially those in control of processing, not only obtained extra profits through credit relations and long-distance trade, but also economies of scale and risk-distribution. They undoubtedly had a vested interest in peasant colonization and commercial production by domestic units, even though the unequal nature of their relations with settler-farmers would lead to conflicts, sometimes over landholding and others over mercantile relations.

During the early stages of settlement, lack of a readily-available labor force, subject to strong economic or extra-economic pressures, hindered the establishment of large, specialized productive units, especially in the more remote, sparsely populated areas. Additionally, even though the Antioqueño elite had accumulated much more wealth during colonial times in mining, trade and livestock-raising than their Costa Rican counterpart,[28] these and other economic activities were profitable alternatives which allowed owners of capital in both cases to diversify, rather than concentrate their capital investments in one activity during the nineteenth century. In Colombia, the Ospinas carried out joint ventures in coffee production with the Vásquez family, but were also involved in sugarcane and livestock, banking, real estate, gold mining and smelting, railroad operation, liquor stores, importing of manufactured goods and retail distribution through local merchants, etc.[29] In Costa Rica, several wealthy merchant-planters from the Meseta Central were active in multiple economic activities, and large landowners in the Northwest were reluctant to single-crop specialization. A limited labor supply and diversified assets were, therefore, among the reasons why large coffee plantations were not the usual outcome of initial landholding concentration on these agricultural frontiers. This, in turn, helps to explain why capital owners actively promoted settlement and coffee production by peasant-farmers.

For peasant colonists, on the other hand, settlement on the frontier and the shift into coffee cultivation were not a cost-free enterprise. Some had the means to cover initial costs, but at least in Colombia, merchants from Medellín provided credit, livestock and equipment, as well as political and legal support to the settlers.[30] In Costa Rica, that may well have been the case too, although advances on inheritance did allow sons of middling

---

27 Palacios (1983), pp. 283-292, gives the example of one such network set up by apparent competitors, the 'X and Y business', which acted as a monopsonic and manipulative 'invisible hand' in Antioquia.

28 Twinam (1982), pp. 41-46, 115-118, 132-141.

29 Palacios (1983), pp. 84-87.

30 Palacios (1983), P. 295.

peasants to cover initial costs associated with settlement. As coffee became a significant crop for domestic units of production, credit certainly became a major tie between producers and owners of processing plants. In both cases, trading networks allowed small farmers to specialize in and within agriculture, get their products to market and obtain those goods which they no longer produced. Even though their participation in credit and product markets involved a degree of vulnerability and exploitation, it allowed settlers to become market- rather than subsistence-oriented farmers in an agro-export economy where prosperity, even if unequally distributed, was associated with coffee production.

To understand agrarian changes asociated with movement of population from previously settled areas to agricultural frontiers, as well as subsequent economic transformations there, we also need to inquire about the migrants themselves: Who were they in their place of origin, why did they migrate, and how does this relate to their degree of success in securing title to the land and developing commercial agriculture?

The early settlers of frontier regions such as those in Costa Rica and western Colombia, where agricultural exports came to be substantially based on peasant farming, were not destitute, landless laborers expelled from the previously settled areas by absolute impoverishment. Quite the contrary, as we have seen for Costa Rica's Central Valley, they were often members of rural households with sufficient means to provide them with advances on their inheritance to establish new productive units on the frontier. In the areas of Antioqueño colonization, as Parsons, López Toro and Arango have shown,[31] initial settlement was often by groups of families with the means to organize an expedition, sometimes seeking gold, and in any case led to the establishment of a limited number of medium-sized farms rather than very many small ones. Successive immigrants found little land available in those areas, and either became dependent laborers there or moved on to unclaimed territories elsewhere.

As land became scarce and rural society more stratified in the former agricultural frontiers, emigrants from these faced greater difficulties in obtaining secure tenure on the new rimlands. They themselves were poorer, the land was already titled, labor was less of a scarce commodity, and overall conditions were not as favorable as for their forebears. The new generations of settlers often found themselves in situations where ownership of the land they were living on was violently disputed. This was the case in many areas of independent colonization throughout Colombia,[32] as it was outside the Central Valley in Costa Rica.

Given peasant access to land on the frontier, by whatever means, how did productive units based mainly on household labor evolve and interact with other productive units and with their various markets, from initial

---

31 Parsons (1979), pp. 97, 103, 114-115; López Toro (1970), pp. 49-50; Arango (1981), p. 71.

32 LeGrand (1980), pp. 164-174.

settlement to gradual specialization in and within agriculture? A somewhat more detailed comparative discussion of this point, for the Costa Rican and Colombian areas referred to above, may help to address certain underlying issues with conceptual implications regarding socioeconomic relations in the countryside.

In the Costa Rican case study, we found that during the initial stages of settlement, variously-sized productive units differed in their scale, but not in their productive activities, intensity of land use, or technological level. Specific research on southwestern Antioquia proper, carried out for comparative purposes in the course of this investigation, showed that large and small productive units on the frontier near the town of Jericó, from 1850 to 1870, shared similar characteristics: they were essentially livestock-raising units, with some sugarcane and maize, and a low level of technological equipment. In the previously settled area near Fredonia, as in Costa Rica's Meseta Central, agriculture proper was beginning to become more important on the various productive units, although livestock was still significant at the time.[33] In southwestern Antioquia, the main commercial crop in the two decades after mid-century was sugarcane. In Costa Rica, it was also significant, but in combination with maize and an earlier expansion of coffee cultivation in the Meseta Central.

Toward the late nineteenth century, a gradual process of agricultural intensification in southwestern Antioquia led to diversified land use patterns, with subregional variations and certain differences between the larger and smaller productive units which were quite like those found in Costa Rica's Central Valley: The relative importance of livestock-raising in the region shifted to the settlement frontier southwest of the Cauca River in Antioquia, while sugarcane and coffee cultivation expanded throughout the region, but more rapidly in districts closer to Medellín, where transport costs were significantly lower. By types of productive units, livestock raising was especially important on the larger haciendas, in association with sugarcane and coffee. On the smaller farms, specialization in agriculture was more complete, as they tended to intensify land use further and had very few head of cattle, mostly draft or pack animals.[34] Generally speaking, these changes are similar to those described for Costa Rica, although swine were much more important in the Antioqueño peasant household economy than in Costa Rica. This may be related to the greater transport difficulties in areas of Antioqueño settlement, or to the fact that coffee became a mercantile option for Costa Rican farmers sooner than for *paisas*.

In the early twentieth century, large and small productive units in southwestern Antioquia, as in Costa Rica's Central Valley, gradually specialized in cofee production. Land previously in forest or pasture was changed over into this tree crop. However, that did not lead to a single-

33 Samper (1985b), pp. 2-3.

34 Samper (1985b), pp. 3-5.

crop regional economy, nor did most productive units specialize completely in coffee. Livestock raising persisisted, not only for consumption or sale but also due to the special transport needs of farms in relatively remote, rugged areas, where mule trails (or rudimentary oxcart roads in Costa Rica) were still the link with the outer world. Sugarcane cultivation was far from disappearing, and the expansion of coffee groves was actually accompanied by foodcrops or *cultivos de pan coger* in Antioquia, as we saw for Costa Rica: plantain as dual-purpose shade, plots for products which it was difficult to bring from other areas, and interplanting of maize, beans and tubers in the growth-years of new coffee plantations, or more permanently on peasant farms.[35] In other words, to use a very appropriate expression applied by María Errázuriz to another coffee-producing region in Colombia, this was a "multicrop system organized around a coffee plantation".[36] Once again, despite major geographical differences and a time-lag in the development of Antioqueño export agriculture, the pattern was very similar to Costa Rica.

By the 1930's, coffee was the main type of land use on most productive units in southwestern Antioquia. Livestock raising, both for human consumption and for work, was still significant in terms of land use on the larger productive units, together with some sugarcane. On smaller and less valuable farms, cattle tended to disappear, and only some had horses or mules. Instead, foodcrops had become more important on domestic units, in association with coffee as the main commercial crop.[37]

As land use patterns became more intensive and, to a certain extent, specialized, labor requirements on the different productive units varied accordingly. More labor was required per area on most productive units, but the yearly labor cycle depended upon specific crop mixes, processing facilities and geographic factors. Insofar as coffee tended to become the dominant crop, harvest labor increased vis-à-vis permanent work. In Antioquia, where there are two dry seasons and two flowerings per year, harvest-related tasks lasted much longer, seasonal peaks were less pronouned and labor exchanges among productive units less frequent than in bi-seasonal Costa Rica.[38] During the early stages of coffee cultivation, when there was more productive diversity, labor requirements were distributed more evenly over the year than later, once specialization within agriculture increased seasonal variations in labor needs and those of the coffee harvest prevailed over others. As processing "bottlenecks" and transport difficulties were gradually overcome, the coffee harvest could be prepared for export more rapidly than before, within the constraints of climatically-defined harvest periods. Generally speaking, from the viewpoint of domestic units, the trend was toward greater family-labor

35 Samper (1987b), pp. 2-3.

36 Errázuriz (1986), p. 52.

37 Samper (1987b), pp. 6-9.

38 Samper (1985b), pp. 7-10; (1987b), pp. 9-15.

surpluses and deficits during the year, although they were probably less pronounced in Antioquia than in Costa Rica.

During land settlement and agro-export expansion in Colombia and in Costa Rica, members of domestic units and owners of capital interacted in ways which led to the strengthening of market-oriented peasant farming through the very processes which placed it under the direct or indirect control of a mercantile elite, which in turn occupied a subordinate position in the world-economy. Based on the rather specific questions discussed comparatively with respect to Costa Rica and Colombia, certain more general issues can best be raised by placing these cases in a broader context. Questions which need to be addressed include:

- To what extent did peasant-farmer access to land and involvement in commercial production help or hinder capital accumulation and the establishment of capitalist-type social relations in the countryside, and viceversa?
- How did domestic units respond to changes in their own balance of material resources, productive capacity and consumption needs, and to those in societal conditions such as degree of landholding concentration, the nature of labor relations, or control over credit, processing, and commercialization of agricultural products?
- How can we characterize social relations in rural societies such as these, where the development of agrarian capitalism was substantially based on a commodity-producing peasantry with multiple and often ambivalent market insertions or interactions with owners of capital?

In the Costa Rican and Colombian case studies, the successful establishment of numerous market-oriented domestic units on the frontier resulted, in part, from the inability or reluctance of capital-owners to directly organize large-scale agro-export production in certain specific areas at the time of settlement. This was due, among other reasons, to local labor scarcity, the existence of a highly mobile and personally free population, initial transport difficulties and the fact that there were other, perhaps more attractive opportunities for capital investment at the time. However, wealthy or well-connected persons did acquire legal ownership of large properties in the areas of settlement and also established some medium-to-large estates in places where transport costs and labor availability made it possible and profitable to do so. Furthermore, the merchant-planters themselves sold or gave land to attract settlers and potential laborers, made loans to the colonists and bought their harvests, effectively stimulating commodity production on domestic units, e.g. coffee cultivation. Governments and local authorities, essentially under the control of these elites, undoubtedly gave merchant-planters and other members of the local elite a preferential treatment, but they also permitted and actively promoted peasant settlement. Far from being "suicidal", this conduct in itself suggests that peasant-farming was, in some way, an extension of capital in geographic and economic hinterlands where domestic units were better suited than supra-family units to develop export agriculture at the time.

As financial and commercial intermediaries, export-import merchants certainly profitted from what some term "unequal exchange", but peasant farmers obviously found coffee production, in particular, to be an attractive, long-term productive option. The survival and vitality of commercial peasant farming thereafter was not and is not an inevitable outcome, but has resulted from complex interactions between collective social actors, whose relationship has involved elements both of complementarity and of exploitation. The future of smallholder production in these areas is not ensured, but neither is its short- or even medium-term demise.

Peasant farmers in the areas discussed took advantage of opportunities not only to obtain land, but also to develop commercial and specifically agro-export production. Agricultural intensification and gradual specialization were the productive components of multi-pronged peasant strategies involving partial reliance wage labor, emigration, and modified inheritance practices. Members of domestic units also played an active role in social movements which sought to control prices, processing and other inegalitarian aspects of their relations with capital-owners. Their relative success in such endeavors did not alter the fundamental nature of class relations in the countryside nor prevent the transfer of value from peasant farmers to owners of capital at home or abroad, but it did define specific limits and force the state to adopt certain regulatory measures. Smallholder commodity production was and still is a basic component of rural society in various parts of Costa Rica and Colombia, despite social differentiation and the parallel development of more typical forms of capital accumulation together with wage labor.

Elsewhere in Latin America, household-scale farming was associated with land settlement and the growth of agrarian capitalism in various other cases during the late eighteenth to early twentieth century. From Mexico to Argentina, there were a number of comparable processes at a local or regional level, but the Mexican *rancheros* and Argentinian *colonos* are paradigmatic in this regard.

In the eighteenth-century settlement of the Bajío in New Spain, studied by Brading, an influx of creole Spaniards and unattached Indians, mulattos and mestizos, uninterrupted despite successive demographic crises, occupied new lands and established many variously-sized holdings.[39] While most productive units combined agriculture and livestock, maize was grown primarily on smaller units, and cattle raising was more important on large, hacienda-type ones. Medium-sized farms were more "capitalized" (i.e., they usually had more oxen for ploughing and transportation), and made substantial investments in clearing of the land and irrigation. Middling *rancheros* relied mostly on family labor, but could probably accumulate some wealth, and hardly fit into the traditional stereotype of the Mexican or Latin American *latifundio-minifundio* polarity.

39 Brading (1978), especially Chapters. 2, 4 and 5.

Aside from the numerous independent *ranchos* or farms, some haciendas in the eighteenth-century Bajío had a growing number of tenant-farmers, who either rented land or entered into sharecropping arrangements. By the beginning of the nineteenth century, tenancy was becoming more profitable than direct cultivation on many haciendas in this region.[40] On the other hand, in contrast to the formerly prevalent image of debt-bondage as a widespread form of control over workers, wage labor in the Bajío was free, not bound by debts or other means of coercion.

The larger landowners in the region during the eighteenth century were merchants and miners, but after 1810 (due to the insurgency and the flooding of the Valenciana mine) a depressed local economy favored sale or subdivision of haciendas belonging to heavily indebted, often absentee owners. At the same time, practical farmers on medium-sized holdings tended to prosper, in what Brading called the "yeoman farmer solution".[41]

During the nineteenth and the early twentieth century, the *rancheros* studied by Schryer and others shared several characteristics with their eighteenth-century predecessors, but were also different in certain important respects.[42] In the Sierra de Jacala, a formerly vast estate which raised cattle and grew wheat on a 20,000 hectare property, and which had come to have many tenants and sharecroppers, was effectively subdivided into *ranchos* during the first half of the nineteenth century. After mid-century, sugarcane and coffee became increasingly important, together with daylabor as agricultural intensification proceeded on the intermediately-sized productive units. New *ranchos* were formed outside the core hacienda, some on former community lands, essentially completing a regional transformation of land tenure patterns. Toward the turn of the century, this area became one of emigration, while the former hacienda was legally subdivided into *ranchos* from ten to several hundred hectares in size.[43]

These *rancheros* were a strong, well-defined group of middling peasant-farmers (Schryer calls them a "peasant bourgeoisie") in various parts of the Bajío, although smallholders were also found in various other parts of Mexico, in a subordinate position with respect to haciendas.[44] As in Costa Rica and Colombia, the relative importance of such rancher-farmers in the Bajío had much to do with the conditions under which land settlement took place and the characteristics of colonists, even if their degree of success was in no way predetermined but rather the outcome of concrete social interactions.

Let us turn now to another, very different situation. In Santa Fe, on the northern margin of the Argentinian *pampa*, the development of agrarian capitalism differed in several important respects from the Bajío, but also

40 *Ibid.*, p. 114.

41 *Ibid.*, p. 148.

42 Schryer (1979), (1980), (1983).

43 Schryer (1983), pp. 46-50.

44 Cf. Van Young (1978), p. 509, and Morin (1979), pp. 212-214 and 226.

shared certain basic features. It was based on late-nineteenth-century land settlement and a predominance of household agricultural production thereafter, in contrast to large, livestock-raising estates further south. The importance of grain as an early market crop in the *chacras* (household farms) of northern Santa Fe was probably due to relative profitability under different climatic conditions, e.g. by comparison with the southern sheep-raising areas.[45] Immigrant *colonos*, many of them from Italy, purchased land at low prices and established productive units which combined subsistence and commercial agriculture. Until the 1930's, maize and wheat were grown alongside flax and groundnuts. After that, cotton became the most significant cash crop in the region, and seasonal labor requirements became more pronounced. Around mid-century, mechanization of agricultural tasks reduced the importance of wage labor once again.[46]

Household labor was clearly predominant during the early decades after settlement, with a diversified crop mix evening-out labor cycles to a certain extent. After 1936, cotton with its highly seasonal labor requirements made hired help increasingly important, with *cosecheros* living on the farm several months a year. Even then, the whole *colono* family would also work on the farm.[47] Once tractors and other machinery were introduced, overall labor requirements and especially harvest-time peaks declined significantly.

While large families and uncontrolled reproduction had been the rule in Santa Fe from initial settlement to the introduction of cotton, demographic patterns afterwards evolved into controlled fertility.[48] Toward the mid-twentieth century, when the local agricultural frontier had reached its end and the land market was "frozen" at high prices, many sons of *colonos* without sufficient land emigrated.[49]

Actual inheritance systems in Santa Fe differed quite substantially from the legal norm. From Archetti and Stölen, we infer that modifications in the productive organization of household units were behind such changes, first to exclude women from inheritance as domestic production of use values lost importance, and then dispossessing younger brothers as mechanization made their labor unnecessary. Mechanisms to by-pass partible inheritance laws in Santa Fe included substitution of the dowry by a vaguely-defined *ayuda* when daughters married a non-farmer, and eventually the gradual elimination of dowries; symbolic compensation for inheritance rights; fictitious sales by the father to third parties, who resold to the favored son; donations, and other means.[50] The result was that viable holdings were

45 Gallo (1969), pp. 93-104.

46 Archetti and Stölen (1975), pp. 50, 106.

47 *Ibid.*, pp. 186 and 192.

48 Archetti (1984), pp. 265-266.

49 Archetti and Stölen (1975), pp. 207-208.

50 Archetti and Stölen (1978), pp. 383-384 and 387-401.

transmitted from one generation to the next in an agrarian society where fragmentation or property would have rapidly undermined the specific productive organization of domestic units.

At least until the 1930s, the lack of cooperative marketing systems in Santa Fe facilitated the transfer of value from producers to capital-owners who controlled processing and marketing of agricultural products. This, in turn, restricted capital accumulation by *colonos*.[51] After the introduction of cotton, favorable conditions for sale of the product and higher productivity due to mechanization, in a context of controlled reproduction, preferential inheritance and emigration, contributed to capital accumulation by farmers in Santa Fe.

Both the Mexican *rancheros* and the *colonos* of Santa Fe obtained access to middle-sized holdings during a process of settlement in rimland geographical and economic areas. Rather than a subsistence orientation, the settlers raised livestock, planted grain and other, specifically commercial crops for the purpose of developing market exchanges. Family labor was predominant during the early stages and continued to be a characteristic of *ranchos* and *chacras* as land use became more intensive and specialized. As the settlement frontier receded, sons of colonists emigrated, and various mechanisms sought to restrict fragmentation of holdings. Although there were some larger productive units and others were subdivided, there was no massive landholding concentration. In Santa Fe, there was more on-farm capital investment in mechanization of agricultural tasks, but this actually strengthened family labor, while family size declined due to controlled fertility. Those descendants of *colonos* who inherited the land, like the *rancheros* of the late nineteenth and early twentieth century, were the winners in a process which required the exclusion of others to ensure the economic reproduction of what we have characterized as surplus-producing domestic units.

We turn now to areas in which agro-export production was substantially based on coffee, under quite diverse social conditions but with a major component of household production. In the Venezuelan Andes, which became the most important coffee-producing area of this country after 1860, large estates were significant in various regions, but there were areas such as Boconó, where peasant farmers played a very major role in export agriculture. The development of smallholder coffee production and, in fact, the local creation of a market-oriented peasantry, was associated with strong immigration into the region and settlement on public lands (without legal title, which was often granted later to merchants), as well as on former Indian reserves (alienated toward the mid-nineteenth century) and colonial *posesiones* (alienable private property after Independence from Spain). During the early twentieth century, continued immigration was associated with fragmentation of holdings.[52]

---

51 Archetti and Stölen (1975), p. 215.

52 Roseberry (1983), pp. 75-76, 84-88 and 95.

In the Venezuelan case studied by Roseberry, as in Antioquia and Costa Rica, merchants were decisive in promoting coffee cultivation. Frequent credit relations between merchants and smallholders led some of the former to acquire numerous separate farms, but this was a last resort. The role of farmer indebtedness in Boconó was basically to ensure the supply of coffee for the merchants. Despite transfer of value from farmer to merchant, coffee production offered nineteenth-century peasant farmers a very real opportunity for material and social advancement. Peasant processing of coffee remained rather rudimentary, using oxen or manual labor to remove the sun-dried pulp. Productivity was probably low, but merchants profited from the geographical expansion of their coverage. [53]

Large farms in Boconó had difficulty mobilizing labor, a factor which was instrumental in peasant access to the land. From the standpoint of domestic units, labor relations involved *callapas* or work parties, in which neighboring farmers' work was repaid in food and liquor; *mano vuelta* or reciprocal labor exchanges; and occasional wage labor. There was, of course, social differentiation within the peasantry, as some benefitted more than others or were in a more advantageous position.[54]

Aside from providing us with a comparative case where coffee was the main cash-crop, Roseberry's discussion of Boconó also raises relevant conceptual issues. Following Harriet Friedman in this regard, he speaks of "specialized household producers" as opposed to subsistence-oriented peasants. However, Roseberry identifies their relationship with merchant capital as the key to understanding the transformation of petty commodity relations: As small farmers acquired long-term debts and were in permanent contact with large merchants, they ceased to be truly independent producers:

> By lending the resources necessary for the establishment of a coffee farm, the merchant established a structural claim to a portion of the suplus product. This penetration of merchant capital into petty commodity relations signified the investment of money capital in production. Merchant capital therefore moved out of circulation and into the production process itself, setting up new production relations based on interest.[55]

In other words, while the form of petty commodity production is maintained, its content is altered by the nature of relations between formally independent producers and merchants who are, in fact, acquiring labor power. There was a structured, exploitative relation between direct producers and merchant capital, but this was not a disguised form of wage labor. Unequal access to resources allowed some peasant producers to

---

53 *Ibid.*, p. 90 and 97.

54 *Ibid.*, p. 91.

55 *Ibid.*, p. 101.

retain a part of their own surplus product, while others had little or no possibility of accumulation.[56]

Regarding the agrarian society in which coffee farmers entered into such relations with merchant capital, Roseberry concludes that it was neither "precapitalist" (since merchants' capital was no longer restricted to circulation, and the independence of farmers had been compromised) nor "capitalist" (as farmers still had significant control over production and resource allocation, while there was no major technical reorganization). Even though free wage labor was not the basis for coffee production in Boconó, the relationship with merchant capital was necessary for reproduction of the family. Boconó farmers were no longer "peasants" in the traditional sense, and surplus value was being transferred, but wage labor was not necessarily a commodity, nor were formally-subsumed laborers therefore proletarians.[57] In Roseberry's terms: "The investment of capital, paradoxically, tied producers more closely to means of production, even as those means of production were alienated from them".[58]

Throughout Roseberry's conceptual characterization of the Boconó coffee economy, loss of independence through debt is the key to socioeconomic relations between direct producers and merchants. However, since Roseberry does not describe credit relations in detail with respect to the various nineteenth-century productive units, it is difficult to assess the actual weight of indebtedness for coffee producers there, or compare it to their situation elsewhere. From the Costa Rican perspective, it would seem that indebtedness had different socioeconomic meanings, and varied over time. In the northwestern part of the Central Valley, for example, peasant-farmer debts were frequent but usually for small amounts and combined with credits in the first few decades after mid-nineteenth-century settlement. From the turn of the century, instead, there is evidence that debt could threaten the viability of a certain number of productive units. Coffee producers in the 1930's were certainly under pressure, as the reaction of *beneficiadores* to the economic crisis made the unfavorable conditions of their credit arrangements and overall relationship painfully clear to smallholders.

In the Greater Antilles and in certain islands of the Lesser Antilles, peasant farming developed on previously unsettled or very sparsely settled inland areas. Although maroon communities had established themselves in some such areas, the main thrust of settlement in these often mountainous and poorly communicated regions came after the decline of the slave trade and abolition. In the British West Indies of the later nineteenth century, it was also associated with problems faced by estates in the context of a weakening of the British market for sugar and a change in local class relations. As a result, states Carl Stone: "The decline of estate agriculture

---

56 *Ibid.*, p. 105 and 110-111.

57 *Ibid.*, p. 106-107.

58 *Ibid.*, p. 109.

was accompanied by the extensive growth of peasant holdings in territories where there was an abundance of land (Jamaica, Trinidad, Guyana, St. Lucia, Dominica, etc.)."[59]

In contrast, the smallest and most densely settled plantation economies of the West Indies, where land settlement processes were minimal, underwent few changes in land ownership. In some cases, island and estate were nearly synonymous, and there was little room for settlement or independent peasant farming. In most such cases, the decline of slavery led to the establishment either of wage labor relations or of a specific social relation which some term "share-wage", in which sharecropping on plantation lands amounts to a continuation of estate owners' direct control over production, and shares were the equivalent of wages.[60]

In Jamaica, the largest island of the British West Indies, peasant agriculture traces its origins to the slave plantation itself, where foodcrops were grown on slopes unsuitable for sugar production. Such cultivation by slaves, often unsupervised, satisfied domestic consumption needs, but also produced small surpluses which reached local markets.[61] Mintz and Hall conclude that even before emancipation, Jamaican slaves were acquainted with and involved in the internal marketing system.[62] Unsupervised work on provision grounds increased, for economic reasons, during the early nineteenth century.

By 1830, it was clear that Jamaican slavery would disappear, not only due to the abolitionist trends in England, but also because creole slaves who had achieved some status within slave society were able to organize large-scale rebellions.[63] After emancipation, even though plantations did not disappear, there was a movement of former slaves away from the estates, which led to the rapid growth of freeholder commercial farming, rather than a reversion to subsistence agriculture.[64]

Within a broadly defined post-emancipation peasantry which produced for self-consumption as well as for local markets, a substantial and growing number of independent small farmers planted one or more of the export crops, both on abandoned estates and on new lands. Coffee, which had been cultivated on some plantations before, became a major crop on these household-labor units.[65] The number of what were in fact domestic units continued to grow more rapidly than population, well into the twentieth century. Not only did their numbers treble between the mid-nineteenth century and 1930, but their share in agricultural output increased from half

59 C. Stone (1983), p. 11.

60 Frucht (1967), pp. 295-300.

61 Mintz and Hall (1960), pp. 3-5.

62 *Ibid.*, p. 19.

63 Higman (1974), pp. 227-232.

64 Hall (1981), pp. 158 and 164.

65 *Ibid.*, pp. 182-189.

to over two thirds. In that same period, gradual specialization increased the export component of peasant farming from 11% to 27% of their own output, and already by the turn of the century smallholders were producing more coffee than the estates.[66]

Despite very different conditions as an island economy formerly based on slave labor and sugarcane, the development of export-oriented peasant farming in Jamaica shares certain characteristics with other coffee-producing areas where domestic units were of major importance in the Caribbean and Latin America.

There are both affinities and critical differences between the Jamaican case and the coffee-producing regions of Puerto Rico studied by Wolf, Picó and Bergad.[67] Sugarcane plantations had been the mainstay of the Puerto Rican economy, but there was also a rapidly expanding frontier where access to land was associated with smallholder coffee cultivation, the financing and marketing of which were controlled by urban merchants. At the same time, coerced seasonal labor and indebtedness contributed to a gradual process of proletarianization in the course of a century. Although slavery as a legal institution lasted forty years longer than in Jamaica, the *Jornalero* law was part of mid-century efforts to make "free" labor truly available for estate-owners. Still, there were few permanent day-laborers in the *Cordillera* during the 1850's; they were usually indebted, and those renting land often had labor obligations too. Landholding was far from egalitarian, yet owner-producers were strongly predominant and medium to smallholders accounted for a major part of coffee production. In the late nineteenth century, coffee acreage expanded, in association with seasonal migration of coastal workers. There were more landless or land poor families, but few year-round wage workers. In other words, members of rural households might often be small-scale peasant farmers and part-time wage laborers.[68]

Actually, the Puerto Rican case is less exceptional than was formerly presumed, and the parallel development of a market-oriented peasantry and a drawn-out process of proletarianization are not mutually exclusive. Agrarian capitalism in Puerto Rico, as in Jamaica, followed the dual path of creating both a modern freeholder peasantry and a wage-labor force in a society where slavery had been the rule. Abolition, land settlement and the shift from sugarcane into coffee cultivation strengthened the peasant component of the local economy in the nineteenth century, despite early attempts to retain or coerce laborers. At the same time, the limited supply of land, population growth, landholding concentration, and direct capital accumulation made wage labor increasingly necessary for members of rural households from the late nineteenth century on. Yet the ambivalence remained, and has been an essential feature not only of socioeconomic

---

66 Eisner (1961), pp. 220-221 and 234.

67 Picó (1981); Bergad (1978 and 1983).

68 Bergad (1978), pp. 69-71; (1983), pp. 89-99.

relations, but also of sociopolitical interactions well into the twentieth century. Despite very different colonial histories, the underlying processes are in many ways comparable to the development of export-oriented smallholder agriculture in continental Latin America.

Within the Caribbean, the development of peasant agriculture in Haiti, like its sociopolitical history, was divergent from other Caribbean cases.[69] Soon after Independence and abolition, obtained early on through active struggle, distribution of public lands in the South, under Pétion and in the context of the early-nineteenth-century civil war, effectively transformed large numbers of former slaves and soldiers into smallholders. Squatting and crop-sharing, which were important in the North under Cristophe, also led to the subdivision of large properties into smaller productive units over the following decades By mid-century, most Haitians had access to land. Unprofitable estates were broken up, sugarcane cultivation declined, and peasant farming became predominant. Although there was some small-scale, untechnified coffee production on peasant farms, export-agriculture gave way to subsistence-oriented production. In the French legal tradition regarding inheritance, large and small holdings were constantly subdivided.[70] In the latter part of the nineteenth century, as in the twentieth, an impoverished peasantry was increasingly subject to new forms of social domination and to authoritarian regimes.

Of all the comparative cases discussed above, Haiti probably comes closest to a "peasant model" such as that proposed by de Vries, where the reaction to population growth and limited trading opportunities is landholding fragmentation and also concentration; labor-intensification with decreasing returns; a productive emphasis on foodcrops and handicrafts for household use; sale of agricultural surpluses but little market-oriented specialization; supplementary daylabor despite low wages, due to insufficient household income; and domination of an urban elite over backward rural areas which do not benefit from their relationship with the cities or external markets.[71] Of course, this is a simplified model which in no way accounts for the complexity of Haitian society, nor does it incorporate historically specific situations, such as a relative abundance of land after independence and abolition, or the socioeconomic consequences of these two events. However, it does indicate the type of agrarian changes which tend to occur when peasant farming evolves via proliferation of primarily subsistence-oriented, often sub-family units, together with some supra-family ones, in a context of demographic pressure on increasingly limited amounts of land, and little or no market-specialization or improvements in productivity of labor on peasant plots.

In contrast, the *colonos* of Santa Fe were clearly much closer to the type of farmer which de Vries' "specialization model" refers to, that is one

---

69 C. Stone (1983), pp. 13-14.

70 Leyburn (1941), pp. 51-79.

71 De Vries (1978), pp. 4-7.

in which peasant holdings are not subdivided nor is there much landholding concentration; there is specialization in and within agriculture; regular agricultural surpluses allow peasant farmers to buy nonagricultural goods; the decline in labor productivity is compensated for by an efficient allocation of the resources available to each household; production is reorganized by the peasants themselves in response to market opportunities; most new population is not admitted to the peasant sector but rather migrates to the cities, and rural productive units benefit from strong intersectoral trade.[72] Once again, agrarian society in Santa Fe was far more complex than such a model, and a historical explanation must take into account foreign immigration, land settlement and numerous other variables. Yet the type of agrarian solution in Santa Fe, via restricted inheritance and population growth, emigration to the cities, productive specialization and, eventually, technification, is certainly very different from a solution based on fragmentation of peasant holdings, local absorption of population growth in the peasant sector, and low levels of specialization, of market orientation and of technological improvement.

All the other cases mentioned in the preceding comparative discussion share characteristics of one and another model, in variable combinations which result from historically-specific characteristics of the "peasant-farmers" dealt with in this study, and of the agrarian societies of which they were a part. From the standpoint of alternative models such as those discussed above, they were, in many ways, contradictory. And that is precisely what challenges analysis, urging us to leave aside preconceived polarities and attempt to comprehend the actions of people who undoubtedly knew what they were doing, even if they seem to have pursued conflicting goals. As William Roseberry has put it:

> "I like to use concepts that embrace existential and social contradictions, rather than separating out contradictory elements into mutually-exclusive categories... It forces me to try to think dialectically. It also helps me to think about and analyze politics, the relationship between contradictory social being and contradictory consciousness. The confusion analysts feel as they embrace a multitudinous reality with a concept like 'peasant' is not entirely unlike the existential and political dilemmas presented to peasants as they get through daily life, plant, cultivate and harvest crops, contract debts, pay taxes, arrange marriages, work off the farm, arrange for workers on the farm and, on occasion and under circumstances not of their own choosing, make history."[73]

In various parts of Latin America, peasant-farmers played a major role in land settlement and the development of commercial agriculture or, more specifically, agro-export production. Searching for opportunities not only to subsist but also to prosper, they established themselves on the agricultural frontiers of the time and devised complex, flexible strategies in

---

72 *Ibid.*, pp. 7-10.

73 Roseberry (1985), pp. 74-75.

response to their changing societal environment. Far from being static, they constantly reorganized production, adjusted material resources, productive capacity and consumption. And they did so not in isolation nor as a passive reaction to external determinants, but as members of interactive economic units within societies which were undergoing deep changes.

From the outset, peasant-farmers in Costa Rica and comparable cases were involved in various markets: for products, land, labor and credit. They bought and sold, hired or worked off-farm, lent and owed, benefitting from these exchanges which at the same time were the vehicle of value transfers.

The successful establishment of commercial peasant farming in various parts of Latin America resulted both from the initiative of a personally free and mobile population, which sought to avail itself of opportunities on the frontier in the context of agro-export development, and of capital-owners who often promoted colonization and productive specialization for their own reasons. To a certain extent, the strength of market-oriented peasant farming reflected the inability or unwillingness of capital to organize production directly in certain regions and periods, but this was no obstacle to surplus extraction from the peasantry through market mechanisms. Nor did it hinder the parallel and intertwined development of larger productive units, in the same or adjacent regions, which peasant-farmers often dealt with on unequal terms regarding disposition of products, land, labor or credit.

Despite major differences in historical background and variations in the specifics of each process, a number of regions in Latin America and the Caribbean followed similar paths, insofar as settlement and peasant access to the land were the basis for commercial, usually export-oriented and increasingly specialized agriculture, with a major peasant-farmer component subject indirectly to capital through various market mechanisms. Subdivision of holdings was partly compensated for by agricultural intensification and gradual specialization in a profitable crop, and partly by emigration to other settlement frontiers or to the cities. Yet in most cases there was, in the course of two or three generations, a substantial reduction in the size of holdings which might be associated with domestic units, as well as the establishment of large, supra-family units and a growing number of micro-farms or sub-family units. Wage labor has become increasingly important for many rural households. Even so, peasant farming has survived in many of these regions, in conflictive interactions with merchants, estate owners, processing firms, and moneylenders, as well as governments and, in some cases, other peasants. Whatever the final outcome, it can at least be said that, in such cases, development of agrarian capitalism has not been incompatible with a predominance of non-capitalist forms of production, which rather than being archaic remnants of the past resulted from that very process. And there may be a need to reconceptualize the classical definitions of capitalism if they are to be meaningful for the type of agrarian transformations dealt with here.

In other parts of Latin America, peasants were also present in previously-settled areas with large indigenous populations, although export agriculture did not develop precisely in those same areas. In such cases (e.g. Guatemala, parts of Mexico, or Peru) indigenous communities with a major component of subsistence agriculture often survived well into the twentieth century or even today, while large estates in neighboring areas recruited seasonal labor from them. Although greater or lesser coercion was frequently involved in such relations over a long period of time, wage labor eventually tends to become a necessity for survival of rural households.[74] Smallholders do sell surpluses, but access to land is so limited that income from independent commodity production is usually insufficient. Clearly, the development of agrarian capitalism in such cases followed a very different path from that described for the Costa Rican and comparable Latin American or Caribbean cases.

Even in situations where independent peasant access to the land was systematically restricted by local estate owners and the state, there was some commercial production by peasant-farmers in geographical or socioeconomic "niches". But the overall dynamics of agrarian capitalism was imposed by the overwhelming predominance of large-scale farming and the specific social relations that evolved on the vast estates which controlled most agro-export production. Whether in El Salvador or in Brazil, for example, to disregard the presence of smallholders in coffee-producing areas would amount to a crude oversimplification of a complex social reality.[75] Yet the socioeconomic and sociopolitical situation of peasant-farmers in such cases was clearly different from areas where smallholders were far more important in agro-export production. The process whereby that situation came about, and the characteristics of agrarian capitalism there, also differed quite substantially.

In a wider comparative perspective, farmer access to land during settlement, and a significant participation of domestic units in export agriculture, can be found in various parts of the world. At different times, under other conditions and in ways which also differed, settlers on such diverse frontiers as mid-western North America and Australia became actively involved in the world-economy. Household labor and productive specialization went hand in hand, while technification often displaced wage labor rather than strengthening capitalist-type social relations within economic units. As a result, the world wheat market, especially, came to be dominated by highly technified units relying primarily on household labor despite a "capitalized" appearance.[76] While these modern-day farmers may seem very different from traditional peasants in many parts of the Third

---

74 For the Guatemalan case see: Flores (1977); Cambranes (1985); and Smith (1987).

75 Regarding the presence of smallholders in El Salvador, see Richter (1976); for Brazil see: Cardoso (1979); Viotti da Costa (1966); de Carvalho Franco (1969); Klein (1969).

76 Friedman (1978) and (1980).

World, their history goes back to a time when the distinction between "farmer" and "peasant" was blurred by many common features.

Many of the people whose lives and labors we discussed in this study were, in a way, part "farmers" and part "peasants". The history of settlers and agrarian capitalism is the history of generations of peasant-farmers who sought both to satisfy household needs and to obtain a profit, to guarantee their families' subsistence and to reinvest in production. They could not easily or rapidly specialize in a single agricultural commodity, yet they often attained higher levels of productive specialization than most large estates, despite the inherent risks. In doing so, they took advantage of opportunities and successfully established themselves as small-scale mercantile producers, while at the same time exposing themselves to various forms of exploitation through seemingly innocuous market mechanisms. They also participated in a process whereby capital extended its control over agriculture and the rural population in a very different way from the classical models of political economy, or the usual stereotypes on Latin America.

The relative importance of peasant-farmers in rural society defines regions where peasant farming is essential to an understanding of agrarian changes, past and present. The significance of such regions with respect to nationwide socioeconomic and sociopolitical development is a key explanatory element to the evolution of each national economy and nation-state, but also to class relations and the way they are perceived and represented. And in Latin Amerca as a whole, a comprehension of these convergent paths as well as of the historical uniqueness of each specific process should help to de-mystify the more simplistic formulations of past and present transformations.

Glossary

Abasto: Marketplace subject to government supervision in colonial times.

Agricultor: A farmer, usually the owner of a medium to large property.

Antioqueño: An inhabitant of the Colombian Department of Antioquia, or a person descended from residents of that region in western Colombia.

Artesano: A craftsman.

Ayuda: In Santa Fe, Argentina, a substitute for dowry.

Ayuntamiento: Town council.

Barrio: Administrative subdivision of *cantones* in Costa Rica up to the mid-nineteenth century; roughly the equivalent of *distritos* toward the end of that century.

Beneficiador: Owner of a coffee-processing plant.

Beneficio: Coffee processing plant.

Caballería: A somewhat imprecise measure for large areas, which in Costa Rica was, in actual practice, roughly the equivalent of 32 *manzanas*, or some 22 hectares.

Cafetalero: A coffee grower. Although the term can refer to small coffee producers, it definitely indicates specialization in coffee as the main economic activity, and is sometimes used with reference only to the wealthier estate owners.

Cajuela: A unit of measure for volume, used especially for coffee berries at time of harvest.

Callapa: In Venezuela, a work party.

Cañaveralero: A sugarcane grower.

Cantón: An administrative subdivision, intermediate between province and district in Costa Rica. Cited in text in English spelling.

Carretera nacional: Main cartroad from the Meseta Central to the Pacific coast.

Cesión: Legal granting or sale of inheritance rights.

Chacra: In Argentina, a household farm.

Código General: Legal code enacted in 1841, also known as *Código de Carrillo*.

Colones: The unit of currency in Costa Rica after the monetary reform at the turn of the century. Equivalent to former *pesos*.

Colono: In Santa Fe, Argentina, an immigrant farmer whose land was cultivated mainly with household labor.

Comal: Iron dish.

Compadrazgo: The religious, personal and social tie between the father of a child and its godfather.

Composición: A procedure by which Crown lands would be obtained at a price during colonial times.

Cosechero: In Argentina, the seasonal harvest workers who lived on the farm several months a year.

Cosecheros: Tobacco growers under contract with the *Factoría* in the late eighteenth century.

Cultivo de pan coger: Foodcrop.

Derecho: An inheritance right, acquired by each heir in probate proceedings.

Dulce: Unrefined sugar cakes.

Estanquillo: Liquor store under government monopoly.

Estera: Straw mat.

Factoría de Tabacos: The governmental institution which regulated tobacco planting in the late eighteenth century and propared tobacco for export.

Fanega: A measure of volume for grain and other products.

Ganadero: A livestock raiser. As in the case of coffee, it indicates that cattle was the main economic activity, and is sometimes applied restrictively to the owners of large cattle ranches.

Gananciales: Joint property acquired after marriage, assessed and reassigned through probate proceedings to the surviving spouse and to descendants or other heirs.

Guano: Manure from bird droppings.

Habilitación: Advance financing of a crop.

Hacienda: An estate, usually large. The term was most often associated with cattle in eighteenth and early ninteenth century Costa Rica, but it was also applied later to large coffee farms.

Hilandera: A spinner.

Información posesoria: Legal procedure, involving witnesses, to prove peaceful, uninterrupted possession of a specific area of land, and obtain legal right to it.

Ingenio: A modern sugar mill.

Invierno: The rainy season in Costa Rica, some seven to eight months long in the Central Valley, from mid-April to late November.

Jornal: Day-labor, whether one day's labor or one day's pay.

Jornalero: A rural worker relying at least partly on wage labor, although he might have some land of his own.

Labrador: A small, independent farmer.

Ley de sucesiones: Inheritance law, enacted in 1881.

Leyenda rosa: An idealized view of historical happenings; applied here to the alleged egalitarianism of *antioqueño* settlement in Colombia.

Logrero: A petty merchant trading in corn or other staple products.

Macana: Planting stick with flat metal end.

Mandador: The direct administrator of a farm.

Mano vuelta: In Venezuela, a reciprocal labor exchange among peasant farmers.

Manos cambiadas: Labor exchange among peasant farmers, without monetary remuneration.

Manzana: Ten thousand square *varas*, or roughly 0.7 hectares.

Meseta Central: That area of the Central Valley which was settled by Spaniards during the colonial period. It extended from the city of Cartago and its surroundings to that of Alajuela toward the west.

Mestizo: A person with mixed, Indian-Spanish ethnic background.

Paisa: A person from the *patria chica* of Antioquia, Colombia.

Palea: Shoveling to prepare the soil in coffee groves.

Parásito: Squatter, literally "parasite".

Peón: A resident or non-resident daylaborer.

Pesos: The Costa Rican currency unit before the turn-of-the-century monetary reform. Equivalent to *colones* thereafter.

Piedra de moler: Grinding stone, often for corn although certain types were for mashing tubers.

Piñuela: A plant used for live fences.

Plaza ganadera: Marketplace for livestock.

Posesión: In Venezuela, an alienable private property after Independence from Spain.

Precarista: Squatter, untitled occupand of land.

Quema: Land clearing with the slash and burn system.

Ranchero: In Mexico, the owner of a medium-sized farm, which usually combined livestock raising with foodcrops.

Rancho: In Mexico, especially in the Bajío region, an independent farm.

Raspa: Cleaning the surface of the land in coffee groves with a shovel.

Rastrojo: Temporarily uncultivated land; the term often refers to corn plots after the harvest, although it could apply to other crops or to land left fallow for longer periods.

Registro de Propiedad: Real estate registry.

Sitio de cercado: Enclosed plot.

Tercena: Tobacco store under government monopoly.

Tierra baldía: Public land after Independence from Spain.

Tierra compuesta: Land bought from the Crown.

Tierra realenga: Crown land in colonial times.

Tierras de propios: Community lands during the colonial period.

Tiquisque: Malanga or spoonflower.

Tortilla: Corn cake.

Trapiche: A small-scale, rudimentary processing mill for sugar.

Trillado: Last phase of coffee processing, once the pulp has been removed.

Vainicas: Green beans.

Verano: The main dry or nearly-dry season in Costa Rica. Usually about four and a half months long in the Central Valley, as short as three or as long as six months elsewhere in the country.

Veranillo: A very short, dry or nearly-dry season in Costa Rica, usually the first two or three weeks of July.

Yuca: Cassava or manioc.

Bibliography

UNPUBLISHED SOURCES

Archivo Nacional de Costa Rica

Complementario Colonial, documents number: 1303, 1307, and 5322.

Gobernación, documents number: 9246 and 7319.

Municipal Alajuela, document number: 896.

Congreso, documents number: 5345, 5424, 5425, 5426, 5428, 5429, 5430, 5431, 6516, 6537, 6545, 6546, 6547, 6549, 6550, 6551, 6552, 6555, 6556, 6557, 6564

Mortual Colonial, Heredia:

Number	*Year*
1379	1728
1674	1732
2969	1770
2050	1779
1830	1787
1722	1788
1547	1789
1856	1789
1983	1790
1438	1792
1692	1794
1443	1795
1986	1795

PROBATE INVENTORIES
(One document may include several probate cases of relatives, in each period)

1850-1859:

Series: Mortual Independiente, Documents:

84-100, 102-103, 105-129, 131-137, 316-326, 453-483, 612-614, 668, 728-741, 829-833, 877-883, 927-942, 1007-1009, 1011-1030, 1032,

1140, 1157, 1165-1175, 1177, 1212-1217, 1269-1272, 1274-1275, 1351, 1354-1361, 1363-1364, 1371, 1531-1535, 1537-1545, 1549-1550, 1554-1558, 1561-1562, 1564-1566, 1569-1572, 1574-1576, 1694-1696, 1710, 1761-1775, 1882-1885, 1895-1901.

1895-1904:

Series: Mortual Independiente, Documents:

294-297, 299, 391-393, 597, 599, 601, 610, 636-637, 670, 685, 816-817, 966-967, 1134-1136, 1251-1252, 1263, 1334, 1461-1464, 1676-1678, 1680-1682, 1686, 1707, 1846-1849, 1851-1852, 1881, 1908, 1914.

Series: Alcaldías, Documents:

1, 3-6, 10-11, 13-14, 18, 23-28, 34-37, 40-42, 47-49, 51-53, 59, 69, 80, 86, 89, 92-93, 99-100, 105, 114, 123, 125-127, 131, 133-137, 140, 142-147, 151, 154, 161-162, 167, 170-172, 176, 178-179, 184-185, 188, 190-195, 199-201, 203, 211, 218, 221, 224, 236, 242-245, 256-259, 264, 266,-268, 270-275, 280-281, 285, 288, 295, 297, 300, 317-319, 327, 332, 335, 340, 342, 345-346, 358-362, 366, 369, 372-373, 380-382, 385, 397, 403, 405, 407, 409, 412, 414, 420, 423-424, 429, 435-438, 443, 450, 465-466, 469, 498, 502-503, 505, 507-508, 512-513, 519, 522, 524-528, 528, 531-532, 534, 537, 540, 543-544, 546, 548-550, 552-553, 556-557, 564, 569, 600, 608, 621, 633, 638, 640, 643, 666, 681, 696, 701-703, 709, 711, 715, 742, 750, 761, 773-775, 780, 782-783, 786, 788, 792, 796, 798, 800, 803, 812-814, 820, 825, 834, 838-839, 842, 897, 989, 932, 964, 1012, 1015, 1024-1025, 1052, 1105, 1135, 1138-1139, 1142, 1145, 1150-1151, 1155, 1174, 1177, 1228, 1302, 1318-1319, 1334, 1352-1356, 1372, 1385, 1396, 1398, 1406, 1416-1418, 1420-1425, 1428, 1430, 1434, 1486, 1496, 1507, 1509-1511, 1514-1516, 1567-1568, 1570-1573, 1616-1617, 1626, 1630, 1666, 1668-1669, 1787, 1793, 1796, 1801, 1807, 1833-1837, 1839-1842, 1845-1851, 1853, 1855, 1858-1859, 1861, 1863-1864, 1867-1871, 1874.

Series: Juzgados, Documents:

2, 4, 7, 12, 15-16, 22-23, 54, 58, 65, 71-72, 76-77, 85, 87, 100, 114, 147, 168-170, 172-177, 181-185, 186-190, 192-194, 196-200, 254, 282, 284, 330331, 339, 341, 348-349, 354-355, 386, 388, 393, 398, 400-402, 406-408, 410, 412, 415, 435, 437, 439-440, 443, 455, 476, 501, 503, 516, 535, 542, 544, 547-548, 555, 562, 575-576, 579-581, 585, 588, 590, 592-593, 596-597, 600, 604, 606, 635, 645, 650, 653, 670, 675, 684, 687, 689, 692, 699, 703, 712, 738, 745, 750, 753, 759, 785, 803, 806, 811, 829-831, 833-836, 868-874, 877, 886, 903-904,945, 971, 979-980, 1021-1023, 1025, 1035, 1038, 1054, 1059, 1063, 1084, 1099, 1144, 1147, 1192, 1194, 1202, 1226, 1289-1290, 1295, 1324, 1409,

1476, 1530, 2013, 2015, 2017-2018, 2020, 2064, 2080, 2101, 2115, 2506.

1926-1935:

Series: Alcaldías, Documents: 1852-853

Series: Juzgados, Documents:

2088, 6096, 6216, 6219, 6222, 6230, 6278, 6302, 6599, 6997, 7771, 8279, 8280, 832, 8326, 8403, 8445-8446, 8498-8500, 8516

Remesa	Documents:
1057	1, 20, 21, 23, 25, 33, 50
1069	43-44, 46, 86
1115	84
1151	60-61, 81, 89, 91
1174	43, 45, 87, 124-126, 140, 143, 169,
1177	441, 510
1210	6, 8, 30, 39
1212	15
1221	13, 16, 18, 20-21, 23-25, 53
1250	783, 806, 885,
1255	39
1257	38
1287	5-6
1330	63, 218, 275-276, 278, 281, 300, 310-311, 322-323, 327, 330, 354-355, 358, 360-362, 403, 405-406, 434, 445, 448, 452, 544, 579, 637, 657,
1358	1
1369	218
1391	19, 82, 121, 130, 161
1395	8, 14-15, 16-17, 20-21, 42-43, 48, 50, 52-53, 67-70, 81-82, 84, 90, 105, 110, 116, 118, 124, 127,
1411	9
1412	39
1428	41, 73
1457	7
1459	501, 613, 772, 116
1468	52, 64
1475	10
1506	4
1521	111, 113, 166, 460

1523 100, 156-157, 189, 200, 214
1556 1, 6
1609 197, 279
1645

PARISH RECORDS:
Libros de matrimonios, parishes of:
- San Anselmo de Los Palmares, 1867-1871 and 1883-1893
- Grecia, 1894-1898
- Naranjo, 1895-1898

REAL ESTATE REGISTRY
Registro de la Propiedad (Costa Rica), Partido de Alajuela, "Indice Antiguo" and "Tomos".

INTERVIEWS
(1984-1985)

Alfaro, Cristóbal; Alfaro, Marta; Alvarez, Anita; Alvarez, Carmen; Alvarez, Idaly; Alvarez, Isabelina; Araya, Elena; Araya, Agustín; Arias, Cristina; Arias, María Cristina; Arias, Esperanza; Arrieta, Adelina; Arrieta, Deifilia; Avila, Orfilia; Ballestero, Isidora; Ballestero, Maximina; Barahona, Bernardo; Barquero, Aquilina; Bogantes, Angela; Bogantes, José María; Bogantes, María Ignacia; Bogantes, María Josefa; Bogantes, Juan Vicente; Bolaños, Nabor; Cerdas, Audí; Corrales, Evangelina; Chacón, Sara; Fernández, Rosa; González, Berta; González, Guillermo; González, Julia; González, Nelly; González, Saturnino; Guzmán, Angela; Herrera, Félix; Herrera, José Lizano, Socorro; Lobo, Andrés; Lobo, Juan; Lobo, Rafael; Lobo, Ramona; Lobo, Rosa; López, Agustina; Marín, Juan Gabriel; Matamoros, María Julia; Méndez, Juan Manuel; Monge, Otilia; Monge, Ramona; Murillo, Celina; Murillo, Hortensia; Murillo, José Luis; Ramírez, Auristela; Ramírez, Berlarmina; Salazar, Asdrúbal; Salazar, Raimundo; Sánchez, Gloria; Sánchez, Francisco; Sánchez, Israel; Vega, Lucila; Verga, Mery

PUBLISHED SOURCES

Acuña, Víctor Hugo (1974) *Historia económica del tabaco; época colonial.* Unpublished licenciate thesis in history, Universidad de Costa Rica.

__________ (1985) "Patrones del conflicto social en la economía cafetalera costarricense (1900-1948)" (Paper presented at the 45th Congress of Americanists, Bogotá, Colombia).

__________ (1986) "La ideología de los pequeños y medianos productores cafetaleros costarricenses (1900-1961)", Paper presented at the Symposium on 'La Costa Rica Cafetalera' (Heredia, Costa Rica, 1986), *Revista de Historia* (Costa Rica), No. 16: 137-159.

Albarracín, Priscilla and Héctor Pérez (1977) "Estadísticas del comercio exterior de Costa Rica (1907-1946)", *Avances de Investigación* , (Proyecto de Historia Económica y Social de Costa Rica, hereafter PHESCR), No. 5.

Alvarenga, Patricia (1986) *Campesinos y comerciantes en la transición hacia el capitalismo. Un estudio microeconómico de la región de Heredia. 1785-1850* Unpublished Masters thesis in history, Universidad de Costa Rica.

Anes, Gonzalo (1978) *La economía agraria en la historia de España.* (Madrid: Alfaguara).

Arango, Mariano (1981) *Café e industria, 1850-1930.* (Bogotá: Carlos Valencia Editores).

__________ (1982) *El café en Colombia, 1930-1958.* (Bogotá, Carlos Valencia Editores).

Araya, Carlos (1981) "La evolución de la economía tabacalera en Costa Rica bajo el monopolio estatal (1821-1851)", in *Avances de Investigación* (Centro de Investigaciones Históricas, Universidad de Costa Rica, hereafter CIHUCR).

Archetti, Eduardo (1984) "Rural Families and Demographic Behaviour: Some Latin American Analogies", *Comparative Studies in Society and History*, 26: 251-279.

Archetti, Eduardo and Kristi-Anne Stölen (1975) *Explotación familiar y acumulación de capital en el campo argentino.* (Buenos Aires: Siglo XXI)

__________ (1978)"Economía doméstica, estrategias de herencia y acumulación de capital: la situación de la mujer en el norte de Santa Fe, Argentina", *América Indígena*, 38, No. 2: 383-403.

Arguedas, Ana Virginia and María Ramírez (1985) *Contribución al análisis de empresas: El caso de Julio Sánchez Lépiz (1862-1934).* Unpublished licenciate thesis in history, Universidad Nacional, Costa Rica.

Augelli, John (1987) "Costa Rica's Frontier Legacy", in *Geographical Review*, 77: 1-17.

Avila, Olger (1971) *La Sociedad Económica Itineraria: 1843-1854.* Unpublished licenciate thesis in history, Universidad de Costa Rica.

Badilla, Patricia (1982) *Estado, ideología y derecho. La reforma jurídica costarricense (1882-1888).* Unpublished Masters thesis in history, Universidad de Costa Rica).

Baires, Yolanda (1976) "Las transacciones inmobiliarias en el Valle Central y la expansión cafetalera de Costa Rica (1800-1850)", *Avances de Investigación*, (PHESCR) 1.

____________ (1986) "El café y las transacciones inmobiliarias en Costa Rica (1800-1850): Un balance", *Revista de Historia* (Costa Rica), Nos. 12-13: 151-162.

Bariatti, Rita (1987) *La inmigración italiana en Costa Rica, 1821-1968.* Unpublished licenciate thesis, Universidad Nacional, Costa Rica, 1987.

Bartra, Roger (1974) *Estructura agraria y clases sociales en México.* (Mexico: Era).

Bergad, Laird W. (1978) "Agrarian History of Puerto Rico, 1870-1930", in *Latin American Research Review*, 13: 63-94.

____________ (1983) *Coffee and the Growth of Agrarian Capitalism in Nineteenth-Century Puerto Rico.*(Princeton: Princeton University Press).

Boserup, Esther (1965) *The Conditions of Agricultural Growth; the Economics of Agrarian Change under Population Pressure.* (Chicago: Aldine).

____________ (1981) *Population and Technological Change; A Study of Long-term Trends.* (Chicago: University of Chicago Press).

Brading, David (1978) *Haciendas and Ranchos in the Mexican Bajío: León, 1700-1860.* (London: Cambridge University Press).

Browning, David (1971) *El Salvador, Landscape and Society.* (Oxford: The Clarendon Press).

Cambranes, J. C. (1985) *Coffee and Peasants in Guatemala.* (Stockholm: Institute of Latin American Studies).

Cardoso, Ciro (1973) "La formación de la hacienda cafetalera en Costa Rica (siglo XIX)", *Estudios Sociales Centroamericanos*, 19: 22-48.

____________ (1979) "A brecha camponesa no sistema escravista", in *Agricultura, escravidão e capitalismo.* (Petrópolis: Eidtora Vozes).

Cardoso, Ciro and Héctor Pérez (1977) *Centroamérica y la economía occidental*. (San José: Editorial Universidad de Costa Rica).

___________ (1981) *Historia económica de América Latina*. (Barcelona: Editorial Crítica), 2nd. ed.

Cerdas, Rodolfo (1978) *La crisis de la democracia liberal en Costa Rica*. (San José: Educa), 3rd. ed.

Chayanov, A.V. (1966) "Peasant Farm Organization", in D. Thorner (ed.), *The Theory of Peasant Economy*, (Homewood, Ill.: Irwin).

Churnside, Roger (1979) "Trabajo, producción y tamaño de unidades familiares: El caso de Costa Rica en 1864-1927", *Documentos*, (Instituto de Investigaciones Económicas, Universidad de Costa Rica), No. 9.

___________ (1985) *Formación de la fuerza laboral costarricense*. (San José: Editorial Costa Rica).

Cortés, Luis Gonzalo (1981) *La crisis económica de 1930*. Unpublished licenciate thesis in History, Universidad de Costa Rica.

Dalton, George (1972) "Peasantries in Anthropology and History", *Current Anthropology*, 3, No.3-4: 385-415.

Dean, Warren (1976) *Rio Claro; A Brazilian Plantation System, 1820-1910*. (Stanford: Stanford University Press).

de Carvalho Franco, Maria Sylvia (1969) *Homens livres na ordem escravócrata*. (São Paulo: Instituto de Estudos Brasileiros).

Deere, Carmen D. and Alain de Janvry (1979) "A Conceptual Framework for the Empirical Analysis of Peasants", *American Journal of Agricultural Economics*, 61, No. 4: 601-611.

de Janvry, Alain (1981) *The Agrarian Question and Reformism in Latin America*. (Baltimore: The Johns Hopkins University Press).

de Vries, Jan (1978) *The Dutch Rural Economy in the Golden Age, 1500-1700*. (New Haven: Yale University Press), 2nd. Edn.

Dirección General de Estadística y Censos, Costa Rica. (DGEC)

- 1864 - *Censo de población de 1864*.

- 1883 - *Censo de población de 1883*.

- 1885 - *Estadísticas varias: 1883, 1884, 1885*.

- 1887 - *Anuario estadístico*.

- 1888a - *Estadística agrícola, año de 1888*.

- 1888b - *Estadística pecuaria, año de 1888*.

- 1892 - *Censo de población de 1892*.

- 1893 - *Resúmenes estadísticos.*

- 1910 - *Resúmenes estadísticos, 1883-1910.*

- 1927 - *Censo de población de 1927.*

- 1932 - *Censo de personas sin trabajo.*

- 1950a - *Censo de población de 1950.*

- 1950b - *Censo agropecuario de 1950.*

Eisner, Gisela (1961) *Jamaica 1830-1930.* (Westport, Connecticut: Greenwood Press).

Errázuriz, María (1986) *Cafeteros y cafetals del Líbano.* (Bogotá: Empresa Editorial Universidad Nacional de Colombia).

Facio, Rodrigo (1975) *Estudio sobre economía costarricense.* (San José: Editorial Costa Rica).

Fallas, Miriam (1978) *Historia demográfica de la parroquia de Atenas.* Unpublished licenciate thesis in History, Universidad de Costa Rica).

Fernández, Mario (1984) "Desarrollo capitalista y formas productivas en el agro: La producción cafetalera. El caso de la zona Alajuela-Grecia", *Investigaciones* (Instituto de Investigaciones Sociales (hereafter IISUCR), No. 4.

Flores, Humberto (1977) *Proletarización del campesino de Guatemala.* (Guatemala: Piedra Santa).

Fonseca, Elizabeth (1983) *Costa Rica colonial; la tierra y el hombre.* (Central America: Educa).

Fournier, Eduardo (1976) *Un análisis histórico-demográfico de la parroquia de San Ramón (1850-1900).* Unpublished licenciate thesis in history, Universidad de Costa Rica.

Friedman, Harriet (1978) "World Market, State, and Family Farm: Social Bases of Household Production in the Era of Wage Labor", *Comparative Studies in Society and History*, 20, No. 4: 545-586.

_____________ (1980) "Household Production and the National Economy: Concepts for the Analysis of Agrarian Formations", *Journal of Peasant Studies*, 7: 158-184.

Frucht, Richard (1967) "A Caribbean Social Type: Neither 'Peasant' nor 'Proletarian'," *Social and Economic Studies*, 16: 295-300.

Gallo, Ezequiel (1969) "Ocupación de tierras y colonización agrícola en Santa Fé (1870-1895)", in E. Gallo et. al., *Tierras nuevas* (Mexico: El Colegio de Mexico): 92-104.

González, Alfredo (1936) *La crisis económica de Costa Rica. Su origen, proceso y factores que la han agravado. Medidas recomendables para procurar el reajuste económico.* (San José: Trejos).

González, Carmen (1982) *Estudio histórico-demográfico de la parroquia de Grecia (1854-1910).* Unpublished licenciate thesis in History, Universidad de Costa Rica.

González, Yamileth (1983) *Continuidad y cambio en la historia agraria de Costa Rica (1821-1880).* Unpublished doctoral dissertation, University of Louvaine.

Goodman, David and Michael Redclift (1982) *From Peasant to Proletarian: Capitalist Development and Agrarian Transitions.* (New York: St. Martin's Press).

Goody, Jack, Joan Thirsk and E. P. Thompson (eds.) (1978) *Family and Inheritance: Rural Society in Western Europe 1200-1800.* (Cambridge: Cambridge University Press).

Granados, Mónica (1986) *Estudio exploratorio para la construcción de una teoría político-económica de la pena en la Costa Rica del siglo XIX.* Unpublished Masters thesis in criminology, Instituto Nacional de Ciencias Penales, Mexico.

Gudmundson, Lowell (1978a) *Estratificación socio-racial y económica de Costa Rica (1700-1850).* (San José: Euned).

____________ (1978b) "La expropiación de los bienes de las obras pías en Costa Rica, 1805-1860: un capítulo en la consolidación económica de una élite nacional", *Revista de Historia* (Costa Rica), No. 7: 37-92.

____________ (1979) "El campesino y el capitalismo agrario de Costa Rica: Una crítica de ideología como historia", *Revista de Historia* (Costa Rica), No. 8: 59-81.

____________ (1983) *Hacendados, precaristas y políticos: La ganadería y el latifundismo guanacasteco, 1800-1950.* (San José).

____________ (1985) "Materiales censales de finales de la colonia y principios del período republicano en Costa Rica", *Revista de Historia* (Costa Rica), No. 11: 173-227.

____________ (1986a) *Costa Rica Before Coffee. Society and Economy on the Eve of the Export Boom.* (Baton Rouge: Louisiana State University Press).

____________ (1986b) "La Costa Rica cafetalera en contexto comparado", *Revista de Historia* (Costa Rica), No. 14: 11-23.

____________ (n. d.) "Rancheros and revisionism: The History of the Peasant Bourgeoisie in Mexico and Beyond", (manuscript).

Hall, Carolyn (1976) *El café y el desarrollo histórico-geográfico de Costa Rica.* (San José: Editorial Costa Rica-Euna).

____________ (1978) *Cóncavas. Formación de una hacienda cafetalera, 1889-1911.* (San José: Editorial Universidad de Costa Rica).

Hall, Douglas (1981) *Free Jamaica, 1838-1865: An Economic History.* (Aylesbury, UK: Ginn and Company; 5th reimpression).

Harrison, Mark (1975) "Chayanov and the Economics of the Russian Peasantry", *Journal of Peasant Studies*, 2, No. 4: 389-417.

____________ (1977) "The peasant mode of production in the work of A.V. Chayanov", *Journal of Peasant Studies*, 4, No. 4: 323-335.

Higman, B.W. (1979) *Slave Population and Economy in Jamaica, 1807-1834.* (London: Cambridge University Press).

Holloway, Thomas H. (1974) *Migration and Mobility: Immigrants as Laborers and Land-owners in the Coffee Zone of São Paulo, Brazil, 1886-1934.* Unpublished Ph. D. dissertation, University of Wisconsin.

____________ (1977) "Immigration and Abolition: The Transition from Slave to Free Labor in the São Paulo Coffee Zone", in *Essays Concerning the Socioeconomic History of Brazil and Portuguese India* (Gainesville, Florida: The University Presses).

Hunt, Diana (1979) "Chayanov's Model of Peasant Household Resource Allocation", *Journal of Peasant Studies*, 6, No. 3: 247-285.

Hymer, Stephen and Stephen Resnick (1969) "A Model of an Agrarian Economy with Non-agricultural Activities", *American Economic Review*, 59, No. 4: 493-506.

Instituto de Estudios Sociales en Población, Costa Rica (IDESPO) (n.d.) *Divisiones administrativas de Costa Rica y del Valle Central de los años 1825-1848-1883-1892-1915-1927-1950-1963-1973 y 1979.* (Heredia: Universidad Nacional).

Instituto de Defensa del Café, Costa Rica (IDC) (1935-37) "Censo cafetalero de la República", *Revista del Instituto de Defensa del Café*, Nos. 1-5.

Johnson, David (1975) *Economic and Social Change in Nineteenth-Century Colombia. Santander, 1850-1885,* Unpublished Ph. D. dissertation, University of California at Berkeley.

Klein, Herbert (1969) "The colored freedmen in Brazilian slave society", in *Journal of Social History*, 3, No. 1: 30-52.

Kula, Witold (1976) *An Economic Theory of the Feudal System: Towards a Model of the Polish Economy 1500-1800.* (London: NLB-Humanities Press).

Kuznesof, Elizabeth (1986) "Comentarios sobre 'La Costa Rica cafetalera: economía, sociedad y estructuras de poder'," *Revista de Historia* (Costa Rica), No. 14: 31-39.

Kuznesof, Elizabeth and Robert Oppenheimer (1985) "The Family and Society in Nineteenth-Century Latin America: An Historiographical Introduction", *Journal of Family History*, 10, No. 3: 215-234.

LeGrand, Catherine (1980) *From Public Lands into Private Properties: Landholding and Rural Conflict in Colombia, 1870-1936*. Unpublished Ph. D. dissertation, Stanford University).

____________ (1984) "Labor Acquisition and Social Conflict on the Colombian Frontier, 1850-1936", *Journal of Latin American Studies*, 16: 27-49.

____________ (1986) "Comentarios sobre 'La Costa Rica cafetalera en contexto comparado', de Lowell Gudmundson", *Revista de Historia* (Costa Rica), No. 14: 41-52.

Lehman, David (1986) "Two Paths of Agrarian Capitalism, or a Critique of Chayanovian Marxism", *Comparative Studies in Society and History*, 28, No. 4: 601-627.

Le Roy Ladurie, Emmanuel (1972) "Système de la coutume. Structures familiales et coutume d'heritage en France au XVIe siècle", in *Annales E.S.C.*: 825-846.

Levine, D. (1977) *Family Formation in an Age of Nascent Capitalism.* (New York: Academic Press).

Leyburn, James (1941) *The Haitian People*. (New Haven: Yale University Press).

López Toro, Alvaro (1970) *Migración y cambio social en Antioquia durante el siglo diez y nueve*. (Bogotá: Ediciones Universidad de los Andes).

Machado, Absalón (1977) *El café de la aparcería al capitalismo*. (Bogotá: Punta de Lanza).

Medick, Hans (1976) "The Protoindustrial Family Economy: The Structural Function of Household and Family during the transition from peasant society to industrial capitalism", *Social History*, 1, No. 3: 291-315.

Meillassoux, Claude (1983) "The Economic Bases of Demographic Reproduction: From the Domestic Mode of Production to Wage-Earning", *Journal of Peasant Studies*, 11, No. 1: 50-61.

Meléndez, Carlos (1978) *Documentos fundamentales del siglo XIX*. (San José: Editorial Costa Rica).

Merz, Carlos (1937) "Coyuntura y crisis en Costa Rica de 1924 a 1936", *Revista del Instituto de Defensa del Café*, No. 4: 603-621.

Mintz, Sidney and Douglas Hall (1960) "The Origins of the Jamaican Internal Marketing System", in *Papers in Caribbean Anthropology*. Yale University Publications in Anthropology, No. 57: 3-25.

Molina, Iván (1984) *El capital comercial en un valle de labriegos sencillos, 1800-1824: análisis del legado colonial de Costa Rica*. Unpublished masters thesis, Universidad de Costa Rica).

___________ (1986) "Habilitadores y habilitados en el Valle Central de Costa Rica. El financiamiento de la producción cafetalera en los inicios de su expansión (1838-1950)". (San José: mimeo).

___________ (1987) "Dinero y capital. El crédito en el Valle Central de Costa Rica (1824-1850)", *Avances de Investigación* (CIHUCR), No. 22.

Monge Alfaro, Carlos (1974) *Historia de Costa Rica*. (San José: Trejos, 10th ed.).

Morin, Claude (1979) *Michoacán en la Nueva España del siglo XVIII: Crecimiento y desigualdad en una economía colonial*. (Mexico: Fondo de Cultura Económica, 1979).

Palacios, Marco (1983) *El café en Colombia, 1850-1970; una historia económica, social y política*. (México: El Colegio de México/Ancora Editores, 2d. ed.).

Parsons, James (1979) *La colonización antioqueña en el occidente de Colombia*. (Bogotá: Carlos Valencia Editores).

Pérez, Héctor (1977) "El ciclo en las economías agrícolas de exportación de América Latina (1880-1930): hipótesis para un estudio", *Revista de Historia* (Costa Rica), No. 5: 9-46.

___________ (1981) "Economía política del café en Costa Rica, 850-1950", *Avances de Investigación* (CIHUCR), No. 5.

___________ (1983) "Las variables demográficas en una economía de exportación: el ejemplo del Valle Central de Costa Rica, 1800-1950", *Revista de Historia* (São Paulo), No. 114: 107-133.

___________ (1986) "Crecimiento agroexportador y regímenes políticos en Centroamérica: Un ensayo de historia comparada" (manuscript).

___________ (1987) "Costa Rica (1866-1973): Tablas modelo de mortalidad", *Avances de Investigación* (CIHUCR), No. 26.

___________ (1990) “Migration and Settlement in Costa Rica, 1700-1850”, in David J. Robinson (ed.), *Migration in Colonial Spanish America*. (Cambridge: Cambridge University Press): 279-294; 380-382

Picó, Fernando (1981) *Amargo café (los pequeños y medianos caficultores de Utuado en la segunda mitad del siglo XIX).* (Río Piedras, Puerto Rico: Ediciones Huracán).

Piñiero, Martín and James Chapman (1984) "Cambio técnico y diferenciación en las economías campesinas: un análisis de seis estudios de caso de América Latina, *Estudios Rurales Latinoamericanos*, 17: 27-57.

Piñeiro, Martín and Ignacio Llovet (eds.) (1986) *Transición tecnológica y diferenciación social.* (San José: Servicio Editorial IICA).

Potter, J. (et. al.) (1967) *Peasant Society.* (Boston: Little, Brown & Co.).

Ramírez, Mario and Manuel Solís (1979) *El desarrollo capitalista en la industria costarricense (1850-1930).* Unpublished licenciate thesis in sociology, Universidad de Costa Rica, 2. vols.

Raventós, Ciska (1986) "Desarrollo económico, estructura y contradicciones sociales en la producción de café", *Revista de Historia* (Costa Rica), No. 14: 179-195.

Richter, Ernesto (1976) "Proceso de acumulación y dominación en la formación socio-política salvadoreña", *Informes de investigación* (Consejo Superior Universitario Centroamericano), No. 16.

Robles, Arodis (1986) "Patrones de población en Costa Rica, 1860-1930", in *Avances de Investigación* (CIHUCR), No. 14.

Roseberry, William (1983) *Coffee and capitalism in the Venezuelan Andes.* (Austin: University of Texas Press).

____________ (1985) "Something about Peasants, History and Capitalism", *Critique of Anthropology*, 5, No. 3: 69-76.

____________ (1986) "Hacia un análisis comparativo de los países cafetaleros", *Revista de Historia* (Costa Rica), No. 14: 25-29.

Sáenz, Alberto (1966) *Suelos volcánicos cafeteros de Costa Rica.* (San José: Universidad de Costa Rica).

Salas, José Antonio (1984) "Liberalismo y legislación agraria: Apuntes introductorios para el estudio de la colonización agrícola de Costa Rica durante el siglo XIX", *Historia* (Universidad Nacional de Costa Rica), No. 8.

____________ (1985) "La distribución y apropiación privada de la tierra en Turrialba. 1821-1900: Un aporte al estudio de la colonización agrícola de Costa Rica", *Historia* (Universidad Nacional, Costa Rica), No.1-85.

____________ (n.d.) "La apropiación de la tierra en el Valle de Candelaria-Puriscal: Características del proceso" (mimeo, Universidad Nacional).

Samper, Mario (1979) *Evolución de la estructura socio-ocupacional costarricense, 1864-1935*. Unpublished licenciate thesis in history, Universidad de Costa Rica.

____________ (1983) "¿Agricultor o jornalero? Algunos problemas de historia social agraria", *Historia* (Universidad Nacional, Costa Rica).

____________ (1985a) "La especialización mercantil campesina en el noroeste del Valle Central, 1850-1900. Elementos microanalíticos para un modelo", *Revista de Historia* (Special issue: *Historia, problemas y perspectivas agrarias en Costa Rica*): 49-87.

____________ (1985b) "Labores agrícolas y fuerza de trabajo en el suroeste de Antioquia (Colombia), 1850-1912", *Avances de Investigación* (CIHUCR), No. 12; also published in *Estudios Sociales* (Medellín, Colombia), No. 2 (1988): 7-43.

____________ (1986) "Uso de la tierra y unidades productivas al finalizar el siglo XIX: Noroeste del Valle Central, Costa Rica", *Revista de Historia* (Costa Rica), No. 14: 133-177.

____________ (1987a) "Fuerzas sociopolíticas en Costa Rica, 1921-1936", *Cuadernos de Historia* (Universidad Nacional, Costa Rica), No. 1-87.

____________ (1987b) "Uso del suelo, ciclo agrícola y unidades productivas en el suroeste de Antioquia (Colombia), 1912-1935", *Avances de Investigación* (CIHUCR), No. 33; also published in *Lecturas de Economía* (Antioquia, Colombia), No. 25-26, 1988: 141-171.

Sancho Riba, Eugenio (1982) *Merchant-Planters and Modernization: An Early Liberal Experiment in Costa Rica, 1849-1870*. Unpublished doctoral dissertation in history, University of California, San Diego).

Sandner, Gerhard (1962-4) *La colonización agrícola de Costa Rica*. (San José: Instituto Geográfico de Costa Rica), 2 vols.

Schminck, Marianne (1984) "Household Economic Strategies: Review and Research Agenda", *Latin American Research Review*, 19, No. 3: 87-101.

Schryer, Frans (1979) "A Ranchero Economy in Northwestern Hidalgo, 1880-1920", *Hispanic American Historical Review*, 59, No. 3: 418-443.

____________ (1980) *The Rancheros of Pisaflores: The History of a Peasant Bourgeoisie in Twentieth-Century Mexico*. (Toronto: University of Toronto Press).

____________ (1983) "From Rancheros to Pequeños Propietarios: Agricultures, Class Structure and Politics in the Sierra de Jacala, Mexico", *Boletín de Estudios Latinoamericanos y del Caribe*, No. 34: 41-58.

Seligson, Mitchell Allan (1980) *El campesino y el capitalismo agrario de Costa Rica*. (San José: Editorial Costa Rica).

Slicher van Bath, B.H. (1963) *The Agrarian History of Western Europe*. (London: Edward Arnold).

Smith, Carol (1987) "Regional Analysis in World-System Perspective: A Critique of Three Structural Theories of Uneven Development", *Review*, 10, No. 4: 597-648.

Spindel, Cheywa (1979) *Homens e máquinas na transição de uma economia cafeira*. (Rio de Janeiro: Paz e Terra).

Stone, Carl (1983) "Patterns of Insertion into the World Economy: Historical Profile and Contemporary Options", *Social and Economic Studies*, 32, No. 3: 1-34.

Stone, Samuel (1976) *La dinastía de los conquistadores*. (Central America: Educa, 2d. ed.).

Tilly, Charles (ed.) (1976) *Historical Studies of Changing Fertility*. (Princeton: Princeton University Press).

Tjarks, Germán (et al.) (1976) "La epidemia del cólera de 1856 en el Valle Central: análisis y consecuencias demográficas", *Revista de Historia* (Costa Rica), No. 3: 81-129.

Twinam, Ann (1982) *Miners, Merchants, and Farmers in Colonial Colombia*. (Austin: University of Texas Press).

Van Young, Eric (1978) Rural Life in Eighteenth-Century Mexico: The Guadalajara Region, 1675-1820. Unpublished Ph. D. dissertation, University of California at Berkeley, 1978).

Vargas, María Mercedes (1978) *Las parroquias de Naranjo y Palmares (1865-1910). Análisis y estudio de historia demográfica*. Unpublished licenciate thesis in History, Universidad de Costa Rica.

Viotti da Costa, Emilia (1966) *Da senzala à colonia*. (São Paulo: Difusão Européia do Livro).

Wagner, Moritz and Karl Scherzer (1944) *La República de Costa Rica en Centroamérica*. (San José: Lehman).

Wharton, Cliffton (ed.) (1970) *Subsistence Agriculture and Economic Development*. (Chicago: Aldine).

Wright, Gavin (1978) *The Political Economy of the Cotton South: Households, Markets and Wealth in the Nineteenth Century*. (New York: Norton).

Yver, Jean (1966) *Egalité entre héritiers et exclusion des enfants dotés: Essai de geographie coutumiére*. (Paris: Sirey)

Index